W9-DIS-789

Sales Management

Operations
Administration
Marketing

SALES MANAGEMENT

Operations
Administration
Marketing

H. Webster Johnson
Wayne State University

CHARLES E. MERRILL PUBLISHING COMPANY
A Bell & Howell Company
Columbus, Ohio

Published by
CHARLES E. MERRILL PUBLISHING COMPANY
A Bell & Howell Company
Columbus, Ohio 43216

This book was set in Helvetica.

The Production Editor was Michael Robbins.

The cover was designed by Will Chenoweth.

International Standard Book Number: 0–675–08598–5
Library of Congress Catalog Card Number: 75–38058
1 2 3 4 5 6 7 8 9 10—80 79 78 77 76
Printed in the United States of America

Preface

This book is designed to give a comprehensive coverage of the tasks of the sales manager as organizer, administrator, and decision maker. It describes many duties which are part of the job and tells how to implement them successfully.

The book covers the sales manager's job systematically. The purpose is to give in-depth treatment in some areas and sketch broad outlines of other areas with sufficient detail to enable the reader to handle the job of sales manager in a small or medium-sized firm.

Part one develops the broad area of a sales manager's responsibilities and duties. The book describes the most used forms of organizations and suggests which ones to use for different types of companies. This material is followed by a discussion of the sales manager as executive and leader.

Part two stresses the operating duties of the sales manager and gives comprehensive information about these activities. Several chapters present approaches, procedures, and methods that are used successfully to hire, supervise, and manage a dynamic sales staff.

Part three covers areas of administration the sales manager uses to implement operating procedures. The material includes elements which aid the sales manager and immediate assistants to develop, guide, direct, control, and motivate the sales force. Related discussion includes proper handling of customer interests and satisfactions.

Part four directs attention to the broader areas of sales management which are part of marketing management. This part covers topics closely related to the sales management functions that define methods, establish policies, and determine the extent of the firm's overall marketing program. This material can be used as a guide for devising sales strategy and direction for implementing sales objectives.

Each chapter gives comprehensive coverage but leaves opportunity for supplementary reading material. For example, the chapter on training can be extended and enriched by adding a compact book on salesmanship.

The cases at the end of each chapter bring the problems of sales managers into sharp focus and present their activities in a working environment. The cases are complete enough to give the beginning student a sample of sales management problems, yet sufficiently complex to extend the thinking of the most able students and sales managers. Testing in the classroom has revealed exciting student reactions to a number of solutions.

The book suggests how the sales manager can extend his or her knowledge and background through experience and by reading some of the excellent sources enumerated. Specific lists, footnotes, and a selected bibliography give a number of reading sources directly related to operating functions as well as areas of a broad nature that relate the sales manager's job to the working environment. Such material not only helps sales managers to work under today's restraints but also prepares them for change so that they are ready to accept new responsibilities, develop new procedures, make social and ethical decisions, retain flexibility in outlook, and make adjustments to people and products.

This book meets the requirements of the college student. Students in community colleges will find this material interesting and instructive; students in business schools will appreciate the direct approach and specific applications. This book is adaptable to students in adult education. It can give valuable information and assistance to the beginning sales manager and is useful in instructing assistant sales managers and sales supervisors in the duties and responsibilities of the sales manager.

I would like to thank Steven Castle, David M. Landrum, Robert R. Smith, Louis Stern, and Wayland A. Tonning for the many helpful suggestions they made after reading the manuscript. Special appreciation goes to my wife Josephine, who worked long periods on many details of preparation, and to Rosemarie Samarjian, our secretary, who handled all the duties of typing preparation.

H. Webster Johnson

Contents

part one

INTRODUCTION

Sales Management Functions

There are numerous functions in sales management. The sales manager's job includes direction and control of sales effort. As top sales executive, he or she participates in decision making at the corporate level.

ROLE OF THE SALES MANAGER

The strength of a firm rests on the effectiveness of its sales operation. The effort of the sales manager and his employees is the major determinant in profitability. This division is the focal point between the firm and the buyer. The buyer sees the salesperson as representing the firm and forms opinions of reliability of product and service by the salesperson's performance.

How well salespeople perform depends on sales management leadership. Guiding and directing a strong selling group requires a person of judgment, leadership skill, and administrative ability.

People who direct sales activities and participate in company decisions are well rewarded financially. Their income is higher than in most other business areas. According to a Dartnell Corporation survey of top sales executives' compensation, vice-presidents of sales in small firms (sales below $5 million) averaged $26,000 a year; vice-presidents in companies with sales between $50 and $100 million averaged $53,000; vice-presidents in large firms (sales of more than $5 billion) averaged $158,000.

The sales manager's role in the business world is exciting, demanding, and challenging. He manages sales in an ever-changing economy and environment. His is a world of action, as he strives to satisfy customers' varied needs.

SALES MANAGEMENT AREA

Sales management, broadly conceived, covers the entire marketing effort; but from the viewpoint of company operations, it is often restricted to the immediate selling area. As a top executive, the sales manager must be able to visualize the company's operations in the economy and plan how to distribute its production profitably.

In a small company, the sales manager has charge of marketing—supervising all activities associated with getting the product to the user. As his duties multiply and increase, he hires assistants to supervise directly major activities, such as managing the sales force, handling sales promotion, directing advertising, supervising marketing research, and analyzing sales performance. Many firms have a strong sales department; others have a few salespeople directing activities of independent salespeople—brokers, manufacturers' agents, wholesalers, jobbers, and large retailers.

In this book we primarily relate the work of the sales manager to management of the sales force, but we also show how he or she must function in related marketing areas to reinforce and support the effort of the salespeople.

Sales Administration

The roles of decision making and management guidance become uppermost when the sales manager acts as administrator, as marketing manager, or as vice-president in charge of sales. He is primarily concerned with establishing policies and developing procedures that free him from details which can be handled by subordinates. His job is to create an organization that controls the functions related to marketing.

Administrative guidance

The sales executive, in his capacity of administrator, must guide subordinates. The director of marketing can discuss major problems and receive sympathetic and perceptive attention; the advertising manager can bring in problems and air feelings, ideas, and ways of handling current activities; the manager of the sales force can present the current situation and discuss particular areas of concern; a regional manager can come to the home office and compare notes with the boss. The sales administrator needs close working relationships with these people because he depends on them for the success of the marketing function. Under the term *marketing function* are major and minor functions and subfunctions related to marketing activities.

Administrative direction

Administrative guidance is initiated by the manager who wishes to consult his superior about his operation. Administrative direction is initiated by the sales executive who wishes to discuss problems, to pass on suggestions, and to give specific recommendations to subordinates.

This specific, direct communication may be originated by the sales executive because of displeasure with current operations or the need for changing procedures to meet new requirements. An executive might readily agree with subordinates that present procedures are satisfactory, but that projected operations mandate certain changes.

Administrative review

The sales executive must constantly review the current marketing situation to assure superior performance. In many firms, changes are so rapid that he must watch daily events to stay current. He receives reports, comparisons, warnings, complaints of major customers, and many other communications which he must read and act upon. As long as operations go smoothly (and they seldom do), he can maintain a hands-off approach; but as soon as trouble arises, he must review, assess, and act. The sales executive should not only review current operations, but also be aware of changes in society that may affect the firm's activities.

Administrative consultation

A significant portion of a sales executive's time is spent in discussion with managers of other company divisions and in consultation with his superior. At this level, each major decision may be very important to the firm's success and usually involves the president and other executives. If there is wide disagreement among top executives regarding a certain policy, the sales executive must have the permission of the president. A decision at this level, unless supported by all top executives, has little chance of succeeding even though the plan may have merit. Therefore, if the president agrees with the sales manager, other executives must carry out their duties within the new framework. For example, the production department prefers to make one model, and the sales executive wants another model which is much more difficult to make. If the executive committee or the president agrees with the sales executive, production must accept this decision, even though it causes manufacturing problems.

Administrative planning

One of the major functions of the top sales executive is planning for immediate needs and long-term needs. Constant planning is essential to meet ever-changing conditions of current operations. Unless that planning is supplemented by intermediate (two or three years) and long-range planning, the sales division is constantly confronting situations which should have been anticipated.

Planning can be restricted in some instances, but it should not be so narrow that it shuts out trends and shifts in demand which may eliminate a firm's present operations. It is of little use to prepare ambitious plans for the future if research reveals the likelihood of an area becoming less important each year.

Administrative creativity

The sales executive must plan and create so that the planning does not become a retread of the past. This creativity may be daring and innovative, or it may merely be pushing existing operations just a bit farther. It will probably be some of both.

Creativity requires vision, thinking, and hard work. Creativity involves ordering and readjusting present operations into new patterns and extending present patterns into new areas. Under the first condition, the executive must ask, "What can we do now that we haven't done before?" In the second case, he thinks, "How can we do the job differently?" or "If it succeeds in this situation, why shouldn't we try it in this other situation?"

The creative manager is successful to the extent that he is able to project himself beyond everyday operations, to project his ideas until they generate something beyond what the firm already has, and to anticipate and prepare for change.

In everyday life most people get along satisfactorily with items that are about right—the knife that is neither sharp nor dull, the car that uses quite a bit of gas but starts easily, the food hastily prepared that does not taste too good but is not bad. Many businesses exist on that same philosophy, but the truly creative manager cannot be content with this approach because he would be muddling along rather than creatively leading.

Administrative decision making

The top sales executive must be a decision maker. How and where decisions are made determines the type of organization. The philosophy of the manager is transmitted through channels to the salespeople, who soon learn where authority is located.

One type of top sales manager maintains close control, makes all major and too many minor decisions himself, and grudgingly grants authority, though he is quick to fix responsibilities down the line. Another type of manager makes a few decisions but expects people lower in the chain of command to make and be responsible for decisions at their level. A third type of manager considers his job to be inspirational—to outline policies, but give very little direct help in the selling operations. He relies on management at lower levels to sell the product, to handle salespeople and sales problems, and to provide effective territory coverage. Of the three types, the first is maximum, and perhaps autocratic, control; the second is strong but moderate and enlightened control; and the third is minimum control. Some managers might consider the last as weak control, but that would not be true if the firm produces few but expensive items that are sold by skilled, highly trained salespeople of managerial caliber.

There is no one best way of control and decision making, but possibly there is one best way for particular firms and particular situations. A manager cannot assume that a present system has merit; it may be inferior, but imposed by the owner. Many firms succeed not because they are effective in selling, but because they are strong in other areas of management which counteract weak sales management.

Administrative organizing

The organizing factor enables easy implementation of activities. The top sales executive needs a properly developed organization to carry on the work. A mark of a good administrator is that his people work effectively and accomplish their jobs with minimum effort. A smooth-functioning organization facilitates work all the way from executive to salesperson, and expedites such jobs as delivery of merchandise, collection of accounts, and service to customers.

Organization is an orderly presentation of work flow, authority, control, and education. It blueprints the steps from decision making to customer satisfaction. If it is carefully constructed, tested, and revised, it becomes an effective work conduit which produces results with minimum disturbance and dislocation. If it is constructed clumsily, it is inefficient, hinders work flow, leads to confusion, and is effective only through infusion of massive effort. The day-by-day organization functions somewhere between these extremes because it cannot be too bad and still permit corporate survival, while the excellent organization functioning perfectly at one period faces new experiences that inevitably require readjustment.

Sales Operating Functions

Daily activities of a sales division are concerned with operations, performance, decision making, and primarily employees and customers. The sales function is to direct employees to do their jobs profitably and to satisfy customers. Sales managers, in their absorption with sales, volume, products, orders, profits, and expenses, may forget that they must control personnel to retain successful operations.

The sales executive must direct and motivate employees so that they will enthusiastically carry out the wishes of management. He must convince employees that their progress, as well as their employer's success, depends on how well they handle the end link in the distribution chain—the buyer. Many employees become so engrossed in their activities that they lose sight of why they are doing certain jobs. Therefore, the sales manager must emphasize service to customers. This should be done so that the most enthusiastic and responsive employees radiate confidence and goodwill, while even the lukewarm employee shows a spark of pleasure in serving customers. Such action is the inspiration of selling—inspiring employees to feel they are truly contributing to customer welfare.

The sales executive has a number of duties and directs a variety of functions; but in his operating role, he is engaged in directing the selling function which moves products or services to final users. His primary effort is devoted to securing, maintaining, and guiding a sales force.

Selecting staff

The sales executive selects the staff of supervisors, salespeople, and other department employees. In a large department, he delegates the selection to subordinates, though he may personally interview many prospects. Of course he might not interview every clerk or salesperson who is hired in a major firm, but he would talk to all individuals considered for key positions in the department, whether employed from outside or promoted from within.

Sales training

Since the sales manager is responsible for sales and the people responsible for making sales, he must be certain that they are prepared for their jobs. People adequately prepared through training become more effective at an earlier period. The sales manager will not do the training himself unless it is a small company, but he is responsible for setting up the training facility and overseeing it to be sure it is giving satisfactory service.

Sales compensation

A satisfied sales force can be expected to respond to sales direction affirmatively. Salespeople work primarily to make a living and are entitled to adequate compensation for their efforts, but how to extend this compensation is neither simple nor static. Sales managers experiment with different patterns of sales compensation, striving to get the best one—a state rarely achieved because salespeople vary and business conditions change.

The ingenious sales executive builds features into his compensation plan that increase motivation and responsiveness to company requirements and customer demands but still maintain a reasonably happy sales force. The plan should be flexible enough to meet the needs of both low and high producers, be sensitive to business conditions, and be suitable for changes in product line.

The compensation plan must be administered, adjusted, and revised to meet ever-shifting requirements. Because of price and product variations, commissions are often open to dispute and arbitration. The sales executive must watch compensation patterns so that the total cost does not exceed a certain percentage of sales.

Sales supervision

In most companies, sales supervision is a major task. A sales manager may employ an assistant whose primary assignment is supervision, but he cannot free himself from all supervision problems.

Planning and implementation are needed to keep each salesperson at his best level of achievement. Constantly the manager faces morale problems common to most employees, but particularly prevalent among salespeople, who must contend with company demands and customer resistance.

A major job of supervision is to keep the sales force following an operations plan outlined by the sales department. Away from the home office, the salesperson usually spends his time as he sees fit. Over a period of time, this practice leads to deviations from the manager's plan. Unless supervision guides salespeople constantly, each man or woman might develop strategies, tactics, and procedures quite unlike those which management desires outlined. The supervisory function is one of the basic sales executive tasks requiring regular surveillance and constant attention.

Sales expenses

The sales manager must oversee sales expenditures and set guidelines regulating salespeople's expenses. An expense plan is not self-administering and must be checked and discussed with individual salespeople if it is to be kept within bounds without sacrificing important features.

Expense accounts may be a temptation to salespeople who feel the pinch from spending beyond income. The sales department may need someone to check expense reports and to question expenditures that deviate from a norm. Periodically, it may be wise to check recorded normal expenditures as well, because a typical salesperson's expense report may be hiding an undesirable expenditure pattern.

Sales territories

One of the difficult problems facing the sales manager is apportioning territories equitably. This problem becomes trying because of changes in territory composition due to number of customers, ability and background of various salespeople, and the importance of some territories in the eyes of management.[1]

Territory adjustment is often a sore point among salespeople, particularly the ones favorably situated. Change is disturbing to "the establishment"[2] and may be resisted vigorously. Territory change to

---

1. It is inevitable that territories will vary. It is not feasible to put a salesperson in a territory when he cannot get his share of potential business. A sales manager cannot afford to put an average salesperson in a strong territory. From the average salesperson's viewpoint, results will be satisfactory; but for the firm, results will be mediocre.

2. This is a term frequently applied to those in power—government, church, society, management, and leaders.

the salesperson assigned a poor territory is welcomed and may not be deferred too long. A firm with a number of poor territories and a very slow turnover of salespeople in the better territories may have a rapid turnover of young salespeople because they soon become disheartened in poor territories. The sales manager must encourage and promote the young, highly-motivated person if he is to retain him. This may become quite an operational problem for a sales manager saddled with a number of poor territories. An attractive salary base may not satisfy an impatient, eager salesperson but will possibly mollify him so that he is willing to wait for something better in the firm.

Forecasting

Effective operation relies on dependable sales forecasts. A number of sales forecasting methods may be used to arrive at accurate data. The forecasting area is difficult to assess and is subject to rapid changes which demand alertness, judgment, and skill in proper handling.

Quotas

Proper use of quotas aids in assigning forecasted sales to territories and salespeople. Salespeople's cumulated sales fulfill quotas and forecasts. Dependable, carefully prepared quotas become targets of salespeople's performance and lead to a firm's success.

Budgeting

Budgeting is planned financial operations. Sales budgets become expenditure guides for the sales department and the salespeople. The sales budget is a plan which shows the framework of financial limitations under which the department and the field people are controlled. It not only shows how far expenditures may go to improve selling effort but also draws a line which more or less defines spending limits.

Customer relations

The area of customer relations is of paramount importance to the sales manager. Daily operations revolve about customers' wishes, complaints, and reactions; procedures and methods are modified frequently to better satisfy customers.

The sales manager stands between the customer and the firm and must bridge this gap primarily through the sales force. Salespeople are the contacts between the firm and customers who have their own priorities and care little about what happens to the supplying firm. The buyer does not worry about the supplier unless a situation develops that jeopardizes the supplier to the possible detriment of the buyer.

The sales manager may have to share responsibilities with top management concerning customer-government relations. For example, if a retailer fails to give correct instructions about a product to a user and damages result, the user may sue both the retailer and the firm supplying the product.

Executive Management Functions

The sales executive makes policy decisions and outlines broad concepts of company procedure which are implemented by management assigned to specific areas. This group of executives truly determine the success or failure of a firm and share in its immediate and possibly long-term future.

The sales executive performing these duties is often one step above the field sales manager, unless he performs both jobs. At the top level he must view the firm as an overall operation and not consider sales as the paramount activity, but as one of several important activities. Some firms depend on quality manufacturing, some on superior purchasing, some on excellent financial support, and some on outstanding selling. Serious weakness in any area may seriously impede functioning of other areas. The following discussion is an introduction to material handled in detail in later chapters.

Marketing strategy

Marketing strategy is the basic task delegated to the sales executive. This assignment includes activities which determine the successful movement of product to the user and varies somewhat by the nature of the product and the firm's organizational structure.

Product acceptance

The sales manager must achieve customer product acceptance and hopefully specific brand acceptance so that he can depend on buyer preference from a considerable segment of the potential market. He has numerous methods to use to reach this objective. Hopefully, customer acceptance increases over time, giving sales stability and permitting the sales manager to concentrate on increasing market share.

Distribution channels

A firm must begin with some channel of distribution to move its product, but this channel need not remain fixed. It is not uncommon to start with one method of distribution and later incorporate a new method or an alternative method along with the older method in some areas and to completely replace the old method in other areas. A third way would be to keep the original approach in some districts, use a new method in some districts, and use both methods in another group of districts. Primarily, the management decision is not what distribution system is best, but which means of distribution is most appropriate at a particular period.

Product pricing

Pricing to maximize profit, to gain market position, to meet competition, and to appeal to the buyer requires careful study, cautious experimentation, willingness to adjust to changing conditions, and flexibility to support a successful product entry. Along with other top executives, the sales manager is part of this decision making. It is also his responsibility to present support data—market research, territory analysis, economic studies—which will be useful in arriving at conclusions. Pricing must be considered within the framework of the firm and its goals.

Sales promotion

It is mandatory to select a variety of approaches to increase sales and evaluate the ones which could be most useful within cost constraints. Certain methods might produce favorable sales figures, but the cost would be prohibitive.[3]

Sometimes the choice of a secondary promotion approach may be more successful because the leading method is being overworked by competitors. Management must judge which approach appears most likely to succeed under current conditions.

Customer services

The area of customer services is subject to careful top management attention, for satisfied customers signal company success. The strategy of keeping customers happy within acceptable cost boundaries requires carefully worked out policies. These policies then become operating management guidelines to be carried out by salespeople or other company representatives. Neglect of this facet of business often leads to snap field decisions which can be disastrous.

Warehousing

Warehouse location, inventories, and delivery methods require major decisions that affect selling plans and create persistent problems. In some industries, certain products must be transported with all possible speed, while others have longer lead periods.

Another element of strategic warehousing is lower transportation cost. Carefully worked out supply and shipping points can realize sufficient savings to influence strongly overall profit.

Product development

Product development is carried on continuously by progressive firms. Seldom can a firm continue without making modifications of present products as well as developing new ones. Since experience has shown that an alarming number of new products fail and others limp along for years, it is important for management to weigh decisions carefully before introducing new products, new product ideas, or drastic modification of existing products. There are not only selling problems to explore in new product development but also manufacturing problems, purchasing problems relative to sources of raw materials, and finance

---

3. A driver training school in Baltimore once used television advertising to secure new students. They did get new students, but the cost was far greater than the results warranted.

problems during an extended expenditure period with minimum returns.

Company growth

The company that remains static is steadily going down. A progressive manager is aware of this fact and takes the initiative to expansion and betterment. Too little initiative leads to stagnation; too much may invite trouble, for there is a thin but not well-defined borderline where excessive pushing may strain a company beyond its limits and introduce serious problems.

A company's growth comes from careful planning supported by strong policies. Management must take action to implement direction of company activity; in this area, the sales manager must be knowledgeable about market potential.

Company production

The sales manager need not be a production expert, but he must be sympathetic to the problems of the production manager. Some products are produced easily and some with great difficulty. There should be no reason for concentrating effort on those that are hard to produce if equal effort would produce similar results with merchandise that is easy to manufacture.[4]

Company finance

Many firms are plagued with financial problems; most firms have periods of financial stringency. If management can coordinate activities and work out optimum scheduling and movement of goods, the burden of financing is reduced. Finance must be concerned not only with everyday operation but also with long-range money requirements which tap a different money source. If the sales manager coordinates his efforts properly, money requirements can be handled more effectively.

Company policies

The sales executive is a prominent member of policy-making management. Some high level policies are created by the board of directors; other policies are developed and put into action by management. Most, if not all, policies are inspired by management.

A policy is a rule of action, a decision to carry out a particular type of activity. Policies are guidelines of operations that establish direction of effort, intensity of application, and expenditure of funds.

---

4. In one small firm, the sales manager was inclined to sell large orders of specialized laboratory furniture, which caused manufacturing many problems and raised the cost so that there were significant losses on many orders. Most of the salespeople concentrated on the regular line of equipment which the company wanted to sell, and on this business there was an adequate profit.

A company has a variety of policies which direct activities toward a goal. These policies may be major or minor, implied or spelled out, rigidly enforced or merely guidelines. They vary in importance and impact not only in the area they cover, but also on how well they are followed.

All policies are not necessarily beneficial to the company. Policies are not inviolate and are subject to change either explicitly through orders issued from the top or implicitly by those who apply them in a fashion not originally intended.

Major policies. A major policy has a strong impact on the company's operation. For example, a decision to add a new product or drop an existing product may alter operations significantly.

A policy to restrict customers to a minimum order size may affect the size of the sales staff. A decision to enlarge or decrease geographic coverage may necessitate hiring many new salespeople or require reducing the force. The decision to change from direct distribution to use of distributors will force a reorganization of the sales department. Major policy decisions suggested by management and passed by the board of directors are presumably enacted to make the company more profitable or to have it conform more closely to other objectives.

Minor policies. Minor policies are closely related to company operations and may affect only particular areas. A minor policy would be one that spells out a salesperson's use of a company car on weekends. A minor policy may be addressed to a salesperson's dress and appearance. How expense accounts are handled may be covered by policy. There could be a policy for handling samples. A minor policy may be instituted for the convenience of the sales manager who wants to carry out some activity but feels the salespeople will accept it better if it is a policy rather than an idea of the boss.

Marketing Innovation

Marketing innovations cover two areas, that which is directly controlled by the sales executive and that which is controlled by top management. Separating the two often becomes a judgment decision. Marketing innovations may be entirely new ways of producing and distributing the product to the consumer or, more likely, will consist of major or minor variations of existing methods.

Marketing innovation relates to a number of facets of marketing. What opportunities exist for improving marketing, where are improvements badly needed, and what are likely directions which appear promising? At one time, efficiency and satisfaction were the measures of new developments, but current society injects other measures which have social relevance.

Convenience and cost appeals

Innovation covers a wide variety of changes. In its simplest form, it may be to add one more size of a package. For example, glue could be packaged for single applications. Innovation might be an entirely new product, or it could be changes in preparing a product to save customer time and effort. Management also looks for ways to improve its products but at the same time lower manufacturing cost.

Improved methods

Ways of improving products and services appear almost limitless. As soon as we feel one product has reached perfection, someone comes along with a change that appeals to the buyer. The actual change may be trifling, but it is sufficient to attract many customers.

Anyone faced with innovating a product should ask himself these questions. Can it be done faster? Can we make it cheaper? Can we make it more compact? Can we make it easier to operate? Can we make it safer? Can we do the same job in a different way? Can we make it more flexible in use? Is there room for another similar product with a more specific application? Can it be made easier to see? Can it be made easier to transport?

Competitive innovation

Competitive factors are present in most marketing activities. The car salesman competes with the salesman of another brand of car; he competes with the real estate salesman. The young family modify many of their original demands because they must spend money for children's needs. Many a family reluctantly change their buying patterns to meet increased medical and dental costs.

Selling innovation

Firms search for the best channel to get their products to the buyer and gain advantage over competing channels. The selling factor may include the tools of the salesperson plus his inducements such as credit advantages, transportation advances, packaging changes, size of order, product order mix, discount patterns, and price inducements.

Product innovation

A firm frequently must change its products because a competitor has brought out something more appealing. This fact is evident in the changes in paper products. It is unlikely that adding color and decorations have increased a napkin's functional advantage, but such changes apparently have appealed to users, forcing manufacturers to add these features to hold their markets. Colors, sizes of packages, and minute quality variations overload supermarket shelves with variety, giving customers greater choice; yet many of these variations have proved to be overly costly.

A new piece of equipment, although more expensive than the one it replaces, more than covers its cost when it improves quality, speeds up production, and operates with minimum attention. It may be more versatile so that it has additional applications; it may require minimum maintenance.

Pricing innovation

A pricing innovation may be new to an individual firm even though it has been used by others. So-called innovations in pricing may be replicas of methods used so long ago they have been forgotten. Most price innovations are modifications of existing methods; few, if any, are distinctly new. The primary purpose of price innovation is not newness, but a fresh appeal to a buyer.

Price innovation may take a number of directions. A firm may quote a complete price for equipment or quote a price for the basic piece of equipment and quote each accessory separately. Price may include variations based on time. Off-season orders are frequently sold at a discount. Contracting in advance may change prices. A variable price for an order delivered over a time period is not uncommon. The cost of raw material precludes a fixed price over a period of time. Manufacturers will often guarantee a dealer against any price change for a definite period.

Pricing innovations appear to be limited only by individual ingenuity. Some do not succeed because they were poorly conceived. Others which appear successful may be transient. The successful innovator does not shout fictitious prices, but develops new ways or substantial deviations from old methods to warrant them being called innovations.

Channel innovation

There are a number of well-known channels of distribution. Channel innovation may use these well-known forms in different situations and thus create an innovation. For example, the industry as a whole may rely on one channel, but one firm may choose another common channel and succeed. Perhaps others might imitate them and fail because this specific channel is very limited.

Hybrid channels may be superior to one channel of distribution. This situation may be true when the market is heterogeneous—many buyers in various size firms manufacturing unlike products. Spotty potential might encourage split-distribution channels.

Some firms with limited production and a narrow line find it advantageous to sell to a similar firm with a good marketing organization. Similarly, a firm with a good marketing organization will seek small firms and offer to do their marketing for them. This procedure is very effective when the products are complementary.

Franchise operations are not a recent development, but their uses and extensions into new areas are innovative. Time innovations are becoming popular; merchants are keeping their businesses open at hours more favorable to customers. Recording devices, such as computer terminals instead of the typical cash register, not only record transactions but give information on customer credit, inventories, and many other operating statistics.

Packaging innovation

Packaging costs often exceed the cost of the product packaged. Some of these costs arise from the packaging requirements, but others arise from the idea that the package should be a good selling tool. Packaging can be bulky and raise costs of transportation. It needs to be monitored constantly to discover ways of doing it better and cheaper. Too often manufacturers forget that most packaging purposes are temporary in nature and merely facilitate marketing functions related to the product.

Packaging costs can also reflect shipping costs. Changes in materials, sizes, and types of containers may reflect great changes in transportation costs. Often a change in packaging permits a lower freight rate.

A package must protect over time periods, against heat and cold, against light, air, insects, molds, and dry and wet environments. Protection makes a product available for longer periods and in different forms—canning, freezing, drying. Protection preserves against undesirable influences—heat, cold, sunshine, spoilage, time, space, poison. The number of ways to protect a product by packaging (which may include change in product form) is limited by nature's provision and by man's ingenuity. Packaging to aid selling adds another product dimension.

Disposing of packaging is growing in importance. This new dimension introduces factors to test people's ingenuity. Too often, new packaging features have been added to enhance the product, but little thought was given to used package disposal. The change from bulk to packaged products has accentuated the package disposal problem.

Advertising innovation

The successful firm will not succeed indefinitely on "me-too" advertising. It must originate new ideas to attract prospects. It must continue to stress fundamentals without stressing boring detail and repetitious boasting.

Fresh and challenging ways to present a product do not come about easily. Government restrictions prohibit some advertising procedures. Statements that appear questionable must be documented. Public complaints about excessive advertising costs must be countered. Innovation demands greater customer response to advertising while holding costs to reasonable amounts. Constant study and cost monitoring are necessary to justify media used, advertisement size, use of color, frequency of insertion, and content quality.

Promotion innovation

Promotion can be directed to buyers as with point-of-purchase aids and to wholesalers, retailers, and others in the channel of distribution as aids to facilitate marketing. There are many opportunities to expand with fresh ideas and devices. For example, the card to which a small item (such as a disposable cigarette lighter) is attached in a transparent enclosure can have an interesting piece of descriptive promotion as well as be a deterrent to a thief because of the size of the card.

Some manufacturers might benefit by using convention exhibits, ethnic festivals, farm auction sales, hospitality parties, fairs, parades, sports contests, and other special occasions. Products are merchandised by church groups, lodges, women's and men's associations, and many other groups. Direct selling by individual salespeople and by mail thrives on new approaches. Many promotions work entirely through the written word.

Promotions have a wider latitude and flexibility than advertising; they may be directed to segments of society, geographical areas, and other specific prospects. They can be pinpointed, measured, controlled, amplified, and directed in many ways. They may be expensive or inexpensive, conducted over long or short periods of time, and their thrusts changed to respond to new hypotheses. Promotion is one of the most flexible tools to create demand.

Finance innovation

Companies frequently gain advantages by introducing new ways of financing. Almost every year, we see a new financing variation which appeals to customers. Most of them are designed to cushion and spread cost over time to permit simultaneous paying and enjoying the product. Manufacturers induce dealers to make payments or even prepayments before they receive the product by offering attractive discounts.

The marketing innovator must think of new ways to offer financial services to the buyer. He must operate within the framework of national, state, and local laws. He should plan new approaches that will increase the number of people who can buy. Twenty-four hour banking, credit cards, extended payments, prepayment discounts, and leasing are a few of the many ways to help prospects become buyers. Dozens of ways have been advanced to make financing easier; some of them are tailored precisely for particular market segments.

Transportation innovation

Transportation has become complex and extended. Through the use of advanced technology, computers, and innovative applications, movement of products has taken on new aspects which result in substantial savings.

Movement by land, water, and air vie with one another for merchandise; trains, trucks, buses, pipe lines, and other means compete on land; barges, freighters, container ships, and rafts compete on water; in the air, there is competition between passenger and freight planes.

Improvements in packaging, crating, and combining shipments lower costs and speed up delivery. Containerization has speeded up shipments and reduced breakage and pilferage. Use of different material has lightened the shipping package. Greater attention to the type of package often reduces freight rates by coming under a different tariff.

Conveyor systems often furnish a low cost way of transporting. Sometimes a firm can arrange for economical hauling by using trucks returning empty to their place of origin. Through trains to one purchaser are economical in hauling coal. Special loading equipment shortens the time equipment is not moving. Around-the-clock use of equipment speeds up shipment and reduces costs in time and money. More efficient and reliable transportation reduces the need for large inventories. Combining and careful coordinating of shipment shortens shipping time, eliminates frequent handling, and utilizes equipment more effectively. Use of computers permits close control of transportation units.

QUESTIONS AND PROBLEMS

1. What opportunities exist for sales managers in the business world?
2. Compare administrative guidance with administrative direction, showing how both are necessary.
3. What is involved in administrative review?
4. Why must a sales manager be creative?
5. Why should the top sales executives be included in top management decisions?
6. Explain why sales operating functions are the most important tasks of the sales manager.
7. Budgeting usually concerns future monetary expenditures. Could one extend this to other areas such as time?
8. What is the role of the sales manager in customer relations?
9. Which areas of policy making demand the sales executive as a member of top management? Why are they so important to the sales department?
10. What is a policy? Give several definitions.
11. Differentiate and illustrate the difference between major and minor policies.
12. Discuss the importance of marketing innovation. Use at least two approaches.
13. Why do you think the author used the approach of this textbook to

marketing innovation rather than listing and describing particular marketing innovations?

14. After reading this chapter, do you see new dimensions to the job of sales manager? Explain.

---

case 1-1   **WILSON COMPANY**

Wilson Company is a family-owned regional household products manufacturer. Its product line is divided into three distinct areas—bleaches, dish detergents, and soap powders.

In December Mr. Oak, the owner, called a meeting to discuss sales, profits, and overall operations of the firm. Mr. Green, the sales manager, began the meeting by saying that although sales were increasing, the company was in trouble. Oak, an old-timer and a former hard-working salesman, interrupted him by saying, "Boy, what do you mean we're in trouble; sales volume is increasing rapidly with no end in sight. You had better be able to back up what you're telling us, or else." Green, somewhat shaken by the remarks, proceeded to show that while sales had definitely increased over the past few years, market share had decreased (Table 1–1). Oak, impressed by the chart, told

Table 1–1
Total sales in region ($ millions)

Year	Company volume	Industry volume	Company share of mkt. (%)
1975	2.25	37.5	3.00
1974	2.10	32.5	3.20
1973	1.95	30.0	3.70
1972	1.70	26.0	3.75
1971	1.60	19.5	4.10

Green to make a study of why the company's share had decreased and what should be done to overcome the situation. Oak was of the opinion that the sales force was not performing and gave strict orders to "fire the loafers."

Green was determined to analyze the problem and ascertain which product lines were the most profitable. Data on sales were collected for the last four years (the results are listed in Table 1–2). It was apparent to Green that soap powders were decreasing in sales even though 40 percent of the company's advertising was concentrated on the soap powder line. The sales manager believed that sales on soap powders were decreasing because of recent product innovations in

Table 1–2
Company sales for product lines ($ millions)

Year	Bleaches	Detergents	Soap powders	Totals
1975	1.1	0.9	0.25	2.25
1974	1.0	0.8	0.30	2.10
1973	0.9	0.6	0.45	1.95
1972	0.8	0.4	0.50	1.70

the field. Green felt that heavy advertising by competitors stressing new product innovation had weakened the market position of Wilson's soap line.

Before recommending new product introduction or the possible dropping of the present line, Green felt a study of contribution to overhead was needed. Oak felt that since the soap powder line had the highest gross margin on sales, it should be stressed most heavily by advertising. He thought that the soap powder line was the most profitable and contributed the most to the operation. Green had an idea that low turnover and sales had discounted the high margin and that this fact, coupled with the introduction of new products, had made the soap powder line actually the least profitable line. The results of a study conducted by Green seemed to bear out these ideas (Table 1–3).

Table 1–3
Gross margin on sales (dollars)

	Year	Bleaches	Detergents	Soap powders
% of Sales		5%	10%	20%
Total gross	1975	55,000	90,000	50,000
margin	1974	50,000	80,000	60,000
($ dollars)	1973	45,000	60,000	90,000
	1972	35,000	40,000	100,000

After making these studies, the sales manager was convinced that advertising costs had been wasted on a dying product line and that the salesmen had been performing as well as could be expected in the face of fierce competition. Green was under strict orders from the boss to "get rid of the loafers," so he felt an evaluation of salesman performance was needed.

The sales manager reviewed his four salesmen to assess each man's sales volume and profitability. The Wilson sales territory was divided into a central city sales district and an outlying sales district. Two salesmen covered the central city, which was smaller in size than the outlying district. The difference in size of the district reflected the management's opinion of market potential for each district. Green felt the potential sales development was smaller for all the regions. The firm, having no previous data on market potential for the region, hired

McCabe Marketing Consultants to determine what salesmen were reaching their potentials and were producing adequately. The study took three months, and the results were summarized by Green in Table 1–4. From this study he concluded that the sales from the two city

Table 1–4
Evaluation of salesman performance, 1975

	Joe	Sam	Dave	Bill
Total sales	$900,000	$700,000	$400,000	$250,000
Calls made	1,500	1,600	1,200	1,000
Miles travelled	20,000	25,000	35,000	40,000
Market potential	$2,700,000	$1,500,000	$800,000	$450,000

salesmen, Joe and Sam, were far below market potential; and although they had high sales volumes, they were not performing as well as the other two salesmen for the outlying district—Dave and Bill.

Just as the sales manager was studying these results, a memo came from Oak stressing the importance of sales volume to the firm and that low sales volume was the result of poor selling by the sales force. He ordered Green to fire the salesman with the lowest sales volume and replace him with someone who could sell. Green knew that Bill was the salesman who had the lowest sales volume, but he also knew that other factors had to be considered in determining sales performance. From the data, Bill had shown himself to be a hard worker because of the miles driven and the number of calls made; but the decision to fire the people who were not performing meant that someone had to go. Green also contemplated splitting Joe's territory and assigning the new territory to another salesman, but he had to prove the logic of his decision to top management.

Green knew his job rested on how well he could prove himself when recommending changes in the selling and product structure. He prepared a chart indicating present profit for each product line (Table 1–5). He felt the chart clearly indicated soap powders should be

Table 1–5

	Bleaches	Detergents	Soap powders	Total
Gross margin on sales	$55,000	$90,000	$50,000	$195,000
Advertising costs	20,000	25,000	30,000	75,000
Handling and operating expenses	5,000	5,000	10,000	20,000
Net profit before taxes	$30,000	$60,000	$10,000	$100,000

dropped before the line became unprofitable altogether. Green assembled his charts and prepared his summary to be presented at the next board meeting. In this summary, he concluded that due to the decreasing unprofitability of the present soap powder line, it should be dropped or new products added quickly to meet competition. He also stated that advertising should be more equitably placed on those products whose profitability was demonstrated. He stated that the present sales staff should be maintained with possible territory re-adjustment. There was a long lull before Oak announced that the plan was weak, adding that to eliminate soap powders would leave Wilson with an incomplete product line far more dangerous than the present situation. He also added that people bought from Wilson because of its long tradition of quality and to change this image product line was impossible.

ASSIGNMENT

1. List the different jobs, duties, and items of sales management presented in this chapter that can be applied to this case.
2. You may wish to return to this case after completing the textbook and try to isolate the problem or problems involved and suggest solutions.

FACING LIFE AS A SALES MANAGER   case 1–2

You have now completed the first chapter of *Sales Management*. It is an introduction to a new area for most of you. You may regard it as just another course or as a step to creating a career which may lead to outstanding successes. Its appeal may present a new direction for your future work. At this point, you have just sampled the breadth and achievement possible if you follow up this opportunity. The whole area of sales management is essentially selling—selling yourself to others in such a way that your work helps them to live a fuller life. Begin now to measure what you may achieve by answering the following questions.

QUESTIONS

1. List the topics you thought this course covered before you registered for it.
2. After reading this chapter, how have you changed your concept of sales management?
3. What genuine opportunity do you believe is open to you in your future career? Keep in mind that all of us must sell ourselves to others—employers, employees, customers, friends, and even competitors.

Organizing the Sales Department

In thousands of small companies, organization develops informally and in response to the need to control particular functions. If an individual started the company, he handled all of the so-called white-collar work himself. If two people started a firm, they probably agreed to share management; one took charge of production and very likely the buying of raw material, and the other took over the sales function and the office. In neither of these firms was there any formal organization, but merely a division of responsibilities. Hiring was the responsibility of the person who was to use the employee. If there were two or more owners in the company, they exercised considerable autonomy.

As a company increases in size, work multiplies, employees increase, and white-collar jobs increase. The person handling office and sales finds it burdensome to supervise office activities; a third member executive is put in charge of all office activities including financial, accounting, hiring, purchasing, and office supervision. By this time, the original owners are too busy to direct any specific activity. As a result, they have the type of organization shown in Figure 2–1.

Figure 2–1

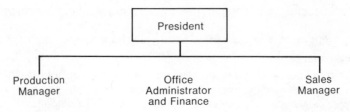

If the company still has two original owners, one is now president, and the other is vice-president in charge of one of the three major activities. Even though the second is shown as subordinate in the organization chart, his authority is equal to the president's. By this time, more owners with additional capital may have joined. Two co-owners may develop conflicts, and one may take precedence over the other if the firm continues.

A growing company needs increased supervision. Other major executive posts are created, such as personnel manager, office manager, and director of purchasing. By this time, the sales department is devoting all its time and energy to the firm's marketing activities, and the sales manager no longer has to control home office operations.

In this description there have emerged at least three, or possibly more, strong administrators to aid the president—sales, production, and finance. These men or women are involved in major decisions and are given great authority. Within this framework we shall now develop the sales function, broadly conceived as the marketing function, which covers all activities of moving products to the final buyer—selling, advertising, promoting, research, distributing, handling customers, and others.

The top sales executive may be known as vice-president of sales, marketing manager, or sales manager. Whatever his title, he is responsible for creating sales and moving merchandise and/or services. In a small firm he has charge of many activities, including direction of the sales force. In most medium-sized firms he has the same assignment with one or more assistants assigned to specific areas. In large firms his job is primarily executive, and most of the work is subdivided and headed by competent managers under his direction. In this text we are primarily concerned with the sales executive who must handle salespeople and be involved in top decisions affecting the marketing function.

SALES ORGANIZATION STRUCTURES

Most sales organizations fall into one of three types—line, line and staff, and functional.

The *line organization* is the simplest and is frequently used by small firms and many new firms. This type has relatively few executives; each has definite authority which flows directly down; and relationships are defined. Often all the decision-making functions are made by one, two, or three executives who work closely together and probably contact one another daily. As long as the firm remains small and all the executives are bound closely together, this organization is quick, flexible, and responsive. When a firm grows, line organization becomes cumbersome because too much must be expedited through one or two narrow channels. In addition, excessive delays result because overburdened executives simply cannot cope with the multitude of duties. This top constriction slows action and frustrates capable subordinates, who may leave for more inviting positions. Thus, the very organization which at first was most useful because it could act quickly now becomes unwieldy.

The *line and staff organization* seeks to get out of the straight-jacket line organization by setting up more functional areas, each under the supervision of an executive who operates in a narrower assignment. As the work grows, more line positions with responsibility are created, and more staff positions are set up to furnish assistance and information to the line executives.

The *functional organization* is based on an individual manager's authority to follow his function through the sales organization. The sales manager would direct salespeople; the advertising manager would give them direct orders relating to his area; the credit manager would tell them how to handle credit, the sales promotion manager would instruct them in placing displays; and other managers would have direct authority in their areas. This system is bewildering and can become distressing to a salesperson, particularly when each product manager insists that he gives more attention to a particular product line.

MARKETING DEPARTMENT ORGANIZATION

The marketing (sales) department is usually organized in a line and staff relationship. The department is headed by a sales executive known as *vice-president of sales, marketing manager,* or *sales manager.* Below him or her are a number of assistants assigned to specific functions. Some of them are known as *line people* because they are directly concerned with activities that sell goods or services; others called *staff* work at activities that help the line employees do a better job. A sales manager is a line man because his duty is to supervise selling. The marketing research manager is a staff man because it is his job to gather information and make suggestions to the sales executive. The personnel manager heads a staff department that provides employees; the advertising manager assists by promoting sales; and the credit manager assists by checking on customer finances. Although staff departments perform facilitative functions, keep in mind that within each department is a line organization to keep it functioning.

In practice, organizations frequently are not so clearly defined, and often there may be confusion as to flow of authority. This confusion is compounded if a strong staff manager usurps authority over a weak line manager. Consequently, employees may disregard the published organization chart and adjust to current situations within the management structure. That is, they recognize how the existing situation operates and not how it is supposed to operate.

Span of Control

Within any sales organization, there are limits to which a manager can supervise individual employees. As long as the sales department is small, one person can supervise all the work. As it expands and duties increase, the manager must delegate more work, authority, and responsibility. Often he does so reluctantly, usually when he becomes overburdened.

How many people one manager can handle depends on the complexity of the task and the capability of each person directing a particular job. If the relationship between a manager and his subordinates is complex, a 1 to 6 ratio might be suitable; if the relationship is less complex, more subordinates can be handled. If the top manager is extremely effective, he may handle more subordinates. Some firms prefer a narrow span of control with few subordinates reporting to one manager; other firms use a wide span of control, where a large number of subordinates report to one manager. Both types are used successfully by major corporations. A wide span of control uses a shallower organization than a narrow span of control, which requires more echelons or layers of management.

Organization Within a Firm

A small company may have a sales manager whose job is to hire, train, compensate, supervise, and motivate the sales force, handle customer complaints, supervise the employees in the sales office, and perform a variety of other duties. In addition, he may do some selling. His entire staff may consist of one secretary and three salespeople.

When the staff grows to two secretaries and six salespeople, the sales manager is likely to designate one person as a supervisor-salesperson who continues to sell part time and assists the other salespeople. By this time, the sales manager may decide to handle most direct salesperson supervision himself and assign many of the routine office activities to a subordinate. As the job grows, the sales manager must share some of the work with one or more subordinates. As the company grows, the job of the sales manager becomes more that of an administrator and coordinator although he retains a line status assignment. Figure 2–2 indicates this transition.

If he still retains the title of sales manager, the person below him receives a title such as assistant sales manager or field sales manager. This person, however, is responsible for handling the sales force and generating sales. The other managers have staff positions which aid the direct selling force.

Marketing Manager

Marketing people suggest that the title of marketing manager should be given to the chief sales executive since his job should be related to

Figure 2–2

Sales Manager performs
all management functions.

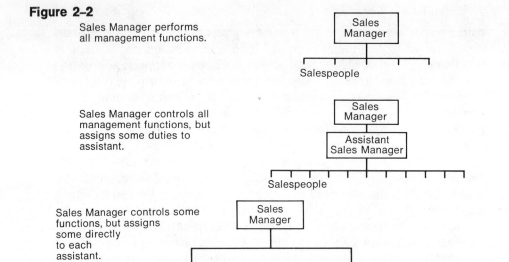

Sales Manager controls all
management functions, but
assigns some duties to
assistant.

Sales Manager controls some
functions, but assigns
some directly
to each
assistant.

Sales Manager has taken the title of Sales Executive.
(Other possible titles: Vice-President of Sales,
Marketing Manager)

all activities directed toward moving goods to the buyer. In practice, however, this title is given to individuals whose duties vary widely. Therefore, the title marketing manager must be equated to the position described in a firm's organization manual.

ORGANIZATION WITHIN A SALES DIVISION

The firm organized into separate production, selling, and finance divisions, departments, or units (a variety of names are used) may find it advantageous to develop a unique organization for sales to meet its requirements. There are different ways to focus selling attention in order to maximize effort, and at times it may be difficult to justify one type of organization over another.

A standard organization plan may be comfortable and seem to fit a sales department quite well. Further examination may reveal that some parts of the sales program are seriously impaired because of the existing organization. For example, a change in product mix could require a different organization; a new type of customer might suggest change; adding or dropping subsidiaries would require some adjustment.

Organizing by Geographical Territory

One common division of sales by geography is the domestic division and the international division. This division suggests itself because distribution abroad is considerably different from that within the country.

When a firm has large sales with salespeople operating in many physical areas, it is often desirable to break the sales area into regions, each headed by a regional manager. If each region is unwieldy, it is customary to divide it into districts, each headed by a district manager, who reports to a regional manager.

Physical areas vary greatly as to sales productivity. Some regions and/or districts may be relatively large but thinly populated; others may be small but heavily populated. Frequently, one city district may be more productive than another state district. Seldom is it possible to set up equally productive areas. Not only may potential sales vary but also the ability of managers and sales forces within districts, the degree of competition, distance from delivery points, and other factors may affect sales. Often territory allocations are changed to reflect economic changes or merely to carry out a change in philosophy or direction of management.

Closer supervision can be one of the major benefits of geographic territories because they are usually small. Hence, salespeople can be made more responsive to executive direction. Another major advantage is to tailor effort and operation to specific territory needs. A third advantage is that it can bring management closer to the customer.

Organizing by Product Categories

A firm may have one or relatively few major products and a number of minor ones. If one salesperson were to handle all products, he might favor some and neglect others. Sometimes one product is so important that it demands the attention of the entire sales organization. Because of the many differences that may be present—customer, volume, profitability, perishability—effort may be grouped by product or product category.

In Figure 2–3, product A could be one that has heavy demand and is sold in large unit volume. For example, a minimum order would be a carload. Products B and C would have several varieties, be sold in moderate volume to the same buyers, and require frequent sales-

Figure 2–3

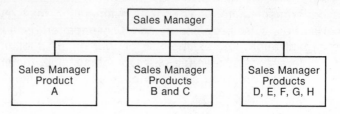

person calls. Products D, E, F, G, and H would be a family of products with wide appeal to many customers and purchased frequently in moderate quantities.

Some firms sell such diverse products that it would be unwise to have one salesperson or one selling department to handle them all. Few people have the ability to push many lines effectively. When salespeople are required to push many lines, they usually give less attention to some products. A further consideration arises when products have a wide price range. It is unlikely that a salesperson selling one item for a thousand dollars and another for ten dollars will give much attention to the latter. Figure 2–4 illustrates organization by products of a major equipment manufacturer.

A refinement in organization by products is introduced when there are direct sales staffs selling several products with each product under the supervision of a product manager with no direct line authority. While this approach may seem disorganized and does present operating problems, it is used when particular products are so important that extra effort is warranted. For example, an appliance manufacturer could have a product manager for television and related entertainment items, one for refrigeration equipment, and one for washers and dryers.

Organization by Customer

Some companies have found that organizing by customer has advantages because of customer differences and because the same channel of distribution may not operate satisfactorily for all.

Industrial customers

A company may sell a universal product—such as flour to bakeries— where quantities are enormous, price highly competitive, and uniform delivery important. A refiner may supply large quantities of gasoline or other fuel to one or several industrial buyers. Processing firms buy fruits and vegetables in large quantities. Some of these products must meet rigid specifications, but other users are not so exacting. For example, certain parts sold to car manufacturers for original installation must meet strict quality control standards, but replacement requirements may not be nearly so exacting.

Many industrial buyers are trained to detect weaknesses in purchases quickly. In addition, they have testing laboratories to check

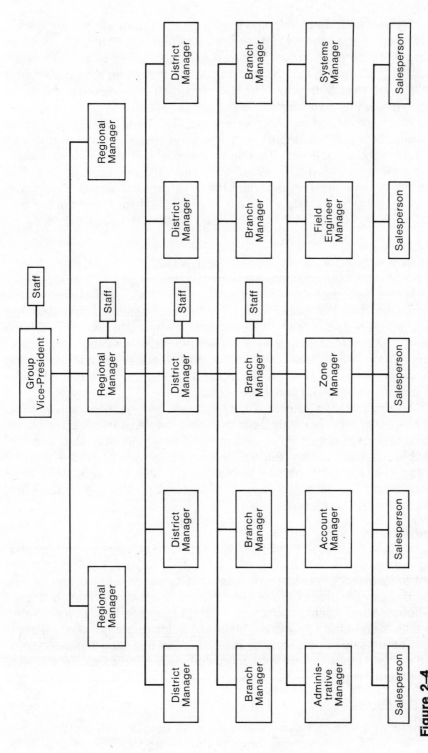

Figure 2–4
Sales Organization for One Group of Products of a Major Equipment Manufacturer
(Only one executive position is detailed at each level.)

quality and uniformity. In some cases, a selling firm will have someone stationed in the user's plant, or the salesman must be ready to go as a troubleshooter if called. For example, one buyer in a major automobile firm stated that he did not want the seller's representative calling too frequently; but if he did want him, the salesman should be available within two hours.

A further division of customers separates large buyers by type of activity. One major computer manufacturer has a salesman in Detroit calling only on schools. Technical salespeople are used to handle many sales requiring specialized skill. Thus, the paint salesman selling his product for use on the manufactured product would have a different job from the man who sells factory paint for maintenance purposes. Both would differ from the man who sells house paints.

Resale customers

When a firm sells to wholesalers and retailers as well as industrial users, it may have separate sales forces calling on each group within the same geographical area. Each group of salespeople may have somewhat different qualifications, and compensation schedules may vary in nature and amount. Supervision may be quite different for each group; expense accounts may differ; length of training period may vary. For example, one large paint manufacturer trained beginning salesmen selling to retailers six months or less, but an industrial paint salesman was trained for three years.

One organization structure may fit well into districts and regions where each area not only sells but also has a warehouse used for deliveries and repair service. Some firms may split lines among salespeople even when they sell to the same customer, because the line is too much for one person to handle. Of course, major firms have many buyers so it is not likely two salespeople from the same firm would see the same buyer.

Home customers

Some firms distribute through several groups of salespeople depending on the product and type of customers. When a firm adds a line that sells directly to homes, it sets up a sales division to handle this distribution. Several of the well-known companies distributing house-to-house have been purchased by larger companies and operated as a division of the new owner. Since the sales operation is so different from other sales operations of the firm, it is operated independently, subject, of course, to overall supervision of the top sales executive of the parent firm.

Service Organizations

Many companies sell service and have no tangible product.

Transportation firms may have a simple organization in which the sales manager directly supervises each salesperson and perhaps spends part of his time soliciting business. A district organization may have one or more salespeople who report directly to the general manager of all operations in the area and have no one who functions directly as sales executive.

The marketing departments of financial institutions can be organized in different ways depending on type of service offered, the aggressiveness of the firm, and its clientele.

Combination Organizations

It is unwise to characterize any one organization as typical, because it may be inadequate in a particular situation. Any firm may develop an organization pertinent to its needs. Hybrid organizations may be preferable to fit the pattern of a firm's distribution. As long as an organization functions effectively, it should be continued.

Sometimes diverse arrangements may prove to be too great a strain on the sales executive, and he will not remain long on the job unless he disassociates himself from many separate activities. His success will be measured by operating at a high level in the organization and appointing strong assistant sales managers to handle each subdivision.

These subdivisions may be separate with a wide range of products. One geographic division may have one district sales manager handling two or three groups of salespeople operating in different fashions. Another arrangement might be a group of salespeople operating under a district manager, but within this district might be one salesperson on special accounts reporting directly to the home office and not subject to the district manager's control. Some firms have two district managers in the same geographic area, each heading a sales force calling on a separate group of buyers. For example, one drug wholesaler has a sales organization for calling on drug retailers and hospitals but also has a separate sales organization to sell heavy chemicals.

Committee Organization

The committee organization is rarely used as the single control in a sales department, although committees frequently supplement present organization. Committee responsibility and authority are difficult to use in a line operation. The committee functions chiefly in an advisory and informative capacity.

The committee may explore the introduction of a new product or different sizes of an existing product. A top level committee can synchronize activities and obtain a mutual understanding of problems of each major division.

Within the sales department, committees can be used to determine sales promotion and advertising objectives and to synchronize these activities with salespeople's work. The sales manager may call his assistants together to explore and finalize policy changes not subject to higher executive decision, or to agree on a uniform approach to aid the sales manager when he must present an important topic to the president. Committees may be set up permanently or temporarily to perform intermittent functions and to furnish advice to supplement a sales executive's background, training, and judgment.

ORGANIZATION, AN EFFECTIVE AID TO SALESPEOPLE

A well-developed sales organization is an effective aid to salespeople and promotes harmony, efficiency, productivity, and profitability because it furnishes a framework in which to fit operations and responsibilities.

Objectives

Building a complete sales organization requires careful planning. Objectives must be detailed specifically and not left in generalizations. For example, it is not enough to say that the firm wishes to sell x amount of products at a profit. It is necessary to determine where to sell, the product mix in each category, the type of distribution, price policies, and other information before an organization can be developed. For example, an entirely different organization would be planned if the firm sold through manufacturers' agents than if it used its own sales staff. There would be a difference if a firm sold through wholesalers or sold directly to retailers. There would be a difference if the firm decided to be price competitive or intended to promote through brand and advertising.

Functions of a Sales Force

The sales force operating functions could be determined in advance and the organization made to fit accordingly. The firm should spell out precisely what a salesperson should do—sell, service, deliver, handle credit, set up displays, handle sales meetings. All of these are possible duties, but most salespeople perform only some of them. The type of selling, number of customers each person should handle, territory size, travel conditions, and other pertinent factors should be given careful scrutiny.

Coordination

Coordination becomes relatively easy when proper assignments are designated and authority, responsibility, and informational flow are spelled out. The ability to coordinate smoothly so that each factor falls in place at the proper time helps assure smooth performance. Without proper direction and a map of operational flow, the job of coordination becomes difficult.

Organization Chart

The organization chart is a drawing or blueprint of personnel planned by the sales executive. Should there be a hang-up in operation, it becomes easy to trace and to alert the responsible individual what he must do. It tells the story of the sales organization not only to management but to every employee in the firm. The salesperson sees the steps in the organization, how he or she can progress, and how many steps there are to the top.

Organization Manual

The organization manual describes the duties of each job shown on the organization chart. It details work, responsibility, authority, and liaison among the staff. With an effective sales organization carefully developed to fit objectives of the firm, with an organization chart to show how it is made up, and with an organization manual that describes the duties of each job, there is a clear map for each person in the department to follow.[1]

QUESTIONS AND PROBLEMS

1. Trace the development of an organization for a small firm. Outline the step-by-step procedure.

2. What are the two basic types of organizational structure? How do they differ and what are the advantages of each?

3. What is the span of control in an organization, and what are some of the reasons for varying its size from company to company?

4. Discuss the changes in a sales manager's job as the company grows (a) in size and (b) in complexity.

5. Describe a sales organization developed by geographical territories. Indicate why this organizational approach is frequently used.

6. When does a firm organize its sales division by product categories? Explain the necessity for this approach and how it benefits both the seller and the buyer.

7. Customers may be so diverse that no one salesperson can handle them effectively. Explain why this is true and how proper sales organization can improve customer relations.

8. Why may the sales organization of a firm selling service be quite dif-

---

1. Rather than detailing the numerous sources used in preparing this material, it is suggested that students interested in pursuing the subject read articles listed in the *Business Periodicals Index, Public Affairs Information Service,* and *Vertical File Services.* These are readily available in most libraries. Also consult the numerous management books that cover organization exhaustively. A variety of such sources will give the reader much greater insight in the area, the changes that are taking place, and new theories being advanced.

ferent from a firm that sells products? Explain why these differences may necessitate individual attention to each buyer.

9. Describe the committee type of organization. Indicate where it is most useful and some of its weaknesses.

10. Explain why it is important to determine specifically the objectives of a sales organization before preparing the organization form.

11. What is an organization chart? What is the purpose of an organization manual? How does one reinforce the other?

---

case 2–1   HEATING AND COOLING SYSTEMS, INC.

The merger between Comfort Air, Inc. and Warm Air Systems, Inc. to form Heating and Cooling Systems, Inc. prompted an evaluation of each segment of the two organizations to determine areas of potential cost reduction or increased efficiency. The recent consolidation of accounting functions, which produced excellent results, made management eager to see a proposal on the sales organizations.

Comfort Air, Inc.

Comfort Air, Inc. was a manufacturer of a full line of air conditioners for home, automobile, and commercial uses. Although Comfort Air had been relatively successful in the air conditioner business, it could not adequately compete with larger competitors without offering heating systems. Sales of the company's products are shown in Exhibit 2–1.

Exhibit 2–1
Comfort Air, Inc. Sales Data
(*In millions of dollars*)

	Total	Automobile	Commercial	Home
1974	$196.3	$5.2	$12.3	$178.8
1973	187.1	5.0	11.4	170.7
1972	178.4	4.1	8.4	165.9
1971	162.4	2.9	6.0	153.5
1970	154.8	2.4	4.0	148.4

(Prior data not available)

Comfort Air depended largely on consumer advertising in selling its products. Its brand was well known for quality and reliability. Brand identification and price are the two chief factors considered by ultimate consumers since service is seldom needed.

Comfort Air depended exclusively on franchise dealers for distribution of its products. Department stores, large hardware stores, major appliance stores, and air conditioning contractors were the principal outlets.

Comfort Air products were sold in all states except Alaska and Hawaii. Sales increases were anticipated by adding dealers in areas where coverage was inadequate.

In establishing new franchise dealers, an executive sales representative, who reports directly to a district manager, contacts the potential dealer. The salesman is thoroughly grounded in product information, company policy, competitive practices, and economic conditions. Prior to making initial contact with the potential dealer, the Corporate Market Research Department makes an exhaustive study of the city to determine population, climate, business outlook, competition, and desirable dealers. The executive sales representative, with the aid of this research data, is fully prepared to solicit a dealer.

After a franchise dealer is signed and initial problems inherent in establishing a new dealer are solved, the account is turned over to a salaried district salesman who is responsible for the territory. A district salesman, on his own initiative, cannot solicit new franchise dealers. He is expected, however, to recommend potential dealers and to identify prime open points in the dealer network.

The sales organization for Comfort Air, Inc. is shown in Exhibit 2–2. Each regional manager is responsible for twelve states; each district manager, four states; and each state supervisor, one state. The number of district salesmen active in a state varies from three in Montana to twenty in California. There are 450 district salesmen employed.

National advertising programs are designed and controlled by the director of advertising. Regional advertising is not a common practice but does occur when engaged in by competitors. If penetration is below desirable limits in a state, advertising is directed at the state in an attempt to stimulate sales.

Advertising copy is available free to dealers for local use. Dealers are encouraged to use the copy, but Comfort Air refuses to share dealer advertising costs.

Credit approval is the responsibility of the corporate finance staff. They determine limits for each dealer whereby approval of specific orders is not required as long as the outstanding account balance plus the new order fall within the established limit.

Technical service assistance from the engineering department or the manufacturing department is available upon request.

District salesmen train dealers to complete orders and to process normal claim reports without having to assist the dealer personally.

Warm Air Systems, Inc.

Warm Air Systems, Inc. is a manufacturer of commercial and home heating units distributed throughout the United States. The product line varies from small space bathroom heaters to large industrial units.

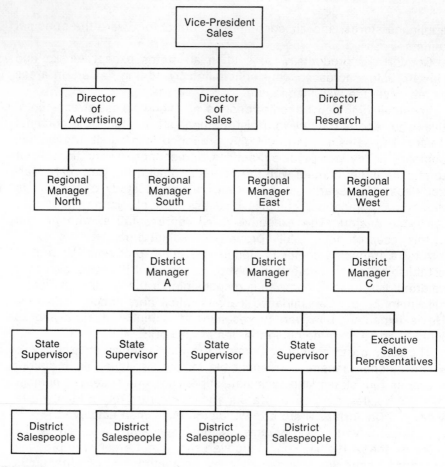

Exhibit 2–2
Comfort Air, Inc. Sales Organization
(*Region East is given in full. Other regions are similar.*)

All products were sold under the brand name "Bear" except when marketed through several large chains which used their own brand name.

Historical sales information is presented in Exhibit 2–3.

Exhibit 2–3
Warm Air Systems, Inc. Sales Data

	Total	*Commercial*	*Home*
1974	$170.2	$7.8	$162.4
1973	168.2	7.6	160.6
1972	178.5	7.1	171.4
1971	181.2	5.6	175.6
1970	171.3	3.2	168.1

(Prior data not available)

Management was convinced that the absence of an air conditioning line was the principal reason for slow sales growth. Competitors were realizing a constant growth rate of about 4 percent each year, but they offered air conditioner products.

Warm Air distributed its products through chain department stores, heating contractors, and wholesalers. Since the bulk of sales were for small home room units, price was the principal influencing factor.

The organization of Warm Air is shown in Exhibit 2–4. Although not shown on the exhibit, technical service assistance from the corporate engineering department is available upon request from a territory supervisor.

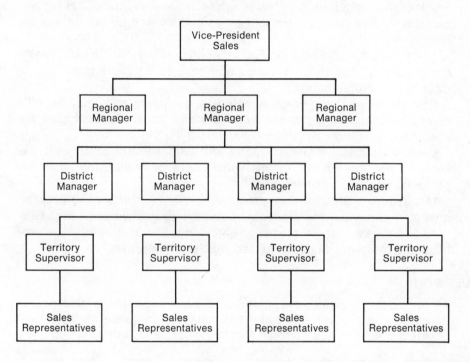

Exhibit 2–4
Warm Air Systems, Inc. Sales Organization
(One district is given in detail. The others are similar.)

Advertising is done exclusively through heating industry journals and direct mailing to potential customers. Advertising budgets are developed by each district manager. Generally it is the sole responsibility of the district manager whether to allocate the total available selling resources toward personal selling effort or advertising. In practice, less than 1 percent of all selling expense is allocated to advertising. The absence of extensive advertising is one factor which enables the company to compete effectively in price.

Credit is approved by the corporate credit department. Since field sales representatives know corporate credit policies, few problems are experienced in granting credit.

Heating and Cooling Systems, Inc.

The merger of Comfort Air and Warm Air Systems is expected to be mutually advantageous. Since each company was previously selling a seasonal product, operating efficiencies are expected in areas such as warehousing and manufacturing. These factors were generally determined before the merger.

Management of the new company is opposed to operating the heating and air conditioner sales organizations separately. However, opposing views have recently been voiced by key corporate executives:

Sales executive: "Since the two independent companies were pretty successful as they were, it makes no sense to integrate them just to make a few people happy."

Finance executive: "We were able to cut costs and improve efficiency by integrating the two finance staffs; so I see no reason for keeping the selling organizations separate."

Legal executive: "Promises made to the board of directors must be kept. To get the kind of results which were promised, the sales organization should be combined."

Management organization executive: "We will probably never be able to evaluate the profit effects of combining the two sales organizations. I suggest that we strive for efficiency, flexibility, and cohesiveness and keep our fingers crossed that sales improve."

QUESTION

1. Should the two sales organizations be combined? Give a detailed discussion on your choice. Point out advantages and disadvantages of both the present organizations and a combined sales organization.

---

case 2–2   **BLANTON FOODS CORPORATION**

Background

Mr. George Case, Detroit district sales manager of Blanton Foods Corporation, is considering a change in the district's organization. Blanton Foods Corporation is among the largest food manufacturers in the nation, selling over one hundred diversified food products. The Detroit district is the third largest in the nation, having an annual wholesale volume of $25,000,000. Sales in the district have been increasing, and control over the sales force has become more difficult. Compounding the current problem is the fact that next year the Toledo district will be dissolved and become a part of the Detroit district sales group under Mr. Case's control.

Current Organization

The current organization (Exhibit 2–5) shows the sales supervisor, account managers, and the combination position of account manager/ sales supervisor reporting directly to the district manager. The sales

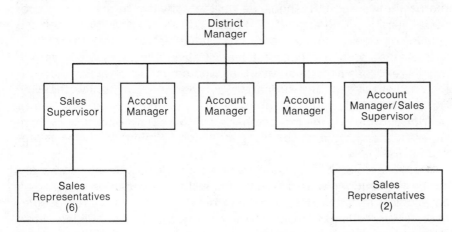

Exhibit 2–5
Detroit District Sales Organization Chart

representatives report to the sales supervisor or account manager/ sales supervisor. The dual role of account manager/sales supervisor was created to fit the needs of the smaller outstate sales force which was not large enough to warrant two separate positions.

The District Manager's Job

The district manager, Mr. Case, coordinates the entire sales effort for the Detroit district. District managers are assigned the responsibilities of setting the district's sales budget (quota) each quarter and guiding the marketing functions. Sales tools used to achieve the budget include buying allowances to meet the local market situations, display allowances, count and recount offers to the wholesale trade, special off-label packs, and special premium packs.

Sometimes the district manager participates in sales presentations to key accounts in an effort to increase distribution, prevent a loss in current distribution, or obtain acceptance of a new product. The time spent with his sales personnel is concentrated with the account managers. This has been a source of irritation with supervisors who have "people" responsibility. Mr. Case feels that the greatest problem with the organization is lack of communication between the account manager and the sales representatives. This problem will be more critical when the Toledo district is merged into the Detroit district since it will add one account manager and four sales representatives.

The Sales Supervisor's Job

The sales supervisor, Carl Nelson, has one of the most difficult jobs in the company. He is two promotions above the lowest job of sales representative and is responsible for the activities of six sales representatives in a 300-mile radius. In addition to "work-withs" when the supervisor rides with the sales representative for a day, he also is responsible for a number of administrative functions, such as approving expense accounts, reviewing and compiling a weekly state-of-the-business letter, and preparing a report on competitive activity. He sets and reviews bonus objectives for his men. He is the Detroit district coordinator for the company's retail data-processing system. He also interviews and selects people for openings as sales representatives.

Mr. Nelson also has account responsibility for wholesalers who are not large enough to warrant key account status and can be serviced by an account manager. He trains and develops new sales representatives. The problem of having enough time to do all his administrative jobs and to spend a "work-with" each week with each sales representative often makes him unavailable for other salesman contacts. Mr. Nelson would like to spend more time with the district manager, who always appears tied up with his account managers.

The Account Manager/Sales Supervisor's Job

Bob Ligget is account manager and sales supervisor in the Grand Rapids, Michigan, area. He handles three key accounts and supervises two sales representatives. He has the same "people" responsibilities as Mr. Nelson. The account manager function requires servicing key accounts in the area in addition to making retail calls on twenty-nine supermarkets. The biggest drawback to the job in Ligget's point of view is that when they have not made quota by the end of the quarter he spends all his time selling. He cannot spend any time with the sales representatives until sales improve.

The Account Manager's Job

The account manager is the next position above sales representative and is performed by people promoted from the sales representative job; or, in some instances, people who were former sales supervisors, but decided to remove themselves from any "people" responsibility and strictly sell. The account manager has three or four key accounts where he attempts to promote additional distribution by use of sales promotions and display activity. The account manager also has thirty to forty retail calls to make per month, where he literally performs the functions of a sales representative. One of the main functions of the account manager is to obtain as much information as possible about competitors' marketing plans, including new products and special offers. This is important because the district manager needs all information available so that he can plan strategy. The account manager is always trying for more shelf space in chains, which will give Blanton products better exposure to the consumer. His efforts are hampered, however, because of small profit margins on his products, although they have very heavy turnover resulting from heavy consumer advertising. Account managers state that they are so busy that they just don't have time to write to the sales representatives and tell them what is going on at chain headquarters.

Sales Representative Functions

The sales representative is responsible for positively influencing the sale of Blanton products in the 100 to 140 stores assigned to him. He attempts to gain distribution, increase shelf space, and promote display activity. These functions are greatly hampered by the strong control chain account supervisors have over their store managers, in that "everything must be authorized by headquarters." Sales representatives also call on two or three small wholesalers who are not large enough to warrant assignment of an account manager. The biggest complaint of the sales representative is that he frequently misses opportunities to get displays because he had no knowledge or no time in advance to plan to make a retail coverage in a chain which has had headquarter authorization to display a particular Blanton product.

Managerial Reactions

Mr. Case is aware that something has to be done to reduce the current problems of lack of communications and people being spread too thin. The district manager is against the account manager/sales supervisor position because it is not fair to all persons and wants this position eliminated in any new organization plan. The regional manager was consulted and gave Mr. Case a free rein to develop whatever form of organization he needs to eliminate the current problem and to consolidate the Toledo district.

Mr. Nelson's Proposal

Mr. Nelson has prepared a proposal for restructuring the district's sales activity. He felt that the first problem existed in the span of control. He noted that Mr. Case had five people reporting to him— three account managers, one sales supervisor, and one account manager/sales supervisor. Each one required some of the district manager's time every day to discuss current conditions in the local market, account status, and personnel situations. As a result, only the most pressing problems were being received with attention. For example, when current distribution was threatened with elimination by a chain, or when a new product needed to be presented to buyers in diversified methods, some account managers were not familiar with new techniques of sales presentations; and Mr. Case would give much of his time to assist them. The sales supervisor was shortchanged because of the district manager's emphasis on getting orders for the quota and neglected sales supervision. One of the people hampered by this situation was Nelson. He knew that his next promotion would be to the district manager's level, and that if he did not receive adequate exposure to district sales management, he would be ill-prepared to handle his own sales district upon promotion.

Nelson knew that account managers disliked assignment to retail stores which they felt beneath them. The time required to make a retail call reduced the time available to communicate with the field sales force concerning current deals, promotions, and product status on the accounts. He felt that the role of account manager/sales supervisor had to be changed.

Nelson's proposed plan is based upon a team. Under this method, a sales supervisor, account manager, and three sales representatives would handle all of the functions related to three or four chains handled by the account manager. This plan would relieve the account manager of his retail store contact responsibility. At weekly meetings with the other members of the team, he could explain what was being done at the headquarters of the chains handled by the team.

Communications was the main emphasis in this program. Nelson felt that the sales representatives could contribute more to district sales and that individual training would be improved. First, the sales representative would still handle small wholesalers, but would also participate with the account manager in calling on key accounts. Upon the sales representative's promotion to account manager, he would be better equipped to handle the larger chains serviced by account managers. This would also solve the district's problem of having someone knowledgeable about the account to call during vacations and periods of illness. Second, the account manager would work more closely with the sales supervisor, gaining insight into the administrative and "people" side of the organization and paving the way for possible promotion to the sales supervisor slot. Finally, the sales supervisor would become involved in all facets of the business, so that upon promotion to district manager, he would know the functions related to the job.

Nelson felt that four "chain teams" would be required, with two teams handling the Detroit and surrounding suburban area, and one each covering the Toledo and outstate Michigan areas.

QUESTIONS

1. What are the basic strengths and weaknesses of the present organization?
2. Give your views of Mr. Nelson's plan for revising the present structure. Indicate the plan's strengths and weaknesses.
3. Prepare your own organization plan for the new district. Explain your reasoning in the plan.

3

The Sales Manager

It is not easy to choose a sales manager because few people can fill the job as it is outlined by a selection committee. Each committee member develops a set of criteria; when these criteria are combined, the requirements are far beyond the capabilities of any individual. The guidelines used may be severely restrictive. Moreover, how much a firm can pay a sales executive often governs the caliber of person available.

THE SALES MANAGER'S JOB

Following a sales manager through a week's activities reveals a bewildering number of duties. Sunday night he calls a number of his salespeople to discover their plans for the week. Monday morning he reads his mail and dictates replies to letters. He has a conference with his boss regarding a bid on a large job the firm needs badly. They discuss how much discount they should quote, when it would have to be delivered, and how it will fit into the manufacturing pattern.

In the afternoon he interviews two applicants for a sales position, looks over a design for some new equipment, and receives a telephone call from a district representative who has trouble closing a sale on a bid made in his territory. That night he plans the strategy to assist the district representative to close the sale.

Tuesday he takes the 8 A.M. plane to meet his district representative to prepare for a final presentation at 2 P.M. They close the job successfully at 4 P.M. He has a final talk with his representative as they drive to the airport and boards his plane at 5 P.M.

Wednesday morning there is an accumulation of two days' mail, several telephone calls, and a committee meeting. In the afternoon he has a chance to start planning for a regional sales conference coming up in two weeks. He is interrupted by a telephone call from one of his best salesmen, who tells him he has just received an excellent offer from another firm and thinks he will accept. The sales manager gets the details of the offer and tells his salesman not to do anything until he calls him that evening. Immediately he makes an appointment with his boss to discuss this problem. In the meantime, he reviews alternatives to be ready with suggestions in the coming meeting.

A short time later, the sales manager talks with his boss regarding this salesman. Had it been a routine request, he would have handled it alone; but he is not prepared to make a decision that might lose a top salesman or upset others in the sales force. The two work out strategy to hold the salesman. Perhaps they will concede nothing and let the man resign if he persists in making a change; they might offer him a small raise (they cannot meet the other firm's reputed offer) and sell him on the opportunities he now has; they might offer him a transfer to a better territory; they might give him a small salary increase plus a new title. All of these possibilities are discussed, and one is agreed upon as most appealing.

That night the sales manager calls his salesman and tells what they hope to do for him. He suggests that the salesman think it over carefully and continue on the job until the sales manager can talk to him personally at the sales conference to be held in his region in two weeks.

Thursday morning he takes a plane to meet a salesman in another city and to work with him on some of his important customers. The sales manager regularly schedules one day a week to be with a salesman in the field.

Friday morning is filled with routine activity. After taking a visitor to lunch, he handles general details. Just before leaving, he gets a memo from the president to be prepared to discuss a policy decision at a conference on Monday afternoon.

This officially closes the sales manager's week, but he knows he will have to come in Saturday to plan his forthcoming conference. This imaginary week is typical of what some sales managers go through every week. Some sales management jobs are more complex; some have greater day-to-day selling involvement.

REQUIREMENTS FOR A SALES EXECUTIVE

While there are many common activities of sales managers, there are duties which may be absolutely essential in some firms, valuable in other firms, and less important in others. For example, one firm would require the sales manager to have a professional college degree; another firm would not be so interested. One firm might require a highly persuasive individual; another would use a channel where the sales manager's job would be basically administrative.

Although a number of traits are valuable for successful sales leadership, the experience factor is of primary importance. Too often a star salesman is given the sales manager's job. While an individual is flattered by getting such a position, he may not be fitted for it. He takes it over with misgivings and hesitation, recognizing his weaknesses. He soon learns that the boss's job is not easy.

Traits That May Hinder Sales Managers

There are many qualities that can be severe hindrances to a person in the position of sales manager. A person without these hindrances has an initial advantage over one who must overcome such traits.

Sluggish thinker

A sales manager who is a sluggish thinker will not be able to think clearly, to think from cause to effect, or to see the real problem rather than the surface problem. Many problems may have two facets—one that appears uppermost and an underlying one which may be hard to detect. Some people never become aware of underlying causes and symptoms.

Shy and retiring

A sales manager cannot be shy and retiring since he must initiate action and contact new people every day. He must be aggressive in originating conversation and be persistently active in advancing the cause of his firm. On the other hand, an excessively gregarious individual may offend by overextending himself in dealing with people.

Introvert

It is customary to think of an introvert as an individual who prefers being alone and wraps himself up in reading material. This characterization would not describe a person who is to be a successful sales manager. Not that the introverted individual shies away from decisions, but the fact that he prefers to work in a fashion that avoids personal confrontation indicates his approaches would not fit too well in a sales management position.

Indecisive

The individual who is unwilling to work hard and to develop new opportunities for his salespeople is unlikely to be a good sales manager. If he is content to let conditions remain as they are, he will not inspire others. A sales manager who cannot make up his mind is not likely to carry much weight with his sales force. His very indecisiveness communicates to the salesmen, who become frustrated and either become ineffective or go ahead and make their own decisions.

Lazy

A lazy sales manager is unlikely to inspire employees. They may imitate him and set up an easygoing pace fatal to success. A lazy person may neglect duties or perform them in a halfhearted fashion. As a result, many activities remain undone, and salespeople must struggle along without assistance they have a right to expect.

Immodest

It is not desirable to have a sales manager who brags more than he performs, who takes credit due others, and who is unwilling to share good fortune with his salespeople. A sales manager's optimism should be tempered with reality.

Superficial

Salespeople are often considered to be somewhat shallow thinkers and may be unwilling to tackle difficult propositions involving deep thought, careful attention to detail, and close attention to customer wants. The sales manager who "hits the high spots" will not wear well, and his weaknesses and lack of attention will irritate both customers and his own salespeople. Lack of depth will prevent a sales manager from fully understanding his job and his personnel and may lead to glossing over situations which later develop troublesome aspects. Superficial treatment of problems may be worse than no attention, since it may arouse anticipations which are never realized because the sales manager failed to carry out his stated intentions.

Gloomy

The sales manager who is perpetually downcast is ill-equipped to generate a salesperson's enthusiasm. Since enthusiasm is an important ingredient in selling, the sales manager should have plenty himself to insure that optimism becomes universal through the sales force.

Some people fail to overcome a habitual negative response to suggestions and fail to look for the problem because their entire attitude is keyed to expect the worst. With a negative outlook, an individual finds it practically impossible to orient his thinking and actions to expect success rather than failure. If a person is unable to overcome failure expectations, he is not good material for sales management.

Qualities That Suggest Successful Sales Managers

Some of the qualities of a successful sales executive are readily determined; others are not so obvious. It is difficult to establish a set of criteria that the individual must possess to achieve success as a sales manager. Nevertheless, there are some traits which are important for a successful sales manager.

Leadership

The sales manager should possess leadership traits. Successful sales performance is often used as an indicator. In appraising a person for the sales manager's position, outstanding selling performance may not be a primary qualification; but a person who has been successful in selling has an advantage, providing he has other desirable managerial qualifications.

Each firm must set up criteria which to them demonstrate leadership. It is good to update requirements to meet current responsibilities. For example, in years past the main job of the sales manager was to get bigger sales and greater profit with little worry about the customer, the government, and society; but today's demands on industry require management to be sensitive to newer areas of environmental significance.

Each firm may require a sales leader of different qualities. For example, a firm selling house-to-house or a firm which depends on salespeople doing face-to-face closing may require a dynamic, persuasive sales manager. A firm that depends on advertising for the major selling input may use its salespeople more as ambassadors of goodwill; then the sales manager may be quite another type of individual. Each firm should set up guides for what kind of leadership they want.

Progressive

A sales manager must be progressive to keep up with changes and different requirements. He knows the fallacies of depending on yesterday's solutions for today's and tomorrow's problems. He knows the value of using past experience not as a crutch, but as a guide to assist in solving current problems. He must be sensitive to changes that alter his sales opportunities, and he must be able to initiate approaches to handle conditions arising from changing patterns in society. The sales manager must be aware of shifting conditions of territory, product, price, and demand. He will be better able to meet tomorrow's problems if he is up-to-date.

Listener

A sales manager often needs to be more of a listener than a teller. He gets so used to talking, explaining, advising, suggesting, directing, and leading that he may never acquire the art of listening.

Some sales managers are so busy hearing themselves talk they fail to even use the most elementary approach to listening—letting the salesperson or the customer talk and courteously hearing him throughout his presentation. In a discussion there may be a tendency for the sales executive to dominate and not permit free expression from salespeople.

A manager must hear not only what is expressed audibly but what may be implied. There are highly charged undercurrents of feeling which may never surface in a conversation but really are the crux of a discussion. To be a good listener, the manager must develop empathy and find out underlying causes responsible for attitudes.

In a selling situation there are the sales manager's view and the salesperson's view, or the sales manager's view and the customer's view. Some sales managers frequently get the idea there are not two legitimate viewpoints to a situation; not his view as contrasted to the salesperson's view, but only his right view and the salesperson's wrong view. The manager prejudges and may be particularly fond of this approach if he is subjected to the same treatment by his superiors.

Communicator

A sales manager should communicate well by voice and through action. There are subtle differences in communicating which motivate and influence individuals. Often a manager thinks he is communicating when he talks to the salespeople, but what he says may not be registering. Some salespeople must be told directly, others can take a hint; some salespeople appreciate a "why" explanation along with an order, others are not concerned with "why"; some avidly accept a suggestion, others must be told explicitly.

The job of the communicator is to get his idea across to the other person. Communication is often difficult because of different backgrounds, different thinking, different economic situations, and different states of mind. For example, as the sales manager talks to a group of salespeople, one hears and understands perfectly, a second hears but only partially understands, a third hears but does not pay much attention, and a fourth hears sound but is so preoccupied with personal problems that nothing registers. A week later conditions may have changed; and while the sales manager is talking to the same people, the individual moods and thoughts may be quite different.

The task of finding a good communicating sales manager is not easy because this ability has many intangible facets. More is required than a strong voice and a dominating personality.

Persuasive

A persuasive sales manager is able to guide thinking in the direction he wishes. He persuades salespeople toward his way of thinking and action. He deals with management to get them to agree with him in his efforts to move the firm's products.

The persuasive manager develops a way of handling people that gets them to change viewpoints without antagonizing them. He presents his points so skillfully that the other person perceives the justice of his position. He tends to agree and concede on minor issues as long as this does not impair his major objective. He often lets the other person maneuver himself into a position where they both see the matter the way the sales manager wishes. He is able to direct and motivate salespeople to broader purposes and assist them to focus on several aspects of company success.

Administrator

In a small company, the sales manager may be a combined sales manager-salesman, but in a large firm his work is largely administrative. His administrative ability will determine his success.

An administrator must be willing to attend to detailed tasks and to operate in situations where small problems are forever appearing. If a customer calls with a complaint and wants to talk to the sales manager, the manager does not casually shift him to a subordinate. If top management wants a report, they expect the sales manager to produce it. If sales employees are upset, reassuring words from the boss will be more effective than similar words from an assistant. These tasks may take up much of the administrator's time and leave him less time for the larger problems.

The sales manager's effectiveness is determined by his administrative and leadership ability, for his success is measured by how well he can direct others to do their jobs. He must plan, organize, lead, settle differences of opinion, make decisions, and exert authority.

Planner

The successful sales executive must be able to plan for the future so that activities of the staff are relevant and effective. He must initiate new ideas to improve existing operations. He must keep his organization functioning smoothly and keep it flexible to meet changing demands of customers. He should plan his office duties so that he regularly reviews performance, evaluates each person properly, gives salary increases, and gives appropriate fringe benefits.

Successful planning includes foresight for short-term change and the ability to look into the future to prepare for contingencies that are not immediately apparent. It requires the ability to assess a variety of changes and approaches, to evaluate and dismiss those which appear uninviting, and pursue the ones which seem to have merit.

Creative

A sales manager must have creativity if he is to head a progressive sales organization. The sales manager must develop an exciting atmosphere for the salespeople so that their work does not become routine. He must keep the field people interested and eager so that they show enthusiasm to customers.

He must be a "dreamer" and generate new ideas frequently. Many ideas may be impractical to implement, but some will be introduced successfully.

Innovator

Successful innovation demands thinking in different ways. It may be essential to break away from standard thinking approaches. Time and change demand new requirements to fit current operations. New performance objectives may require formulating new operating patterns. The sales manager cannot afford to be locked into one behavior pattern. He cannot depend on the answers to yesterday's problems to answer tomorrow's operations.

MARKETING CAPACITIES OF SALES MANAGERS

Many of the traits already mentioned apply to the sales manager in handling the sales force and sales routine, but the important area of relating to other top executives must be considered if he is to be successful. Much of the sales executive's time is spent with other executives at his level in working on corporate problems. He must recognize the other necessary functions of the firm and be ready to adjust to the requirements of others. While being firm on his own requests, he must accept similar requests from other executives; when conflict arises, he must be willing to compromise. Compromise may not be easy, and many bosses do not willingly adjust.[1]

The need for empathy and a willingness to adjust at high executive levels is difficult to achieve, particularly for a strong sales executive. Often when a man is forced to retreat, he may sulk or even lose much of his effectiveness particularly when he must fit into a situation he dislikes.

There are a number of facets to a sales manager's job, and it is important that each facet receives proper attention and sufficient consideration to keep it strong and viable. Most sales managers tend to be strong in some areas and weak in others and may intentionally or otherwise fail to devote adequate attention to areas they especially dislike. The provident manager recognizes these weaknesses and provides counteracting forces to overcome them by hiring an assistant or assistants to specifically handle such areas or to reinforce them in some other way.

---

1. Dr. Charles Austin, in a lecture before the Greater Detroit Area and Michigan Hospital Personnel Directors Symposium in the spring of 1970, said that from 60 to 90 percent of today's bosses are not considered organizational assets by their peers and subordinates. If this is true of a cross section of executives, it is not likely that sales executives are an exception.

Figure 3–1
Performance Review and Evaluation, Branch Manager

Burroughs Corporation Ⓑ

BUSINESS MACHINES GROUP
PERFORMANCE REVIEW AND EVALUATION
BRANCH MANAGER

DISTRIBUTION:
ORIGINAL - BMG EMPLOYEE & INDUSTRIAL RELATIONS
DUPLICATE - DISTRICT FILE

REVIEW PERIOD:
FROM _____ TO _____

NAME	BRANCH		LOCATION
JOB TITLE	STATE OF HEALTH	MARITAL STATUS	AGES OF CHILDREN
AGE DATE EMPLOYED	EFFECTIVE DATE OF PRESENT ASSIGNMENT		

PREPARED AND DISCUSSED WITH BRANCH MANAGER BY:

DISTRICT MANAGER _____ DATE _____

EMPLOYEE'S SIGNATURE _____ DATE _____

WHAT ARE THIS MANAGER'S AMBITIONS AND DESIRES AS EXPRESSED IN THE INTERVIEW? _____

BRANCH SALES RECORD DECEMBER 31				PERSONAL SALES CURRENT YR.		KNOWLEDGE BY LINES OF BUSINESS			
	TOTAL ORDERS	QUOTA	UNITS SOLD	ACTUAL	%		TRAINED	EXPER.	EXPERT
GROUP I	$	%				FINANCIAL			
GROUP II	$	%				GOVERNMENT			
GROUP III - S	$	%				EDUCATIONAL			
TOTAL GP	$	%				MEDICAL			
GROUP III	$	%				TRANSPORTATION			
GROUP V	$	%				COMMUNICATION			
GROUP VI	$	%				PUBLIC UTILITY			
GROUP VIII	$	%				MANUFACTURING			
TOTAL EDP	$	%				WHOLESALE			
TOTAL	$	%				RETAIL			

BRANCH OPERATIONS	CURRENT YEAR		PERCENT OF		LIST NEW SALESMEN HIRED BY BRANCH SINCE LAST REVIEW (INDICATE MINORITIES WITH *)
	ACTUAL	ASSIGNMENT QUOTA	ACTUAL / QUOTA	CURR. YR. / PRIOR YR.	
TOTAL ORDERS	$	$	%	%	
TOTAL REVENUE	$	$	%	%	
TOTAL EXPENSES	$	$	%		
% OF TOTAL REVENUE	%				

EXPLAIN FACTORS RELATED TO ACHIEVING OR NOT ACHIEVING ALL AREAS OF EXPECTED
RESULTS - - REMARKS:

_____

LIST THOSE SALESMEN PROMOTED TO
MANAGEMENT POSITIONS IN PAST YEAR

* Courtesy Burroughs Corporation

Figure 3–1 (Continued)

THIS FORM IS DESIGNED TO HELP YOU APPRAISE EACH EMPLOYEE UNDER YOUR SUPERVISION WITH RESPECT TO SPECIFIC GOALS AND STANDARDS OF PER-FORMANCE. IF EACH APPRAISAL IS CARRIED OUT IN A SYSTEMATIC MANNER, THE PROGRAM WILL ASSIST YOU IN MAINTAINING AN EFFECTIVE ORGANIZA-TION THROUGH EMPLOYEE DEVELOPMENT AND IMPROVED JOB PERFORMANCE.

CHARACTERISTIC (PLEASE RATE THE MANAGER ON THE FOLLOWING CHARACTERISTICS)		EXCEPTION.	VERY GOOD	SATIS-FACTORY	NEEDS IMPRV.	UNSATIS-FACTORY	COMMENTS USE SEPARATE SHEET FOR ADDITIONAL COMMENTS
SELECTION & EMPLOYMENT OF PERSONNEL	1						MANAGERIAL ABILITY
AFFIRMATIVE ACTION TAKEN TO HIRE MINORITIES	2						
TRAINING AND DEVELOPMENT OF PERSONNEL	3						
EFF. TERRITORY ASSIGNMENT; LINE OF BUSINESS COVERAGE	4						
PROMOTION OF ALL PRODUCT LINES	5						
INVENTORY MANAGEMENT	6						
COLLECTION RATING, TERMS, CANCELLATIONS	7						
ACCURACY OF FORECASTING	8						
MANAG'T OF DISC./ALLOW. & SEC'D HAND EQUIPMENT	9						
COMMUNICATION WITH SUPERIORS & SUBORDINATES	10						EXECUTIVE ABILITY
EFFECTIVE DELEGATION OF RESPONSIBILITY	11						
JUDGMENT, BALANCE, STABILITY	12						
ABILITY TO TAKE TIMELY & DECISIVE ACTION	13						
LEADERSHIP – ABILITY TO MOTIVATE	14						
ABILITY TO EXPRESS SELF IN WRITING	15						
ABILITY TO EXPRESS SELF IN SPEAKING	16						
HANDLING CUSTOMER COMPLAINTS & CRITICAL ACCOUNTS	17						
PLANNING AND MANAGEMENT OF TIME	18						ADMINISTRATIVE ABILITY
RESPONSIVENESS AND TIMELY REPORTING	19						
FOLLOWS INSTRUCTIONS AND COMPANY POLICIES	20						
COORDINATION BETWEEN SALES, F.E., OFF. & TECH. DEPTS.	21						
UPKEEP & MAINTENANCE OF FACILITIES	22						
APPEARANCE OF OFFICE & DEMO ROOMS	23						
USE & CARE OF ADVER. & PROMOTIONAL MATERIAL	24						
PERSONAL PRODUCTIVITY	25						OVERALL EFFECTIVENESS
MARKET PENETRATION	26						
BRANCH PRODUCTIVITY	27						
REVENUE GROWTH	28						
ECONOMY OF OPERATION	29						
OVERALL EFFECTIVENESS OF BRANCH OPERATION	30						

WHAT ARE THIS MANAGERS STRONG POINTS? BE SPECIFIC

WHAT ARE HIS WEAKNESSES? BE SPECIFIC

COMMENT REGARDING THIS EMPLOYEE'S DEVELOPMENT NEEDS.

IS THIS EMPLOYEE WELL PLACED? _____ IS HE PROMOTABLE? _____

WHAT WOULD YOU RECOMMEND AS HIS NEXT ASSIGNMENT? COMMENT.

OVERALL PERFORMANCE APPRAISAL

EXCEPTIONAL	VERY GOOD	SATISFACTORY	NEEDS IMPROVEMENT	UNSATISFACTORY
Consistently does an excellent job. Performance approaches the best possible for the job. ☐	Exceeds requirements for satisfactory performance for the job. ☐	Meets all job requirements in a satisfactory manner. ☐	Performance must improve to meet job requirements. ☐	Performance does not warrant continuing in present assignment. ☐

HIS PERFORMANCE GENERALLY HAS _____ IMPROVED _____ NOT CHANGED _____ GONE BACK SINCE LAST REVIEW

CHOOSING THE SALES EXECUTIVE

We can set up a series of overall performance criteria which include those already discussed and other criteria that show up in the sales manager's work.[2]

1. He shows a number of strengths that fit him to his work. His strengths overbalance his weaknesses.
2. He is competent, knows his job, does not behave erratically, stands up under abuse, and thrives on work.
3. He is liked, or at least respected, by his sales force. He protects them when problems arise.
4. He handles customers well and takes appropriate action to keep them happy without criticizing his firm or finding fault publicly with his salespeople.
5. He is strong on suggestions and implements new approaches that keep the firm as one of the leaders in the industry.
6. The firm and sales force would dislike losing him because he would be hard to replace.

Understandably, no person will qualify in all categories, but the people selecting a sales manager must have confidence that the applicant can fit most criteria well. In fact, the people hiring must conclude that the applicant is far better fitted for the job than any other available applicant. To anticipate less would be doing an injustice to the firm.

A NEW DIMENSION IN SELECTING SALES MANAGERS

In the January 26, 1974, issue of *Business Week* is a review of an intriguing study on psychic research. A study by two scientists indicated that successful business executives had qualities of ESP (extrasensory perception) not possessed by less successful ones. It is often repeated that successful executives have better intuition than others; some call it better judgment. There is a beginning in testing the ESP of applicants for executive positions. Further research may reveal differing individual characteristics which will aid in choosing the better applicant for a sales manager position. If a company is lackluster in performance, use of ESP testing may reveal weaknesses in present executives. *Executive ESP,* published by Prentice-Hall, goes into detail on research findings of the two scientists.

The author does not suggest this technique will be a panacea in selecting successful sales executives, but it may be another spoke added in the selection wheel to strengthen selection procedure.

---

2. J. V. Fort and George E. Anderson, "Sales Manager: Man on the Griddle," *Marketing Times* 22 (July/August 1975): 10–12.

QUESTIONS AND PROBLEMS

1. Why is it important to have a description of a sales manager's daily activities?

2. What are some of the reasons we have incapable sales managers, and how can we avoid such situations?

3. Why does the text include a section on negative traits which would affect sales management performance? Is it helpful to list a person's negative as well as positive traits in selecting a sales manager?

4. Discuss character and physical traits as aids or hindrances in a sales manager's effectiveness. Include discussion points on such topics as ethnic influences, male and female prospects, college trained individuals versus individuals with less formal training, intellectual capabilities, experience, and age.

5. Does a successful manager have traits and capabilities not possessed by managers of production, finance, or personnel? How are they unlike? How are they similar? Can these managers be rotated and still be successful in their new positions?

6. Compare the relationship of a sales manager to his salespeople with the relationship of a production manager to his employees. Point out the similarities and the differences of the two managerial jobs.

7. Is being persuasive an important trait for managers in most positions? Explain your answer.

8. Why is planning considered so important in the work of a sales manager? Do you think planning is less important for other types of managers? Explain your answer.

9. Is it as important to evaluate a sales manager periodically as it is to evaluate salespeople? Would you consider successful sales operation the true evaluation criterion of a sales manager, or need there be other measures? Discuss why you might wish a number of ways to evaluate a sales manager.

10. Why do we stress innovation as an important factor in a sales manager's work? Is he expected to be more innovative than other company managers? Should a sales manager be content with a strong sales department operation and leave innovation to a separate department (research and development) in the company? Justify your answers.

11. Prepare a sales manager job description that could be used to guide the selecting committee in choosing a new sales manager. Choose your own particular type of company, and indicate why your selection criteria are important.

WESTERN MANUFACTURING COMPANY   *case 3–1*

Andrew Morris, sales manager for Western Manufacturing Company, is appraising the qualifications of Arthur Freeland for the position of district manager in the states of Virginia, North Carolina, and South Carolina.

Western Manufacturing Company produces a variety of tools and small equipment, such as garden tractors, chain saws, space heaters, and particular types of equipment suitable for different sections of the United States. Retail prices for their line vary from $1 to $650.

The company has sixteen sales districts in the United States, each under the direction of a district manager. Each district varies in size, employing from five to fifteen salesmen. The district of Virginia, North Carolina, and South Carolina employs five salesmen. The primary users of the products are farmers and suburban dwellers.

Salesmen sell to farm equipment dealers, large hardware stores, dealers in sports equipment, garden supply stores, marinas, and other stores which may feature some of Western's items. They also handle wholesale and distributor accounts. It is not unusual for a Western salesman to compete with a wholesaler salesman on the same retail account. The wholesaler buying from a Western salesman gets an additional discount which enables him to compete with the same salesman selling to a retail account. Wholesale salesmen with their extensive line sell to many small buyers; a Western salesman would find this unprofitable because of his much narrower line of merchandise.

Mr. Rathbone, the present district manager in Virginia, North Carolina, and South Carolina, will retire at the end of the year. Since this is July, Mr. Morris would like to have a new manager by August to work with Mr. Rathbone before he leaves.

Mr. Morris has discussed this opening with the other district managers and received their recommendations from their sales staffs. He has finally narrowed his choice to one salesman, Arthur Freeland.

Arthur Freeland has been a salesman for the company in the Texas district for five years. He is thirty years old, of medium height, weighs about 150 pounds, has brown eyes and dark hair, and has a ready smile and a pleasant voice. His sales record is encouraging, but not tremendous. He gets along well with customers and fellow salesmen.

In analyzing Mr. Freeland's qualifications and following a personal interview with him, Mr. Morris has prepared a list of strengths and weaknesses, which he is weighing carefully. Some of Freeland's strengths indicate he would handle customers well, get along with salesmen satisfactorily, and maintain a harmonious spirit in the district. His weaknesses indicate he might lack firmness, be too easygoing, and be unable to be severe with his salesmen. In other words, he would not crack down on his men if occasion demanded it.

Mr. Freeland was somewhat careless with detailed work, but Mr. Morris believed that trait could be corrected easily. What concened him most was Mr. Freeland's desire to be friendly, kind, helpful, and considerate even at the expense of sales performance. Mr. Morris knew that a sales manager is seldom liked and admired by all his men; but no sales manager should be upset by this situation as long as he has the respect of his men.

If Mr. Morris did not choose Mr. Freeland, he would have to go outside the firm to find a new district manager.

QUESTION

1. What should Mr. Morris do? Analyze the situation carefully; give advantages and disadvantages for both approaches; and justify your selection by careful reasoning.

MORLEY, INC.   *case 3–2*

Morley, Inc. was a large manufacturer of metal containers. Its main offices were located in New York City, although it had several manufacturing plants and sales offices throughout the country.

David Martin, sales manager, received a phone call from Jackie Sample, a secretary in Detroit. His Detroit sales office frequently plagued him with problems which he felt should have been resolved at the local level.

The Detroit sales office consisted of one office manager, Jay Bond, four secretaries, one teletype operator, and four inside sales assistants. The office serviced salesmen in the area, and the sales assistants handled inside accounts. Jay Bond was in charge of all of the people in the Detroit office with the exception of the salesmen, who reported directly to the sales manager.

The Detroit office was located in one of the company's factories. Several other sales groups which were a part of other divisions of the company and which sold entirely different products had just moved into this same location. Mr. Bond was given the additional responsibility of attending to their needs.

Jay Bond

Jay Bond had been in the army for a number of years before joining Morley. He was initially stationed in the Chicago office, where he was quite happy since his wife's relatives were from that area. He was promoted from assistant office manager in Chicago to office manager in Detroit, a move which he felt was most advantageous. However, as time went by it did not appear to be as enjoyable as he had originally hoped. His wife did not enjoy the Detroit area and longed to return to Chicago.

In the office, Mr. Bond operated much as he did in the army. At times he got along well with people. Yet there were times when he did not particularly care to be bothered with others' problems, even those of his subordinates who sought his advice. He prided himself on his years of service with the company, but remained somewhat ignorant of its policies and regulations. He would much rather discuss sports with one of the salesmen than read newsletters dispatched from New York containing changes in policy. The inside assistants soon realized that it was futile to seek his assistance, because he usually did not know the answer to their questions and would merely tell them to call someone in New York for help.

Jackie Sample

Ms. Sample was one of the secretaries in the Detroit office. She had been there the longest (twelve years) and had seniority over the other secretaries. Consequently, she was chosen by Mr. Bond to be his private secretary, though this was an informal position and not specifically recognized. When he sought assistance in procedural matters, he asked her advice since she had been in Detroit for a longer period of time.

Ms. Sample was divorced and had one son. She was loud and sarcastic and enjoyed arguing for its own sake. She and Mr. Bond constantly argued, though they enjoyed it immensely. Each loved to chide the other, and the entire office seemed to enjoy this feud. However, the constant bickering made working extremely difficult.

Ms. Sample was often absent due to either her own or her son's illness. Her son had contracted a terminal disease and was not expected to live past the age of twelve, although he was presently thirteen. To properly care for her son, Ms. Sample found it necessary to work two jobs, but the additional money barely covered her son's medical expenses.

To lighten her burden, Mr. Bond pointed out that it was not necessary to maintain her family Blue Cross Blue Shield insurance since the company provided maximum insurance at minimal cost to each of its employees and their families. Consequently, she dropped her Blue Cross Blue Shield insurance.

Remaining Office Staff

The other members of the office staff were Sarah Mason, Donna Wilson, and Janis Smith, secretaries; Sally Walker, teletype operator; Bill Stevens, Al Larson, Alice Wessels, and Frank Mandel, sales assistants.

Of the other secretaries, Sarah Mason probably presented the largest problem. She was approaching retirement and often complained of aches and pains which annoyed the other office personnel. Her typing was poor, and she was generally slow in all of her work. Yet she had been with the company over ten years, and Jay did not think it would be right to fire her since she was near retirement. Donna and Janis were both good workers. They did their work without fuss and were well liked. Sally, the teletype operator, was recently hired. She too worked hard but the quality of her work needed improvement. Jay felt that she would improve and since she was well liked and pleasant, he decided to keep her.

Of the sales assistants, Alice had been with the company for thirty years and was also approaching retirement. Though she did not do as much as the others, she worked hard and knew her accounts well. She also knew a great deal about the company, and others often turned to her for advice.

Bill and Al had both been with the company for two years. They were both young, ambitious, and hard-working individuals who hoped to progress rapidly. However, they often felt discouraged since they received little credit for their efforts from their immediate supervisor, Mr. Bond.

Frank was the newest sales assistant, having been hired recently. He worked hard and enjoyed joking around with the others. Jay felt this was permissible so long as he did his work. In time Jay felt Frank would become a good inside man.

Problem

When Mr. Martin received the telephone call from Ms. Sample, she was quite upset. Apparently, she had called Mr. Bond the previous morning at the office to tell him she would not be in since she was not feeling well. He told her that if she did not come in she would be fired. When she reported for work the following day, Mr. Bond told her to leave. Ms. Sample did not think Mr. Bond was being fair and decided to go over his head to his superior.

As Mr. Martin sat in his office, he wondered what to do. He knew that both Jackie and Jay were hotheads and that they probably had both been caught off guard that day. He also knew that Jackie frequently was absent from work due to illness and that the Detroit office was extremely busy at that time. Jackie had pointed out that she was now in a terrible bind because if she lost her job she would also lose her insurance. Since she might not be able to insure her son, she knew that she could not afford to lose her job and regretted that she had let Mr. Bond talk her into disposing of her Blue Cross Blue Shield. Mr. Martin was concerned about the impact this might have on the Detroit sales assistants, especially two who were both in the last part of their training program. After serving as inside assistants for approximately two years, they would soon be eligible to move in the direction of sales or management. Both were well qualified. Mr. Martin knew their training program was long, and he did not want either of these men to become dissatisfied with the program itself or with Morley, Inc. as represented by the Detroit sales office.

QUESTIONS

1. What is the immediate problem? What should Mr. Martin do?
2. What changes, if any, would you recommend be made in the office?
3. What type of sales manager would handle this problem successfully? Could two strong sales managers handle this problem quite differently? Discuss, pointing out strengths and weaknesses of sales managers.

part two

OPERATIONS

4

Recruiting and Selecting Salespeople

The importance of selecting superior salespeople cannot be over-emphasized. There are enough problems in selling without saddling the sales organization with people who will never measure up to expectations.

GENERAL CONSIDERATIONS IN SELECTION

The sales department, in selecting applicants for sales positions, tries to choose the best people possible. However, every hiring situation is surrounded by peculiar conditions and by company restrictions which narrow choice.

Conditions Outside the Firm

Many restrictive measures may work against hiring the kind of sales-people wanted. If favorable, the reputation of the hiring firm may bring many applicants for sales positions; but if the firm has created an un-favorable image, the response may be poor. Certain times of the year may be less favorable for hiring than other periods; and the same may be true for different periods in the economic cycle.

In today's hiring market, society demands that we pay attention to minority groups and give them representation on our sales force. Yesterday's freedom of wide selection is a luxury not given to hiring today. Yet within these limitations, one must still hire an individual who seems capable of handling the job.

Considerations Within the Firm

Any firm undoubtedly has a number of unusual hiring restrictions. They may or may not be spelled out, but they have been expressed in some way by top management. These restrictions cannot be ignored.

Salesperson compensation level is a factor of governing importance. It is easy enough to say that one ought to hire the best people, but the practical fact is that the offering salary usually is not sufficient to attract the best.

An applicant must be able to get along with people in the sales force. He must adjust to a pattern and work under prevailing conditions within the firm. If he has superior strengths in some areas but possibly would not fit in the group, it would be unwise to hire him. Not only would he become upset, but also he would upset others on the sales staff.

RECRUITING FOR SALES POSITIONS

Recruiting Fundamentals

Recruiting is developing sources of applicants to fill sales positions within the company. It consists of providing suitable raw material (applicants) to meet the needs of the finished product (successful salespeople). Effective recruiting uses various tools, specifications, sources, literature, and approaches. Successful recruiting is a continuous effort not only to fill immediate needs but also to build up backlogs of suitable applicants. It can create a feeling within the community that a firm is a desirable place to work and thus encourage a constant flow of applicants.

There may be special requirements that must be met—physical strength to handle equipment; a physical stature requirement; an age factor; marital status; climate adjustment factor; educational factors; voice and diction control. The sales manager should set up a profile or image of an applicant. The danger of this profile, however, is that he may overlook strong people who may not fit the image too well, but have some qualities in such abundance that their overall worth more than makes up for deficiencies in some areas.

Developing a Want List for Future Salespeople

It is essential to determine what type of people are needed. In general, there is little difficulty in pinpointing requirements; but when it comes to exact qualifications, the selection process may be quite volatile. In specifically outlining qualities, it is important to delineate the various job requirements. What is the job? What is the salesperson's work? Where or on what must the salesperson concentrate efforts, attention, and time? What qualifications are necessary to avoid offending certain customers? What are the main duties, responsibilities, demands, and activities of the new salesperson? The sales manager should prepare a job description which clearly states the requirements.

JOB DESCRIPTION

Senior Sales Representative

Senior sales representative, under direction of the branch manager, conducts the sales of assigned products in an assigned geographical territory and/or to specified named accounts or lines of business as defined in his contract.

Job requirements

This job requires proven equipment sales ability; thorough sales knowledge of the products assigned, including quality, features and applications, superiority and prices, as well as general knowledge of all products, their uses and applications; sound knowledge of his assigned territory, its business potential and best sales prospects; and the ability to make and maintain contact with customer personnel who influence or make equipment purchase decisions.

Typical duties

Plans personal coverage of his territory to make most effective use of time.

Calls on customers and prospective customers at planned intervals to sell assigned products. Interviews key personnel to determine customer's computing, data-processing, and management information needs, to explain the advantages of equipment in meeting those needs and to persuade the customer to buy equipment.

Demonstrates or arranges for demonstration of equipment to customers and prospects. Points out desirable features, quotes prices and terms. Answers questions and explains company policy and practice relevant to the transaction.

Writes equipment orders for customer's signature in conformance with authorized pricing and all other provisions of company policy. Prepares order preparation work sheet, form layouts, operation sheets, and other supplemental information as required. Submits equipment orders and attachments for management approval. Makes no agreement expressed or implied which would make the order unacceptable to the company.

Prepares written proposals as a means of soliciting orders. Clears proposal with his manager prior to presentation to the customer. Organizes and maintains an attactive sales portfolio for use as a visual sales aid. Makes effective use of advertising, competitive information, and sales reference material.

Keeps his manager informed of sales activities and the business situation in his territory. Seeks management assistance when necessary. Submits prescribed activity reports. Keeps an up-to-date territory management record and reviews same periodically with his manager to plan adequate, profitable territory coverage and to exchange ideas for improving sales.

Keeps abreast of new products and new applications for existing products. Uses knowledge to upgrade current accounts, develop new prospects, and obtain new business.

In cooperation with field engineering personnel, tests and prepares equipment for delivery to customer. Oversees installation. Supervises training of customer personnel who will operate the equipment. Maintains customer contact after installation.

Promptly investigates any customer complaints. Works toward a solution equitable both to the customer and the company.

Solicits or assists field engineering personnel to obtain maintenance agreements on equipment sold.

Contacts customers for collection of accounts.

Keeps accurate records of and properly cares for equipment assigned to him.

Cooperates with sales technical personnel, sales promotion representatives, specialists and others who may be assigned to assist him. Assists in training new salesmen.

Exercises good judgment in the use of time and expense. Submits expenditure reports as required.

Builds good will. In all relationships, conducts himself in a manner so as to earn the confidence of customers in himself, the company, and its products.

Accountability

Accountable to the branch manager for conducting the sale of assigned products within his territory.

JOB OF RECRUITING

Recruiting involves finding applicants of the right kind. One good way of screening applicants is to recruit so that most undesirable people would not bother to reply. Such recruiting is beneficial to the firm and to the job seeker. However, the recruiting should not be so restrictive as to eliminate many good prospects from applying.

Specific Sources for Recruiting

There are many sources of sales applicants, some of which may be far better than others for particular needs. In the following examples, there is no attempt to rank the methods since the method best for one firm may not be equally successful for another firm. Each firm must experiment to find out which source, which type of wording in advertisements, and which time of the year may be most suitable for recruitment.

Advertising

Many firms have found selective types of advertising an advantageous way to recruit salespeople. For lesser selling jobs, the classified advertisement may be adequate; a display advertisement may be used to attract applicants of a higher caliber.

Classified advertisement. Classified advertisements are usually placed in the "Help Wanted" columns under appropriate newspaper headings.

The theory of this advertising is that there is always someone looking for a job either because he is presently unemployed or is dissatisfied with present employment and is looking for something better.

Many people use the newspaper as a first resort in looking for employment. While the preceding statement is probably true for all sections of the United States, it might not hold for other countries. Therefore, firms operating abroad must learn which medium is best for a particular nation.

Sometimes multiple listings at one time may be useful, since some people read one category of classified advertisements but not another. If a major city has a morning and an evening paper, one may be better in specific instances. The time of week may be quite important. For example, a Thursday or Sunday edition may be superior to other days in one city, but not so successful in another city.

Display advertising. When the sales positions are of greater importance, it is common to use display advertising. Business papers are frequently used, as are business sections of daily and Sunday newspapers. This type of advertising stands out, is specifically directed to a segment of the market, and is clearly oriented to particular people. For recruiting within a city, such advertisements are used successfully in daily newspapers, but particularly on Sunday. For national newspapers and business papers, such advertisements can be used daily; experimenting will indicate which day is most suitable.

Wording is important in both classified and display advertising, but should be carefully evaluated in the display advertisement because of the cost. Contrast the wording of these two advertisements:

> A firm needs an energetic person for selling in a wide territory. Salary and benefits commensurate with age and experience. Phone 633–1246 or write Box 476. Include your background and experience.

> Are you looking for a sales position that is challenging, rewarding, and fascinating? Are you interested in joining a rapidly growing firm that needs people in new territories? Would you like to work for a company that offers you a good starting salary, generous commissions, fringe benefits, retirement pensions, and car allowances? If you would like to join a company that is going places and has numerous open-

ings for advancement and promotion, phone 633–1246 or write Box 476. Include in your letter a brief resume of your background and experience.

Undoubtedly each firm would modify such advertisements, but it is preferable to make it too inviting and get a large number of applicants, most of whom must be rejected, than to have it too restrictive so that only two or three replies come in. Through experience one soon learns how to temper advertisements to achieve optimum success.

Magazine advertising.   Magazine advertising for salespeople is common in direct selling magazines, which are full of requests for direct selling personnel to homes and industry. It is also used in many business publications to recruit salespeople in special fields, such as industrial salespeople and manufacturer's representatives. This medium of advertising is a highly selective tool to be used after careful consideration and evaluation. Many recruiting sources are highly selective and frequently helpful only in narrow ranges, but within these limitations they can be productive.

Special papers.   This group includes weekly papers, suburban papers, church and lodge publications, school papers, programs, and others. Many of these are of dubious value, but some may be quite influential and helpful in specific instances. Most of the time, it is more advantageous to use the large daily newspapers.

Convention recruiting

Conventions have much to offer for certain types of recruiting, particularly for higher level positions. Frequently, better employees of firms come to conventions to participate in meetings and work in exhibit booths. A large convention may have hundreds of salespeople working in the trade show exhibition; thousands of other salespeople and agents attend to keep up with developments and to investigate possibilities of employment. Studies reveal that perhaps 20 percent of the attendance is made up of people interested in investigating new opportunities.

School recruiting

Many major firms recruit regularly in colleges and universities. Definite periods are scheduled for each firm, and recruiters usually have opportunities to talk to a number of prospects. A major university may have more than one recruiting location; so it is advisable to find out the arrangements for each school. It is not uncommon to have the business school recruiting handled separately from other recruiting in the university.

Government sources

National, state, and local governments are taking increasing roles in aiding people to find jobs. Firms may find particular government agencies have many people available under specific classifications. State agencies may be useful not only in general selection but also in securing people from particular groups or disciplines.

Friends

Friends and acquaintances are quite useful in drawing applicants. If a firm has an enviable reputation, present employees are glad to tell others about existing opportunities. Present, capable employees may enlist others of equal capability. A danger to anticipate is that a certain number of inferior applicants will apply. The rejection of such people must be handled judiciously in order to avoid embarrassment. Dealing with friends is a sensitive area; consequently, rejection must be handled diplomatically.

Competitors

It has often been said that when you hire people away from a competitor he considers it piracy, while you think of it as giving people greater opportunities. There is typically some turnover in the sales force because of dissension, desire for change, ambition, stagnation at present level, and many other reasons. Just as one firm finds some attrition inevitable and perhaps desirable, so will competitors find a similar situation.

In recruiting from competitors, management must be careful not to get drifters, weak salespeople, and those who constantly upset harmony. But just because a salesperson wants to change does not mean he is inefficient or unhappy. Consequently, one should investigate the desire for change and try to determine whether the change will benefit him and the firm. Unless both benefit, merely to change is disadvantageous in the long run; in the short run it could be advantageous to only one.

Even if a salesperson's performance with a competitor has been modest, he could easily develop as a top producer with another firm. This could result from a change in attitude on the salesperson's part, from better leadersip in the firm, from a happier environment, or from the fact that the individual has progressed to a higher plateau of performance and a higher level of maturity.

Employment agencies

Firms frequently develop close relationships with particular employment agencies. The agency learns much about the type of sales applicants preferred and is alert to send the proper people for consideration. One sales manager will find the employment agency to be one of his superior sources of applicants; while another will not have this experience. A willingness to experiment will aid a firm in determining whether this source should be one of its prime resources.

Walk-in applicants

In any major city and often in smaller cities, there will be people who walk in to apply for sales positions. While this may be considered a random approach, it should not be discouraged. People who try this way may have qualities sorely needed by salespeople. At least it indicates desirable initiative, even though a more astute applicant might have employed a more subtle approach.

Treating each applicant courteously and ascertaining what he has to offer are a welcome way to impress him and create a pleasant feeling. Even if he does not become an employee, he likely will be a customer in some way.

The company

The sales manager ought to look closely in his own firm for possible sales recruits. It may be easy to overlook this source either because present employees seem unsuitable for sales jobs or because employees are doing so well where they now are that the sales manager is reluctant to upset the organization by taking a capable employee from another job. Yet some inside salespeople for wholesalers and distributors are impatiently waiting for an opportunity to get an outside selling job.

SELECTING FOR SALES POSITIONS

After securing a number of applicants for sales positions, the sales manager must sort them and select the most suitable ones. This may be a continuous or intermittent activity depending on the number to be hired. In a large firm hiring may be fairly regular, but a small firm may hire infrequently.

Selecting Fundamentals

Selecting employees consists of carefully reviewing the qualifications of available applicants and choosing the ones who appear to meet the requirements of particular jobs. Selecting is a crucial step because it determines the type of employee entering the firm.

There are a number of steps in selection and a set of standard tools frequently used in the selecting process. Each firm may use many common procedures and techniques, but will vary in assessing the importance of each step.

Application Blank

The application blank can be used to furnish basic information that would otherwise be secured in the interview or elsewhere. The employing firm should carefully design such a blank as to provide the maximum information it needs without violating the law and without prying into private affairs. It is good to be cautious in accepting all information as given. Some data may be slanted in favor of the applicant, and some may be incorrect. The following areas are important: personal data, education, work experience, references, military service, financial data, and interests and future ambition.

Personal data

Personal data include name, address, telephone, and social security number. If desirable, a person's height and weight can be included.

Prospective employers want to know marital status—single, married, divorced, widowed—and number of dependents. Age data is usually helpful although discrimination edicts may rule that out. If not secured in this way, it can be picked up in the interview. Experience shows that people with dependents are usually better performers than people having minimum obligations.

If the spouse or other family members are working, it would be interesting to find out where. This may help in focusing on the social position of applicants. It is also useful to know if family members or other close relatives are working for the firm or for competitors.

The applicant's health is significant because a salesperson may be exposed to conditions and situations that test physical stamina. Often, long days and late evenings allow a salesperson minimum rest.

It might be more difficult to detect mental health hazards, but these hazards might be tied in with physical health. Thus, if a salesperson is subjected to a grueling physical job plus one that threatens his emotional state, the two together could break down his health. However, mental stress alone might be sufficient to upset an individual's performance and destroy his effectiveness. For example, a salesperson might do very well selling tangible products, but the same person might fail miserably in selling intangibles, such as insurance where one must not only sell but first awaken buying desire. To what extent it is possible to link perseverance and persistence with physical stamina is debatable, but it would seem that salespeople with inward staying qualities must have some reserve of physical and mental strength.

A firm may wish to avoid hiring applicants with exceptional qualifications. Such people quickly become dissatisfied and quit, unless promoted to more desirable positions.

A wide range of information on the application blank plus other selective tools may uncover a prospect for the marketing department or elsewhere in the firm, even though he may not seem suitable as a salesperson.

An individual with a record of several law violations bears careful scrutiny. Many traffic violations may indicate a particular temperament or a disregard for rights of others. Occasionally an applicant may have been in serious trouble; but, having paid for his indiscretion, he may now be excellent selling material. Such knowledge about an applicant may be important in supervising him on the job later.

Education

Most applicants have completed high school or its equivalent. In high school, however, it is becoming common for teachers to do what they can with pupils and then pass them to the next grade and eventually high school graduation. Therefore, high school graduation may be significant as a standard of performance, or it may merely be an age and exposure factor with little formal training. Nevertheless, such schooling has social implications which may help people to adjust in society. Graduates may attain a degree of social maturity denied those who did not complete high school.

Applicants with college training have, for the most part, been exposed to a more rigorous type of training and become more self-dependent. Many students successfully complete a terminal education program in community colleges but are not interested in, or may be incapable of, completing a four-year program. Of those who complete the four-year college program, many go on to complete their master's degree. This situation is becoming increasingly common for engineers who, having completed their engineering requirements which tend to make them "thing" oriented, go on for their master's degree in business, where they become "people" oriented.

In a recruiter's eagerness to select promising candidates, he may oversell the job and recruit too well. Hiring overcapable people is just as unrealistic as hiring incapable people. If a recruiter secures a person far above the demands of the job, he will soon leave unless promoted to a more challenging position. A person who is inadequate will never measure up to the job.

Since all salespeople hired cannot be promoted, it is sufficient to select those who have adequate potential for the salesperson position. For many sales positions, recruiters may confine their efforts to the community or junior college and not to the four-year college graduate. If a firm's salespeople receive average compensation, recruiting in top educational institutions puts the firm in competition with recruiters who are willing to pay more. They may siphon off the better prospects, and the remainder in four-year colleges may be less effective than stronger ones in community colleges.

One reason for interviewing college graduates is to take advantage of natural selection to some extent. Presumably, one who completes college shows greater ability, perseverance, or other traits which mark him fundamentally superior to ones who do not attain this mark of educational excellence. While there may be numerous flaws in this reasoning, the fact is that if a firm hires one hundred sales applicants with satisfactory qualifications plus a college degree and hires another similar group of people without the college degree, usually more of the people with degrees succeed than those without degrees. Thus, if out of the first group seventy-five out of one hundred succeed, perhaps out of the second group fifty out of one hundred succeed. Since the selection, training, and breaking-in process is long and expensive, it is preferable to concentrate on the better group.

For certain types of sales positions, some firms concentrate only on people with master's degrees or better. Presumably, these people have superior capabilities and are more articulate. They have learned to think, write, and express themselves better than applicants without a master's degree and will probably be excellent material for executive positions once they have had adequate sales experience on the jobs.

Some students prefer to round out their education after high school by a year or more of training at a business school. People with this type of training can become excellent salespeople and may be more content working in the selling organization instead of constantly striving for the managerial position.

Work experience

People tend to build up a pattern of behavior that carries into the future. Since it is unlikely that an individual will radically change from his past performance, it is helpful to find out about an applicant's past work experience.

The work experience of young people is limited and subject to variation. Many first jobs were spur-of-the-moment choices. Even at an early age, however, and certainly later, one can begin to evaluate individual work performance.

If the applicant changed jobs frequently (one must exempt temporary jobs) was it because he lacked staying qualities? Was he easily discouraged? Dissatisfied? Overly ambitious? Self-centered? Did he exhibit loyalties to employers, or did he concentrate solely on selfish desires? Were job changes horizontal or vertical? Was there steady progress in salary and responsibility, or was it merely job-hopping?

An applicant with an experience of infrequent job change may have weaknesses. He may be afraid to change jobs; he may be satisfied with the present one; or he may lack aggressiveness in trying to change. An employee may have confidence that the boss will recognize superior performance and promote accordingly. This employee should recognize that no one is as interested in his welfare as he is and should act accordingly.

Significant time gaps in work experience should be checked. Such unemployment periods could arise from illness, difficulty in changing jobs, losing a job through inefficiency, and other possible reasons. Even if a person lost a job because he was at fault, was it because of poor performance, lack of attention, or was he thrust into a job beyond his capability?

If a person with many years' work experience applies, he should not be automatically rejected because of age or the fact that he may be out of a job. Many people are lucky to be in aggressive companies which expand fast and have many job promotions; equally good people in another firm may be handicapped by lack of opportunity.

References

It is common to have a section of the application blank for references. One may anticipate that the references will be favorable. References from close friends of the applicant have little value because of the obvious personal bias. A reference from a student's former teacher may be quite accurate, but probably will overstate his qualifications.

In checking references over the telephone, the person calling must be able to interpret replies. If the reference called hesitates and gives reluctant favorable replies, this can be interpreted as being almost neutral. If replies are neutral or evasive, one might suspect difficulties. A firm can hardly expect any person to give derogatory information in a letter. It is quite dangerous to give information that might be used later in a court suit.

Sometimes during the interview the applicant is asked for additional references. These probably would not be as favorable as the original ones. If the applicant gives reluctant consent to contact his former employer, any information received from the former employer should be evaluated carefully. If the information is unfavorable, it might be that the applicant and his former employer did not get along, and who is to say which one is to blame. If the former employer gives a good recommendation, the applicant may be really strong; or the former employer may feel sorry for him and may want to help him. If the applicant is weak, a former employer may be delighted to see him hired by a competitor. Most firms are glad to reciprocate with one another in hiring information, credit information, and other areas. Occasionally a present employer will give a glowing recommendation, for he would like to get rid of the salesperson. References should be treated cautiously as one indicator in selection.

Military service

Many application blanks have a section on military service to determine what the applicant has experienced in the military or if he is eligible for future military service. If a person had rapid promotions, it is well to ascertain whether they occurred in war or peacetime periods. A strong individual during a quiet period might be promoted slowly, while an ordinary individual might receive rapid promotion in an expanding army.

Financial data

Some applicants may minimize their financial requirements in order to get a job. They have obligations that require a definite income. Should they be started for less, their personal problems will be worrying them and gnawing at performance. Had the new employer been aware of the financial situation, he might have started the person at a higher salary.

Interests and future ambition

Some application blanks have space where an applicant can express his thoughts, ambitions, interests, and future progress. This section can be most revealing not only for what is written, but also for what is omitted. This section may reveal the depth of the applicant, what he sees in the future, how he views the business world, and other items that reveal character, strengths, and perhaps weaknesses. While an intelligent applicant might use this space to impress the reader, a discerning reviewer readily separates meaningful statements from those which are written to create an impression.

Preliminary Application Blank

Using a short preliminary application blank that screens out many applicants obviously unsuited for the position eliminates much of the effort involved in using a long application blank. Such an approach saves time and money for the firm and prevents the applicant from receiving false hopes.

The hiring process can be expedited by using a preliminary application blank. When matched with the job description, it will immediately reveal favorable or unfavorable aspects.

Testing Program

The use of tests in selection varies from firm to firm. A promising tool, testing has been used and abused, praised and criticized, used carefully and recklessly, and is regarded with suspicion by many.

It is likely that testing in the future will be most helpful in selecting certain kinds of salespeople. As long as testing is used as one of several selection criteria and is placed in its proper perspective, it can be advantageous in aiding in selection; but too much dependence on it can be harmful.

Testing might have greater use as a rejection tool. After repeated use, it may be possible to determine that applicants below a particular

Figure 4-1
Salesperson Application Blank

PARKE-DAVIS

AN EQUAL OPPORTUNITY EMPLOYER

PROFESSIONAL
EMPLOYMENT APPLICATION

PRINT PLAINLY IN INK

LOCATIONS:

DATE _____

DETROIT, MICHIGAN		GREENWOOD, SOUTH CAROLINA
LOS GATOS, CALIFORNIA		WALTHAM, MASSACHUSETTS
ROCHESTER,, MICHIGAN		LIONVILLE, PENNSYLVANIA
HOLLAND, MICHIGAN		KANKAKEE, ILLINOIS
RESEARCH LABORATORIES	—	ANN ARBOR, MICHIGAN
DISTRIBUTION CENTERS		
SALES OFFICES	—	MAJOR CITIES IN U.S.
INTERNATIONAL	—	MAJOR COUNTRIES

GENERAL

NAME _____ SOCIAL SECURITY NO. _____

PRESENT ADDRESS _____
STREET   CITY   STATE   ZIP   TELEPHONE NO.
(INCLUDE AREA CODE)

☐ OWN HOME   ☐ RENT   ☐ BOARD   ☐ LIVE WITH PARENTS _____
HOW LONG

PERMANENT ADDRESS _____
STREET   CITY   STATE   ZIP   HOW LONG

DATE OF BIRTH _____   U. S. CITIZEN ☐ YES   ☐ NO

STATUS: ☐ SINGLE   ☐ MARRIED   ☐ ENGAGED   ☐ DIVORCED   ☐ WIDOWED

NUMBER OF PERSONS DEPENDENT UPON YOU FOR SUPPORT ? _____

HAVE YOU PREVIOUSLY BEEN EMPLOYED BY PARKE-DAVIS ?   ☐ YES   ☐ NO   DATE _____

HAVE YOU EVER BEEN DENIED A SURETY BOND ?   ☐ YES   ☐ NO   EXPLAIN _____

HAVE YOU EVER BEEN CONVICTED OF ANY CRIMINAL OFFENSE ?   ☐ YES   ☐ NO   EXPLAIN _____

WHAT PROMPTED YOU TO APPLY AT PARKE-DAVIS ? SPECIFY _____

IN WHAT PROFESSIONAL OR SPECIALIZED FIELDS ARE YOU MOST INTERESTED ? _____

AVAILABILITY DATE _____   SALARY REQUIREMENTS _____

GEOGRAPHIC PREFERENCES _____

HEALTH

HEIGHT _____   WEIGHT _____   WHAT IS YOUR PRESENT PHYSICAL CONDITION ? _____

LIST ALLERGIES, IF ANY _____

HAVE YOU BEEN HOSPITALIZED IN LAST 10 YEARS ?   ☐ YES   ☐ NO   EXPLAIN _____

HAVE YOU EVER APPLIED FOR OR RECEIVED WORKMEN'S COMPENSATION ?   ☐ YES   ☐ NO   SPECIFY _____

HAVE YOU EVER BEEN REFUSED EMPLOYMENT FOR HEALTH REASONS ?   ☐ YES   ☐ NO   EXPLAIN _____

Page 1

* Courtesy Parke-Davis

Figure 4–1 (Continued)

EDUCATION AND TRAINING

TYPE OF SCHOOL	NAME AND LOCATION	MAJOR	MINOR	CHECK LAST YEAR COMPLETED				GRADUATE DEGREE		DATES ATTENDED
COLLEGE				1	2	3	4	☐ Yes	☐ No	
GRADUATE				1	2	3	4	☐ Yes	☐ No	
				1	2	3	4	☐ Yes	☐ No	
OTHER (Include Service Schools)										

CLASS STANDING QUARTILE ☐ TOP ☐ 2ND ☐ 3RD

UNDERGRADUATE GRADE POINT AVERAGE _____ GRADUATE GRADE POINT _____

LIST PROFESSIONAL, SOCIAL & HONORARY SOCIETIES, MEMBERSHIPS OR OFFICES HELD _____

SPECIFY FOREIGN LANGUAGE ABILITIES _____

PERCENT OF EDUCATION SELF-FINANCED _____ HOW _____

MILITARY SERVICE

SELECTIVE SERVICE NUMBER _____ CLASSIFICATION _____ LOTTERY NO. _____

LOCAL BOARD NUMBER AND ADDRESS _____

IF EXEMPT OR REJECTED EXPLAIN _____

BRANCH OF SERVICE _____ ENTRY DATE _____

SEPARATION DATE AND RANK _____ TYPE OF DISCHARGE _____

WERE YOU HOSPITALIZED WHILE IN THE SERVICE ? ☐ YES ☐ NO EXPLAIN _____

REFERENCES

LIST PEOPLE WHO MAY BE CONTACTED FOR AN APPRAISAL OF YOUR PROFESSIONAL ABILITIES & WORK PERFORMANCE. STUDENTS SHOULD INCLUDE FACULTY.

NAME	POSITION	ADDRESS	TELEPHONE (Area Code)

Page 2

Figure 4–1 (Continued)

EMPLOYMENT HISTORY

BEGINNING WITH YOUR MOST RECENT POSITION LIST ALL PREVIOUS EXPERIENCE IN CHRONOLOGICAL ORDER FOR THE LAST 10 YEARS. INCLUDE SELF EMPLOYMENT, SUMMER JOBS, AND MILITARY EXPERIENCE. PLEASE BE ACCURATE AND IF UNEMPLOYED LIST THE DATES.

From: _____ To: _____   Description of your job (include responsibilities and accomplishments)

Job title: _____

Company: _____

Address: _____

Name of Supervisor: _____

Supervisor's title: _____

Last salary: _____

Reason for leaving: _____

From: _____ To: _____   Description of your job (include responsibilities and accomplishments)

Job title: _____

Company: _____

Address: _____

Name of Supervisor: _____

Supervisor's title: _____

Last salary: _____

Reason for leaving: _____

From: _____ To: _____   Description of your job (include responsibilities and accomplishments)

Job title: _____

Company: _____

Address: _____

Name of Supervisor: _____

Supervisor's title: _____

Last salary: _____

Reason for leaving: _____

From: _____ To: _____   Description of your job (include responsibilities and accomplishments)

Job title: _____

Company: _____

Address: _____

Name of Supervisor: _____

Supervisor's title: _____

Last salary: _____

Reason for leaving: _____

– IF MORE SPACE IS REQUIRED, USE SAME FORMAT AND ATTACH SEPARATE SHEET TO COMPLETE YOUR EXPERIENCE RECORD –

Page 3

Figure 4–1 (Continued)

SUPPLEMENTAL INFORMATION

USE THIS SPACE FOR ADDITIONAL INFORMATION THAT WOULD BE USEFUL IN EVALUATING YOUR ABILITIES AND INTERESTS. INCLUDE LONG RANGE CAREER PLANS, BUSINESS OR ACADEMIC HONORS OR ASSOCIATIONS, SEMINARS, HOBBIES, TECHNICAL ARTICLES PUBLISHED, PATENTS, ETC. EXCLUDE ANY ORGANIZATIONS WHICH INDICATE RACE, COLOR, RELIGION, NATIONAL ORIGIN OR ANCESTRY OF ITS MEMBERS.

THE STATEMENT BELOW IS PART OF THIS APPLICATION AND SHOULD BE READ CAREFULLY

IN SIGNING, I SWEAR OR AFFIRM THAT I DO NOT ADVOCATE NOR AM I A MEMBER OF ANY ORGANIZATION WHICH ADVOCATES THE OVERTHROW OF THE GOVERNMENT OF THE UNITED STATES BY FORCE OR VIOLENCE OR OTHER UNCONSTITUTIONAL MEANS. I CERTIFY THAT THE FOREGOING INFORMATION IS CORRECT TO THE BEST OF MY KNOWLEDGE AND BELIEF AND I AUTHORIZE PARKE-DAVIS TO INVESTIGATE AND VERIFY THE ABOVE MENTIONED INFORMATION IN REGARD TO EMPLOYABILITY. I ABSOLVE THE COMPANIES, SCHOOLS AND PERSONS NAMED IN THIS APPLICATION FROM ANY AND ALL CLAIMS OR LIABILITY IN FURNISHING THIS INFORMATION AND UNDERSTAND THAT ANY MISREPRESENTATION OR OMISSION OF INFORMATION IS SUFFICIENT CAUSE FOR DISMISSAL. I UNDERSTAND THAT EMPLOYMENT WITH PARKE-DAVIS IS CONTINGENT UPON MY SATISFACTORILY PASSING A PHYSICAL GIVEN BY THE COMPANY PHYSICIAN OR A PHYSICIAN AUTHORIZED BY THE PARKE-DAVIS INDUSTRIAL MEDICAL DEPARTMENT. I CERTIFY THAT I HAVE NEVER USED, NOR PRESENTLY USE ANY ILLEGAL OR ADDICTIVE DRUGS, OTHER THAN THOSE PRESCRIBED SPECIFICALLY FOR ME BY A PHYSICIAN.

SIGNATURE _____   DATE _____

Page 4

grade seldom are profitable. However, that does not say that all those above that score will succeed.

Test measurement

Before discussing types of tests, it is helpful to indicate how tests are designed to measure particular characteristics and how they are reliable and valid.

A reliable test consistently measures that quality or characteristic it was designed to measure. Used with different individuals, it should give accurate information in a particular area.

The more important test characteristic is its validity. Is it relevant to the job? Does it give precise, useful, dependable information? Even if the information is accurate, how useful is it in selection? Unfortunately, much data uncovered by tests have not been particularly relevant in selection. The background and environment of applicants may cause different patterns of reaction.

Concurrent validity. Concurrent validity means that the results of today's test are indicative of the applicant's potential and are a safe indicator of success on the job. A test of this kind overlooks the possible effects that may occur in transforming the applicant with one background experience to an entirely new way of living and work. Thus, the sales applicant coming from a small town or rural area assigned to a big city might be overwhelmed, while the salesperson reared in a metropolitan area might not fit in a rural environment.

Prediction validity. Prediction validity is the relationship between today's score and work performance in the future. Presumably the tests have been tried on successful salespeople first and their scores used for comparison with applicants' scores. The weakness is that an experienced salesperson would not answer the questions in the same way a beginner would.

As an example, if the applicant is a young, inexperienced person, a test of predictive validity might be useful; but if the applicant is supposed to be a mature, experienced salesperson wanting to change jobs, a test with concurrent validity is suggested.

Content validity. Content validity refers to the makeup of the test. The material in the test should have a relationship to the job. While many characteristics of salespeople are universal and desirable, it is not likely that such information is inclusive enough to cover individual job variations. At least a part of the test should be directed at particular areas that are important for a specific job. It is recommended that a psychologist be employed to assist in developing a testing program.

In developing specific information, one must be careful to distinguish between significant major deficiencies and relatively minor weaknesses. The latter, even though presently unknown to the ap-

plicant, may be corrected in a short time; but the majo.
may be fundamental and part of the applicant's makeup.

How to use tes.

Tests may be useful when used as one indicator or as one of
criteria in selection. If other criteria are favorable and the tes.
favorable, hire the applicant. If other criteria are favorable and
tests are unfavorable, check again carefully before hiring or reject.
the applicant. If the tests are favorable but other criteria are unfavorable, it is unlikely the applicant would be hired.[1]

How many tests should be used

For predictive purposes, a battery of tests is preferred over a single
test. However, additional tests have little value or may be dangerous
if the data they contribute is of little significance or if they are not
reliable. Choose only those tests which can be helpful. Avoid certain
tests unless skilled psychologists aid in interpretation. A test, like any
other tool, is useful in its own particular application where its superiority has been proved; but when transferred to another area, it may
become an inferior and perhaps useless tool. The tests briefly described in the following paragraphs are some of those used in selecting salespeople.

Intelligence tests

Intelligence tests measure learning ability and other characteristics
that indicate ability to grasp information and use it in the sales effort.
Both low intelligence and extremely high intelligence can be detrimental in most sales jobs. The person with high intelligence may become impatient with a customer and unconsciously develop antipathy
which the customer senses. In a majority of sales jobs an individual
with average intelligence can readily learn his job. Most salespeople
who might find the job difficult at first soon gain facility and knowledge
through repetition.

Weschler Adult Intelligence Scale (WAIS). It is made up of several
subtests, each with a separate score which can be combined to give
a verbal I.Q., a performance I.Q., and a full-scale I.Q. Because of its
length and difficulty, its primary use is in selection of managers or
potential managers.

---

1. An individual in a major firm related this incident to the author. When he applied
for a sales position, he was rejected by the head of the personnel department on the basis
of tests but hired anyway by the sales manager. He became a successful salesman and a
district sales manager. In this latter position, he had to hire additional salesmen. During
the testing program in his district, he again took the tests under a fictitious name and
included his tests with the others. When the results came back from the home office, he
was one of the men rejected. Some time later at the home office, he told the head of the
personnel department what had happened. He said that from that time on he has had a
strained relationship with the head of the personnel department.

Otis Self-Administering Tests of Mental Ability. These tests have been used extensively. They are easy to administer and can be given to a group simultaneously. They have several revisions.

Wonderlic Personnel Test. This is a test of general intelligence. It has several revisions and many validities because of its wide use.

For a list of psychological tests, consult O. K. Buros, ed., *Tests in Print* (Highland Park, New Jersey: Gryphon, 1974).

Motivation tests

Motivation tests are used to help determine interests and attributes. When a young person is uncertain about what to do, such tests can aid counselors in helping an individual to see his strong and weak points.

Strong Vocational Interest Blank for Men. This form has been widely used for many years. It has eight parts. The first five include lists of occupations, school subjects, amusements, usual activities, and peculiarities of people. Part 6 groups ten activities, from which the applicant selects the three most enjoyable and the three least enjoyable. Part 7 gives a choice of paired items in such areas as occupation, personal characteristics, and leisure activities. The individual tested may indicate preference for one; in some cases, both paired items are equally acceptable. Part 8 is a personality inventory which emphasizes ability to discriminate in relative importance, ability to remain composed under pressure, and similar traits. The scoring or grading is done by comparison with satisfactory scores of others in a particular occupation; in sales, it would be in a particular sales area. Thus, there is one grading key for insurance salesmen, one for wholesaler's salesmen, one for manufacturer's agents, and others.

Kuder Preference Record-Vocational. It has been used to a limited extent in choice of sales personnel. At best, its use has not been too successful in this area.

Guilford Zimmerman Temperament Survey. This personality survey is based on ten factors of measuring scales: general activity, restraint, ascendance, sociability, emotional stability, objectivity, friendliness, thoughtfulness, personal relations, and masculinity. This test is widely used and apparently has merit in aiding in the final judgment in selection. It has been used as a rejection tool in some sales areas with considerable success.

Many other tests are being used and developed so that choice is enormous. A cynic has remarked that the continued influx of new tests and modifications of existing ones indicate a need for better testing tools because of dissatisfaction with present tests.

Suggestions on the use of tests

Before one can choose tests, it is necessary to study the sales task and separate meaningful differences. Accepting raw performance scores on tests as criteria may give too much attention to some factors and too little attention to other factors important on a sales job. Such tests may gloss over specific performance characteristics that determine success of a salesperson.

The use of the terms *soft sell* and *hard sell* has been greatly overworked. It would be better to have a scale of aggressive selling which would illustrate activity desired at various levels. Even so, one can find numerous examples where toward the same product two customers will respond to different degrees of aggressiveness. The mood of a customer at a particular time may dictate the degree of aggressive selling.

Prepare a number of models of test responses and try variations and adjustments to see how they might be improved. Set up conditions or characteristics that appear relevant. Finally, do some experimental testing before adopting a test or tests. Unless there is predictive validation in certain areas, testing becomes distinctly marginal. "Where predictors are attitudinal, concurrent validities offer no advice for selection. Success and failure are as likely to be the basis for attitude variation as to be results of it. Concurrent validities say nothing about the direction of the relationship."[2]

The sales manager should be skeptical of many tests purporting to select salespeople. Frequently, employers are sold testing programs by specialized firms who select personnel. Sometimes tests developed and used with some reliability by psychologists deteriorate to no validity in the hands of the average personnel department. Newer tests tend to follow the same patterns of preceding tests and present minimum innovation. Continuous validation is desirable.[3] What might be true one year may change the next. Often one finds implicit trust in a test by the user when even the test maker would label parts of the test experimental.

Administering the testing program

It is not likely the sales manager or his immediate staff would administer the testing program. That would be handled by the personnel department or the personnel section of the sales department. While the mechanics of testing, which is important, would be primarily a personnel function, in choosing tests a number of departments and individuals might be involved. Certainly, the sales manager would be vitally interested.

---

2. Robert M. Guion, *Personnel Testing* (New York: McGraw-Hill, 1965), p. 446.

3. "Failing System-Job Tests Are Dropped By Many Companies Due to Antibias Drive," *Wall Street Journal,* 3 September 1975, p. 1.

The Interview

The interview is usually the first meeting of the applicant and the interviewer. The two inspect, question, and appraise each other. Too often, people have the impression that those prerogatives belong to the interviewer, but under circumstances where an applicant may be investigating several good job openings, it is clear that he has considerable leeway in accepting or rejecting.

Types of interviews

The *preliminary interview* is a screening device to determine if an applicant should be immediately rejected or passed on for further consideration. This interview may be used in connection with a brief application form. It would be a waste of time and money for the firm and quite unfair to the applicant to go through a long prehiring procedure if, from the beginning, the chance of hiring appears remote.

The *patterned interview* follows a carefully laid out approach which covers all the essential data the interviewer should obtain. The approach is uniform and used repeatedly. Since there is a minimum of variation among interviewers and a uniform approach to each interviewee, the resulting data can be uniformly dependable unless false information is given. The big advantage is avoiding the omission of important data.

The *unstructured* or *free interview* does not follow a single pattern, but consists of conversation and questioning in an informal manner to bring out the necessary information. Each interview varies, and the order of information received is not uniform. The interviewer may need to spend more time in bringing the attention of the applicant back to pertinent information. This type of interviewing may seem easy, but actually is more difficult than the structured approach.

The *depth interview* would be more commonly used for hiring people for difficult selling jobs and people the firm would hope to promote to managerial positions. This probing type of interview attempts to find out the applicant's ideas about many problems and situations and how he thinks under certain conditions. Skilled interviewers are required for this work.

How many interviewers

One interview is used for relatively simple sales positions. As the selling job increases in complexity and importance, multiple interviews are in order. It is unlikely that a sales manager would hire a new salesperson without a personal interview by himself or his assistant, even though an earlier personnel department interviewer had recommended the applicant. As the position increases in importance, the number of interviews will increase in proportion. At high levels, it is not unusual to have joint interviews in addition to a number of single interviews.

Information furnished from interviews

The purpose of the interview is to supplement and extend information derived from other sources. The interviewer should not use his time searching for data which is adequately presented by an application blank or can easily be secured in other ways.

Information from 273 respondents to a study indicates that interviewers feel they are most successful in securing data on appearance, personality traits, temperament, attitudes, interests, ability to communicate, experience, job training, job education, poise, and some degree of intelligence and motivation. They are least likely to gain information on job skills or actual ability, personality, character, intelligence, work habits, initiative, adaptability, and motivation. It is obvious from these data that there was disagreement among interviewers in some areas. Interviewers did feel that the most useful information obtained pertained to personality, temperament, attitude, experience, and appearance.[4]

Conducting the interview

Since the sales manager, his assistants, and district managers must conduct interviews, they should be trained to do an effective job. Wide variation in interviewing skill indicates need for training.

Often, the sales applicant has been interviewed by someone in personnel before he is finally interviewed by a sales representative. However, in district offices and in small firms the first interview will come from the sales manager or someone designated by him.

Many applicants are nervous at the interview, particularly if they are young people or salespeople who have failed elsewhere. It is advantageous to develop a cordial, relaxed atmosphere.

In the patterned interview, follow the directions but provide some informal conversation and an occasional digression which may relieve tension. In the unstructured interview, develop one area or topic at a time. Avoid jumping around since that can lead to a chaotic situation. The interview may be unstructured, but certainly it is not a hit-and-miss operation. The depth interview allows the greatest latitude and requires the greatest skill, since the conversation can easily be diverted from pertinent areas and become a pleasant conversation with little information received. Every interview is expensive and has an important purpose, which the interviewer must keep in mind so that he extracts significant data pertaining to the individual's qualifications for a particular job.

The applicant should talk about himself, his work experience, his home life, his likes and dislikes. The interviewer soon learns to catalog

---

4. AMA Research Study 47, *The Employment Interview* (New York: American Management Association, 1961).

people by their conversation. Is the interviewee a detail person? Is he interested in punctuality and preciseness? Is the voice clear or garbled, and is sentence structure smooth? Do thoughts flow readily, or is he repeating himself? Does he seem open? Does he talk in a worried tone? Does he portray confidence? Does he avoid certain topics? Is he evasive in some things? Does he display strong likes and dislikes? Does he become tired and show resentment at times? Does he get aroused emotionally about some topics? Is he willing to admit some shortcomings? Is he opposed to overtime and Saturday work, long evenings away from home, and separation from family?

Probing the educational background is helpful to the extent that the education is important in selling. A person without college training can be as successful in selling as one with a college education. The customer is interested in himself and what the product will do for him and cares little about the preparation and background of the salesperson except as it shows in his presentation.

While outside activities may have been valuable in school, all extracurricular activities are not equally valuable. If a person was extremely active, he might have neglected his subjects in school.

Conversation may reveal communication strengths or weaknesses; careful probing may bring out mathematical or statistical weaknesses.

Discrepancies in data in the application blank should be clarified in the interview. As the interview progresses, the applicant should become more relaxed and will appear in a more normal setting. While testing gives some insight to the applicant, the interview gives an opportunity to assess him more closely to try to determine qualities of perseverance, motivation, and personality and to try to judge him as he will appear on the job.

The interviewer should write down information during the interview. A special form is often used to record an interviewer's findings and conclusions. This material is entered during and after the interview. This procedure will not upset the interviewee.

Physical Examination

Some type of routine physical examination is helpful. Some routine physical examinations uncover difficulties that the applicant did not know about himself. Some physical problems may be handled satisfactorily when both the firm and salesperson are aware of them. It is unfair to the applicant and costly to the firm to hire a person who cannot physically cope with the job.

Final Selection

The final selection should not be delayed any length of time, particularly when hiring beginning salespeople. In many situations, the applicant can be selected or rejected the same day he applies. If time is required to check references, give tests, and take other steps, there may be a delay of a day or several days. When hiring managers, one might not check references until he is quite interested in the applicant. He may be applying for several positions, and it would be disconcerting if several firms inquired about the same person from the same reference. References can be contacted speedily by telephone, and the replies may be more frank than if written in a letter.

Multiple interviews may slow up selection, and they should be arranged with little delay. The convenience of the applicant may be more important than the convenience of the interviewer. Some executives adjust interviewing to fit their schedules and seem to forget that capable personnel are the most important ingredient in their firm's success. The sales field and the business field as a whole are failing to attract the great majority of top level young people. Executives cannot afford to accentuate this loss of talent by being stuffy and unresponsive. Just as the salespeople of a firm must make their product attractive to buyers, so must the sales department make their sales positions attractive to applicants.

WOMEN IN SALES

Women have held a predominant position in retail selling for many years. Now they are moving into selling jobs which previously were all staffed by men.

Statistics in 1975 indicated that about 10 percent of sales jobs were staffed by women. This trend is likely to increase as women demonstrate capacity to sell machinery, automobiles, factory supplies, and many other types of merchandise.

In this text, the author uses "salesperson," "him," "he," and other expressions which should be interpreted as referring to both males and females. Just as the term sales clerk in a store may refer to either a woman or a man, so do terms used in this text refer to individuals applying for or working on a sales job.

QUESTIONS AND PROBLEMS

1. Most firms have restrictions which limit freedom in hiring salespeople. Discuss these restraints, pointing out how they might develop and why it is necessary to follow them.

2. Hiring may be governed by both stated and implied instructions. Indicate how such directions may cover a wide variety of factors.

3. A firm wishes to hire the best possible salesman "within a framework." This implies limitations and conditions which eliminate immediately

some individuals. What are some of these limitations, and how do they affect the hiring process?

4. One of the first steps in successful recruiting is to get a sufficient number of suitable applicants. What are some of the approaches used to meet this requirement?

5. How does a display advertisement differ from a classified advertisement? Which one is more commonly used for executive talent?

6. Is there any one best source for applicants? Discuss, bringing out implicit factors that favor one source over another.

7. Tom Jonas, sales manager for Olson Sports, Inc., had been managing the sales force of twenty men for the past ten years. He was successful in hiring, training, and supervising the sales force. One day in reviewing sales activities with Mr. Jonas, the president of the firm discovered that Tom had no written job description for a salesman. The president chided Tom for this and asked, "How can you possibly hire satisfactory men when you have no written job description to follow?" How would you answer this question? How do you think Tom solves this problem?

8. Can a job description ever adequately describe a job to guide hiring? Explain your answer.

9. Indicate the many ways an application blank assists in hiring and how it can shorten the task.

10. What applicant deficiencies may be revealed by an application blank that requires careful follow-up? Why should one explore such areas cautiously?

11. Discuss the use of references, indicating possible strengths and weaknesses of reference individuals. Suggest approaches to strengthen the value of references.

12. In his eagerness to get the position, Fred Winters failed to give information concerning some of his financial obligations. Later on the job, it was discovered that Fred cut corners on his expenses but reported full expenses. When discovered, he told his supervisor about some of the desperate home problems and the money bind he was in because his salary did not cover his many needs. Fred was developing satisfactorily, but not spectacularly, as a beginning salesman. His supervisor felt that he would become a good average salesman. Discuss alternatives for solving this problem. What recommendations should the supervisor make to the sales manager?

13. Why might a firm use a preliminary application blank?

14. The whole area of testing is praised and criticized by various users of sales tests. Why does this controversy exist, and how would you suggest resolving it?

15. Is there a distinct relationship between testing and the quality of salespeople hired? Explain.

16. How can you justify using a test that a person answers one way when applying for a job but answers quite differently after five years' experience on the job?

17. The interview may be thought of as the key to selection. Why is it stressed so much?
18. What are the advantages of multiple interviews? When should multiple interviews be used? What are their chief drawbacks?
19. Discuss the various types of interviews, indicating problems involved in using each and the advantages in using one over another.
20. Discuss the proper way of conducting an interview, showing how to secure the most favorable applicant responses and indicating how and when to record data before it fades from memory.
21. What is the value of a physical examination? Is this a discriminatory technique?
22. The final selection or rejection culminates the selection procedure with an applicant. How rapidly should the final decision take place? How do you soften rejection to an unsuccessful applicant?

SEARCHMONT COMPANY   *case 4–1*

The Searchmont Company had been manufacturing and selling lamps for fifty years. They sold nationally to department stores and furniture stores. Searchmont's products were of high reputation and quality. Basically, they designed floor and table lamps with metal or ceramic bases. These lamps were priced at retail from $55 to $300.

The Searchmont Company had a national sales force of sixty salesmen and six district managers. Total sales for 1975 totaled $18,000,000. Salesmen were paid between $8,400 and $12,000 per year plus 3 percent commission for sales volume above quota.

Mr. John Ranther, district sales manager for the Illinois district, had twelve salesmen under him. A week ago Mr. Kirk Rainey, a salesman, passed away. He had been selling for the Searchmont Company for the past fifteen years. His territory had included most of central Illinois, and his sales volume for 1975 had totaled $300,000.

Mr. Ranther was now in the process of selecting a replacement for Mr. Rainey. Mr. Ranther had narrowed his candidates to three people. He saw good points in all the candidates, and he knew this decision would be a difficult one. Mr. Ranther once again reviewed the job description, hoping it would help him in his selection. Some of the points he had to consider were:

1. The salesman had to be personable and easygoing with people.
2. This job would sometimes require the salesman to be away from home from one week to two weeks at a time.

3. There were no complicated technical skills involved.
4. The salesman must have completed high school or have an equivalent education.
5. A person who was stable and would stay with the job for at least three years was preferable, because it took a while to get acquainted and establish a working relationship with customers.

Following are descriptions of the three people from whom Mr. Ranther had to make his selection.

Wanda Blake

Age 22, single, completed two years of community college majoring in business. Has a lot of enthusiasm. Five feet 6 inches tall, weight 120 pounds. Has been working for two years in the lamp department in the Elwood Department Store. Is a successful sales clerk. Gets along well with fellow employees.

Ronald Kavock

Age 40, height 5 feet 10 inches, weight 160 pounds, married with two children, home in Chicago. Lost his previous position as a furniture salesman because of a company merger. Did not finish high school, but has completed a number of sales and allied courses in night school. Has been selling since he was 20. Has a home on which he still owes $1000. Home life appears pleasant; is well accepted by neighbors. Active in church and boy scouts.

Gerard Ronson

Age 21, height 6 feet. Weight 140 pounds. Has just been discharged from the service, married his high school sweetheart, and is now looking for his first full-time position. Is a pleasant, likable young man with an easy smile and cheerful disposition. Is energetic and not easily upset. In high school, participated in sports and had good grade average. Enlisted in the army just before he was 18 and was discharged at age 21 with rank of sergeant.

QUESTION

1. Which one would you select? Give your reasons.

---

case 4–2   **ANDOVER CORPORATION**

Mr. Stanford White, national sales manager, and Mr. Robert Stephens, the personnel manager of the Inorganic Chemicals Division of Andover

Corporation, were considering the qualifications of several men for the positions of sales representative. Due to expansion and turnover, there were presently three vacancies in the field. In addition, the Fresno area salesman had just received an M.B.A. and was being reviewed for a staff position in the corporate offices. Therefore, there was a good possibility of a fourth opening.

The Inorganic Chemicals Division of Andover Corporation, with sales of $1.5 billion, manufactured a wide line of heavy inorganic chemicals including alkalies, phosphates, peroxygens (hydrogen peroxide), dry bleaches (chlorine and oxygen), bariums, phosphoric acid, solvents, and sodium sulfate. The customers for these products were located throughout the United States in the automobile, chemical, food, drug, glass, paper, textile, agricultural, and detergent industries.

Andover products were sold nationally by thirty-five salesmen operating out of ten district offices located in Boston, New York, Philadelphia, Charlotte, Cincinnati, Chicago, Houston, San Francisco, Los Angeles, and Atlanta. There were as few as two salesmen assigned to the Boston district and as many as six in Chicago. The Cincinnati, New York, and Chicago offices had an assistant sales manager in addition to the district sales manager because of the large volume of business and number of contacts to be made. These three districts also required the services of an office manager to assist in processing orders and writing routine memos.

All the current salesmen were four-year college graduates with backgrounds mainly in chemistry and chemical engineering. Several of the men held business degrees, and a few had liberal arts backgrounds. The salesmen called on research directors, technical directors, company presidents, and engineers, in addition to purchasing agents or buyers. Although salesmanship was the primary characteristic sought, technical background seemed to increase a salesman's chances of establishing a better rapport with buyers, who were almost all in the industrial manufacturing areas.

The demand for technical people in chemical engineering and chemistry placed a high price tag on recent college graduates. A chemical engineer was averaging $13,000 per year starting salary, and a chemist averaged about $12,000 per year depending on class standing, major field, and other personal qualifications.

The salesmen were paid a salary, given unlimited use of a new car every two years or 50,000 miles, and had adequate expense accounts. The travel time depended on the district and ranged from no evenings away from home to three evenings per week in some areas of the Midwest and Northwest.

Each salesman was responsible for about $2.5 to $3.5 million in sales. Each was responsible for preparing weekly itineraries of his proposed activities in addition to reporting (via standard forms) competitive situations, events affecting a product line, new start-ups, and other information which would be of concern to his district sales manager and others within the Andover Chemicals Division. He prepared status reports on all accounts and prospects once each year, usually the first call of the year. These reports were keyed to EDP systems which kept on tape pertinent data on products used, quantity, competitors, and prices. He was also required to prepare a monthly sales forecast and a yearly sales budget. The salesman had available the facilities of a large research staff located at the home office. Analysis of samples, product applications research, and process improvement recommendations were services a salesman could use in gaining new sales and bettering his position with established accounts.

Prices were competitive, and quantities varied so that an order could range from $600 a truckload to over $25,000 a truckload.

There were five senior salesmen who had been with Andover for over twenty years. They were either not considered ready for management positions, or had expressed a desire to remain in the field when positions on the marketing staff at the home office became available. They received higher compensation than the younger men. The average age of the senior salesmen was fifty-two years. The other men ranged in age from twenty-three to forty.

There was no standard path of progression upward in the hierarchy, but most of the district sales managers (nine) had served as an assistant product manager in the home office, as an assistant district sales manager, or as a product manager before becoming a district sales manager. The product managers were all exsalesmen and were considered on the same level in the organization as the district sales manager. There were then two avenues of advancement—to a district sales manager or to a product manager responsible for the marketing mix of a specific line or lines of chemicals. All higher levels of management were chosen from the ranks of the sales and product managers.

Mr. White had an opening in the Boston office, which covered all of New England; one in the Cincinnati district, where the salesman would cover the state of Indiana working out of Indianapolis; and an opening in the Los Angeles district involving southern California. He was also aware of the possible promotion of the Fresno area salesman, Dave Chase, and felt that four men should be hired.

Within the past year, it had been necessary to recruit nine new salesmen since three men had left and seven were promoted to new positions. The disparity in numbers occurred since a Houston salesman, Bill Strapp, promoted to the home office, decided he didn't like the "big city life" and quit. Three weeks later, he was rehired as a salesman and assigned to the Cincinnati district.

Mr. Stephens traveled the college circuit starting in October to interview prospective college graduates. He also recruited for the Organic Chemicals Division, which was growing at a more rapid rate. Because of the highly specialized nature of the organics sold, a chemical degree was necessary. He recruited for both technical and sales positions.

Stephens interviewed candidates who had expressed an interest in Andover by signing up for a prescheduled interview. This interview, conducted on an informal basis at the college or university, allowed Stephens to spend twenty to thirty minutes with a man and review his grades, interests, and reasons for desiring a career in production, marketing, or research.

The age and maturity of a salesman were very important. A twenty-two-year-old college graduate could find himself calling on purchasing agents old enough to be his father, in some cases his grandfather, yet he had to gain their confidence. Though Bob Stephens visited many campuses searching for technical people for both sales and production and research, only four of the last nine men hired were recent college graduates.

White and Stephens had a close friend, John Collins, a marketing consultant with Jensen, Horn, and Allen. One evening while riding the train to Connecticut, the three were talking about hiring personnel and the four men whom White would need. Collins said that one of his clients had tried a few new areas to find salesmen and had come up with several excellent prospects.

Further discussion revealed that the client manufactured and sold fabrics and carpeting nationwide, selling to both industrial and retail outlets. The areas for prospects first involved exmilitary men, i.e., men just ready to leave the service. Almost all officers were college men, and quite a few enlisted men were also college graduates. These individuals, especially the officers, had enlisted rather than wait for the draft and were quite stable and mature for their age; most of them were around twenty-five or twenty-six. Stephens and White were well aware of this type of prospect and had hired several some years earlier from men just leaving the military service. All were married with children. All but one of this group were still with the company.

White was interested in a second area covered by Collins, that of community college graduates. In the past, all salesmen were hired as future high level management potential. The company demanded the highest qualifications for a job which at times could become quite routine, and in fact, White had several men tell him that they were bored with the job and wanted more challenging work. The position's only incentive was a desk in the home office, as no one had ever been promoted from the field directly to district manager or assistant district sales manager. White felt that the company had possibly "overhired" in the past and had forgotten that there was nothing wrong with having a professional salesman the backbone of the marketing organization. A junior college man with a background in chemistry, especially one who had served three or four years in the military and then attended a junior college, would be an excellent prospect. He could first attend the standard sixteen-week training program in the home office and then either go directly into a sales position or spend some time in a district sales office as an assistant to the district manager. In this way, he would receive a sound background concerning company product lines, sales policies, and the variety of customers. When a sales opening occurred in that district, he would fill it. The more White thought about it, the more he liked this second approach.

A third area discussed was hiring men from minority groups. Collins said he now knew of two highly qualified black college graduates with chemistry degrees who had to turn to teaching because "there was nothing else for a man of your qualifications." Both were married with children. White and Stephens were quite interested, yet had some reservations.

A fourth area Collins brought up was experienced salesmen. His agency had résumés of many salesmen dissatisfied with their present positions and desiring a change. There were also employment agencies which specialized in placing sales personnel. White had thought of this area many times before and felt that a "fresh mind"—a man just out of college—was most eager to learn and the easiest to train. Too many experienced salesmen had acquired a specific technique. If this technique lent itself to the sale of Andover's inorganics, fine; but in most cases these salesmen were too interested in applying their old principles to the new job. Although this was a good area for prospects, White still thought his present system superior.

Hiring women as sales personnel was a final area which merited further thought. Hundreds of women graduate from colleges with degrees in chemistry each year. They automatically go into teaching or research because the field of business is assumed closed to women. White thought that there were many areas of business where a woman could excel, but that sales of heavy chemicals was not one of them. Hiring a woman would be more controversial and revolutionary than hiring a member of one of the minority groups.

QUESTIONS

1. What types of individuals should Andover hire as salesmen?
2. Should possible future management potential of the candidates carry such heavy weight?
3. Do any of Collins' suggestions have any merit? Which ones? Why?

5

Training

Sales training is a billion-dollar-a-year operation. As the cost of selling increases, it becomes prohibitively expensive to send untrained personnel into the selling field.

NEED FOR TRAINING

Bringing in a new sales employee can be disruptive to an organization and disconcerting to him. He is brought into a new environment, working with people who are already welded into a behavior group. His background and experience may be dissimilar to those of the people now working in sales. His views and orientation may be different from the majority of the sales group, and he has not had an opportunity to "breathe the air of success" of his new firm.

The new salesperson needs training before he can fit into his new group. Some skills need honing, and other skills must be acquired. There is a broad field of knowledge about his new job that he must acquire. He will need assistance in building proper attitudes to enhance his success and make him productive, congenial, and cooperative.

The new salesperson may have to change in many ways—develop new work habits, gain new perspectives, adjust to a different set of problems, fit into a new pattern of operations. Above all, during the transition period, he will have to learn a whole new set of rules, procedures, and methods in order to become productive on the job. To become successful, most beginners need a variety of training to equip them to meet the demands of a new, exacting job.

Skills Training

The beginning salesperson comes into the firm with certain qualities. While he undoubtedly has basic potential, it is difficult to bring his capabilities into profitable use until his efforts are properly channeled. He may waste his effort in aimless trials which not only hurt him and his employer but also upset buyers.

It is expensive and sometimes dangerous to use customers as a training ground for the new, inept salesperson. Many firms inflict inexperienced salespeople on valuable customers.

Whatever degree of selling skill is required must be determined by establishing some norm of skill performance and measuring each salesperson by this scale and training him to meet these minimum requirements. The beginning salesperson must be trained over and over if necessary until his performance has reached an acceptable level.

Product Training

Product training is necessary to familiarize the trainee with the products. In some instances, this procedure may require only a few minutes; other situations may require three years. The salesperson must know fundamental facts about his product and its uses. At the other extreme, some firms hire technical people who overwhelm buyers with detailed information. The danger in having a wealth of detailed knowledge is that the salesperson may talk too much and confuse the buyer with irrelevant data. A salesperson should have sufficient knowledge about his product to meet the buyer's requirements.

Orientation Training

A new salesperson must learn how his new employer operates. He must learn new policies, procedures, and approaches. Product policy, service policy, guarantee policy, and many other policies vary from firm to firm. He must learn selling tactics and methods used. Differences in territory, quotas, expense allowances, discounts, transportation, and return privileges are a few of many policies which may be different from the previous employer and entirely new to the beginning salesperson.

Personal Adjustment Training

Personal adjustment training is a highly critical and sensitive area for the beginning salesperson. Many people find it easy to communicate facts and information about a company but difficult to communicate intangible values which are essential to develop esprit de corps.

Much personal adjustment assistance is passed on by the sales manager or a supervisor, who will be able to present useful behavior patterns along with other information in discussion with the new salesperson. For example, the manager would say, "Bill, usually one would handle a customer like Mr. Roth in this way, but we have learned that our best results came when we did it this way." He would tell him the best way to handle Mr. Roth.

A salesperson may not understand why some company personnel deal with him in a particular fashion. Someone in the organization will then explain to him the idiosyncrasies of certain company individuals and how to adjust to each. The new salesperson may be sorely tried on delivery of his sales, on following up complaints, and in handling requests for information and assistance. The words "at once," "immediately," "in a short time," and others may not be used in the same way as the new person has understood and used them, but the firm's customers are well aware of their meaning. The young beginning salesperson learns over a period of time that words take on a variety of meanings, that a promise may have great latitude in interpretation, and that angry customer expressions are subject to interpretation. Thus, if a firm sells a highly competitive product, immediate delivery may mean delivery today; but to the buyer, immediate may mean anytime during the coming week. Personal adjustment training is designed to keep the salesperson happy and effective under conditions that may differ from the ones he is familiar with.

TRAINING OBJECTIVES

The goal of training is to improve sales activity through using a more effective sales representative, who is competent and knowledgeable.

Develop Salespeople Faster

Salespeople need training to meet their job requirements in a shorter time. Training tends to eliminate errors and centers a salesperson's attention on correct ways of handling his work.

Leaving salespeople to their own devices permits them to experiment in a variety of ways. While a limited amount of experimenting might be beneficial, it is impractical to let them try approaches which the sales manager knows cannot succeed. An orderly, carefully controlled approach eliminates pitfalls and smooths the way to adequate performance.

Improve Customer Relations

If customers are a firm's and a salesperson's most valuable assets, it seems logical to protect this asset by careful attention to customers' wishes.

Buyers are busy people immersed in their own problems and activities. Buying should be made as easy as possible. Salespeople must have knowledge of products, prices, terms, deliveries, and the use of a product for a particular application. The buyer purchasing hundreds of items cannot be familiar with each item and must rely on the salesperson. If the salesperson does not know, the buyer is exasperated because he must know before he can make the correct decision.[1]

Increase Sales

The sooner the salesperson knows what he is talking about and the sooner a buyer develops confidence in the salesperson, the quicker the salesperson's orders will increase.

A salesperson who ties in rapidly with a buyer not only has the opportunity to get choice orders; but, if he is observant, he may also get peripheral sales which might be given to someone else later. The trained salesman is alert and aggressive and sees opportunity others pass by. He helps to smooth the path of customers, makes buying easier, prevents overbuying and underbuying, assists a storekeeper in moving merchandise, and keeps abreast of special sales and overstocks. He assists the industrial buyer in keeping inventory flexible, expedites rush shipments, makes samples and trial amounts available quickly, and supports the buyer.

Lower Turnover

Discouraged salespeople quit; losing salespeople is expensive, particularly if such losses could be prevented by proper training.

The beginning salesperson has many problems on his new job. At the beginning, he is unaware of some problems which may breed customer hostility. As he finds sales do not increase as hoped for, he may sense that something is wrong, but be unable to analyze the situation and isolate his problem. He faces buyer resistance and does not understand why. Bewildered, he surveys the situation—lost orders, too small orders, unprofitable orders, failure to get a proper buyer audience, poor home office backup (he thinks), and other difficulties he had never anticipated. Lonely, embittered, discouraged, battered in every direction, and with nothing but problems staring him in the face, is it any wonder he quits?

To keep the beginner in a selling mood, it is essential that he be kept in a pleasant frame of mind, encouraged to see the opportunities ahead, taught as much about selling as possible, and encouraged to keep trying. Any salesperson will expect to meet a number of problems and be expected to cope with a variety of situations; but the fewer he meets unexpectedly, the easier it will be for him to stay until he makes the transition from beginner to producer.[2]

---

1. Physicians frequently depend on pharmaceutical manufacturer representatives for information on new products for prescriptions.

2. A producing salesperson can be defined as one who generates sales that give sufficient profit to cover expenses of his territory, including his salary and expenses, and contribute to overhead of the firm. Experienced salespeople cover overhead and contribute to profit.

Increase Morale

Morale is contagious. The buoyant, cheerful, confident salesperson radiates a feeling that wears favorably on the buyer, but the dispirited salesperson is half licked before he starts. Since success helps morale, it is logical to provide a favorable situation for salespeople.

One major area supporting success is to develop a salesperson's self-reliance and attitudes. Surrounded each day by opportunities, the salesperson learns to develop himself and expand his usefulness, to demonstrate ability, to increase customer satisfaction, and to contribute to the buying situation. Sharing this optimism with others becomes contagious; successful sales are made which increase the salesperson's enthusiasm and make him happier. Success and improved morale go hand-in-hand and grow to maximum effectiveness. Much of this inspiration effort depends on the training provided at the beginning of the company-salesperson relationship.

Improve Selling Patterns

There are many ways for a salesperson to improve selling performance. If a salesperson is shown these ways, he has a big advantage over the one who must learn on his own.

The trained salesperson is taught to discriminate in products so that he will take orders for goods that have little profit but will push high-profit items. He will be able to distribute his time equitably among his customers, not by equal number of calls but by profitable volume from each customer. He will know how to use the telephone and mail to substitute for personal calls as occasion permits.

The trained salesperson will learn early the importance of planning, of laying out activities, and of maintaining a schedule that will force him to do required tasks without shirking those of lesser importance. He will know how to optimize time, his most precious asset. He will adjust his schedule so that his important selling time will be spent talking with buyers, not in driving or in filling out reports. He will discipline himself to contact difficult customers, look for new buyers, spend time in territory development, and maintain a constructive appraisal of new opportunities.

The trained salesperson will never be too busy to handle customer problems, expedite orders, handle buyer complaints, and give proper attention to buyer wants. He will go out of his way to develop a pattern of service that will please customers.

HOW SALESPEOPLE LEARN

Learning is a process which can aid a salesperson to change his pattern of performance. Learning does not necessarily create changes, but it makes change possible if the individual wishes.

Learning Stimulation

Before a salesperson learns, he must be stimulated to want to learn. In a sales training situation, such a stimulus must be strong enough to make training feasible. A trainee's interest is raised by showing him what training can do for him. He sees that training opens the door to successful performance, which is a requisite for the financial rewards he seeks.

Participatory Learning

In participation, the trainee takes an active role in the training and learning process. Through reading, observing, testing, discussing, and practice selling, the trainee is exposed to a number of situations focusing on the same general problem and concerned with getting him to learn to express himself successfully in a selling situation. Using a number of tools exposes the trainee to some which he may find more advantageous than others.

Participation reveals weaknesses and strengths and enables the trainee to correct weaknesses. In the training process, activities are spaced over a period of time permitting reflection, observation, study, and polishing. If a salesperson shows weaknesses in a training demonstration, he can see that they do not recur. In a real sales situation, this weakness could mean a lost sale.

Continuous Learning

Learning is a continuing process. The trainee learns continuously in his training period; and if he becomes a successful salesperson, he will learn every day of his selling life. Much of this learning is subtle and scarcely visible, but it becomes evident in a salesperson's performance over time. When this learning stops, the salesperson's performance slips.

Systematic Learning

Training should be systematic and regular. Forgetting may be a factor of a number of conditions, such as how busy the individual is, how many distractions occurred at the time of learning, and what was the impact of learning. Remembering becomes easier when it is connected with some strong impact. Thus, it is easier to remember what took place in the illustration of a successful sale if the trainee not only read about it but also saw it demonstrated.

Forgetting can be a blessing. Over a period of time, people have not only pleasant happenings but also distressing events. If all is kept to clutter up their minds, they would soon be hopelessly mired in a welter of thinking that would be upsetting. It is better to forget and reestablish remembering by fanning their memories with desirable attributes and by judicious repetition at particular intervals—that is, by retraining.

This process reinforces the positive, while the negative is allowed to fade away.

What Affects Learning

Each trainee has a varying capacity to learn; it is necessary to pitch the training at a level that all can grasp. Probably most of the trainees are eager, but all are not equally conscientious. Some have greater obligations and pressures which reinforce their success attitude. Some have the capacity to concentrate and pick up information readily; others lack many of the characteristics conducive to learning. If the training is given in groups, a skilled trainer and a pleasant environment can affect learning favorably. If these conditions are lacking, learning may be slow and spotty.

COST OF TRAINING

Training is an expensive process. Therefore, it is necessary to balance training cost against using salespeople without training. Experience shows that the no training approach is more expensive overall than the cost of using trained company representatives.

Trainee Wages

In most cases, the trainee is put on the payroll as soon as he starts working for a firm. Prevailing sales wages are often higher than those of other employees. When the trainee remains relatively unproductive for three years, and some programs last that long, the cost in salary alone plus fringe benefits mounts rapidly. A major cost comes from the training of many salespeople who drop out. Some will drop during the training period; others, during the first years of selling before they become fully productive.

Trainer Salaries

In formal training programs, company personnel are used full-time and part-time to handle training activities. This cost is considerable in most cases and high in others. Major firms have large staffs involved in sales training. Many of these people have been successful in other areas of the firm, but have been transferred to the training function.

Where training is a small operation, certain people are designated as trainers on a part-time basis. While no exact cost can be attached under these circumstances, there are indirect costs since some regular employees cannot do their own work as well or must put in extra time to catch up on their regular assignments.

Executive Time

Certain executives in the firm must spend some time with sales trainees to demonstrate friendliness and teamwork. This training cost is difficult to measure, but it cannot be ignored.

Training Location

In small training situations, the training can be conducted at a desk, near someone in the sales department, or in the territory with another person. Major training is carried on in special rooms or buildings. Some firms have training establishments in separate locations from the plant or office. Some with offices and plants throughout the United States and abroad will conduct most of their training in one or more central locations. Living costs are included in training away from trainees' home areas.

Equipment

Training facilities must be suitably equipped for the comfort of trainees. Most trainers use aids varying from the ordinary chalkboard to expensive motion picture and slide techniques. Much material is needed, such as paper, notebooks, syllabi, programmed texts, and other texts. Many firms provide trainees with manuals for their individual use.

Junior–Senior Salesperson Arrangement

Some companies send their junior salesperson into the field with a senior salesperson to get experience and seasoning. If each sale is relatively important, it is unwise to send the beginner out alone. How much the new person contributes or detracts by burdening the experienced person is problematical. To assign a dollar cost to this area is practically impossible, but most sales managers will admit to a hidden cost.

Hidden Costs

Trying to assess hidden costs becomes a matter of estimating. But the cost of lost sales through inept selling can be staggering if there are a number of beginning salespeople.

Customer dissatisfaction arises when they have to deal with salespeople who do not know their jobs. Buyers in retailing often let salespeople make up orders based on the salesperson's experience with such retailers. A new person usually cannot perform this service. Older salespeople have learned customer idiosyncrasies and know how to handle particular problems.

A new salesperson may be a poor merchandiser. He has not learned techniques of display and promotion well enough to take advantage of opportunities offered by retailer promotions; he is not adept in using manufacturer promotions.

Inadequate territory representation is characteristic of lack of training. The beginner may handle customers poorly, neglect some customers, fail to call on potential customers, ignore specific requests, shirk difficult responsibilities, route his travels awkwardly, and fail to spend enough time on the job. He may report trouble spots too slowly or not at all. He may fear that if he complains his boss will think he is ineffective. In industrial sales, the salesperson may be timid with the buyer and feel inferior. The salesperson may recognize how little he knows and how much he thinks the buyer knows. The salesperson may not recognize that the buyer has limitations; and if he is a new buyer, he may be inexperienced on his job.

TRAINING CONTENT

Training content covers the area of subject matter. To cover this area adequately would require several chapters devoted to skills training. Rather than hastily touching this area, it is preferable to handle this instruction in salesmanship texts.

Other types of training, such as product and company orientation, are pertinent to each company and do not lend themselves to a standard approach. This training is very important but must be adapted to each firm. A firm's training schedule need not include basic skills training to newly hired, *experienced* salespeople, but it would stress particular applications of sales skills to company products and customers. The newly employed skilled salesperson would require thorough training in product, company policies and procedures, and other information pertinent to the industry and the particular firm.

A FURTHER LOOK AT TRAINING

The salesperson must continue to train if he is to grow on the job. Changed environments, new products, and different sales problems all dictate the necessity to alter sales approaches and techniques to fit new situations.

Introduction of new products makes regular training application essential. Developing and selling new uses for existing products calls for additional training. Deletions of some products (modifying the line) may require direction in new ways of handling old customers as well as in obtaining new customers.

When a company enters a new market or directs its attention to a new segment of buyers, different sales techniques may be necessary. The firm largely dependent on government business finds it must use different sales tactics when it enters the industrial field. Changes in customers, in channels of distribution, in product emphasis, or in conditions of sale may require a drastic overhaul of selling.

The firm that has relied on price as its most effective sales tool must quickly revise its sales tactics when competition removes price advantage. A new sales effort based on other strengths must be taught the sales force. The firm that rests on its dominance in the field as an assured supplier of high quality and excellent service must teach its salespeople new, aggressive approaches when smaller companies seriously nibble away major segments of its sales.

The whole area of retraining salespeople is receiving greater attention. After several years of successful selling, many salespeople develop the attitude that they are top producers. Often, they actually are average or mediocre salespeople in an area of inferior selling by a whole industry.

Retraining is necessary in highly competitive companies. Many firms counter competition with more advertising, greater sampling, larger selling forces, better promotion allowances—spilling "financial blood" needlessly because they are inept at increasing sales effectiveness through ingenuity, inspiration, and originality.

PREPARING FOR TRAINING

Adequate training preparation is essential to a successful program. It includes careful attention to specific areas and subjects.

Training Aids

Training aids are helpful when used properly; but they must be considered as assisting in, not substituting for, forceful teaching. There are a number of training aids. Some of the ones used currently are:

Textbooks and manuals	Feltboard
Printed materials	Magnetic board
Photographs	Control (progress) board
Graphs	Phonograph and tape recorder
Overlay	(cassette)
Flip chart	Movies
Chalkboard	Models
Projectors (slide, filmstrip, micro, overhead, opaque)	Teaching machines

Where to Train Salespeople

Where to train salespeople depends on the complexity and length of the training program, number of trainees, amount of money allocated, caliber of the program, level of trainee, size of firm, locations of the firm, and other individual contingencies. Before making any decisions about where to train, it is advisable to study training needs in great detail. Analyze the training problem and the difficulties of bringing trainees up to an acceptable standard. Study the type of trainees to ascertain their background, present educational level, and ability to absorb training. If the training is complex, the location can be quite different from that if the training is simple. Even in a single training program, there may be variation in locating different segments and even in handling particular trainees. Thus, part or all of a particular program might be handled differently between neophyte salespeople and experienced salespeople.

Centralized training

Centralized training refers to schools or training facilities located in a central location or locations. Usually, centralized training refers to one particular spot, but there is no reason why a major firm cannot use more than one central location. Thus, if a firm operates in several continents, training might be centralized within each country.

Some companies carry on a continuous training program; others train intermittently as the need arises. It is unlikely that formalized training is carried on longer than a number of weeks or months as occasion demands. The trainees then go to another form of training, where they may perform some tasks while sharpening sales skills.

Advantages of centralized training. Centralized training enables a firm to concentrate its training skills, equipment, and energies at one physical location. Since cost of training is high, it becomes financially impossible to duplicate extensive training facilities. When executives are called to participate in training sessions, it is far easier for them if the training facility is nearby.

Trainees from various areas and with different backgrounds are put together to learn about one another and to broaden their outlooks on life. Too many trainees may come to a firm with a narrow view of life and with minimum contacts with people of other races, religions, nationalities, and customs. Removing the trainees from home environments may create some loneliness, but they will have time to view the new environment objectively and can devote all their attention to training.

Centralized training gives excellent opportunities to build morale and indoctrinate trainees with the thinking of the executives and with corporate objectives. Centralized training at the home office is close enough to top executives to keep the trainees alert and is stimulating to trainers. The whole training operation is subject to scrutiny and evaluation on a continuing basis by the executives who appropriate funds for its operation.

Disadvantages of centralized training. Centralized training is expensive, particularly when trainees must be maintained away from home. A centralized training program takes time and keeps people out of production and in a training atmosphere rather than in a sales-oriented atmosphere. As a result, some trainees shine during the training period but quickly become disillusioned when meeting real selling.

There usually is much pressure put on trainees when they devote all available time to training activities. Often, the training is operated as a crash program rather than a leisurely program of learning which the trainees hoped for. It may be difficult to choose an appropriate balance of activity because of the diversity of trainees. A centralized, costly training program under constant executive surveillance can become so rigidly structured that it overlooks the fact that trainees are individuals, each with a different set of values and aspirations.

Decentralized training

Decentralized training is conducted in the sales area or close to it. It can involve training in the field, at the branch or district office, and in the trainee's home, where he is expected to spend time in the evening studying. Frequently, training is given by a part-time local trainer, sometimes by a local manager, and often in the field by supervisors and senior salespeople. Such training is spiced with a local flavor and permits trainees to get in touch with realities early in the training period. Unfortunately, a trainee may be exposed to trainers with varied experiences and backgrounds. The local trainer may not be nearly as adept in handling trainees as trainers from the central office. His effectiveness is weakened by other demands on his time, and his personal training commitment might be lukewarm because he has been assigned the job against his will. The senior salesperson may fill the trainees' ears with much talk, but not much useful information. The trainee may absorb not only what the senior salesperson says but also some of the weaknesses a senior salesperson has. Thus, a trainee may pool his and his trainer's weaknesses as well as strengths.

Sometimes the central office may send trainers from district to district to conduct training programs. This method should give greater continuity and better teaching since such people are professional trainers. This approach permits part of the decentralized training to have professional teaching and the use of training aids, which can be transported along with the training staff.

Since the manager of a branch has the ultimate responsibility for trainee success, there can be a close liaison between the two. The manager can oversee the trainee's control, adjust training activities, and direct the trainee in fashioning himself to meet individual needs.

Decentralized training probably is most suitable when the training job is short, when it is not complex, when cost prohibits extensive training, and as a follow-up part of central training where it must be done on the job. Continuous training would also lend itself to this approach.

Training Methods and Procedures

A number of training methods and procedures should be considered in developing a training program. Some methods may be better than others, but one may be better than another in a particular situation.

Lecture

The lecture approach is economical of time for both the lecturer and the trainees. A skilled trainer can present the best material in relatively short periods in the same environment to a group under the best training conditions.

Lectures should contain information and stimulating data that pertain to all the trainees. Frequently, a lecture is reinforced with special aids to portray factual material. If the content of a training session is diverse, part of it may be given in lecture and the remainder developed in small groups. If a portion or mass of relevant data is essential to all trainees, the well-done lecture does a faster and more complete job than any other approach. Some material is of such a nature that it can be used repeatedly for several trainee classes.

The content of lectures needs careful preparation. Because a lecture is given formally and to larger groups, it warrants careful attention to detail and its effect on the trainee. The best speakers in an organization should be used to lecture. Sometimes, it is worthwhile to bring in a powerful speaker from outside the firm, who can be called a consultant. Poor delivery is damaging to training, and reading a prepared talk is not advised. If the lecture is read, it would be better to give printed copies to trainees and have them read it individually.

Discussion

The procedures used to implement discussion can be oriented to the trainees in a particular group. The entire group, if it is not unwieldy, can be kept together for a discussion. They can be seated in a classroom fashion, in a circle, around a large table, or arranged to give the greatest teaching effectiveness.

The material should lend itself to discussion and be developed so that trainees find it easy to understand. Discussing cases involving actual sales problems is interesting; in solving them, trainees learn different ways of meeting sales situations.

Another approach is to have the discussion leader make a statement describing a sales incident. Then he stops, and trainees are expected to develop the situation and isolate the problem by raising questions, getting more information, and analyzing the cause of the trouble.

Small groups will secure participation by all, but invariably some will dominate and others say little. A larger group, a group of twelve instead of two groups of six, can be more beneficial if it is directed by a skilled leader who plays down the more talkative members and forces timid members to participate. Each member of a group can be forced to participate by directing questions at every trainee. This approach forces participation from the ones who are too timid to talk or the ones too lazy to prepare their assignments. The lazy one may not have much to offer the first time, but he soon realizes he had better prepare.

Demonstration

Demonstrations are dramatic ways of presenting information to people. If the trainee needs to know more about his product and how it works, he can learn from a well-performed visual presentation. If a trainee wishes to see the best selling techniques, he can see others do it, usually on slides or in motion pictures.

The trainee sees and hears through demonstrations. He learns the best ways of selling, accurate production information, and effective ways of tying the sales presentation to the product.

It is often difficult to convey precise information about a product or procedure without showing the trainee. Word descriptions simply cannot convey the finer points of selling. The trainee must experience these finer points.

Role playing

By simulating an actual presentation and putting the trainee in a selling situation, he gets to feel what the work is like. If several trainees are present, each can alternate being buyer and salesperson. This method can be used for advanced training as well as retraining, so that the individual can polish his regular work and adapt it to new products and conditions. When role playing is done before a panel, helpful suggestions can aid immeasurably in detecting weaknesses, mannerisms, repetitions, and other offensive habits.

On-the-job training

No training can take the place of the real situation. Seldom can any training anticipate all of the conditions that arise in selling. Training cannot duplicate the required intensity of the selling which varies from buyer to buyer, at different points during a sale, and among buyers by what they face at the moment. A normal, pleasant buyer one day may be a quite different individual another day because of peculiar circumstances.

Often, a beginner will accompany the regular salesperson on his calls and observe. Frequently, the trainer or supervisor will accompany the new person to observe his work and make suggestions. In one instance, the young salesman of a well-known soap company called on a storekeeper who had been selling its product for forty years. The young man came in with enthusiasm and proceeded to tell the storekeeper what and how to sell his company's products. In no uncertain terms, the storekeeper soon took charge of the conversation and told the young salesman a few facts of life. In relating the incident later, the storekeeper remarked that the supervisor accompanying the young salesman stood a distance away in the store and listened to the conversation with a smile on his face. The young salesman received one lesson from the storekeeper and undoubtedly another from the supervisor later.

On-the-job training is expensive because the supervisor's whole time is tied up with one person, the cost of traveling is considerable, and the selling is not very productive. If possible, most of the training should have preceded this period, so that the actual on-the-job experience could be used to give the salesperson his first exposure and to sharpen his skills and overcome weak areas. If the company is small and the sales manager sells, trains, and manages, he may have to take the young person with him because time and job pressures are too insistent to permit the manager to do any outside training.

The goal of training is to bring about a positive change in the trainee and improve techniques. At the same time, when he is shedding his own weaknesses and building up selling ability, he must be insulated against weaknesses of present salespeople with whom he might train. Successful salespeople have more or less insulated themselves against their own weaknesses, but a newcomer might pick up some of these undesirable traits.

Training by mail

Formal correspondence courses will perform some training jobs quite well. When little training is sufficient, this approach can be helpful. When direct-selling salespeople are recruited by mail and work full-time or part-time on a commission basis, this type of training may be all that can be cost justified. Distributor salespeople and salespeople selling independently, but handling lines of several firms, can be reached by this method.

Trainees may pay greater attention to this type of training if they contribute to its cost. When a standard selling talk is used and the approach is more or less routine, this training can be developed successfully. Also, it is well suited for supplementing incomplete product information and for introducing product changes to the regular sales staff.

Developing the Training Program

There is no training program that will fit the needs of all firms. There are general programs which can be adapted readily to fit the needs of many firms, particularly if they are in similar lines of selling or are all members of one industry group. Thus, a program for electrical wholesalers could no doubt be used by such firms with minor adaptations. However, some larger manufacturers in the same industry might use unlike training approaches.

Before developing a training program, management should specifically outline the goals of the sales function and what they want a salesperson to do. The approach the sales department takes is largely governed by the directions of management. When the sales manager has a firm grasp of the selling direction, he can develop a training program that will prepare beginning salespeople for their jobs. While it is impractical to pinpoint one precise sales training program, generally any program would incorporate the following features.

Skills training

The beginning salesperson must learn how to sell. He can learn it in a hit-and-miss fashion, or he can be prepared through careful advance training.

It is not the purpose of this text to give a skills' course in selling. Various books have been prepared covering the area thoroughly.[3] A company could use material already available and supplement it with specific skills' data pertinent to its customers and operations.

Since skills training teaches the trainee how to meet and handle the customer and how to close the sale, it is really the most important segment; the rest of training merely facilitates salesperson-customer contact.

Product training to aid customers

Too many salespeople do not know their product well enough; a few know it too well and, as a result, talk too much product and not enough customer application.

A trainee should know his product well enough so that he can discuss its use with customers. Seldom does he need extensive knowledge of intricate parts and components unless the product is extremely technical. In such circumstances, the salesperson can call in an engineer from his firm to handle involved discussion. For example, a retail clerk may not know how or where a piece of cloth is woven, but he should know whether it is colorfast and how much it will shrink; the car salesman may know little about the material and fabrication used in the car, but he should be able to answer a wide range of questions on equipment, performance, comfort, and options; the industrial salesman may not know the exact specifications of each material going into the tool he sells, but he should be well versed on exactly how to use the tool and its limitations; the industrial salesman should know how his paint will stand up under different atmospheric conditions, what type of paint to use in specific applications, problems in applying the paint, and its expected life. Important areas in industrial selling are the size of a machine in terms of installation, its rated capacity, how long one can expect trouble-free operation, how many spare parts are necessary, how expensive these parts are, whether the plant maintenance man can keep the machine in repair, and whether they must call in men from the machine manufacturer.

The product complexity is one of the determining factors in training, as is the salesperson's ability. When a product is complex, such

3. H. Webster Johnson, *Creative Selling*, 2nd ed. (Cincinnati: South-Western Publishing Co., 1974).

as machinery installations, the trainee is a high-caliber person who can be taught such information readily. In a simple selling situation where product knowledge is easily acquired, the caliber of trainee is lower; and teaching is more difficult. Thus, the amount of time required in training is governed by the amount of product knowledge and by the trainee's ability to learn.

When teaching product information, it may be desirable to incorporate a market background of future customers. Teaching product knowledge isolated is not nearly as effective as training in a job environment. A brief experience in the field is helpful because the salesperson learns firsthand about the problems he will face and is more willing to learn, because he knows he will use such information.

Company relations to customers

Each firm has a body of information each salesperson needs. Management has a philosophy and a series of objectives a salesperson should know. How a salesperson treats his customers depends on how the company operates. Thus, one firm may give meticulous attention to each customer, while another firm determines its services by the size of the account. One firm may depend on wholesalers to handle smaller accounts and concentrate salesperson attention on important buyers. One firm may be careless in handling customers, but maintain its position by giving lower prices on quality products.

Some firms may have carefully developed policies, which help salespeople to guide their work and answer buyers' questions; other firms may have indefinite policies, which give salespeople greater leeway but may also contribute many uncomfortable moments with the buyer. Even the company that says it has no definite policies in certain areas does have a policy, which may be to devise a solution expedient at the time. Salespeople sometimes forget that *no policy* is a policy.

Policies are guides to chart the path of operation. Some policies may not be written or clearly expressed, but the young salesperson soon learns they are very real. He learns that some things must be done a certain way, that he must conform carefully under some conditions, and that in some areas there is a minimum of restraints but also a minimum of company assistance. Thus, he may find the peculiar situation where the boss says "Suit yourself, but do not come to me if you get into trouble."

Hopefully, company information is complete enough to guide the salesperson. It should make it possible for him to make proper decisions within his framework of authority and permit him to establish strong working relationships with his customers. The salesperson should not be in a position where he has minimum authority, cannot make any promises without first contacting his home office, where he is hemmed in by petty restrictions, and where company procedures frustrate both him and the buyer. Neither should company information be so vague or unresponsive that the salesperson gives the impression he can act for his firm without restrictions, without regard for consequences, and without considering the best options for buyer and seller.

Human information

The trainee becomes a salesperson loaded with product and company information and prepared in skills training, but he also is an individual, who needs training and understanding of himself. It is, therefore, essential that attention be given to the one who is to profit from training. While he may be chosen carefully and embody many of the characteristics of successful salespeople, he nevertheless must use his ability, background, and training in the most effective manner.

To achieve this goal, training should inject a catalyst that will bring training into focus. This catalyst must be motivation—which is inherent to some extent in each person but which must be stimulated, spurred, teased, coaxed, and cajoled into superior performance. Unless training is spiced with qualities that wake enthusiasm and drive, it will be like a powerful machine used improperly. Some sales managers feel that providing basic requirements is sufficient, forgetting that there must be a series of sparks that will not only set the trainer in motion but jolt him and inspire him to even greater achievement. Since salespeople frequently work alone and away from direct contact with the boss, they must be self-energizing. Many salespeople themselves do not possess enough of this quality and need training, instruction, and constant attention to develop this to a point where it becomes as much a part of them as does skill in selling and handling the firm's problems in the territory.

Other training

The trainer must include a generous amount of teaching on trainee self-development. The trainee must develop perseverance, aggressiveness, and other traits. It is necessary to instill correct attitudes, develop proper working habits, and teach proper dress and behavior. He must realize that he is the connecting link between his firm and the customer and that it is his job to communicate how his product or service will benefit the buyer.

Physical facilities

The physical area where the training is given should be properly prepared. If carried out in a separate room or facility, the space should be adequate, chairs comfortable, and tables of proper height with necessary writing materials available. The lighting should be regulated and focused on objects so that vision is clear and unimpeded by obstructions. Temperature control throughout the year brings comfort and makes learning easier. Equipment should be kept clean and in excellent working order, and spare equipment must be convenient to replace worn-out projection bulbs or mechanical equipment. There should be enough printed material for each trainee.

A trainee cannot sit through hours of lecture, observing, and reading without periods of sufficient relaxation. Trying to sandwich in too much training defeats the learning process and cannot be tolerated. Repeat training must be carried on to bring all trainees to a minimum knowledge level. Careful testing will indicate the progress of each trainee and the amount of repetition needed.

Class training conditions may be worked out carefully, but if there is only one trainee, the conditions may deteriorate or never be prepared properly. Unless careful attention is given to training details for one trainee, chances are that many of the steps may be done carelessly, at odd times, sandwiched in with the trainer's other work, and skipped or slighted.

Inviting trainee participation requires thought and effort from each individual and provides better instruction. The instructor should encourage questions and participation. Some trainees must be literally forced to participate by using direct questions. Such trainees need encouragement because they may be timid, are not used to voicing their own ideas, and are reluctant to express what they fear are weak suggestions. Superior training comes as a result of following carefully prescribed methods and procedures, utilizing approved educational techniques, and aiming for predetermined objectives and goals.

EVALUATING TRAINING

The value of training may be questioned by executives; they may compare costs with results that presumably overshadow costs. Therefore, measuring sticks should be developed which give general impressions of increased selling effectiveness and, if possible, incorporate concrete measuring devices that can be assessed in sales dollars or gross income.

Measuring Training

Although the training program is not an end in itself, it has been established to perform a service to the trainee. To be an effective program, it must cover various activities that will make him a better salesperson. Therefore, it will consist of a number of different parts, each relating to a particular segment of information. The trainee's progress is measured at a number of checkpoints through examinations or other means which can determine how well he has progressed.

In evaluating the salesperson on the job, his weaknesses can be compared to his training performance to discover if there is a correlation between the individual's training weaknesses and particular weaknesses displayed on the job.

Trained and untrained groups

One obvious comparison of training results is to use a control group of salespeople who did not receive the regular training and measure their results with those who have been trained. In such a comparison, the results should be watched closely in early selling periods since the trained salesperson should respond more quickly than the one not trained. For the first few weeks, months, and even years, the trained person should progress faster than the untrained one. Eventually, there would be little if any difference between them. Over a longer period, there would not be noticeable differences.

The salesperson who did not receive regular training would fall into the category of self-trained. If he succeeds, he trains himself through experience and learns by his successes and failures.

Handling territory problems

A practical way to evaluate training is to assess the trainee's response in the field. If the training program is workable, it should reflect in earlier selling maturity, a better selling pattern among the items handled, and customer satisfaction. If, for example, many customer complaints occur when a beginning salesperson takes over a territory, there apparently is a training deficiency or a salesperson weakness. If a salesperson has price troubles, he has not learned to meet quality competition emphasis. Competition may outsell him badly, because of inexperience, inadequate preparation, or both. On some occasions, of course, company policies may affect territory sales regardless of what the salesperson does.

One way of assessing a salesperson's response to training is to have a supervisor accompany him periodically to check his performance against standard performance. How much is the beginner improvising rather than following procedures he was taught? How far has he strayed from accepted procedure? Unless the new person is checked regularly, he may deviate so far from original instructions that the teaching has become nonexistent in his mind. On the other hand, a supervisor may find a salesperson adhering so rigidly to his training that he lacks flexibility and is unable to adapt to a variety of situations.

The supervisor can also determine how well the beginner can improvise and adapt to situations he never faced in training. Some of these situations would be ones he ought to recognize from training, which now appear in a slightly different form in the field. He should be able to adjust and meet them. Others are entirely new, and he would have to improvise. Skill in meeting such a situation would indicate he had native ability and/or had digested his training to learn the correct appoach. The trained person hopefully would have an answer similar to that of an experienced person.

FUTURE OF TRAINING

Training will continue to broaden, increase in intensity, and enter new areas as its effectiveness becomes more evident. Huge as the present training effort is now, it may in the future expand dramatically because it tends to remove areas of uncertainty in distribution. The whole area of understanding customers better, learning to anticipate their wants, and developing products and services that can make living more pleasant is tremendous. There are many customers with different wants. This situation makes segmenting the market easier and can lead to specialized training for various groups of buyers.

Each successive generation should improve sales training. Sales trainers of the future will look back at current training with tolerance because they will recognize that improvements were helped by improved training aids and a broader psychological understanding of people.

QUESTIONS AND PROBLEMS

1. Discuss the need for sales training, pointing out specific benefits of training to both the buyer and the salesperson.

2. Why is skills training imperative? Why can lack of skills training prove expensive?

3. Discuss the often repeated statement of buyers talking about salesmen, "They don't know their product."

4. How can you tie orientation training to personal adjustment training? What does this training accomplish?

5. How can training (a) develop salespeople faster, (b) improve customer relations, (c) increase sales, (d) lower turnover, and (e) increase morale?

6. Discuss the importance of improving a salesperson's selling pattern. Would you agree this is essential to his success? Why?

7. Is there a difference in learning ability among salespeople? Justify your answers.

8. What factors stimulate and improve learning? Describe several and indicate their importance.

9. Discuss training costs, pointing out why this expense may be prohibitive in some situations. What cost elements must be recognized and appraised in a training situation?

10. What are some hidden costs resulting from improper training?

11. Indicate the need for retraining. Explain how time affects salesmen's knowledge.

12. Discuss the relative strengths and weaknesses of training aids, and indicate where each one might be superior.

13. When should training be centralized, and when should it be decentralized?

14. Under what conditions is the lecture the preferred training method? Why?

15. What are the advantages and disadvantages of the discussion approach to training? When is it most effective?

16. Why is demonstrating superior to most types of training? If you disagree, explain your reasons.

17. What is a major defect in role playing? Does this destroy its usefulness? Explain.

18. Is on-the-job training really a training device? Discuss and indicate why it can be dangerous and also helpful.

19. Why is product training second only to skills training? If you think it is the most important training, give your reasons.

20. What is policy?

21. Training should be carried on in an inviting environment. Discuss this statement, giving a number of factors to be considered.

22. Discuss approaches to use in evaluating training. Point out ways of measuring training.

---

case 5–1   **THE MORGAN COMPANY**

The Morgan Company is a large manufacturer of electrical and electronic equipment. It maintains sales offices in major metropolitan areas throughout the United States, Canada, and Europe. The firm was started in a garage shop in the late 1800s by an inventor who had developed several devices used to control electrical current. These devices were the forerunners of much of today's sophisticated electrical and electronic equipment. The company has grown from this humble beginning into a diversified corporation engaged in international activity with annual sales of over $150 million.

A continuing emphasis on product improvement and research into many seemingly unrelated fields has contributed to this growth. Recent major acquisitions have helped to reduce the significance of business cycles in the capital goods industries and have helped the firm diversify into new areas.

The firm now manufactures a complete line of electrical and electronic equipment. Products range from tiny solid state devices such as transistors, diodes, and integrated circuits to complete computer control of a steel mill, aircraft radar installations, and complex satellite tracking equipment. Several separate divisions produce this wide range of products. The industrial division is responsible for complete process control and related auxiliary equipment. The specialty division produces all of the solid state devices sold separately, as well as those used in the other divisions. The aerospace division produces all military and aviation equipment, and the distribution division manufactures all switchgear and control components.

Much of this growth has occurred in the past several years. Sales in 1974 were the highest in the company's history, and a doubling of 1974 sales by 1976 is anticipated. Because of this rapid growth, district offices have expanded their sales forces to serve adequately the new markets.

Early in 1975, Mr. D. F. Ambler, district manager of the Atlanta sales office, began a program to add several salesmen to the Atlanta staff. It is a company policy to hire recent college graduates for any sales openings; each district manager has the responsibility to recruit personnel. Over the past several years, Mr. Ambler has put together a fairly well trained and closely knit organization. Since it is often necessary for salesmen to work closely together, the new salesmen would have to fit in well and be compatible with those in the existing organization.

Hiring three new sales trainees was complicated in the Atlanta market, which was rather unique in that it represented industries spanning all the firm's divisions. It was necessary for each salesman to have some knowledge of the entire product line and each division's operations since he would be calling on a wide variety of customers. One customer might require a standard catalog item, such as a pushbutton or pilot light, while another would require a complete engineering analysis of a complicated problem.

Therefore, extreme care was essential in selecting new sales trainees. Because of a wide range of work activity, Mr. Ambler placed strong emphasis on scholastic achievement and on extracurricular activities.

By early June, three new sales trainees had been hired. Lester Richard, twenty-one and newly married, had received a B.A. degree from a small midwestern university and had majored in marketing. Walter Barko was twenty-three years old, married, and the father of one small boy. He had just graduated with honors from Georgia Institute of Technology, where he received a B.S. degree in mechanical engineering. Charles Williams, thirty-one years old and the father of three children, had received a B.S. degree in electrical engineering from Auburn University in 1966 and was presently working toward a master's degree in marketing. Of the three, only Mr. Williams had previous industrial experience. Since graduating, he had worked in several supervisory capacities for a large steel company and had spent the past two years in charge of electrical maintenance in a rolling mill for that same firm.

Mr. Ambler and other company officials felt that the training program would be most effective if it was geared to each individual's background and needs and not stereotyped. As a result, the training received by each of the new trainees was quite varied. A quotation from the first page of the standard instruction manual given to each new salesman illustrates this point.

"The Sales Education Program represents a departure from the usual training programs. Our program is an adult approach to the learning process based on the premise that given sufficient responsibility an adult will respond with whatever self-application it demands for success. Our program is not the typical spoonfed learning process with great dependence on the instructor. It reverses this concept and places the total responsibility for learning on you. This is accomplished by using a carefully developed program complete with all materials, text, films, catalogs, and instructions, permitting you to progress as fast as your abilities and application demand."

Phase 1 of the training program was conducted in the Atlanta office with all three trainees participating and lasted approximately six weeks. This basic introductory course had the following objectives:

1. Learn about the company, its marketing philosophy, its distribution channels, its "way of life."
2. Establish a foundation of product knowledge on which to build through personal effort and further product training at the home office.
3. Develop familiarity with terms, pricing, estimating, circuitry, wiring diagrams, and standard symbols.
4. Develop ability to sell professionally with honesty, sincerity, and conviction, emphasizing product benefits and develop an awareness that each sale represents an individual problem.
5. Provide the initial framework of knowledge of competition.
6. Provide a familiarity with district office procedures.
7. Provide a variety of basic information on the company and its products.
8. Provide an initial knowledge of the job requirements of a sales engineer.

The following is a condensed program of phase 1:

Company history, purposes, division of responsibilities, and long-range objectives
Company organization, physical and functional
Distribution organization
Salesmanship
Catalog use

Estimating procedures
Communication techniques
Individual product analysis
Building block and language of control
Basic electricity

Phase 2 lasted three months and took place in the home office. Mr. Barko and Mr. Richard attended this phase, which had the following objectives:

1. Develop a broader span of product knowledge.
2. Develop greater familiarity with terms, pricing, estimating, circuitry, wiring diagrams, and symbols.
3. Provide vocational directional training to focus attention and learning on a specialized basis to help determine future assignments.
4. Complete a working knowledge of the functions of a Morgan Company salesman prior to assignment in the field. This includes work habits, time management, reports, and customer relationships.
5. Develop skill in the proficient use of all sales aids provided by the company.

The following is a general program of phase 2:

Company purposes and aims
Company organization, including tours
Distributor operations
Speech
Salesmanship and sales techniques
Review use of catalog
Communications, reports
Distribution apparatus
Engineered control
Special industry control systems
Specialty products
Competition

Phase 3 lasted another three months and was attended only by Mr. Barko. This part of the program also took place in the home office and was designed to provide an in-depth engineering and marketing training specifically geared to the industrial division, its products, services, and capabilities. It was felt that this phase was too technically involved for Mr. Richard. He returned to Atlanta and began on-the-job training, calling on carefully chosen companies. He also worked on a series of correspondence courses designed to improve his electrical and technical background.

Because of Mr. Williams' industrial experience and electrical engineering background, Mr. Ambler felt the training time in the home office would be unnecessary. Instead, he felt an emphasis should be placed on on-the-job training. As a result, Mr. Williams began making calls on small companies which were not assigned to any regular salesman. These firms may have written or phoned expressing an interest in one of the company's products or may have wanted someone to look at a specific application. Mr. Williams' experience with a wide variety of equipment was very helpful in dealing with these firms and their problems. After a short initial training period, he was given 200 accounts, which were undeveloped but represented considerable potential business.

QUESTIONS

1. Evaluate the training program of each new salesman.
2. Was the training program fair to each man? Discuss.
3. Should Mr. Ambler have hired Mr. Richard? Why?
4. How important is selling ability as contrasted to technical background?

---

case 5–2   **NORTHSTAR SKI COMPANY**

In July, 1976, Ray Otto, owner and manager of the Northstar Ski Company, was in the final planning stages of his marketing strategy. Mr. Otto had recently hired Ernst Bjork from a leading ski manufacturer to function as sales manager. The Swedish-born Mr. Bjork had worked in this country as a ski instructor until an automobile accident ended his career. He was thereafter hired as a sales representative for the previous company, where he sold skis successfully for the last ten years.

The Product

Mr. Otto, an engineer with one of the automotive corporations in Detroit, had been experimenting for the last five years with various metals and alloys with the hope of inventing a new type of ski. This was a hobby at first, but became a driving ambition which occupied all his leisure time. After four and one-half years of experimenting, he combined an aluminum alloy with fiberglass and produced what proved to be a very practical ski. Mr. Otto then perfected his ski and hired a market research firm to analyze the market and product acceptability.

After three months, the research firm reported to him that his ski proved acceptable to beginning and intermediate skiers, because they reported that they felt more in control with the Northstar skis. However, expert skiers, including ski professionals, seemed to dislike the ski for the fast movements of racing because they were lighter and were unnaturally easy to maneuver through the gates of a slalom course. This, the experts claimed, threw off their timing. For this reason, Mr. Otto could not get a renowned ski pro to represent or provide a testimonial for his ski. The research firm also explained that with the sport of snow skiing growing at such a rapid rate, there was room in the market place for his skiing innovation.

The innovation that contributed to the success among rookie skiers was the special camber. He called this feature a "personalized camber" which distinguished Northstar skis from all other brands. Whereas most other ski companies stress the proper length of the ski to correspond with the buyer's height, Mr. Otto's ski was specifically engineered to stress the stiffness of the camber to the buyer's weight. If the skier used the Northstar ski with the personalized camber for his weight, the edges of the ski would contact the snow with equal pressure, thereby reducing the chance of catching an edge in the snow when the skier was too light. Mr. Otto decided to manufacture the Northstar ski in one model only, in 20 lb body weight increments ranging from 50 lb to 250 lb and in standard lengths from 5 ft 1 in. to 7 ft 3 in. They were to be priced competitively with the least expensive model of the top three American metal ski manufacturers.

Competition

Three well-entrenched national ski manufacturers have been in operation for at least fifteen years. These companies sell, promote, and advertise nationally and are the giants of the American ski industry. Many foreign-made skis have penetrated the American market over recent years, and three of these have gained considerable sales in the United States. In addition, many specialty and department stores have added their own private brands of skis and have achieved remarkable success because of their competitive quality, somewhat lower prices, and charge account convenience. In total, the Northstar ski was coming into an ever growing yet extremely competitive industry. As previously mentioned, the Northstar ski will be priced at wholesale to sell at approximately the same price as the bottom line of the top three ski manufacturers. Retail price is flexible among ski dealers, depending upon their desired profit margin.

Distribution and Promotion

Being on the ground floor of his venture and possessing little capital for national distribution, Mr. Otto narrowed the scope of his marketing activities to five midwestern states, Michigan, Indiana, Ohio, Illinois, and Wisconsin. He decided to distribute the Northstar ski through ski shops exclusively. His reasons were (1) he didn't have the financial or productive capacity to saturate the market; (2) the more specialized staff of a ski shop would probably do a better job with explaining the "personalized camber"; and (3) most ski shops rent skis, and Mr. Otto saw a tremendous advantage to getting the Northstar ski placed in these shops.

Mr. Otto felt strongly about getting his skis placed as rental equipment because, according to the research study, they should be able to sell themselves once they're used by a beginner or intermediate skier. Since most advanced and expert skiers own their equipment, it is the novice and seminovice skier who will be, for the most part, renting the skis. These are the people that the Northstar is segmenting out of the entire market. Mr. Otto believed that people rent skis only so long, and when they decide to purchase they naturally will purchase a brand that they have previously used and liked. He also believed that once a person has purchased a set of Northstars, that person will become so accustomed to their unique performance that he will never purchase another brand, even if he progresses to become an advanced and expert skier.

Because of limited finances, Mr. Otto will have to forego advertising and promotion at this time. He will rely exclusively on his sales force to get the Northstars into the ski shops, to convince the proprietors to rent them, and to teach the salespeople how to sell the personalized camber in the midst of tremendous competition.

Sales Organization

Along with Mr. Bjork, Mr. Otto has hired five recent college graduates for his sales force. Each man will be assigned one of the midwestern states as his territory. The new salesmen had degrees in various subjects—two in business, two in liberal arts, and one in political science. As a prerequisite for this position, each man had to be at least an intermediate skier since some of their work would require the demonstration of the ski under actual conditions. Mr. Otto reasoned that the young prospective salesmen could be molded into successful ski sales representatives because of their background and interest in skiing plus their youthful exuberance. Besides, he couldn't afford the salaries necessary to hire experienced salesmen. The sales staff was guaranteed $500 per month plus a commission of $1 for every pair of skis they could sell.

In January, 1976, Mr. Otto informed Mr. Bjork that he had two months starting April 1 to train these recruits in the fundamentals of salesmanship and in the particulars of selling the Northstar ski. Furthermore, he suggested that Mr. Bjork use his experience working for the previous ski manufacturer to develop a training program which would establish confidence before they actually challenged the hard, cold world of sales. This left Mr. Bjork with approximately two and one-half months to organize the training program. Since he never authored a program like this, he anxiously set about his task.

Training Program

Mr. Bjork believed that in order to establish confidence he would primarily have to instill in the salesmen a comprehensive background in all phases of the origin and development of skiing. He reasoned that discussions with potential customers are bound to uncover some areas involving the history and terminology of skiing. In order to effect this preparedness, Mr. Bjork's first month of the training program was devoted to the history, terminology, and background of skiing. The second month was devoted to handling the customer and practice presentations.

Each training session totaled eight hours. During the first month, Mr. Bjork would lecture from 8 A.M. until noon. Starting at 1 P.M., the salesmen were allowed a question-and-answer period of not more than two hours and would then be given an essay examination on the morning lecture. Mr. Bjork would correct the papers and post the scores on a chart the following day. This chart was to be a cumulative measure of comprehension (the first month) and of presentation finesse (the second month); scores would be totaled at the conclusion of the training period. As an immediate bonus, the highest scorer would receive $200; second place, $150; third place, $100; fourth place, $50; with the last man receiving nothing above his regular salary of $500.

Since Mr. Bjork did not believe in a "canned" presentation, he impressed upon the trainees during practice presentations to individualize their approaches. During the last two weeks of training, each man would present a sales presentation to Mr. Bjork every day, after which the trainees and Mr. Bjork would evaluate, criticize, and suggest improvements. Mr. Bjork suggested that the men vary their sales approaches from day to day and thereby discover which methods best suited their abilities and personalities.

The monthly and weekly topics were as follows:

I. First month
   A. History of skiing
      1. First week
         a. Origin of skiing and the Nordics
         b. Evolution of ski types and designs
      2. Second week
         a. Invention of ski competition and its progression
         b. Styles of skiing

    B. Terminology of skiing
       1. First week
         a. Clothes, customs, and equipment
         b. National and international ski lodges and owners
       2. Second week
         a. Skiing professionals, their specialties, and where employed
         b. National and international races, events, and conventions

II. Second month
    A. How to handle the customer
       1. First week
         a. Acting with confidence, examples
         b. Using skiing jargon frequently, examples
       2. Second week
         a. Emphasizing product features, examples
         b. Never taking no for an answer, examples
       3. Third and fourth weeks
         a. Putting it all together in individualized presentation

Anxious to see the progress of Mr. Bjork's training program, Mr. Otto paid an unexpected visit to one of the presentation sessions. To his disappointment, none of the trainees gave a similar presentation. In fact, he noticed that they really didn't stress the personalized camber or the ease of skiing for beginners and intermediate skiers. Instead they seemed to linger on about various ski names, events, and places before they even attempted to sell the product. He invited Mr. Bjork to dinner that evening and expressed his surprise at the presentations. Mr. Bjork, however, assured him that the best way to gain a customer's confidence was to snow him with your knowledge of the subject and then present the product after he sees that you know what you are talking about. He assured Mr. Otto that the five men had progressed rapidly and that their sales would show it. With only two weeks before the new sales staff was to start, Mr. Otto believed that it was now too late to try to change anything. He hoped Mr. Bjork's prediction would come true.

ASSIGNMENT

Analyze and appraise the training program. Discuss the program for each week and suggest possible changes.

6

Supervising the Sales Force

The term *supervision* has a variety of meanings to different sales managers. Some managers include most of their tasks; others consider it as checking reports, giving directions, and watching sales and expenses. In this text, supervision directs performance through suggestion, demonstration, observation, instruction, and authority.

There is a considerable difference between supervising a salesperson on the job and supervising people in the office or the factory. The office supervisor has employees where he can see them and be ready at any time with assistance. This situation creates a close relationship and can lead to cooperation or friction. In sales supervision, the supervisor is with the salesperson very little. He can travel with him at periodic intervals to see how the salesperson performs, but most of the time the supervisor is not physically present when the salesperson meets customers. He must therefore depend on means other than observation. The supervisor's inspiration is given at contact intervals and may not coincide with a time of low morale for a salesperson. When he is desperately needed in the field by one salesperson, he may be elsewhere working with another person who needs help or working in the office.

PURPOSE OF SUPERVISION

There are a number of reasons for establishing supervision. Some of them may be universal for all firms; others may appear only under special occasions that are unique to certain firms.

Control Salespeople

One of the primary reasons for supervision is to control salespeople. This task may include selling activities and personal behavior. How a salesperson acts reflect on his firm. It is not likely a large number of salespeople will behave at all times in a manner the firm approves without regular supervisory surveillance.

Few people are able to discipline themselves to act in an approved way regularly, and salespeople are no exception. Unless controls are maintained, there is a tendency to let work slide, become careless with customers, cut selling time, procrastinate in work, and indulge in activities that do not promote the firm's image. Just the mere fact that the salesperson knows he is being checked keeps him alert. If he is reminded immediately when he fails to perform certain assigned duties, he is unlikely to develop a lackadaisical attitude or to slough off duties that may be annoying.

When a salesperson starts in his territory, he receives instructions on handling expenses. As time passes, these instructions blur, and he begins to interpret expenses in his own way. If the supervisor checks on the salesperson's expense handling, it is not likely he will stray too far.

A salesperson may become careless in his appearance and be unwilling to spend money to appear professional on the job. Sometimes a gentle nudge from the supervisor is sufficient to alert the salesperson that he is slipping in this respect.

Increase Morale

Unless a salesperson has a chance to meet a supervisor occasionally, he becomes involved in a maze of selling and other duties, which may in a sense divorce him from contact with the office. All he may see are the headaches he receives from the home office and the constant prodding to do more, do better, and work for greater company profits. If a supervisor gets to the person in the field, he can bring him up-to-date on what is going on at the home office and make him feel he is an essential part of the organization.

The salesperson works alone, handling a variety of problems, frequently under difficult circumstances. He is being plagued by customer demands and is receiving indifferent response from his firm. He begins to wonder if what he is doing is worthwhile. But once he sees what is actually happening and what he considers company indifference is mostly the company's inability to follow up on its demands, he becomes more comfortable, realizing his job is to accept more territorial responsibility and that he is only sharing company problems.

In house-to-house selling, the salesperson faces so many discouraging turndowns that he needs frequent supervisory encouragement if he is to continue. Some jobs require far more supervision because the selling conditions are quite discouraging.

Check Selling Techniques

An important supervisor assignment is to watch how salespeople use approved selling techniques. Salespeople may be encouraged to modify what they were taught so that it becomes more applicable to specific customers. However, some salespeople soon take this privilege to mean they can make wholesale changes or even revamp the entire approach.

Once they are given latitude to improvise and adapt, some people will go to great lengths to make changes far beyond their permission. Occasionally, such extreme positions may become successful. Unless checked, however, some of these approaches will be so individualized that a chaotic situation may develop. If modifications proliferate, the result is a hodgepodge of ideas that are usually detrimental.

The supervisor in touch with his salespeople can stay close to their selling, make suggestions for using approved techniques, and show the salesperson how far he has strayed from the superior methods. Salespeople forget much of what they learned and must have their memory jogged by the supervisor so that they will reinstate some of the better techniques.

One very successful salesman told the author how on his first selling job he strayed from the standard technique, substituting what he felt were superior procedures. His sales decreased, and not until his supervisor brought him back to what he should have been doing did he again become successful.[1]

Prevent Selling Problems

Salespeople without adequate supervision can build serious problems which become embarrassing to the firm. Their selling techniques may grate on customers until finally they lose out but never know why because the buyer never tells them. If the salesperson does not sense he is irritating the buyer, it is not the buyer's duty to tell him; but a supervisor accompanying the salesperson could detect that something was amiss.

A salesperson may be giving prices and services to which customers are not entitled. After a time, this comes to the attention of the home office; and, in correcting the situation, much customer ill will may arise.

The salesperson might be careless in writing orders or write them so the people in the home office find them difficult to read. He might be slow on following up customer requests and irritate buyers, who turn away from his firm. These are a few selling weaknesses that can arise.

Direct Selling

A salesperson may have much latitude on how and what he sells. In choosing from a large number of items, salespeople develop favorites, which they push to the neglect of others. Sometimes these choices are

---

1. This man was vice-president of sales of a different firm when he told the author this incident. However, the standard approach and techniques he used on his first selling job would not have worked on his present job.

not rational and are particularly expensive to the employer because the salesperson is not producing profitable sales.

A salesperson has many possibilities in selling a product mix. He can develop order patterns which reflect careful thought, or he can sell merchandise in no particular pattern. This latter approach may soon degenerate into selling anything that sells easily, and the salesperson may be content to settle for almost any order as long as there is volume. The author knew one salesman of expensive equipment who frequently sold specially fabricated pieces which were costly and difficult to make instead of emphasizing the standard line. Since he did not get enough additional money for these special items, the company got volume but little profit.

The supervisor knows what items to stress and can guide the salesperson to sell those most advantageous to the company. These products may consist of high profit items, too large inventories of merchandise in particular groups, products the firm is discontinuing and wants to sell rapidly, or merchandise lines that need to be moved because of obsolescence or deterioration.

Increase Outlets

Salespeople readily settle into a rut of calling on only a set number of customers. They also can get into the rut of selling particular merchandise to each customer. Thus, they limit themselves in number of customers as well as items sold to present customers.

Developing new outlets is challenging, but frequently difficult and frustrating. It is easier to give reasons for not calling on an outlet than it is to keep on trying to sell him. Thus, a salesperson can justly report that an outlet does not want to buy from him because he is too small, he already has satisfactory suppliers, his son-in-law sells for another firm, or prices are out of line. The salesperson listens to these reasons and after a few calls is reluctant to keep on trying. In one particular case, a representative of a tool and die firm in Detroit wanted a chance to bid on particular requirements for one of the major automobile firms. The buyer refused to put him on the bidding list, saying, "I'm not questioning the quality of your work or your ability to perform, but I already have thirty-five qualified firms on my bidding list and I don't want to add any more." If the supervisor or the firm feels that it is essential to get on this bidding list, the supervisor may try to gain entry or, even better, work with the salesperson to develop an approach that will make him successful. If the total purchases of this buyer from the thirty-five possible sources are thousands of dollars, the effort may not be worthwhile; but if the yearly buying amounts to over a million dollars, getting on the bidding list would be important.

A student who was a buyer in one of the big automobile firms mentioned that in his particular area he would buy over two million dollars a day at certain periods in the year. One student walked into class one night and said he had just sold a bakery its yearly supply of dried eggs, 250,000 pounds at $0.97 a pound. In one night class, a student who was a salesman came in late and after class explained to the teacher that he was delayed because he had just closed a transistor sale for $200,000. These examples certainly are not typical, but they do illustrate the importance of securing new customers.

On the other hand, a salesperson may step into a situation without good judgment and get into trouble unless a supervisor advises him. Thus, one student related an incident in which a salesman came to his firm hoping to sell a small order of textiles for a particular industrial use. The buyer was interested and asked for a price on 100,000 yards. The salesman gasped and had to admit his firm was in no position to handle such a large order.

HOW MUCH SUPERVISION

There can be no categoric assumption that a certain amount of supervision is necessary. In a house-to-house situation where new salespeople are hired frequently, close supervision helps. Close supervision may mean daily supervision in some instances. One successful distributor of vacuum cleaners called his men into a meeting every morning, gave them juice, donuts, and coffee for breakfast, inspired them with a pep talk followed by a rousing song, and then sent them out. For him this approach was very successful; and, of course, he followed up with new salespeople by going out with them.

Contrast that approach with supervision of skilled, widely scattered salespeople of high caliber. Perhaps the sales manager visits each person once a quarter to discuss problems and give new information. Occasionally, the sales manager is called in on a particularly difficult sale. Most supervision is conducted by mail, and a minimum of skills and personal training is given.

Between these two examples are many degrees of selling and many qualities of salespeople. Frequently, if the selling is house-to-house or at a lower level, the quality of person recruited requires close supervision, even though the product may be easily understood and demonstrated. If the product or service is complex, management recruits higher caliber people who would need less personal attention, but might require considerable supervision because of selling complexity.

A salesperson works alone and is subjected to sales involvement that can be discouraging. He can become lonesome, tired, and have a feeling of not being appreciated. He is expected to be cheerful, smiling, and optimistic facing a series of buyers' refusals. Unless the salesperson is a strong individual, he will need periodic supervisor visits to give him a feeling of belonging.

A salesperson needs a supervisor to talk over personal problems, family problems, and company-related problems wholly separate from field-selling problems. Sometimes a supervisor must give the salesperson permission to go home more weekends to build up his morale; he encourages the salesperson to attend concerts or social activities in his territory; he shows the salesperson how he can have more personal time by better handling of reports, routings, and procedures.

Of two salespeople, one may require much more attention than the other. Even if one does require much attention, it is worthwhile because this is one way of keeping a good salesperson in the field; and good salespeople are always scarce. It may be possible to maintain a successful field force of somewhat lesser quality by reinforcing it with excellent supervision. Or lacking supervision, it will be necessary to hire stronger people and pay them more.

WHO SUPERVISES

In a small firm with a few salespeople, the sales manager supervises. As a company grows and the sales force expands, the sales manager lacks time for direct supervision and delegates this task.

Assistant Sales Manager

In a smaller company, an assistant sales manager is frequently designated to give supervision. On the rare occasion that the sales manager prefers doing much of the supervising, he can hire an assistant to take over administrative detail. As the sales force grows, additional people are employed as supervisors. They could be designated by various terms, such as assistant sales managers, regional managers, district managers, and sales supervisors.

District Managers

A district manager may be a sales supervisor spending most of his time working with salespeople, or he may be responsible for many sales activities in a particular geographical area or for a particular product. If he is the latter type, sales supervision will be only one of many duties, and in a large branch, he will hire specialists for supervising salespeople.

Special Supervisors

Companies with large sales forces divided into geographic areas usually have more carefully developed supervision. These companies have a regular pattern of supervision and build a staff to supervise and assist salespeople.

Supervising Distributor Salespeople

Supervising distributor salespeople can be a delicate job since these people are not company employees and usually sell products of a number of manufacturers.

The supervisor or salesperson from a firm must usually confine his assistance and suggestions to his own line and be careful not to overstep his authority. Actually the supervisor in this situation has little direct authority and must exercise supervision through persuasion. Frequently, the only practical supervision of a distributor sales force is through a group meeting which may be held in the distributor's home office.

METHODS OF SUPERVISION

To supervise is to oversee, to observe, to guide, to explain, to suggest, to persuade, to insist, to order, to direct, to motivate, to stimulate, to reason, to interest, to inspire, to irritate, and to use aids that will improve sales performance. Sometimes kindness and consideration will accomplish much, but at other times a sales manager needs to be almost brutal to get results.

Home Office Supervision

In many smaller firms, it becomes expensive to send a supervisor or the sales manager to handle a field problem. Much of this supervision is personal discussion when salespeople report to the home office by telephone, by letter, and through printed literature.

Correspondence helps to keep regular contact with salespeople in the field, to give uniform directions to all at the same time, to inform each person of action desired from his territory, and to develop a feeling of belonging. While a wealth of useful information can be given through letters, they should not dwell on what the salesperson must do or how he is expected to improve. Undoubtedly, this often sets the tone of a letter, but it ought not to dominate so that even before the salesman opens the letter he says to himself "I wonder what he wants this time?" A telephone call, even in the evening or on weekends, is appreciated when the sales manager talks in a friendly, cheerful tone because he is genuinely interested in the person.

Field Supervision

All supervision is in a sense personal because it is directed by a supervisor, but personal field supervision is usually thought of as the physical presence of the supervisor.

When a supervisor travels with a salesperson, he is devoting his time and attention to him. The salesperson may be pleased or apprehensive, but he knows that he is being observed and his work is assessed.

The work of the supervisor can vary in field supervision from aiding in selling a difficult job to handling an unhappy customer. It can take the form of cold calls to get new customers, or it can be used to build up weak customers. It can be used as a pretext to introduce the buyer to the salesperson's boss or can serve to straighten out price problems.

A number of problems may be personal to the salesperson. He may have acquired bad habits which are injurious to sales performance; he may never have learned properly how to handle particular sales techniques; or he may be in a comfortable rut because he is earning enough money but not maximizing territory potential. Even the dynamic and aggressive salesperson needs reminders to counteract being overbearing, stiff, unpleasant, too familiar, or abrasive in his selling traits.

The supervisor, being closer to the head office, can give the salesperson accurate information about what goes on in the firm and explain any new products or selling drives that will appear. He can also give personal information about other salespeople and employees in the firm, which is indicative of success. A supervisor would be cautious about spreading derogatory information unless it was fundamental to selling effectiveness. Thus, if one salesman is no longer with the firm, the supervisor might tell the salesman he is working with, "Joe is no longer with us. Seems he got a job with another firm," or "Joe got to the point where he just couldn't handle his customers so after talking it over with him he resigned." It would be unwise and perhaps dangerous to say "We caught Joe stealing and fired him." A supervisor does not publicize unpleasant situations.

Group Supervision

Group supervision can be handled at the home office of local firms and in district locations in large firms. It frequently is a supplement to other methods and is economical and effective for certain activities.

If there is a tendency for several salespeople to slight a particular phase of presentation, they can be taught in a group. How to present a new product or handle a specific problem lends itself to group presentation. In fact, much sales training is group presentation. Since individual supervision is slow and expensive, a supervisor can clear up confusion and weaknesses by telling a group of salespeople about certain dangers and hope that most of them will take the initiative to avoid such procedures. Additional group supervision methodology will be discussed in chapter 8 under the discussion of conferences and conventions.

Built-in Supervision

Built-in supervision is a device to make supervision automatic. Such supervisory features are part of the salesperson's operating procedures and can be used for close control on a daily or weekly basis.

Reports can be used to establish a salesperson's pattern of work. Daily reports will show the supervisor how a salesperson operates. Weekly reports develop a representative description of activities and highlight those of major importance. Other types of reports have special uses and, properly handled, are informative and helpful.

Routing plans

Routing plans (call schedules) indicate that salespeople do some forward planning. A call schedule shows not only how much time a salesperson gives to each customer but also how much attention he gives to reviving former customers and how much to building new customers.

When fill-in sheets are mailed to salespeople to keep their manuals up to date, some firms require the salesperson to return the old sheets as a check to determine if he actually inserts the new sheets. Some firms may request territorial information which requires the salesperson to study potentials and estimate future sales possibilities.

PROBLEMS OF SUPERVISION

A supervisor's problems can be listed with a degree of reliability, but how they occur and recur varies with salespeople, territories, products, customers, and types of selling.

Handling Salespeople

The sales supervisor's primary problems obviously concern the salesperson. Some of these fall into patterns; others must be solved in an individual fashion. Even the common problems require somewhat individualized treatment.

Selling problems

These problems relate directly to selling skills. The supervisor usually can observe a salesperson in action and discover selling weaknesses. When it comes to correction, the salesperson may disagree with the supervisor, may resent some of his suggestions, may have grooved himself so hard into a rut he can hardly change, or seem incapable of understanding what the supervisor means. To avoid unpleasantries, he will tell the supervisor he understands, but later performance will reveal he probably did not understand the supervisor or else refuses to follow suggestions.

Family problems

The supervisor should know to what extent he ought to enter into personal problems relating to family. He should be able to assess major and minor problems and be able to relate to them impartially. He should sense when circumstances force him to invade the salesperson's privacy and retreat from those areas as quickly as possible. If such situations persist, it may be necessary to discharge the salesperson.

Personal problems

Some salespeople find it difficult to maintain proper equilibrium in the territory when away from home; such people may forget that selling is a difficult job requiring all their capacity. What a salesperson does on his own time is his business does not hold true if his actions reflect unfavorably on his firm. Some salespeople are unwilling to conform to supervisory suggestions. In such a case, the supervisor must weigh various factors—how serious are a particular salesperson's transgressions and how important is he to the firm. Unfortunately, a supervisor often has to compromise. In two similar cases, one salesman will be discharged while another will be retained but continually admonished, because discharging the latter might be critical to a firm's existence.

Inspirational Leadership

One of the main jobs of the supervisor is to keep the salesperson alert, optimistic, and aggressive. While he may have to correct the salesperson and make him do some jobs better, one of his primary tasks is to be the inspirational link to higher performance. He must praise, encourage, vitalize, and inspire the salesperson to perform better and more effectively. Leadership is the act of inspiring the poor performer to better performance, the successful performer to increasing his performance, and the top performer to achieving higher levels which he is capable of doing.

Dealing with Customers

The supervisor must rely on his ingenuity to show the salesperson how to handle a variety of customers. In his daily contacts, the salesperson manages to get along satisfactorily with his customers, but there are always a few who resist him. At times, the customers who normally buy become upset, and the salesperson does not know how to restore empathy. Careful supervision can aid the salesperson to hold such unfortunate situations to a minimum.

Handling Reports

Many salespeople are slow in mailing reports. Reports are often late, skimpy, and inadequate. Such reports may omit pertinent information that would be valuable. The sales manager then has a fuzzy picture of what goes on in the territory.

Some firms burden salespeople with too many reports which require too much of his time and energy and contribute little to the sales manager's knowledge of territory, salespeople, or customers. The supervisor can observe what effort the salesperson puts forth in handling reports and can discuss intelligently the reasons for particular reports. He may suggest elimination of particular reports by incorporating necessary information in other reports or by special mailings at infrequent intervals.

Satisfying Sales Office

Whether it is the home office or a regional, branch, or district office, the supervisor has a boss to whom he reports. He is between the salesperson and the appropriate sales manager and conveys information from above to the salesman. He can also funnel salespeople's problems up to the boss. While the supervisor may not be directly responsible for a salesperson's performance, he is inevitably tied in with sales performance. A salesperson is responsible to his manager for sales and other activities, but the supervisor must share some of the displeasure of the boss for mediocre sales performance by the people he supervises.

Satisfying Company Executives

The success of the firm is ultimately decided by the effectiveness of the sales force. In a small firm with a few very important salespeople, the president may exert as much or more influence than the sales manager. If one salesperson provides orders to operate the plant for three months in a year, it is not likely the president or vice-president will remain quietly aside waiting for orders. More likely, the top executives will tie in their ideas with those of the sales manager, who in those situations will personally work with the salesperson in the field. It is quite common for the sales manager to aid the salesperson and help him close an order. The salesperson may or may not appreciate this procedure, but he can do little about it because of the critical nature of each order. Top executives may feel the risk is too great to let the salesperson handle it alone. The sales manager himself gets nervous on such occasions, for his job may depend on one or two orders of this kind each year. Practically this may be a wise action by management, particularly when the sales manager or some other supervisor is an excellent salesperson.

SELECTING AND TRAINING SUPERVISORS

Although it is common to promote a salesperson to a supervisory position, a good salesperson will not necessarily become a capable supervisor. On the other hand, using a weak salesperson or bringing in a person with no selling experience to be a supervisor will build up resentment and hostility from the sales force.

It is unwise to take a successful salesperson out of his territory to become a supervisor against his will. He may be unable to supervise, or his half-hearted efforts may lead to failure. In a rising group of salespeople, some undoubtedly will have the basic qualifications requisite for successful supervisors. In a smaller firm where none of the salespeople seem suitable for supervision or prefer remaining salespeople, it is possible to go outside the firm to hire someone already in supervision or acquire a salesperson anxious to go into supervision.

Qualities of a Successful Supervisor

The supervisor is at the beginning of the management ladder. Hopefully this person has a satisfactory sales record, but it need not be outstanding. He should have leadership qualities.

If a person with successful sales experience is willing to become a supervisor and if he has abilities in teaching, guiding, and inspiring, he may be excellent supervisory material. In addition, he must have self-control and be self-energizing so that he can push forward with patience and work with people with varying personalities, capacities, and commitments.

Training Supervisors

If a salesperson has been selected from the field to be a supervisor, he should undergo a period of training. He may have developed techniques somewhat different from standard approaches taught when he was a trainee.

When a supervisor trains for his job, he must reorient himself to standard techniques. He must refamiliarize himself with the many facets of training. He must disassociate himself with some of the pets of the line of merchandise and develop selling aptitudes for the entire line. He must recognize that some methods he put in mothballs as a salesperson actually have merit. He must try to get rid of his personal likes and dislikes for types of customers and products and overcome personal idiosyncrasies.

The new supervisor must train himself to work with a variety of salespeople and have them adopt patterns of behavior that have been proved successful. He must not force his personal pattern on others.

The supervisor must adjust his pace to the salesperson; if the salesperson's pace needs change, it must be done gradually. When a supervisor finds it necessary to change a salesperson's way of doing specific tasks, it should be done so that the salesperson sees the advantages. This type of supervision requires sensitivity to the salesperson's feelings, which many supervisors do not have naturally. They must train themselves to respond to salespeople.

When a salesperson becomes a supervisor, one of his major problems will be to adjust to salespeople in this new relationship. While he can learn much from reading books and articles on supervision, he should also study material that tries to explain the actions of people. Reading books in psychology and sociology should help him gain a better understanding of his people. Counseling by the sales manager and others above him in administration should open new areas of understanding.

The alert supervisor can learn by observing other supervisors and asking them questions. He may reconstruct how his supervisor dealt with him and recall what he liked and disliked about his supervisor. Probably what bothered him with his supervisors are the very things he should avoid.

The supervisor must learn how to listen. As a salesperson, he was taught to listen to customers in order to get selling clues. As a supervisor, he must listen to his people to find out what the real problems are. Often he thinks he hears, but words can have several meanings. What is implied, but remains unsaid, may be more important than what is said.

Dealing with a salesperson's personal life is a sensitive area and one most supervisors prefer to avoid if possible. Therefore, he must sense when to intervene in a salesperson's personal habits because they are injuring the company image. He must learn how to work smoothly with salespeople who ask for help on personal problems. He might prefer to avoid such problems that recur frequently with certain salespeople; but, if the company insists on retaining these people, he must continue his efforts with them. The supervisor cannot fire weak individuals, but can only report his feelings to the boss.

IMPROVING SUPERVISION

Supervision is not a static job carefully laid out and detailed in execution. The new supervisor who depends on the training of his predecessor soon finds himself thwarted in new situations. If the new supervisor could see the changes that took place in his predecessor's supervising experiences over the years, he would recognize the versatility and adaptability of his predecessor.

The supervisor should think of his job as starting where his predecessor stopped. He may not be as successful at first as his predecessor, although he is equipped with technical know-how. But he lacks experience, which is acquired on the job. The new supervisor should not be content to achieve the same success of his predecessor, but should strive to become a stronger leader. The new supervisor must improve constantly in better execution of his duties. He must enlarge his horizon of performance. He should recognize increasing dimensions of his job and grow to respond to these newer demands. Business conditions, laws, unions, competition, and more aggressive buyers will impose new selling problems. If he is alert, he will anticipate new problems and originate solutions before his salespeople become frustrated. He must remain flexible to respond to unanticipated contingencies and make appropriate adjustments in his immediate assignments.

The supervisor who prefers relaxing pressures on himself by accepting convenient "truths" from others may soon find such "truths" imaginary but convenient. The supervisor who retains an open mind and constantly questions that which presently exists in practice keeps himself alert to possible changes looming on the horizon to which he must adjust in the future.

QUESTIONS AND PROBLEMS

1. There are a number of objectives in supervising salespeople. Discuss each reason for supervision, and indicate how different conditions can make one more important than another.

2. Why is the search for new customers a continuing job? Why not be satisfied with present customers?

3. How can you reconcile the need for considerable supervision both in simple and complex selling situations?

4. Does the amount of supervision required often depend on the individual salesperson? Explain.

5. Which member of the sales staff can give the best supervision? Justify your answer.

6. Can a manufacturer's sales staff effectively supervise distributor salespeople? Describe the relationship and problems involved.

7. Which method of supervision do you believe is most effective? Discuss, indicating why one method may be better than another. Is there one best method?

8. How can a series of salespeople's reports aid supervision?

9. Discuss salespeople problems that supervisors must handle. Point out what the supervisor should do in each situation.

10. What qualifications should be uppermost in selecting supervisors?

11. Training supervisors is a distinct job often done haphazardly. Why does this situation exist, and how might it be remedied?

12. Why might a new supervisor find difficulty in adjusting to salespeople? What are some of the ways he may overcome this problem?

13. Why should a supervisor strive for greater results in supervision than his predecessor? What is the danger of maintaining status quo?

ROY TRAILER COMPANY   *case 6–1*

George Phelps had been promoted to the position of sales manager of the Chicago division of Roy Trailer Company. He replaced William McMichaels, who retired at the company's retirement age of sixty-five.

After the monthly sales meeting held on the last Friday in March, John Masters came in to talk to Phelps about staying a couple more years rather than taking the planned early retirement when he turned sixty in six months.

Masters' decision to continue work posed a problem to Phelps, because Richard Benson had been brought into the sales organization six months ago to replace Masters when he retired.

Company Background

The Roy Trailer Company was a manufacturer of a full line of commercial trailers, including refrigerated trailers, moving van trailers, and common carrier trailers. The company was started in 1936, with its real growth starting in 1940.

The philosophy of the Roy Trailer Company was that it should be a leader and an innovator in the commercial trailer manufacturing field. It was one of the first manufacturers to develop its trailers to be hauled piggyback on rail cars. It was also one of the first to develop a van that could be detached from the axles and frame of a trailer and be stacked in the hull of a ship for transportation overseas. Because of this dynamic philosophy, it had grown to be one of the top manufacturers of commercial trailers in the United States.

Chicago Division Sales Force

Prior to Phelps' promotion to sales manager, the sales force of the Chicago division consisted of eight full line salesmen and two trainees. The two senior salesmen were John Masters and Phillip Mailer. Both had come into the sales force in 1940, and along with Bill McMichaels were considered to be the main reason for the Roy Trailer Company being in the high position in the Chicago area. John Masters was fifty-nine years old, and Phillip Mailer was fifty-six.

George Phelps had joined the Chicago sales division in 1950 at the age of twenty-six. He first worked behind the parts counter in the branch office. He learned the technical aspects of the job quite fast and showed a real interest in going into sales. At this time, Bill McMichaels was thinking of getting out of the sales part of the business and getting more into the area of managing the sales force.

Phelps came into the sales force in 1956, and after six months of training conducted mainly by McMichaels and Masters took over a large
part of McMichaels' accounts.

Two more salesmen were added to the sales force in the late 1960s,
Gary Bloomfield and Mike Hamilton, both in their late 30s.

Between 1970 and 1973, three more salesmen were added, Robert
Kingsley, James Amer, and Gary Schwann. These men were brought
in mainly to cover the increase in commercial hauling.

The two trainees were Lawrence Wilson and Richard Benson. Wilson
had joined the sales force in June, 1974, and Benson had joined in
November, 1974.

Training of Sales Personnel

The training program consisted of two parts, the initial training of new
salesmen and the continuous training of more experienced salesmen.

The continuous training consisted of a meeting every other Friday.
The program usually explained new products and services offered by
the company, pointed out new markets for the salesmen to cover, and
interpreted general economic conditions with the market area and how
they affected the salesmen. This was also a good time for a salesman
to discuss some of the problems that he might be having with a certain
account and to get the opinions of other salesmen on how to solve the
problem. The meeting would usually last from one to three hours,
depending on the amount of material that had to be covered.

Initial training of new salesmen consisted of meetings on the Fridays
that the general sales meetings were not held. The training period
usually lasted from six to nine months. Since most of the salesmen
were recruited from inside the firm, very little time was required to
explain the items being sold. The majority of the time was spent
instructing the sales trainee in the aspects of selling. The training
program was made up of personal experiences of the sales manager,
selling material sent in from the home office, and occasionally send-
ing the trainee to an independent sales training school.

A trainee was usually not brought in unless there was an expected
vacancy coming up in one of the territories. Once the training was
completed, the new salesman would take over the territory of the salesman leaving after certain modifications in the territory were made.
It was felt that some of the better accounts in the territory should be
given to the older salesmen to reward them for their efforts and to
make the new salesman develop some accounts of his own.

Compensation

The compensation plan consisted of straight commission with a draw
that was balanced out every three months. The computation of the

commission consisted of taking 2½ percent of the net sales less taxes and trade-in, if applicable, plus 10 percent of the gross profit with an upper limit of 30 percent of the gross profit of the sale. Then 15 percent was added onto either the 30 percent of gross profit or the 2½ percent of net sales and 10 percent of gross profit, whichever is less. An example follows:

Selling price	$5750.00
Taxes	600.00
Trade allowance	1000.00
Net selling price	$4150.00
Profit	$ 500.00
Commission:	
2½ percent net sale of $4150	$ 103.75
10 percent gross profit of $500	50.00
	$153.75
or	
30 percent gross profit	$ 150.00

Since the 30 percent of gross profit is the lesser of the two, it will be used as the commission base. Fifteen percent will be added to it to make a total commission of $172.50.

For the first three months of 1975, the commissions and draws were as follows:

Salesman	Commission	Draw
J. Masters	$5,700	$4,000
P. Mailer	6,350	5,000
G. Bloomfield	4,690	4,000
M. Hamilton	5,210	4,800
R. Kingsley	4,840	4,600
J. Amer	4,160	3,900
G. Schwann	3,970	3,800
R. Benson	2,490	3,200
L. Wilson	3,630	3,400

The Chicago Division had developed an informal system of assisting those trainees who had drawn more than their commissions. The system consisted of crediting the trainees' accounts with sales sold on a fleet basis. Fleet sales were usually sold below branch cost and therefore were not eligible to a normal commission, but there was a minimum limit of $6.50 commission to all of the salesmen whether the trailer was sold above or below branch cost. The older salesmen usually did not want to be bothered with this type of sale, and therefore the sale was credited to the branch itself. If a new salesman had drawn more than his commission for a quarter and if the sales manager felt that the trainee deserved some assistance, enough of the commission from fleet sales would be credited to his account to bring him up to the amount that he had drawn. Phelps did not know if this system was used in any other branches, but he felt that it was a good way to assist a younger salesman.

A Conversation with Mr. Masters

Half an hour after the normal Friday meeting, Masters entered Phelps' office. Phelps had been expecting a call from Masters, since his sales seemed to have been dropping off for the last two months. Phelps asked Masters to have a seat while he finished filling the weekly sales sheet that had to go out to the main office that afternoon.

After he had finished, Phelps opened the conversation by saying, "Well, John, what do you think of the new men?"

"I think they will work out all right," replied Masters. "I don't know if they could have done as well as we did back in the beginning, but considering the situation now, I think they will make out okay."

Phelps paused here, waiting to see if Masters wanted to tell him the reason for his sales decrease. After a few seconds of silence, Phelps realized that Masters wanted to chat a while longer before getting down to the real problem.

"Well, are you getting ready for your retirement? You've been talking about it for a long time now," said Phelps.

"That's what I have been wanting to talk to you about," replied Masters. This took Phelps by surprise. Masters continued, "The more I have been thinking about it, the more I have been wondering if I am ready for retirement yet. You know, George, I can still get around and cover all my accounts, and I am not sure I am ready to be put out to pasture yet."

"You sure aren't talking the way you were six months ago, John. What made you change your mind?"

"Six months ago I didn't know you were going to take over Bill's job as sales manager. I thought the main office was going to send down one of their 'whiz kids' to show us old timers how to do our job and just didn't think that I could put up with it."

"Why didn't you tell Bill that you didn't want to retire early back in November when it was announced that I was going to take over his job?"

"At that time I began to think that I might reconsider retiring. I would be able to enjoy some of my retirement while I was still young enough. But since then I have been thinking that I would really miss the job after all. You know that I am still a good salesman and can beat any one of these kids at selling."

"Yeah, I know you are still good, John. In fact I was sorry to hear your intentions to retire, but since then we have set the wheels in motion to have a man ready to take over your territory when you retired. Richard Benson was supposed to get the larger part of your territory. You have given me a real problem, John, but I'll see what I can do about possibly shuffling territories, and I will get in touch with you next week sometime."

After Masters left, Phelps began to think about his problem. He didn't think that the Chicago territory could use an extra salesman, and he didn't feel that he should force Benson to handle just the marginal accounts, even though he could supplement his income with commissions from fleet sales.

QUESTION

How would you handle this problem? Give a detailed explanation. Include possible adverse effects of your decision. Indicate other possible alternatives.

MEREDITH TOOL COMPANY   case 6–2

After ten months as sales manager of the Meredith Tool Company's Detroit office, Mr. Jason was having problems with several of his salesmen not making quota. He didn't know why they were having problems and didn't have time to find out the reasons until he hired a new salesman.

Company History

The Meredith Company was in the business of manufacturing and selling carbide and aluminum oxide tips, wear parts, and mining bits. It produced a quality product, in some cases superior to that of competition. The company had arrived at its present size through the acquisition of the RV Tool Company in the fall of 1970. The main office was in Omega, Illinois, and the manufacturing branches were in Omega and Knoxville, Kentucky. Total employment was 650.

In 1972 the company decided to change slightly from its policy of selling to distributors only. With increased manufacturing ability and increases in carbide tool usage, it decided to sell directly to some of the larger users as well as to their distributors. After a study, Detroit, Michigan, was chosen as a prime city to open a sales office. This location would capitalize on the automobile industry and other manufacturing operations.

The company salesmen were technically trained in all phases of machining and cutting operations. They were sometimes called upon to troubleshoot machining problems in customers' plants. The salesmen were required to make calls on their accounts in a missionary capacity. They were also required to help distributor salesmen in any technical problems they might have. The salesmen managed their territories with a minimum of guidance from the district manager.

Don Jason was chosen to be sales manager of the new Detroit office. The president, director of marketing, and personnel director of the company made the choice. They felt that Jason would be the logical choice since he had sold successfully to distributors in the Detroit area and had lived in Detroit during most of his sales career.

The marketing director came to Detroit to spend some time with Jason so that they could study the potential in the area and decide upon the number of salesmen that would be required. From the facts and figures of an American Machinist survey, an analysis of past sales to distributors, and the projected increases due to direct sales, they mapped out six territories with equal potentials.

They also decided that the Detroit office should have a specialist in mining bits to handle sales to the salt mines in the area, the drilling operations of the oil companies, and the mining equipment distributors (sold to Upper Michigan mines) that were based in Detroit.

After looking at the present salesmen of the company, they decided that John Williams of the Kentucky office would fit the job as mining bit specialist. Bill Irwin, from the home office, could be transferred to the Detroit office for his first sales position. Robert Long would be kept in the Detroit office as he was presently selling to distributors there. Three sales positions were to be filled.

Jason felt that an advertisement in the newspapers would be helpful in securing salesmen. The marketing director felt the job required more than the newspaper advertisement and suggested they list the position with an agency. After discussing the means available, they decided to use both the agency and the newspaper advertisement in an attempt to hire more salesmen.

The marketing director filled out a job description along with the qualifications for the position that he felt were needed and placed it with a local agency. He also decided upon the format and size of the advertisement to be placed with the *Detroit News* and *Detroit Free Press.* Then he went back to the home office, leaving Jason in charge of the office and the hiring of the new salesmen.

Jason thought he might hire a friend of his who was a tool engineer with one of the automobile companies. After a few weeks, the Detroit office sales staff was almost staffed. There was one territory that wasn't accounted for, and Jason took over the accounts in that area.

Detroit Sales Staff

John Williams was the mining bit specialist brought from the Kentucky sales office. The Kentucky operation consisted of 150 production and office workers and four salesmen. Williams had done a good sales job for the Kentucky office.

Williams was thirty, married, with two children under the age of five. He was born and raised in the coal mining area of Corbin, Kentucky. After spending two years in college majoring in business, he dropped out and went to work in the sales department of the Central Tool Company in Knoxville. After learning the sales office routine, he was offered the position of salesman. Most of his sales in the Kentucky office were direct and in mining tools. A small portion of his sales was in carbide tools to a couple of distributors in his territory.

Mr. Williams was given the salt mine accounts in the Detroit area, along with several oil drilling accounts and a couple of industrial tool distributor accounts in northwest Detroit.

Bill Irwin was transferred to the Detroit office also. He was twenty-three years old, a business administration graduate, married, and without children. Since graduation he had spent two years on a training program which consisted of six months in the advertising and sales departments, six months as assistant to the marketing director and one year as assistant and junior salesman in the Milwaukee, Wisconsin, territory.

Mr. Irwin had joined the company after graduation because he felt he could sell carbide tipped tools and wear parts. He had worked in his father's machine shop while attending school. Irwin was given the territory of southern Michigan. His accounts consisted of three distributors and ten automotive accounts to which he sold direct.

Robert Long had worked in the Detroit area with Jason, selling to the distributors for twenty years. When the Detroit office was formed, he was allowed to keep five of his distributors and was given five more automotive accounts on the east side of Detroit. For the past several years, Mr. Long's total earnings had risen by about 10 percent per year.

Joe Keller answered the newspaper advertisement and was hired. Keller's résumé showed twelve years' experience selling carbide tools and wear parts for a company in the Detroit area that went out of business. He had a B.A. degree in philosophy from Detroit Institute of Technology. He was married, had three children, and lived in Madison Heights. Under activities he had stated that he was on the church council, a Boy Scout leader, and a member of a P.T.A. committee.

Jason had assigned Keller eleven automotive accounts in the tricity area of Bay City, Saginaw, and Midland. He was also assigned one tool distributor account in the area.

Ralph Bacon, the fifth salesman of the Detroit office, had no prior selling experience. Bacon had been one of Jason's contacts when he was a salesman, and the two had become great friends. When Jason found out about the new Detroit office, he asked Mr. Bacon if he were interested in a sales position. Mr. Bacon immediately accepted the offer, as he felt there were more opportunities in sales than in manufacturing.

Mr. Bacon had ten years' experience as a tool engineer for an automotive company. He was given eight automotive and truck accounts in the Flint and Pontiac areas. Jason had felt that Bacon would be a natural salesman with these accounts due to his background.

At the time of the formation of the new Detroit office, Ken Wilson had been slated to be the sixth salesman. He had been with Meredith for sixteen years, selling to the industrial distributor accounts. His sales record had been quite good as far as the company was concerned. When he found out who was to be the Detroit office sales manager, he decided to join a large competitor whose home office was just outside Detroit.

Don Jason the sales manager of the Detroit office, had been with Meredith for twelve years and had been very successful in the Detroit area. He started as a clerk in the sales department of the home office and was made a salesman after two years with the company. His sales territory had been the industrial and mill supply houses in downtown Detroit and west of Woodward. He was a cheerful, friendly individual whom customers appreciated.

Jason decided to take over the accounts in the sixth territory until a new salesman could be hired. Most of the accounts were ones that he serviced before he became sales manager. He felt that he could hire a new man before too long and that he would then be able to devote all his time to managing.

Sales Situation

In June, 1972, the Detroit sales office officially opened. Jason held a series of sales meetings with the men, outlining the new sales policies and objectives of the Detroit office. He also informed each of the men of their quotas for the coming six months. The older, experienced salesmen were aware of the quotas and had to be convinced they could easily make their quotas to obtain a commission. The new salesmen were on salary but were given quotas to aim for as an incentive. Jason said they would probably be given a small bonus for exceeding their quota.

After the first two days of sales meetings, the older salesmen were allowed to go into the field. The new men were kept for the remainder of the week while Jason attempted to explain the intricacies of selling carbide tools and wear parts to them. Jason felt the new men would learn salesmanship through experience and allowed them to cover their assigned accounts after the first week.

Jason didn't require call reports of the salesmen and didn't spend too much time with them, as he was too busy selling to the accounts he had and making out sales reports to the home office. During the first couple of months, none of the salesmen did as well as he had expected. Jason felt that this was due to inexperience on the part of the new men and the new accounts and territories for the older men. With time, he felt they would produce up to the company's expectations.

As the months went by, Jason noticed that Williams, Keller, and Bacon were not doing too well. He called them to find out why they weren't coming close to their quotas. Each of them mentioned something about poor accounts, keen competition, and too high quotas. Jason didn't believe any of these excuses. He had hoped to go around with the three men who were having problems and find the causes of these difficulties, but he had to service his own accounts.

ASSIGNMENT

Discuss the steps Jason must take to build satisfactory sales volume. Give details on what he must do to overcome weak sales.

7

Analyzing and Evaluating Salesperson Performance

Effective sales management appraises salesperson performance regularly to insure maximum results and to give equitable consideration to each salesperson's contribution. Judgment factors and general observations are insufficient to evaluate performance accurately and may lead to unjust individual assessment as well as overlooking major work discrepancies. Sales managers become better leaders when they have the essential information to assess the real strengths of each person.

OBJECTIVES OF ANALYZING SALESPERSON PERFORMANCE

From the practical standpoint of operating a successful sales force, it is essential that a sales manager learns the strengths and weaknesses of his salespeople. He must be able to pinpoint potential trouble areas and be prepared to implement remedial measures as well as to act promptly to stop costly lapses and weak procedures. Analyzing salesperson performance is a thorough examination of the work of each salesperson measured by predetermined performance criteria.

Maximize Salesperson Performance

Every sales executive strives to get the most from his salespeople. Maximizing salesperson performance is not a static condition, but consists of a changing emphasis on various activities in response to current conditions. For example, in the first quarter of a year, volume may be emphasized; in the second quarter, profit may be the goal; the third quarter may be concerned with one or more specific lines; and the fourth quarter with balancing inventories.

Eliminate Weak Performance

Eliminating weak performance is not necessarily the same as maximizing performance, although in the end they may amount to the same. Eliminating weak performance is applying corrective techniques to improve salespeople's work. One might increase performance by a great effort; and, in spite of weak spots, the overall result would be increased sales but at a high expenditure of effort. The better way to improve performance is to find and eliminate impediments, allowing normal operation to function smoothly.

Weak performances mean expensive ways of doing a job that can become serious profit drags; weakness indicates improper functioning in sales operation; weakness indicates indecision by someone responsible for assigned tasks. Weakness might just be laziness. Whatever the causes, it cannot go on for any length of time without impairing corporate vitality.

Give Proper Attention to Customers

Salespeople do not treat all customers alike, nor do they necessarily direct their energies to satisfy important customers and make them even more profitable. Even worse is a salesperson's tendency to favor some customers at the expense of others without any particular reasons. It is far easier to work with pleasant, friendly customers than with disagreeable ones, even though the latter may be more important.

Many salespeople unintentionally slight some customers and miss many orders because they do not follow a well conceived customer-handling plan. Chance rather than plan becomes the directive force, and the result is a hodgepodge of activity with serious gaps in customer attention.

Realize Territory Potential

Many salespeople seriously undersell the potential of their territories by improper customer approach, by lack of imaginative innovations and ideas to nonusers, and by failure to push products favorable to their employer. As soon as a salesperson steps out of the familiar territory path to explore other potential areas, the going becomes rough, perhaps unpleasant, and surely harder. It creates a struggle, an uncomfortable exposure to vexing problems that require extra effort, and makes demands on a salesperson that interfere with his many other activities.

Performance Geared to Employer's Interests

The sales department gives salespeople directions on how to achieve particular sales objectives. Too frequently, they follow these directives generally rather than specifically. Many salespeople follow directives but do not follow through to get the results needed for maximum performance.

Within a framework of sales department direction, a salesperson may have much latitude of execution. As a result, it is imperative to supervise the salesperson so that his efforts are in tune with company objectives; he must be impressed with the importance of focusing on work that will promote company success. Too often, there is a scattering of effort among company personnel and a lack of coordination toward a common goal. While some firms operate successfully under such conditions, the wasted effort is enormous and costly and could be avoided with more precise attention, direction, and control.

PERFORMANCE STANDARDS

Performance standards are useful as a guide in analyzing salesperson performance. A pure analysis without any guide is of little value until a comparison is made with a norm. Even comparing the performance of one salesperson with another means little unless there is a basis of comparison.

Job Description as a Guide to Preparing Standards

A job description details the job and duties of a salesperson. It is a starting point from which standards can be set up, and it is important because it is the same for all the salespeople. Someone has taken the time to study and prepare the salesperson's job and what is expected in the way of performance. Presumably, no job applicant is hired unless the manager feels the person has the potential for fulfilling the requirements.

Kinds of Standards

A large number of standards can be set up to measure characteristics and to meet objectives. Standards can be mutually exclusive; they can dovetail with one another; they can overlap; they can be arranged to operate simultaneously; one can begin when another is fulfilled. They can vary in emphasis from season to season, by the business cycle, by competitive factors, and by individual salespeople.

Because of the diversity in sales situations, it is essential to develop a cross section of measuring devices so that each salesperson's contribution can be assessed. Volume, profit, quantity, and product mix are some standards. The salesperson is assessed as an individual in relationship to customers and to associates.

Performance Measurement Limits

It is unlikely that any standard ever does justice to the salesperson or is completely informative to the boss. Standards at best are limited because no one knows precisely how to set them up, what to measure, or how to assess each salesperson accurately.

QUANTITATIVE STANDARDS USED IN ANALYZING SALESPERSON PERFORMANCE

Quantitative standards are used to measure tangible performance and to assess the value of each sales job in contributing to the success of the firm and the effect on profits. Company management and stockholders are interested in profits and dividends.

There are a number of these standards that can be used profitably by many firms. Since all are not equally applicable to a firm, a brief description of each will enable the sales manager to choose the ones most useful for his purposes.

Time Standards

The salesperson must learn to use his time to best advantage, concentrating on those areas where he can spend time with expectation of adequate return.

Number of sales calls

Each sales manager can develop a norm for the number of sales calls to be made daily, weekly, and monthly. If it becomes impractical to pin a salesperson down to daily calls, it may be possible to establish weekly or monthly call quotas.

The salesperson who is persistent, conscientious, and disciplined finds time to make more calls. Since a relationship between calls and sales can be established, it is important to have the salesperson increase effective calls. The hardworking salesperson makes one more call before lunch or before closing time; the lackadaisical person thinks of excuses not to make these calls. If a standard is used, it may be easier for the weak salesperson to meet his call quota than to think up excuses for not making it.

Use of time in sales calls

Studies of salespeople at work reveal tremendous wastes of time on sales calls as well as between calls. Waste of time on calls includes waiting for interviews, broken interviews, general conversation, and just doing nothing. It is not unusual to find a salesperson spending less than half his time (in some cases, only two hours a day) in face-to-face selling. Studies show repeatedly that weak salespeople are poor time users as compared to the more successful salesperson.[1] It was said

---

1. For two such studies see Harold H. Maynard and James H. Davis, *Sales Management,* 3rd ed. (New York: The Ronald Press, 1957), 467–71; and Wayland A. Tonning, *How to Measure and Evaluate Salesmen's Performance* (Englewood Cliffs, N.J.: Prentice-Hall, 1964), chapter 11.

of one particularly effective wholesale drug salesman that he never spent time in general conversation. Most customers would gladly forego idle conversation to talk about what they need to improve their operations.

Travel time

Some salespeople have a tendency to jump around in establishing a travel schedule. Admittedly, customer demands often require extra travel, but too often salespeople are unaware of the time wasted in driving. One salesperson may spend an hour going from one customer to another, while another salesperson spends a half-hour because he chooses a different hour of the day or goes by a different route.

Some salespeople use the noon hour for travel because this may be a slack period. If a long distance must be traveled between towns, the salesperson might drive after the last afternoon call so as not to waste valuable selling time. A time-consuming trip can be made early in the morning before the office opens.

Other time factors

Time can be saved by making appointments, using time waiting for interviews to perform useful work on records, postponing some activities until evening or after regular working hours. The salesperson should use prime time in face-to-face selling and relegate supplementary activities to free time. He must avoid situations where valuable selling time is usurped. He should set up a pattern of time use where each activity is graded and the important ones are given the time they deserve and require.

Volume Standards

One of the common ways of appraising sales performance is on the basis of volume. Often this is the only way a person is truly judged, although it may be a weak measurement unless volume is weighed from several vantage points.

Dollar volume

Sales in dollars is often a guiding criterion because it is easily understood, may reflect substantial performance, and is often the basis for commission. The simplicity of basing success on dollar volume is appealing and often obscures dangers which are revealed only when an analyst studies the salesperson's profitability to the firm.

Increasing dollar volume looks inviting, but it does not reveal such conditions as inflation or a growing economy. For example, a salesperson's dollar volume may increase, but the physical amount sold may not have increased; dollar volume is greater absolutely, but relatively the salesperson has decreased his share because competing salespeople's sales have increased more. Dollar volume may have increased, but price cutting may have made such sales relatively un-profitable.

Unit volume

Unit volume may be more meaningful than dollar volume because it represents changes in physical movements of merchandise. A unit volume has merit if the units have some degree of uniformity so that they correctly measure change; if great variation occurs, the solution is not simple. For example, a salesperson sells 100 units of A and 100 units of B in a particular month. The following month, he sells 50 units of A and 200 units of B. It is true that volume in units increased; but if A sold for $10 a unit and B for $5 a unit, the gain may be more apparent than real.

A rapidly changing price structure may cloud a physical unit standard. In one instance, a firm selling an electronic component for $10 in January had dropped the price to $1 in December of the same year because of technological change. In another situation, a pharmaceutical product came on the market at a high price with an inviting sales outlook, but it was superseded in a year by a competitor's product which gave the same results at much less cost.

Product category volume

Product category in dollar or unit volume may be one of the most useful standards for judging performance. Product category is usually based on factors that stress profitability, difficulty in selling, production balance, or other distinguishing characteristics that make such division helpful.

Setting up standards by categories is inviting to the firm because it stresses sales patterns that maximize company interests. This type of standard is more difficult to establish and maintain than either volume or unit standards because there may be a different set of factors to adjust. It is more rewarding because it more accurately portrays existing conditions and ties current performance to these conditions.

Method of sale volume

While salespeople may have a regular customer call schedule, many sales come into the home office directly. Because of the nature of a business, many sales are called in or solicited on the phone by a salesperson or someone in the home office. Some firms have heavy mail orders, and salespeople write few direct sales. Where such sales patterns exist, a volume standard may have a number of variations.

Volume may consist of sales by the salesperson, by telephone, by mail, and by personal customer visit. These methods may be common in some types of wholesaling. Volume may be measured by merchandise on consignment, sold on time, sold for cash, or volume generated by special promotional commissions.

Method of sales volume is a useful, but complex approach that can be especially appropriate when more precise distinctions are needed and when the more common methods may not give adequate measure. Lumping too much under one heading or category can be self-defeating because too much remains unexplained. Making too many and too fine distinctions may give seemingly excellent data, but in essence compounds analytical work without yielding a commensurate return.

Customer Standards

Customer measuring devices can take a number of forms and involve intricate study in order to implement them properly. Numerous surveys, readily available in marketing literature, have pointed out wide profit disparities among customers and how firms have benefited by becoming more selective in their customers.

Number of orders

The number of orders can be a decisive measure value of a customer For example, an occasional order as a fill-in on merchandise purchased from other sources is usually unprofitable unless it is of considerable size. Customers taking advantage of only specials are not particularly helpful unless such specials are clogging inventory and must be moved regardless of profitability.

Size of orders

Size of orders can make a marked difference in profitability. Small orders are seldom profitable because of fixed costs. Some firms refuse orders below a certain minimum. Very small orders for repair parts on machines and equipment are sometimes handled without charge. It costs the firm less to give the customer the merchandise than it would to put it through the office and bill him for it. The minimum charge would upset the customer because even to cover part of the handling cost the customer would be greatly overcharged for the item itself.

Small orders may be handled profitably if the company is geared to such an operation. A bakery making daily sales to a store may not get much daily volume, but it can be lucrative. Some firms tie up customers with a cumulative discount system that justifies accepting many small orders, but such operations reflect a way of doing business and would not be typical of firms with a wide range of order size with intermittent sales.

The wholesaler can have a sliding discount to encourage sales in original cartons. A manufacturer rarely would break case lots in his sales. To encourage salespeople to work for profitable orders, a firm can set up a sliding scale which penalizes the salesperson by giving him reduced commissions. For example, if a salesperson turns in many orders with line extensions of less than $2 (a line extension is one line on an invoice), he would receive no commission on such lines. An occasional line below $2 would not be questioned, but many such orders would be objectionable.

Quality of orders

Some customers give salespeople consistently profitable orders; others seem to give only unprofitable orders. One retailer trying to satisfy two wholesale drug salesmen followed the advice of one and gave him all his pharmaceutical business. The other got miscellaneous business of equal dollar volume, but it was much less profitable.

In addition to basic profitability of orders, there may be conditions that make a normally profitable order unprofitable. Some customers may be slow in paying and create additional expense; some abuse return-goods privileges; some want special delivery service free; some may give a large order but have it shipped in small amounts over a period of time, which increases the seller's costs. Sometimes the season of the year can be decisive in the quality of an order. At some seasons a firm may be lenient because it needs business badly. In the busy season, some customers may expect the same treatment, and a salesperson is hesitant to refuse unless his firm's policies forbid such privileges.

Number of demonstrations

Some types of selling are aided by demonstrations. The automobile salesman demonstrates his car; the equipment salesman demonstrates his equipment; the typewriter salesman demonstrates his typewriter. The salesman of tangible goods can demonstrate how to use his product, a privilege denied the salesman of intangibles, who must rely on word descriptions.

Making effective demonstrations requires some skill by the salesperson in addition to adequate preparation. Often, salespeople are reluctant to put forth this effort, particularly when sales results are doubtful. A salesperson may be inclined to omit demonstrating too frequently. If the sales manager sets a minimum number of demonstrations, the salesperson usually tries to meet this standard.

Number of new accounts

It is to be expected that there will be a turnover of customers. For a number of reasons customers are lost and must be replaced, or the remaining ones made better to take up the lost sales. Most salespeople find it necessary to seek new customers to maintain the present status and to show sales gains.

To seek new customers requires greater effort than to call on present ones. A salesperson may shun the job unless he has a standard for new calls. Sometimes a firm will put a missionary salesperson in a territory to work new accounts exclusively, which will later be given to the person in the territory. Each sales manager will soon learn how many new accounts are necessary to remain successful.

Number of lost accounts

A sales manager would set a standard or quota of lost accounts reluctantly. For example, a sales manager may be concerned but not take strong action as long as a salesperson's lost accounts stay within a 2 to 5 percent yearly range. Beyond this range, he will start an immediate investigation to determine the problems. Losing accounts may signal a serious situation in one territory. If this situation prevails in most territories, it is an indication for change—to meet new competitive factors, to alter the price structure, to revise the product line, to reassess selling techniques.

Number of accounts sold

Some salespeople are content to develop or take over a fixed number of accounts and accept this load without questioning whether it is adequate or whether improved sales techniques would give time for additional accounts. Usually, there is room to add new accounts and reestablish former ones.

Some calls are made regularly on accounts that give very few orders, give minimal orders, or orders with little or no profits. This situation can be changed by setting a standard for the number of accounts sold in relationship to their profitability. This method of appraising a salesperson's efforts would pinpoint a person who was going through the motions of selling and accepting anything thrown his way.

Number of complaints serviced

Each salesperson with a cross section of customers will have a number of complaints. How many, and even more important, how effectively he handles these complaints may be a determining factor in his success. The salesperson has the delicate task of satisfying a customer without injuring the image of his employer.

Regular calls on repeat customers may make servicing relatively easy. When a buyer makes a purchase once or makes purchases years apart, a salesperson may not call on him for a year. When such a buyer registers a complaint, a salesperson probably has no personal advantage to make the call. The company wants the salesperson to follow up, to protect company reputation, and to fulfill its agreement with the buyer. Since the salesperson may consider this a nuisance or fringe activity, how well he responds to this demand is an excellent measure of his willingness to serve.

Customer assistance

Some salespeople take an order and feel their job is completed. Others become interested in their customers' welfare and spend time helping them.

In the retail area, a wholesaler salesperson or a direct selling manufacturer's salesperson may work with customers in taking inventory, arranging merchandise on shelves, setting up displays, making demonstrations, and even aid in selling. A salesman to industry may show how his product can be used more advantageously, assist in getting equipment into operation, and make special trips with repair parts. A salesperson may assist a customer to move excessive inventory by a special sale or by transferring merchandise to another dealer; he may help a manufacturer to sell his used equipment; he may help by suggesting sources of personnel.

The individual salesperson should report extra activities to his sales manager, who would appreciate such efforts. Some salespeople would report each activity they perform in glowing terms. Other salespeople would report only significant ones in a brief manner. This category has quantitative aspects with qualitative overtones which require subjective evaluation.

Company Standards

Many standards are directly related to company success and progress. These standards are basic and must be closely watched if the firm is to prosper.

Profit standards

Management sets up measures of profitability to measure each salesperson's contribution. These standards range from overall profitability of a salesperson's territory to specific analysis of customers, orders, terms of sale, or other variations. It gives little comfort to know that specific sales in a territory are profitable if such sales are overbalanced by a host of unprofitable ones. Pockets of profitability may not justify working large, adjacent unprofitable areas. If there is no successful way to work widely scattered profitable accounts, it may be necessary to abandon the entire territory.

Expense standards

Sales operations analysis often reveals excessive expenses. These expenses include salesman travel, entertainment, delivery, and return of merchandise. If a particular territory shows an expense factor far in excess of average territories, it calls for exacting analysis to determine if such expenses are indigenous to the territory or result from lax administration. If analysis shows that a territory normally generates high expenses, the solution may be to withdraw altogether or increase prices. For example, one company sold a particular school chemistry instructor's desk to two different schools in widely separated states in the United States. Had the company been permitted to ship FOB factory, the prices would have been identical; but both schools wanted to have the equipment installed. Since installation expenses in one city were three times the cost in the other city, the final price in each instance reflected that variation.

Quota standards

A quota is a volume standard based on slightly above average performance. Since a quota is an individual standard, it may not be fair to use it as a comparison with other salespeople's quota standards since there may be different bases for each quota. A salesperson's quota may be broken down into subquotas or divided into product groups which reflect sales potential of his territory.

Difficulty standards

A salesperson's tasks vary in difficulty, pleasantness, and amount of application. A salesperson may neglect tedious details, procrastinate in solving complex adjustments, put off calling on difficult customers, and give excuses for not calling on competitors' customers.

A perceptive sales manager can catalog sales jobs and set up working standards which will point out how well each person handles his whole job, where he concentrates on specifics to his liking, and where his sales work is below standard. If a salesperson is strong in some standards and weak in others, the sales manager may work with him to remedy his weaknesses, transfer him to another territory or type of work, or terminate his employment.

Other Standards

The kinds of standards that may be established are numerous; some are applicable only under special situations.

Use of display material

It is common for a manufacturer to send display materials to dealers to aid in sales. Frequently, these displays are never used. How well a salesperson guides customers and gets them to use such materials is a mark of sales success. If the salesperson cannot get the dealer to set up displays, he may secure the dealer's permission to arrange displays himself. Some salespeople are far more skillful and zealous in arranging attractive displays than others, and some are willing to inconvenience themselves and work with the dealer in effective display use.

Servicing dealers

Many firms sell through dealers, and the primary sales contact is between sales representatives of the firm and dealers. The dealer then sells to retailers or to final users, such as industrial purchasers. The primary task of a company's sales representatives is to motivate dealers to move more merchandise. Sales representatives can work against established standards which measure dealer visits, training dealer salespeople, accompanying dealer salespeople in the territory, and personal sales calls in which orders are secured and turned over to a dealer.

When a salesperson's effort only indirectly influences sales, his skill must be exercised in working with dealers to sell his products enthusiastically. The amount of support he gives the dealer and the effort he uses to make sales easier will go far toward insuring success. A sales representative working through a dealer must convince him that their interests are identical and that they work as a team toward a common end.

Distribution of company literature

Distribution of company literature may be sporadic, or the work may be considered an important segment of sales performance. Some salespeople pass out literature reluctantly and not enough; others give it away without any thought of its final use. Effective use of company literature can be promoted if standards and distribution approaches are carefully developed.

QUALITATIVE STANDARDS USED IN ANALYZING SALESPERSON PERFORMANCE

Qualitative appraisal uses subjective methodology and results in opinions made by the sales manager and other executives. The factors measured qualitatively may contribute the most to sales success, which is demonstrated quantitatively. These factors may be elusive to measure and may be given different values by each member of management.

Product Knowledge

Purchasing agents complain that too many salespeople do not know their product. Furthermore, they do not know enough about competing products to give useful comparisons. As a result, they use unsubstantiated statements in comparing competing products.

The amount of product knowledge a salesperson needs depends on the use and the user. An industrial buyer may want to know not only how a product is used but also conditions of use, length of use between maintenance service, composition of material used in making the product, and other pertinent facts. The individual consumer may want only one or two specific points. Many retail salespeople have so little product knowledge that a customer must depend on attached labels or point-of-purchase informational literature.

A sales manager may not realize how well a salesperson knows his product unless he accompanies him on field trips, but he will have a fair impression through customer comments, how well this salesman keeps up on literature, how orderly he keeps his catalogs, and how he participates in sales meetings. In a casual product discussion, a salesperson can be led to reveal his knowledge or lack of it.

Company Policies and Programs

Some people tend to read much company information cursorily, particularly if there is considerable volume. Consequently, many new programs are only partially understood.

Before a salesperson can act intelligently, he must understand how his company operates. Misinterpretation causes numerous customer problems. If a salesperson is in constant trouble with customers, he either does not know company policies or is indifferent in bringing them to the attention of customers.

Competitive Efforts

Sometimes a salesperson may become excited about a competitor's effort in his territory, but he does not try to evaluate its impact. A salesperson should be aware of competitive effort and try to measure its effectiveness, length of time, and whether it is intermittent or continuous.

A salesperson should report any change of competitor effort immediately because a lapse of a few weeks may give the competitor an impetus that will be difficult to counteract. Sometimes competitors use particular territories as test markets for new products, different terms of sale, different delivery schedules, selective advertising programs, or introduction of new sales techniques. The sensitivity of a salesperson about what is occurring in his territory and his speed in communicating to the home office are marks of sales awareness.

Organizing and Planning

How well a salesperson plans his work and organizes his efforts help to determine whether he will be ordinary or outstanding. The person who is disorganized, acts on the spur of the moment, does not plan calls, does not use an orderly approach, and is careless in follow-up lacks the discipline essential to success.

A careful analysis should be made on the depth and variation in planning. If a salesperson plans one year and then repeats himself, it is an indication of laziness or inability to be creative. Most territories are not static, and the aggressive salesperson must alter his approach to meet the diverse needs of his customers. The skill shown by a salesperson in managing himself can be measured by a number of performance criteria—sales, customer satisfaction, breadth and depth of coverage, and responsiveness to home office directions. Subjectively, analysis of a salesperson's organizing ability can be ascertained by his meticulous approach; his firm, assured way of handling work; the way he divides his time to tasks graded by their size and importance; and his personal control of territory problems.

Selling Skill

While the results of a salesperson's efforts can be measured in profitable sales, how he accomplishes these results must be analyzed. Observation of a salesperson will reveal his ways of persuading customers to buy. Each person works out an individual pattern of behavior to influence buyers; each pattern has strengths and weaknesses. These approaches can be evaluated, and parts that seem superior may be interwoven into the selling patterns of less effective salespeople in order to improve their presentations.

Study of the successful salesperson may show detailed preparation before each presentation. The strong salesperson may have studied the buyer or the buying committee to be aware of personalities involved, but the weaker salesperson approaches buyers without any knowledge about them. The better salesperson is prepared with all the ranges of price adjustment and may have asked the head office for a special concession. The weak salesperson is armed only with his standard approach and shows no initiative in attempting to propose variations. The analyst must be prepared to assess many variations and alternatives in an attempt to arrive at success criteria not readily seen or perhaps even suspected. He must try to tear down the veil of difference that some may attribute to luck or good fortune and show that sales differences result from superior, but difficult to trace or define, techniques.

Creative Selling

Some salespeople are able to create, improvise, and adjust as occasion demands. The creative salesperson will demonstrate new approaches and better product use and bring ideas to the buyer. The creative salesperson studies his customers to determine how to be of greater service. He may study the communities of his customers and make contributions to these communities that will reflect favorably in the eyes of his customers, or even better, he may suggest steps the customer can take to improve his status.

Uses Good Judgment

A sales department operates under a set of rules established by management. Sometimes these rules must be followed literally; other times they are subject to interpretation. It is unlikely that a company's rules are carried out exactly as stated because they will not apply perfectly in field selling. Rules must be interpreted by the sales staff.

A few salespeople may use latitude in carrying out directives as license to do almost anything; others may deviate as little as possible. The salesperson with good judgment will bend rules when he sees that it is necessary. Some salespeople scare at every buyer threat; others handle threats in a more mature manner by giving a little under some circumstances, but mostly through maintaining successful relationships by superior service and attending to each buyer's needs.

Relations with Customers and Competing Salespeople

The effective salesperson builds a close relationship with his customers. He builds rapport, establishes empathy, and creates confidence. His relationship with top-level customers is excellent. He does not stoop to unethical practices to meet competition, even though urged to do so by unscrupulous buyers. Yet he will continue to sell to such buyers in a proper way as long as these sales benefit his employer.

The strong salesperson is not easily ruffled by efforts to get especially low prices or extra service because someone else does it. A strong salesperson is able to keep the demanding customer in his place without losing his business; he holds the unscrupulous buyer as a customer not by giving in but by furnishing strong reasons why this buyer needs his products or services; he handles the dishonest customer by keeping everything so clearly spelled out that there is little chance for misunderstanding. Better salespeople are not easily offended by customers because they take insults and unprovoked criticism as a business problem, not a personal insult. If a salesperson conducts himself properly, there will be few complaints from the territory. If he vacillates, gives improper attention to requests, and neglects his work, criticism mounts.

Friendly relationships with competing salespeople are desirable, but it is unwise to have frequent association with them because of the risk of divulging company information. Some astute salespeople may cultivate less astute salespeople of competitors merely to draw them out and get them to talk recklessly.

Self-management

The successful salesperson has learned to manage himself. He has learned the dangers relating to neglecting duties, the price paid for forgetting to do essential jobs, and the penalty for talking too much or in the wrong places. He has learned the importance of fulfilling obligations, meeting promises, preparing for appointments and interviews, and countering unpleasant proposals. He has learned to say no graciously without offending a customer who may be trying to receive a concession to which he is not entitled.

Qualitatively, a salesperson must be appraised by his appearance, his language, the way he maintains his equipment, the disposition of available time, the satisfaction created in customers, and other factors. Whatever attributes he may show or however favorably he may impress customers, the salesperson must still be capable of directing his energies into profitable customer response.

Communication with Management

In evaluating a salesperson's record, management may emphasize communicating with the home office. This communication includes call reports, expense reports, follow-up on sales directives, telephone communication, and reports on competitors. Management is interested in field response and in how rapidly and effectively a salesperson follows directions.

The sales manager judges a salesperson by his willingness to respond to requests—meetings on Saturdays and in the evening, making special reports, reading information on new products, contacting people who send in requests for information, requests for information on difficult cases. A salesperson's willingness to follow directions even though they seem to have little merit and his ability to cement customer relationships even if such customers have been improperly handled by the home office indicate the type of cooperation he gives.

PROBLEMS OF SALESPERSON PERFORMANCE ANALYSIS

Each employer has similar problems in analyzing salesperson performance, but he also has individual problems pertaining to his type of operation. Furthermore, each employer has a number of analytical jobs applied to all his sales staff and a number which apply only to specific individuals and territories. And there are random, unexpected problems.

Change in Customers

Customers are not a firm group of followers behaving in a predictable way. A steady customer may behave in a certain way and be depended on for a certain amount of business, but often a salesperson is unaware that the relationship is not as close as he thinks. What he thinks are large orders could be increased if he was more perceptive.

Sales to retailers are subject to competition from many manufacturer representatives. Consumer demands force the retailer to change his inventory. For example, sales of phonograph records vary rapidly and a successful producer may be leading one month and trailing the next.

Some salespeople service a relatively stable industry; others, a rapidly changing one. Some businessmen are active for years; others change frequently because they are unable to cope with their problems. Firms with purchasing agents and staffs of buyers have turnover so that almost any salesperson with a number of customers will have some new buyers every year. Larger firms will rotate buyers to prevent too close a relationship between buyer and salesperson. Decisions in purchasing may change from one office to another, from one city to another, or from a buyer to a buying committee.

Change in Product Demand

Product demand changes are typical in many industries. A customer may drop one supplier and choose another because the suppliers do not supply identical items or give the same service. A market may become segmented, and a firm may continue a present model too long; a soft-goods manufacturer may come out with garments in the wrong color or style; a toy manufacturer may misjudge the market and have too few of one item and too many of another. Even relatively stable items can take new dimensions. It may be hard for a salesperson to push his old standard line against competition with bright, new, attractive alternatives. In assessing a sales decline, an analyst may be forced to judge between salesperson performance and relevance of product line. The analyst may be in the delicate position of balancing sales performance against management judgment in manufacturing a line of merchandise which may have lost its appeal.

Changes in Purchasing Power

Sales do not constantly spiral upward, particularly when increasing living standards make greater demands on customer income. As the luxury of yesterday becomes a commonly accepted standard of today, such requirements take priority on limited consumer income. Even though people have larger incomes, they may be assigning a greater share to areas considered of lesser importance in the past.

Competitor Strategy

A salesperson's performance must be analyzed in terms of the environment of his territory. Therefore, his work and customers must be analyzed, and an appraisal of competitor strategy must be considered. A shift in competitor approach by increasing sales representation in the territory or by assigning a superior salesperson to the territory can affect a salesperson's performance.

When a company structures changes, a customer may be purchased outright by a larger firm that has a subsidiary furnishing the same product. Pressures may be applied indirectly, and a salesperson is helpless. Unforeseen conditions may demand extra effort which a firm is unable or unwilling to give. Realignment of production facilities, opening or closing warehousing units, or drastic changes in transportation may give a competitor overwhelming advantages in one territory, have minimum impact in a second territory, and cause a loss of competition in a third territory. Such varying impacts are of great significance, but the salespeople themselves may be unaware of what is happening. The salesperson in the least affected territory will be unaware or less sympathetic to the plight of his fellow salesperson whose territory has been drastically altered by competition, although remaining the same geographically.

Company Strategy

Management does not always take salespeople into their confidence when altering strategy. For example, management may be urging the sales force to push a particular model because of excessive inventory or because it is presently profitable. The salespeople are not told that the firm expects to discontinue the model the following year, leaving present buyers with an orphan model. The repercussions of this action may leave a bitter taste for both salesperson and customer and seriously shake sales for some time. However, it might prove dangerous for the analyst to attribute sales decrease to this action since it would be unpopular with management. He might realize the damage caused by the previous action and assess it correctly, but he might have to attribute decreasing sales to upsetting market conditions rather than to the unwise actions of management.

Changes in company strategy might be ultimately successful, but temporarily they might have serious repercussions on the sales force. Possibly, the effects would vary from territory to territory and on each salesperson. The analyst would try to assess effects of this new strategy on each territory and each salesperson, but he would be aware that with two variables the effects would be difficult to determine. He would hesitate to challenge individual sales performance when the measurements appear of doubtful validity.

At best, analysis of salesperson performance using qualitative factors would be recognized as attempts to evaluate important areas with rather crude tools. But even imperfect measurements have value, for they serve to focus management attention on sales problems and stimulate salespeople to improve their performance.

EVALUATING SALESPEOPLE

How valuable is a salesperson to his employer? How much does he contribute to the firm? How much would the firm suffer if it lost his services? Can he be replaced easily? These and many more questions must be answered about each salesperson.

It is difficult and at times embarrassing to answer questions about a salesman's performance. The sales manager has an impression of how John is doing; he knows that Brenda had some big orders last year; he knows that Pete lost one of his best customers a month ago. This information, although relevant, is not exact enough to draw definitive conclusions. Unfortunately, the sales manager's current viewpoint might be swayed by an immediate event. As a result, the salesperson might be given a salary increase or refused one, promoted or fired, benefited or rejected by a fluke that is not truly representative.

The sales manager needs a history of a salesperson's performance to avoid hasty decisions and faulty judgment. Evaluating salespeople performance is collecting and appraising sales performance data measured by established criteria and measurement devices. Evaluation is dependent on judgment influenced by evidence which can be rated. Sometimes this rating is quite tangible and precise, based on quantitative data; at other times, it is intangible and highly subject to judgment and impression.

There is a problem of setting up performance measurements and the necessity for establishing weights for each criterion. To make weighting more difficult, it can be unfair to assign the same weight for a salesperson for a certain criterion because age, skill, and experience vary, as do territories, competition, and customers. Thus, a series of weights may be necessary as well as variations in weights from time to time as each year brings new sales problems and opportunities. For example, one year a salesperson is expected to call on four customers daily. The next year he is given another territory, where he must make six calls a day. This latter number might actually be an easier assignment than the first. Thus, the four-calls-a-day assignment might get a 2 weighting, and the six-calls-a-day assignment might get a 1 weighting because of inherent territory problems. Thus, even the weighting assigned becomes dependent on objective and subjective criteria.

Before evaluating a salesperson, it is necessary to determine the job in considerable detail. Then the manager must separate the job into groups of activities or series of operations subject to measurement. He must separate a job of continuous activities into discrete parts or components to isolate each activity and set proper measuring sticks. If this can be done satisfactorily, it becomes relatively easy to add up performance and come up with a quantitative answer. While he may rank qualitative criteria independently, in the end these criteria should reflect satisfactory quantitative performance.

Even with a job description which gives an accurate picture of duties, the sales manager still cannot completely define a salesperson's job because the job description inadequately describes a salesperson's job in a specific territory. Thus, a salesperson ought to be evaluated on those factors within his control, even though other territorial factors might deserve careful attention for purposes of stimulating performance.

Purpose of Evaluation

Evaluation is a necessary preliminary step before a supervisor can discuss performance with a salesperson because it gives fundamental data about the salesperson in his territory. Evaluation enables a supervisor and salesperson to discuss intelligently what the salesperson is doing well and what he can improve. It prevents blind discussion, recrimination, careless accusation, and thoughtless statements.

Evaluation can be used to determine the thrust of new training or retraining because it can be directed to areas of demonstrated weakness. Evaluation is useful in pointing out where a salesperson should be motivated to improve because it shows his slack and blind areas. The supervisor should isolate the causative factor or factors responsible for poor results and work on these specific areas.

Evaluation is most useful when the salesperson really believes what he sees and is told and takes steps to strengthen himself in specific areas. If the supervisor can get the salesperson to see himself as the supervisor sees him, both can work together toward a common goal.

Evaluation is an essential part of appraisal leading to salary increases, territory adjustments, promotions, and other rewards, as well as determining when a salesperson should be discharged for his benefit as well as the firm's benefit. Often, being discharged is the best thing that happens to the salesperson. If he is convinced of his own ability, he goes elsewhere and demonstrates it; if he feels he is in the wrong slot, he goes into another type of work where he may become outstandingly successful.

Who Evaluates

The salesperson's supervisor, the district manager, and the sales manager evaluate. Anyone who bears responsibility for or relationship to the salesperson evaluates.

There is usually an informal evaluation made by other salespeople in the firm. These comparisons are inevitable and may have considerable influence, even though they are unofficial. Their effect may be indirect, but powerful if there are evidences of favoritism or discrimination. Salespeople may use their own comparisons or intimate knowledge to defend their positions or to buttress their requests. So Fred might say, "I know that Greta sells more, but did you actually compare our territories? Greta drives ten miles a day when I drive 100 miles." How can the supervisor really explain that Greta is in a crowded city where she must fight traffic, hunt for parking, and put up with inconveniences that may make her ten miles equivalent to Fred's 100 miles? Distinctions of this nature are numerous. The salesperson should be his own most careful evaluator. If a salesperson loses an important sale, no one knows the details of the sale as well as he does; and no one can analyze what happened as carefully as he can. Others can comment, but no one can determine what went on in the salesperson's mind. Superior salespeople often remark that they may learn little from a successful sale, but learn much when they lose a sale.

The customer evaluates a salesperson and indirectly the firm the salesperson represents when he gives or does not give an order. Somewhere during the sale attempt, the buyer is convinced one way or another.

Each buyer may develop his own criteria of selling. The astute salesperson recognizes individual differences and adjusts accordingly, but the less sensitive salesperson plows forward, oblivious to warning signs. If the salesperson is creative and sensitive to the buyer's needs, he will tailor his presentation to information the particular buyer wants and discard irrelevant data and conversation. The salesperson is acute enough to recognize when to push and when to listen.

If the salesperson is sensitive to a buyer's need, he will present items which benefit the buyer and not push items he would like to sell. This approach becomes increasingly important on repeat buyers, where success is predicated through a continuing friendly relationship. Even if a salesperson-buyer relationship is not warm, at least it can be respectful. A buyer may not personally like a salesperson, but he can respect him and buy because it is advantageous.

The buyer also evaluates the salesperson on his follow-up work. Does he live up to his promises? Is he available when needed? If difficulties in delivery arise, does he inform the buyer in time and work with him to avoid problems?

When to Evaluate

Evaluating should be a continuous process by the salesperson himself. Such evaluations need not always be critical, but should be objective.

The customer is unconsciously evaluating and rating a salesperson whenever he sees him. The customer forms opinions which are modified from time to time as he sees the salesperson under different conditions.

The supervisor or sales manager tends to evaluate each salesperson continuously, but this informal way creates impressions which may be accentuated by infrequent favorable or unfavorable events. Thus, one unfavorable spectacular event might wipe out a series of smaller favorable actions and obscure the sales manager's vision to the real worth of a salesperson.

This approach exists, but it must not substitute for the carefully developed approach which gives solid, carefully weighed factual data plus carefully considered subjective factors.

The frequency of formal evaluation varies among firms, depending on type of selling, closeness of supervision, and the personal views of management. High caliber salespeople operating alone over long periods and selling large orders are not rated as often as those in firms with numerous salespeople under close supervision. For all salespeople, a yearly evaluation should be the minimum. Some sales managers prefer two ratings a year, and some use quarterly evaluation. There can also be individual ratings for special purposes, for example, to find someone to promote or to reward with a new territory.

The weakness of infrequent evaluation is that much passes unnoticed in the early part of the rating period. Events occurring just before the evaluation period take greater importance than they deserve. Too much of a decision may be based on the last month and very little on the first month of the period. A weakness of frequent ratings is the effort involved, which may lead to superficial rating or delegating the job to a subordinate who is not equipped for the task. Poor evaluation is definitely unfair to the salesperson and may be costly to the firm. It may lead to the retention of weak people or frustrate a capable salesperson, causing him to resign.

Where to Evaluate

A supervisor may rate in the office, in his home, or even in hotel rooms. The sales manager probably would do the evaluation in the office or at home. It is quite possible to split the rating job, handling objective ratings at the office or wherever the information is available. Subjective ratings require reflection, thought, weighing alternative factors, and fitting together bits of information and behavior.

How to Evaluate

Two general rating approaches, subjective and objective, are commonly used.

Subjective evaluation

Subjective evaluation is rating the salesperson by observation and appraisal. Quite likely, one salesperson receiving ratings from several supervisory officials will find they do not agree in some aspects, but these ratings may be similar.

The supervisor in the field will have better knowledge of the salesperson's daily behavior, operations, performance, and ability to get along with customers. The district manager will be able to appraise other characteristics better, such as sales performance compared to other salespeople and their potential. In a very large firm, the sales manager would have so little contact with a salesperson that his subjective appaisal, if any, would draw conclusions from submitted data.

Intuitive guess.　Some supervisors and managers often use a feel for the answer, or what is commonly called a hunch. One frequently hears the expression "I know, but don't ask me how I got it," which signals a so-called educated guess. Unquestionably, some raters can be somewhat successful using this approach, but such results can be sporadic and vary in quality depending on how well the rater knows the salesperson.

Subjective yardstick appraisal. Subjective ratings are better when they follow a set of guides. Relying on memory is dangerous, for at any one time the rater will not recall all the pertinent information he needs. Later incidents may be recalled more forcefully than those of previous months or quarters, and too often one event will remain indelibly stamped in the rater's mind. While this event may loom strong in the rater's memory, from the company standpoint it is minor. For example, if a salesperson got into a strong disagreement with his superior that one incident would remain unfavorably in the superior's mind. If one salesperson made a spectacular sale, the rater would be favorably impressed; but it might have been a windfall sale. Supervisors giving ratings try to be fair and work for accuracy, but they are human.

In setting up a subjective appraisal, the rater should have a number of criteria at his disposal. First he should have a set of values in mind so that when he uses such terms as excellent, good, fair, and poor, each fits a segment of the scale from top to bottom. If the salesperson is being graded on communication, he should consider sound of voice, clearness of diction, freedom from slang, courtesy while the other speaks, and other factors which spell out effective communication. During a demonstration, does the salesman go logically step by step, or does he jump around in his explanations? When the salesperson talks about customers, is he objective or does he tend to explain away all lost orders? Does the salesperson tend to cover up often, or is he frank in admitting some weaknesses?

Even though a salesperson creates an impression of good, bad, or average, using a blanket assessment is too crude for a critical appraisal. The rater should break down an overall impression into specific traits and characteristics and evaluate each.

There can be a marked discrepancy between raters, depending on the responsibility criterion. Thus, a supervisor or sales manager may rate favorably or overrate salespeople under their jurisdiction because to do otherwise would reflect unfavorably on them. A rater not having close ties to the salesperson and not being responsible for him in any way might give ratings considerably lower. Both could be right because of differing viewpoints, or both could be wrong. Beware of trying to average two viewpoints; they both might be wrong; one could be right; or both could be right but reflect different standards.

Objective evaluation

Objective appraisal is based on measurable quantitative data. Data could include time, profitability, performance against a yardstick of quotas, and budget standards.

It may be much easier to rate a salesperson on these bases because of tangible evidence as contrasted with intangible factors in the subjective approaches.

The objective yardsticks may jeopardize evaluation. Are the measuring devices accurately determined? Are they relevant; that is, do they measure performance? It may be quite possible to develop measuring devices that measure accurately but then the question arises: what is to be measured? Drop-offs in sales performance or erratic behavior in the market demand application of corrective factors in the measuring devices before they are valid again.

The degree of quality should be determined by the use of the evaluation. If the evaluation is used merely to establish whether or not a salesperson is making a contribution to the company, the accuracy need not be as great as in evaluating a salesperson on a number of specific factors. Too often, a careful objective evaluation is predicated on measuring devices which are not reliable enough to be used precisely. For example, a salesperson may be judged by his quota performance; but the quota may not be accurate and should be used as a guide, not a precise performance indicator.

What to Evaluate

In subjective rating, the appraiser bases his opinion on a number of factors that appear relevant to the particular situation; in objective ratings, he uses tangible, measurable performance. The rater may choose the factors that apply to the salesperson he is evaluating. The sales manager should develop a list that most effectively represents a true measure of his sales force.

Comprehensive Evaluation Program

A measurement and evaluation program should be adapted to the salesperson in his particular job. There is little merit in installing such a program unless it fits the task being judged. This rating should be based on the job as described in the job description and include actual sales activities in the territory.

Evaluating a salesperson's performance must be done in the interests of both company and salesperson. Evaluation may aid a salesperson and spur him to increased effort. Evaluation should benefit the company because the information tells what a particular territory contributes to profits. It should tell the company what it needs to know about relations with customers; it should give a clearer indication of attainable potential; and it should be a performance guide of individual salespeople. Figure 7–1 is an example of a salesperson's evaluation form.

QUESTIONS AND PROBLEMS

1. What are the objectives of analyzing salesperson performance? How do these objectives fit into the salesperson's life?

Figure 7–1
Salesperson's Evaluation Form

Burroughs Corporation Ⓑ
BUSINESS MACHINES GROUP
PERFORMANCE REVIEW AND EVALUATION
NON-MANAGEMENT SALES PERSONNEL

DISTRIBUTION:
BRANCH – ORIGINAL AND DUPLICATE TO DISTRICT MANAGER; TRIPLICATE, BRANCH FILE.
DISTRICT – REVIEW, INITIAL AND FORWARD ORIGINAL TO BMG EMPLOYEE & INDUSTRIAL RELATIONS; DUPLICATE, DISTRICT FILE.

REVIEW PERIOD:
FROM _____ TO _____

NAME			
BRANCH		LOCATION	
JOB TITLE	STATE OF HEALTH	MARITAL STATUS	AGES OF CHILDREN
AGE DATE EMPLOYED	EFFECTIVE DATE OF PRESENT ASSIGNMENT		

PREPARED AND DISCUSSED WITH EMPLOYEE BY:

ZONE/ACCOUNT/SA MANAGER _____ DATE _____

BRANCH MANAGER _____ DATE _____

REVIEWED BY: DISTRICT MANAGER _____ DATE _____

EMPLOYEE'S SIGNATURE _____ DATE _____

WHAT ARE THIS EMPLOYEE'S AMBITIONS AND DESIRES AS EXPRESSED IN THE INTERVIEW? _____

_____

	LINES OF BUSINESS	DATE TO BE TRAINED	TRAINED	EXPERI-ENCED	EXPERT (SPECIAL-IST)	COMMENTS
KNOWLEDGE BY LINES OF BUSINESS USE ADDITIONAL LINE FOR SPECIFIC APPLI-CATIONS BY LINES OF BUSINESS AS REQUIRED	FINANCIAL					
	GOVERNMENT					
	EDUCATIONAL					
	MEDICAL					
	TRANS., COMM., & PUBLIC UTILITY					
	MANUFACTURING					
	WHOLESALE					
	RETAIL					

*SALES RECORD YR-TO-DATE - - Month _____ 19 __

	PRODUCTS	DATE TO BE TRAINED	TRAINED	EXPERI-ENCED	EXPERT (SPECIAL-IST)	TOTAL ORDERS	QUOTA	UNITS SOLD
	GROUP I					$	%	
	GROUP II					$	%	
	GROUP III-S					$	%	
	TOTAL GP					$	%	
PRODUCT KNOWLEDGE						$	%	
	GROUP V					$	%	
	GROUP VI					$	%	
	GROUP VIII					$	%	
	TOTAL EDP					$	%	
	TOTAL SALES					$	%	

	YEAR	ASSIGNMENT	DATE ASSIGNED	TOTAL ORDERS	QUOTA	UNITS SOLD
SALES RECORD	PRIOR YEAR 19			$	%	
	PRIOR YEAR 19			$	%	
	LAST YEAR 19			$	%	
	CURRENT YR 19 ___ (___ MOS.)			$	%	

* FOR LAST YEAR, OR CURRENT YEAR IF REVIEW IS PREPARED AFTER FIRST QUARTER - - FROM ZONE SALES PERFORMANCE REPORT.

* Courtesy Burroughs Corporation

Figure 7-1 (*Continued*)

THIS FORM IS DESIGNED TO HELP YOU APPRAISE EACH EMPLOYEE UNDER YOUR SUPERVISION WITH RESPECT TO SPECIFIC GOALS AND STANDARDS OF PER-FORMANCE. IF EACH APPRAISAL IS CARRIED OUT IN A SYSTEMATIC MANNER, THE PROGRAM WILL ASSIST YOU IN MAINTAINING AN EFFECTIVE ORGANIZA-TION THROUGH EMPLOYEE DEVELOPMENT AND IMPROVED JOB PERFORMANCE.

CHARACTERISTIC (PLEASE RATE THE SALESMAN ON THE FOLLOWING CHARACTERISTICS)		EXCEPTIONAL	VERY GOOD	SATISFACTORY	NEEDS IMPRV.	UNSATIS-FACTORY	COMMENTS USE SEPARATE SHEET FOR ADDITIONAL COMMENTS
LEADERSHIP ABILITY	1						PERSONAL QUALITIES
WILLINGNESS TO ACCEPT RESPONSIBILITY	2						
DEPENDABILITY	3						
COOPERATIVENESS	4						
AGRESSIVENESS, PERSEVERANCE, PERSUASIVENESS	5						
GENERAL APPEARANCE	6						
RELATIONS WITH SERVICE & OFFICE DEPARTMENTS	7						
LEARNING ABILITY	8						
WILLINGNESS TO ACCEPT AND TRY NEW IDEAS	9						
WILLINGNESS TO ACCEPT CONSTRUCTIVE CRITICISM	10						
CIVIC ACTIVITIES	11						
PLANNING AND MANAGEMENT OF TIME	12						TERRITORY OPERATION AND SALES ABILITY
THOROUGHNESS	13						
QUALITY OF INSTALLATIONS	14						
QUALITY OF DEMONSTRATIONS	15						
QUANTITY OF DEMONSTRATIONS	16						
ABILITY TO ANALYZE PROSPECTS NEEDS	17						
ABILITY TO CREATE INTEREST - ENTHUSIASM	18						
CLOSING ABILITY	19						
ABILITY AGAINST COMPETITION	20						
ABILITY TO HANDLE LARGE ACCOUNTS	21						
CUSTOMER RELATIONS	22						
ABILITY TO EXPRESS SELF IN WRITING	23						
ABILITY TO EXPRESS SELF IN SPEAKING	24						
COLLECTION RECORD	25						
SOFTWARE REVENUE	26						
EXPENSE CONTROL	27						
RESPONSIVENESS	28						

WHAT ARE THIS SALESMAN'S STRONG POINTS? BE SPECIFIC. _____

WHAT ARE HIS WEAKNESSES? BE SPECIFIC. _____

COMMENT REGARDING THIS EMPLOYEE'S DEVELOPMENT NEEDS. _____

IS THIS EMPLOYEE WELL PLACED? _____ IS HE PROMOTABLE? _____
WHAT WOULD YOU RECOMMEND AS HIS NEXT ASSIGNMENT? COMMENT. _____

OVERALL PERFORMANCE APPRAISAL

EXCEPTIONAL	VERY GOOD	SATISFACTORY	NEEDS IMPROVEMENT	UNSATISFACTORY
Consistently does an excellent job. Performance approaches the best possible for the job. ☐	Exceeds requirements for satisfactory performance for the job. ☐	Meets all job requirements in a satisfactory manner. ☐	Performance must improve to meet job requirements. ☐	Performance does not warrant continuing in present assignment. ☐

HIS PERFORMANCE GENERALLY HAS _____ IMPROVED _____ NOT CHANGED _____ GONE BACK SINCE LAST REVIEW

2. What is the purpose of a standard of performance? Can standards be applied to a number of activities?

3. Discuss the advantages of using a job description in determining kinds of standards.

4. Do standards fit salespeople exactly? Point out limitations that at best are partially resolved.

5. Many sales managers prefer to use quantitative standards in measuring. Why?

6. Do salespeople use time well? Illustrate effective time use and poor time use.

7. Sales volume is an inviting standard to use. How can volume be interpreted, and why are various interpretations useful?

8. Discuss customer standards with special reference to size, value, and importance of individual customers.

9. Why is it necessary to gain new accounts? Is loss of accounts inevitable? Do you think there is a "batting average" in accounts sold?

10. Explain the need for clear company standards. How useful are they?

11. What is the purpose of stressing difficulty standards? Do you believe sales managers give much attention to them? Explain.

12. Are there individual standards that might have little advantage in one company but be quite helpful for another firm?

13. Define qualitative standards. Are they a measure of a salesperson's awareness? Do they measure motivation? Are they primarily a measure of the individual salesperson?

14. Can qualitative measures be appraised in quantitative performance? Explain.

15. Choose three qualitative characteristics and explain why they are important to a salesperson.

16. Analysis can be of great help in determining performance in some areas, but in other areas analysis is not too helpful because it is primarily based on historical data. What are some of these problem areas, and why do they hinder performance evaluation?

17. What effects on sales performance can be triggered by a change in company strategy?

18. Discuss the task of salesperson evaluation emphasizing standards, weighting, differences in territories, and other factors within the salesperson's control.

19. What are the purposes of evaluation?

20. Who is best equipped to evaluate a salesperson? Name several.

21. How often should salespeople be evaluated? Discuss advantages and disadvantages of different time periods.

22. Compare subjective evaluation with objective evaluation. Is one more important than the other?

23. A salesperson's performance must be evaluated both in the interests of the salesperson and the employer. Explain why this is necessary.

SARDON DRUG COMPANY   *case 7–1*

Sardon Drug Company is a drug wholesaler located in Westmore, Ohio, a town of 300,000 inhabitants. Their salesmen cover the city plus adjoining territory within a 100-mile radius. Ten salesmen cover Westmore and the surrounding area.

The salesmen make regular calls on customers, take routine orders, and attempt to sell additional items to increase order size. Salesmen make some calls every week on prospects to get new accounts. Small accounts are a nuisance, particularly the ones that split their buying among other wholesalers. Salesmen try to capture a greater share of such accounts.

Salesmen are paid commissions on sales plus traveling expenses. Commissions vary from 1 to 6 percent, depending on the profitability of the item. There has been some discussion about penalizing salesmen on orders that are unprofitable.

Emanuel Borg, the sales manager, has never been able to develop a satisfactory evaluation system for his salesmen. No matter how he adjusts his system, he finds some salesmen benefit more than others; and he is not convinced this is always equitable.

ASSIGNMENT

Develop a form with pertinent criteria that would aid the sales manager to accurately evaluate each salesman.

SONAR ELECTRONICS COMPANY   *case 7–2*

Warren Thomas, sales manager of the Sonar Electronics Company, is dissatisfied with the practice of evaluating and rewarding salesmen solely on the basis of sales volume. He is devising a system built upon five factors he has found to be important in evaluating industrial salesmen. He recognizes that his firm faces different challenges at different times, and he would like his evaluation plan to be useful in influencing salesmen's behavior consistent with company's objectives.

Present Evaluation Plan

The Sonar Electronics Company, a relatively small firm, makes a broad line of electronics components which it sells to original equipment manufacturers through a field sales force of twenty technically trained salesmen. There are approximately 3,000 original equipment manufacturers throughout the United States. Sonar's main competition comes from two larger electronics firms and several smaller firms, of which Sonar is one of the leading companies.

Mr. Thomas has been using sales volume as the criterion for rating salesmen performance. Although he occasionally tries to indoctrinate his men with a balanced view of the firm's sales objectives, the company awards salary increases, bonuses, prizes, and praise solely on the basis of sales volume. If sales fall off in any territory in a particular month, the salesman immediately receives a telephone call from the home office asking why.

Although this method of rating and motivating salesmen has been successful in raising sales volume, certain undesirable behavior has developed. Some of these side effects are:

1. Increasingly, salesmen are reluctant to make the investment in time and effort necessary to open new accounts.
2. In their eagerness to make sales, salesmen have increased pressure on the home office for price reductions. More frequently then ever, they report losing orders because of competitors' lower priced offerings. The home office people doubt the truth of this and feel that they can no longer trust the pricing information obtained by their salesmen.
3. A number of less active accounts have been complaining about a deterioration in service. Salesmen's calls have declined in frequency, and answers to inquiries have slowed noticeably.
4. The company has been finding it more difficult to introduce new products. New products usually present dangers of technical difficulties that take time, patience, and some engineering assistance to correct. Thus, new products take a disproportionate share of salesmen's energy and cut into available selling time.
5. The salesmen tend to resist any suggestions or proposals that would not have an immediate favorable effect on sales volume.
6. From time to time, the company falls behind on delivery on popular items. When this happens, salesmen cajole or even try to bribe company personnel so that their orders are given priority.
7. Salesmen have become increasingly vehement in their objections to the practice of the credit department in placing low credit limits for slow payment of invocies. The salesmen believe that a restrictive credit policy tends to inhibit sales.

Proposed Plan

Mr. Thomas is developing a plan based on six important factors and assigning various weights to these factors. (Weighting is assigning points, such as 1, 2, 3, to show relative importance.)

The six factors are:
1. Salesman reaches or exceeds his annual sales quota.
2. Salesman regularly opens new accounts.
3. Salesman gives superior service to his accounts and thereby cements customer loyalty to the company.
4. Salesman provides home office with good intelligence data about customer's buying plans and competitor's prices.
5. Salesman shows consistently high year to year sales growth in his assigned territory, of which a substantial portion is accounted for by the introduction of new products offered by the firm.
6. Salesman strives to upgrade his technical and selling skills with respect to services of customers' problems.

The salesmen are to be informed of the multiple criteria upon which they will be judged and the weights to be assigned to these factors.

Mr. Thomas is pondering what weights to assign these six factors. He has developed four different situations that could be used. These situations are:

1. Because of the difficulty in assigning weights, all criteria are considered equally important.
2. Because the company's management has placed great stress on a rapid build up of sales volume, both sales volume and new accounts are given greater weight.
3. The company wants to introduce a line of products new to it, but now being sold successfully by its competitors. Greater weight is thus placed on factor five.
4. An emergency situation arises that requires sales volume with existing customers be given overwhelming emphasis.

Even though the assigning of weights to the various factors is not necessarily rigid, Mr. Thomas must now decide how best to assign the weights. Once a proper assigning of weights is established, Mr. Thomas proposes to set up a bonus fund of $15,000 and award shares of the fund in proportion to each man's ranking. The ranking will be based on points, or weights, assigned to the six factors. The salesman with the highest point total for the year would receive a $4,000 bonus; the second highest man, $3,000; the third man, $2,000; the fourth man, $1,500; the fifth, $1,000; and five additional ones ranging from $100 to $500 in $100 steps.

In reviewing his proposed plan, Mr. Thomas is aware of some flaws. There is the problem of assigning weights to the six factors. Next, there is the difficulty with establishing factor 1 (annual sales quotas). How can he arrive at a fair quota for a salesman?

Because of the difficulty of assigning weights and the problem with factor 1 (annual sales quotas), Mr. Thomas is considering dropping his proposed plan for evaluating salesmen.

QUESTIONS

1. Should Mr. Thomas use the proposed plan? If so, how can he overcome the flaws?
2. Compare multiple versus single measures for evaluating salesmen.
3. Is assigning weights to various factors a good way of controlling salesmen?
4. Should the bonus plan be used?

Conventions, Conferences, Group Meetings, Workshops, Clinics

Salespeople appreciate meeting with management and other sales-people to share problems, viewpoints, apprehensions, and successes. Since they have much in common, they should be able to talk with other salespeople.

Sales meetings are called by different names, but all have the purpose of getting salespeople together to share mutual concerns. These meetings may be called conventions, conferences, group meetings, workshops, or clinics; some of these meetings may be similar, although each company chooses to use different names; some may vary considerably, depending on the size of the group and the purpose of meeting.

CONVENTIONS

Conventions are one of the more formal types of meetings scheduled for salespeople. A convention can be the highlight of a salesperson's year. A convention becomes a rallying point, a topic of conversation, and an event a salesperson plans for. To some, it may be a source of inspiration; to others, a chance to have fun at company expense; to some, serious business and a chance to grow; to others, a bore. The sales manager cannot judge the usefulness of the convention from the comments of salespeople, for any salesperson with good judgment will tell management what management likes to hear.

Purpose of Convention

A convention should have a purpose. It is wasteful to have a convention if there is no need for it, but the effective sales manager should find needs for periodic conventions. He does not create these needs, but the demands of the sales department are such that a convention is the best way to meet certain problems. While there can be numerous reasons for having a convention, there are a number which are basic every year.

Product changes

Many companies have new products which will appear on the market. That is not to say that products can only be introduced after a convention because many firms do not follow this practice. A convention is an excellent way to give the salesperson a preview so that when a new product appears, he can tell the customer and not the reverse. Too often, buyers learn about changes before some of the salespeople.

Sales strategy changes

Selling strategy is not likely to remain static very long. Although changes are communicated to the field rapidly, major changes may be held in advance until they can be explained to the whole sales force at once. If the explanation is made by one person at one time, all will receive the same message, but that does not mean they will all interpret it in the same way. A uniform single presentation followed by explanations and discussion will clear many aspects. In one meeting, a number of salespeople will raise different questions, all of which might occur to each salesperson sometime in the future. This process is informative to salespeople, and it may surprise management and make them aware of problems which had not occurred to them.

Presentations and demonstrations

Presenting fresh approaches and presentations may jar a salesperson into recognizing his sliding performance. The salesperson seldom realizes how far he has deviated from the standard, but rather feels his minor changes improved his selling techniques. Standardized presentations by experts revive the salesperson's desire to perform better.

Company information

Salespeople are stationed long distances from the home office and know very little about what goes on. A convention can be the means of getting the latest information; when it is given by a top executive, it lends authority. This inside information gives the salesperson a warm feeling of belonging and makes him feel that the home office thinks of him as a member of the team.

Individual conference

Since a convention is a gathering of executives and sales leaders with the rank and file salespeople, it is an excellent time to schedule individual conferences. While this practice may detract from the main events, few salespeople are pulled from general meetings; and many conferences can be scheduled during free periods.

Many salespeople may spend years with a firm before meeting some executives. Many firms have executive changes each year so that there is always opportunity for a salesperson to meet a different executive. It may do much for a salesperson to meet someone from the home office and find out that, in spite of directives and communications through the mail which may have been critical, the individual is warm and approachable.

Who Should Attend

All salespeople should attend the convention. Often, firms set up conditions so that only a few of the most successful people attend. If the firm feels that it is too expensive to bring most or all the salespeople to the convention, it probably is too expensive to have in the first place.

In addition to the sales force, the sales management group will probably attend. In a small firm, this may be the sales manager only or perhaps an assistant sales manager. The other extreme would be several members from the home office as well as regional, district, and local managers and sales supervisors. Sometime during the convention, certain top officers will be present to speak and to talk with various people who want information. The presence of a number of top management lends importance to the convention and develops empathy among members of the sales organization, for it emphasizes teamwork.

When to Hold a Convention

The time to hold a convention varies from firm to firm. Some companies hold their annual convention between Christmas and New Year's because that is a quiet time in their operation. Some hold it in July or August if this is a quiet time in the year.

Many firms pick a time when salespeople's absence from the territory will be least harmful. That time would usually coincide with slack periods in selling, though it could easily coincide with periods of maximum use of company products. Frequently, the nature of the convention determines when it should be chosen to get the most benefit from the location.

Length of Convention

Conventions may vary in length from two days to a week. Of course, there may be some of shorter or longer duration, but the expense may prohibit calling such a gathering for less than two days. The expense cannot justify prolonging it for more than a week because of the money involved as well as keeping salespeople from their territories.

A convention should be long enough to meet the purpose for which it is set up. Often, a crowded calendar of events with tight scheduling does shorten the overall time, but defeats the primary purpose for the convention. Conventions are often scheduled improperly with too many meetings.

Multiple meetings scheduled simultaneously and sometimes repeated can be used when smaller groups are desirable. It is not necessary that all the salespeople attend the same meeting, because there may be special purpose interests to attract particular groups. For example, there could be a meeting only for salespeople who have worked less than a year for this company. Special meetings can be sandwiched in at odd times in order to make the convention shorter; such meetings would affect only limited groups.

There should be sufficient diversity in content of meetings to appeal to everybody. No one should go home feeling the convention was useless, a farce, or the same old stuff stirred up a little differently. Some activities should be scheduled for those not participating in the main activities.

Convention Cost

Conventions need to be budgeted carefully so that the expenses do not overweigh benefits. If the time of the year is not too important, conventions can be held to take advantage of low hotel rates. If the sales convention is held in the city of the home office or plant, it can be fitted into a regular time plan. Often the plant location or multiple plant locations are not in the same city as the home office, and none have adequate convention facilities. Many cities and hotels are ready to assist in handling convention requirements. Large firms with numerous salespeople may find it cheaper to have several smaller regional conventions.

Advantages of regional conventions
Regional conventions are smaller than a national convention. Usually, they are held in particular areas to facilitate travel and save time. Because they are smaller, each salesperson gets some individual attention and feels freer to participate in smaller group meetings. Cost is reduced for each person because he spends less time and money in travel.

Disadvantages of regional conventions
Regional conventions are expensive and time consuming to the sales officials who must attend. Top sales management officials can spend weeks of their time at these conventions when they should be home plotting new sales strategy. It is usually feasible to bring top manage-

ment to a single convention, but not to regional ones. Often, a regional convention cannot justify the lavish equipment and presentations used in a single convention.

Convention Appraisal

The sales manager should do some serious appraisal after each convention. While much of his appraisal remains subjective, he should not content himself with the belief that it must have done some good. Sales increase or decrease after a convention is not a reliable measure because there are so many other possible causes for change. How can he measure change?

A perceptive sales manager can set standards of performance to measure convention results objectively. For example, there have been numerous complaints from customers about the breakdown of a particular machine in use. At the convention, one meeting is devoted to instructions on how to operate this machine, and salespeople are given on-the-spot training. If this particular customer complaint diminishes, the manager could attribute this fact to better salespeople efforts resulting from their instruction. One meeting could be used to explain how quotas are determined and to illustrate that sound bases, not guesswork, are employed in such work. If salespeople grumble less about quotas, this could be a positive convention contribution.

CONFERENCES

A sales conference is held for a specific purpose or purposes to improve a particular area of the sales program. Some firms use the terms convention and conference interchangeably.

A sales conference may have fewer frills and a minimum of entertainment. Most of the time is allocated to specific subject matter presented in a learning situation. The agenda requires careful planning and assigning work periods for specific topics.

The purpose of a sales conference should be clearly stated so that both the leaders and the salespeople know what is expected. The meetings are set up to discuss or consider particular topics, and the leaders should endeavor to keep everyone's attention on one topic. If a conference has been called for one purpose, it is of sufficient importance to demand the entire attention of the group. Possibly, if the main topic is exhausted and further attention contributes little, it would be proper to take up some other topic which is particularly relevant.

The length of the conference, whether in hours or days, should be gauged by the apparent difficulty of the topic to be discussed and the probable time needed to treat it thoroughly. If the topic or problem is broad, it might be useful to break it down for consideration at several meetings simultaneously using one phase for each subgroup. In bringing the groups together later, each subgroup can have its thinking reported by a spokesperson.

In many instances, it is unnecessary to have all the salespeople attend a conference. Rather, it would be preferable to involve the group of salespeople most concerned with the particular objective.

Quarterly home office sales conferences could be used to spell out operations for the coming quarter. In a major company, only district managers would attend from the field. They might go back to their districts and hold district sales conferences to discuss how to implement the work decided at the home office.

A sales conference can be serious, but at the same time more intimate than a national convention. It can be geared to meet immediate problems of a particular territory and the salespeople in that territory. These differences occur because the problems in one district may be unlike those of another district, and even the sales staff may differ among districts. Thus, a concentrated district with high potential may have the better salespeople, while another sparsely populated district with smaller potential may be staffed with less experienced people.

A sales conference might well lend itself to a variety of problems and different groupings of salespeople. It could vary in length and be readily adjustable to district or regional problems. The location of conferences will largely be dictated by the personnel who will attend. A district conference would be in the district; a state conference, within a state; a regional conference, within a region; a manager's conference might be rotated among home office and various plant locations.

GROUP MEETINGS

Group meetings can be any type of sales meeting where a number of salespeople are gathered for a specific purpose. They are less formal than the convention and conference, are preceded by less preparation, and often are only for a day or a few hours. Such meetings are often used to bring wholesalers' salespeople together to hear a salesperson of one of the firms they represent. Thus, drug salesmen would listen to a manufacturer of beauty preparations; industrial salesmen would listen to a representative of an abrasive manufacturer; and grocery salesmen would hear a representative from a food-processing plant.

The purpose of a group meeting may be rather narrow. Time is too short for a variety of subject matter, and presentation and discussion are centered on one area. Frequently, the topic concerns a new product or a new sales effort, and the speaker is trying to inspire the wholesaler salespeople to give it a special effort.

Meetings of this type may be held on a Friday evening or a Saturday. Frequently some type of refreshment is furnished. Attendance is usually excellent because the wholesaler expects his people to be there.

A similar type of meeting can be held by the wholesaler for his own group or by a district manager for his salespeople. Such meetings are common and occur weekly in some firms. In rare situations, group meetings are held daily.

In most sales forces, group meetings are useful. Few salespeople can go on indefinitely without supervisory stimulus. Most salespeople benefit from getting together because it gives a spirit of unity and a feeling of belonging.

WORKSHOPS

Workshops bring together interested parties to discuss mutual problems, isolate deficiencies, and seek tentative solutions. Each person in the group has an opportunity to express himself, and hopefully each group is small enough that each person can participate frequently. Such an interchange may bring forth a variety of ideas. Sometimes the discussion reaches an impasse, and nothing tangible comes forth. Then management steps in with suggestions or implements some approach it thinks feasible.

An area group of salespeople can be brought together and subdivided into small groups to discuss a specific problem that affects them. A workshop implies discussion and study. Therefore, each salesperson is expected to do advance preparation. If a particular discussion is not resolved at the workshop meeting, it can be retained for further home study and put on the agenda for a future workshop.

A well-handled workshop is an experience no participant ever forgets. It is an exhausting and demanding approach that expects and extracts much of each member. If an individual does not perform, it shows. Since no salesperson wants to show weakness in the midst of his group, he will try his best to perform.

An example of a workshop in a firm could be a series of workshops in different areas to discuss the sales of a new deodorant that was introduced to the market with heavy promotion. After its initial impact, sales declined except for a few areas. Each area has a workshop to consider why the sales declined.

Such a workshop would have sales statistics, customer analysis, the product, and competing products available at the meeting. The territory workshop would consider each aspect of the problem and come up with suggestions. Later, an area workshop made up of supervisory personnel would advance their ideas. Finally, a home office workshop would consider suggestions and ideas from the field and, together with their own suggestions, evolve a new approach.

CLINICS

A clinic is most often a group meeting used to analyze problems or isolate certain factors that are responsible for success or failure. People think of a clinic as analyzing what is wrong, but it can be equally effective in breaking down successful sales approaches or actions and trying to isolate those factors that contribute to success. It is just as worthwhile and much more pleasant to have a success clinic analysis as it is to have a failure clinic analysis. Usually, the latter is more meaningful, however, for people tend to learn much from failures and little from successes.

A sales clinic should be rewarding to the participants because they should learn how to improve performance. Ordinarily, sales clinics would not be held frequently with the same group unless performance was dismal. Clinics should be scattered infrequently throughout the sales force and used sparingly, sandwiched in among other types of meetings. When a clinic is used, the sales force should know why it is being held. It may be narrower in scope than a workshop, but for some companies it may substitute for a workshop. When used as a motivating force, the clinic may substitute for group meetings.

PREPARING FOR MEETINGS

Careful advance preparation for sales meetings pays rich dividends in accomplishments and prevents unfortunate experiences that reflect unfavorably on management. Careless preparation is unthinkable for a small meeting or a large convention, for each is equally important in its own area.

Purpose of Meeting

Unless a clearly defined purpose is stated, it becomes difficult to plan because no one seems to know exactly what the objectives are. Many sales managers decide on a sales convention without clearly knowing what they are trying to accomplish. Early in the planning stage of a convention, the responsible parties should write down precisely what they want to accomplish.

Who Will Attend

Who will attend the meeting will be determined by the objectives. The meeting may be a sales convention where the salespeople and their spouses and top executives from the home office attend. It may be strictly a working convention attended by salespeople and a select group of home office personnel. It may be a district meeting when the district manager meets with all his salespeople, or it may be a special type of district meeting where the manager meets with some of the salespeople.

The meeting may be held for wholesalers' salespeople only, in which case salespeople from one or several wholesalers may attend. Each year automobile manufacturers have a meeting for dealers to announce the new models. This meeting is conducted with fanfare to create enthusiasm and often is a showy affair to attract attention.

The number attending will determine the size of the meetings or meeting. For some purposes, large single meetings are preferable; but many objectives are best attained through multiple smaller groups. Even some of these smaller groups can vary in size, depending on how the meeting is conducted. A group of twenty-five to fifty can easily hear a speaker and participate in discussion, but if the group members must learn how to operate and demonstrate a piece of equipment, ten may be the maximum that can be handled. Thus, it would not be improbable to have half a dozen meetings simultaneously, thereby maximizing the effectiveness of every executive and speaker—that is, trying to use all the time of all the leaders as much as possible. Even at lunch and dinner periods, the executives can be helpful by sitting among the salespeople rather than clustering in a group.

Responsibility for Meeting

A sales meeting or convention is the responsibility of the sales manager or top sales executive. Depending on the size and purpose of the meeting, the direct responsibility will be delegated to one individual or a group of people working together, for the top executive would not have the time to handle such work personally.

Many firms have a variety of meetings going on throughout the year, but other companies may have only one important meeting a year. When meetings are numerous and widely scattered, a staff would be employed the year around merely to handle and coordinate the work. When meetings are held infrequently, someone is designated to take over this job on a part-time basis along with his regular assignment. Whoever is assigned the task must carry on most of the detail himself, but he should check with his superior frequently enough so that both agree on the direction the meeting is to take.

PLANNING A MEETING

Once the purposes for meeting, the people who will attend, and the responsibility for setting up the meeting have been established, the detailed planning can start. Management sketches what it wants accomplished through a meeting or series of meetings, and designated individuals take over the task of working out details.

Size and Makeup of Meeting

The number of people attending the convention or meeting will usually determine how large a room or auditorium will be needed. The number of group and subgroup meetings scheduled concurrently will determine the minimum number of rooms required for meetings and the sizes of rooms.

The number attending will also determine the night accommodations necessary when the meeting lasts several days. Transportation used may determine convenience of location. If people come by plane, a hotel or motel near an airport may be ideal. If people drive, parking may be a problem. Facilities should be convenient so that salespeople do not waste time that should be spent in sessions.

Presentations may be so complex that equipment must be brought from the home office. Stagings may be so elaborate that only certain facilities in large cities are adequate. Frequently there is a conflict as to size, length, and elaborateness of a meeting or convention and the money available. It is useless to plan a convention knowing that management will veto the plan because of expense.

Location and Time of Meeting

Adequate meeting facilities are not always available at the time and place chosen. Timing well in advance often overcomes this problem; many major conventions are set up years ahead.

Many firms choose a period when their business is slow and salespeople can leave their territories with minimum or no danger. It would not be wise to pick a busy time of the year because business would be neglected. Avoid religious holidays or special periods which might seriously interfere with an individual's personal life.

If a certain amount of entertainment is needed, a downtown location is preferred; but if it is strictly a working meeting, suburban, small town, or even secluded settings are desirable.

Length of Meeting

The entire meeting should be carefully planned to maximize the use of time without impairing effectiveness. Since the cost of keeping salespeople away from home at a meeting is expensive and the possible loss of being absent from sales territories cannot be ignored, the timing should be sufficient to cover meeting objectives but should not be dragged out. Many meetings begin to lose force after two or two and one-half days. Specialized or technical meetings can continue as long as the objective demands, since this meeting may truly be an applied work period.

Physical Facilities for Meeting

There must be adequate space for the largest meetings, concurrent smaller meetings, and exhibition areas if needed. To be certain that all requirements are met precisely, spell out details beforehand and use a checklist that fits the needs.

A frequent source of embarrassment is scheduling meetings so that they overlap or giving insufficient time between meetings to set up for the next meetings. It is not unusual to have last-minute luncheon arrangements, latecomers who wish to be served, and clatter of dishes after a meal which interrupts the speaker. Meeting stragglers are a common occurrence, as are interruptions which distract attention.

Tight scheduling is common and often defeats its instructional purposes. Holding a group all day in one meeting after another does not lead to effective learning or understanding. It is better to have sessions loosely spaced so that individuals have a short period in between. Equipment must be adequate and in excellent condition. Equipment breakdown, faulty pictures on screens, and poor lighting may seriously impair a demonstration; and a speaker may find his efforts almost wasted because of these malfunctions.

Handling Meetings

While some speakers and meeting chairpeople may be seasoned veterans and know how to adjust to circumstances, others may be upset if they do not know each procedural step. Therefore, it is helpful to provide each speaker and person responsible for the meeting with a résumé of what is to take place.

If an unexpected emergency arises so that the speaker cannot come, be prepared to substitute some worthwhile speaker or activity. If a session tends to get out of hand, be prepared to inject something that will terminate discussion. A session that seems to be leading to unpleasantness should be redirected or gracefully terminated.

An opening general meeting may be truly an introductory meeting preparing members for what is to follow, or it may be a special feature of general interest.

Opening requirements before meeting

Many details must be worked out in advance regarding registration, welcoming people as they arrive, room registration, badges, and meeting places. It is common to have a preconvention session to work out last-minute details. Many not involved in this meeting will be arriving with nothing in particular to do. It is gracious to arrange a general meeting place where such people may get together informally.

Convention participants are usually informed about the program through advance publicity. Checklists with data sufficient to stage almost any type of meeting are available from some airlines and from magazines such as *Magazines and Conventions* published in New York.

MOTIVATING SALESPEOPLE

Most activities that promote successful salesperson performance can be included under motivation. It is an integral factor essential to long-range progress.

Most of the chapters in this text weave in motivation, some very forcefully. Proper motivation based on study, planning, continuing effort, new approaches, and salesperson participation upgrades morale and increases efficiency. Improperly used motivation efforts can cause costly mistakes and hinder effective sales operation.

Most motivating factors are covered in several chapters, where specific information is presented. However, it may be helpful to reinforce this topic by some applications singled out for emphasis.

Individual Salesperson Attention

Complimenting the sales force as a group has merit, but it is better to single out each salesperson for meritorious service.

Recognition

Complimenting any salesperson gives him a feeling of satisfaction. When he is awarded recognition by the sales manager in a meeting or a convention, all his fellow salespeople see him honored. When he is mentioned in the company house organ, all the company employees read about him. Appropriate personal notes from senior executives give him a great feeling of pride. Publicity in local newspapers and trade journals announces his success to outsiders.

Planned Motivation

The well-managed sales department does not depend on spontaneous motivation, but has a number of methods to recognize each salesperson when he deserves it. Such procedures are designed to produce a balanced, sound, and welcome effect to emphasize and reward meritorious service. Even though financial rewards are often forthcoming, intangible ones reinforce superior performance.

Dynamic Motivation

Successful motivation calls for regular use of approaches already used, but it must introduce original ways to spearhead innovations. Suggestions from salespeople on how to improve motivation are often welcome to management.

Negative Motivation

The positive approach to motivation is the most pleasant and usually the most common. Negative motivation tactics may be unpleasant, but disciplinary and effective. Threats, loss of job, and losing a good territory are a few drastic measures that may be used as a punishment or to stimulate better performance. Often a salesperson can be goaded to improve his work.

A sales manager cannot overlook the pleasant, cheerful, encouraging approach, nor can he be adverse to using negative tactics if occasion suggests them.

QUESTIONS AND PROBLEMS

1. There can be a number of reasons for having a convention. Discuss several, pointing out the advantage of a convention for specific purposes.

2. What are the reasons for scheduling conventions during different periods in a year?

3. How long should a convention last? Are there exceptions? What is the effect of multiple simultaneous meetings?

4. Under what conditions are regional conventions superior to a national convention?

5. Is it imperative to appraise the results of a convention? Discuss, bringing in such factors as time, cost, accomplishments, and inspiration.

6. Point out how a convention and a conference may vary. Is it important to use the correct name?

7. Explain the purposes of group meetings. What is one particular purpose of a group meeting?

8. Discuss the use of workshops for salespeople. Are workshops significant?

9. Does a clinic meeting have a particular purpose? Explain in detail.

10. Trace the steps in preparing for a convention. Is there any difference in preparing for a convention than for other meetings? Explain.

11. Why should one individual be responsible for a convention? Does this mean he has all the responsibility for a convention's success?

12. What are some convention problems that cause trouble?

13. Can a convention manager depend on the local people to have physical facilities that are adequate? Can he leave certain decisions to others without worrying about their response? Discuss some situations that may arise to create unforeseen contingencies.

14. Discuss some advantages of positive motivation.

15. Is negative motivation useful in handling salespeople? Explain.

---

case 8–1 ALLIED AIR, INC.

Allied Air, Inc., in Portland, Oregon, employs approximately 45,000 people in thirty separate plants and supporting facilities. The company's four major plants are located in different cities and are engaged in air frame manufacture under government contract.

The company early saw the need for development and application of the atom to peaceful purposes. Using its own funds, the company set up an organization staffed of leading atomic scientists and engineers to conduct work for the United States government. The company has initiated many new developments in nuclear applications. Two types of research reactors produced for the United States government are used for advanced development study of reactor designs and general nuclear research.

The company does extensive work in guided missiles, rocket engines, and electronics. More than twenty percent of the company's employees, an unusually high percentage, are engineers and scientists working in widely diversified and advanced technical activities necessary to design and develop the company's products.

The company is organized by functions, such as engineering, material, manufacturing, and sales, with the senior executive in charge of each function reporting directly to the president. The functions are duplicated in the operating or geographical divisions, each centering around a major plant. Each operating division manager reports directly to the president, and the heads of each of the local functional divisions report to the local division manager. In addition, senior executives of the functional divisions coordinate policies and procedures with the heads of the local divisions.

Communication within the company presents a serious problem because of its wide geographical decentralization, its widely diversified technical activities, duplicate organizational structures, and the fact that nearly all of the work of the company involves defense items for which military security imposes serious communication restrictions.

The public relations department has concentrated on establishing sound communication channels for the dissemination of information about the company's policies, activities, and progress to all employees.

The objective of Allied Air's internal communications program is aimed at the long-range goal of teamwork through broad understanding and short-range goal of effective daily action. To achieve this objective, the company employs a wide range of communication techniques to fit its particular problem. Four basic policies are the guiding principles of its communication program:

1. Anything affecting Allied Air is the business of all management personnel. A minimum of secrets and free spread of informa-

tion help to achieve an environment of confidence and understanding.
2. The functions and responsibilities of each individual in management must be clearly defined to avoid confusion, misinterpretation, and conflict.
3. Each subordinate member of management, particularly foremen
   and supervisors, must assume heavy responsibility for horizontal communication.
4. Lines of communication throughout the company must be simple and direct.

The basic stimulus for a free flow of information emanates from the
president of the company who follows a policy of being available to
subordinates for discussion of any matter they consider worthy of his
attention. In addition to direct discussions of specific operating
matters, a regular pattern of informational contacts is maintained
through daily luncheon discussions and a weekly meeting attended by
top management.

The weekly management staff meeting is duplicated by various
management levels and operating divisions throughout the company,
providing a weekly fanning out of essential information from top management. Notes of the top management meeting are distributed weekly
to key executives who, in turn, route this information to their subordinates.

The company follows a basic policy of starting the flow of information from top management through the executive level staff and line
supervision, then to all employees, and lastly, to the community and
general public.

Communication between top management and supervisors is an
important feature of the Allied communications program. The president
of the company has met with each of the 2,000 supervisors at headquarters in Portland to give every member of supervision a feeling of
closer identification. Thirty supervisors were invited by the president
to a series of weekly two-hour meetings. The meetings were opened
by the president with an informal talk on the current status of the
company and were followed by questions from the supervisors on
any subject they chose.

Following the supervisors' meetings, the president wrote a periodic
"confidential" letter to supervisors discussing company affairs. Both
supervisors' meetings and the following "confidential" letter made it
possible for management to circulate to supervisors a great amount
of classified information. The company's supervisors are now trained
to use the president's letter as a basis for keeping employees under
their supervision currently informed on special information concerning
company operations and policy.

Another medium of communication with supervisors is a basic management course for supervision of the rank of assistant foreman and above. This forty-hour course features lectures by executives representing engineering, material, manufacturing, and other functions of the company. Following each lecture, supervisors have an opportunity to ask questions and engage in discussion, out of which comes much information about the company's operations.

Communications with all employees are furthered by means of four weekly newspapers, one published in Ohio where an Allied plant is located, and the others in Portland, Oregon—one for the Portland division; one for the division at San Francisco, California; and one for the division at Salt Lake City, Utah. These publications are primarily intended to report company activities and developments; they also devote space to employee news. The company also publishes a quarterly magazine which is sent to all employees and to the press and a selected list of industrial, governmental, and armed forces personnel.

When important news of company operations breaks before it can be reported in the weekly newspapers, employees get the information from special news releases posted on bulletin boards in all plants and offices. In exceptional circumstances, form letters are mailed to each employee. When a new union contract was signed, employees were notified by letter less than twenty-four hours after conclusion of the negotiations.

To inform the families of employees about the company, Allied Air periodically holds open house at its various plants. Attendance is limited to families and friends of employees. Special displays are arranged throughout the plants, and guides explain the various operations.

QUESTION

There are five different types of meetings described in this case. From the material presented in this chapter, how would you characterize the five types of meetings held? Use the five types in the chapter title.

A. Daily luncheon discussions
B. Weekly staff meeting
C. President's meetings with supervisors
D. Management course for supervision
E. Open house

---

case 8–2   PITKIN, INC.

The sales manager of Pitkin, Inc. has just finished a meeting with the president, during which they agreed that a sales convention should be held in February.

Fifty salespeople comprise the sales force. They cover the United States east of the Mississippi River. They sell paints, finishes, and allied products to retailers, chain stores, discount houses, and wholesalers. Ten salespeople concentrate on industrial sales. The home office and plant is located in Columbus, Ohio.

It is now June and time to begin preparation for the forthcoming convention. A complete plan must be sketched, including finalizing a location and meeting place. The president has suggested a location somewhere along the Gulf coast. There are many hotels and large motels in Mississippi, Alabama, and Florida. As one goes farther south in Florida, the weather is warmer. The east coast of Florida has been rejected because of crowded facilities.

ASSIGNMENT

The sales manager has selected you to handle details. Outline the steps and procedures to follow. Include what you would do immediately. Follow with successive steps up to the time of the convention, that is, until you leave the home office to go to the convention. This assignment occupies only a portion of your time since you must also carry on your regular duties.

9

Sales Contests

Salespeople are constantly handling customer problems, smoothing over difficulties between company and buyer, and struggling to convince buyers to channel their purchases to their companies. To accelerate the salesperson, to sharpen his approach, to broaden his horizon, to turn greater potential of his territory into sales, and to give him an opportunity to improve his own status, the firm introduces a contest. A contest is a mutual sharing experience which benefits at least three parties—the firm, the customer, and the salesperson.

WHY TO USE CONTESTS

Contests stimulate salespeople to greater performance. They cause a salesperson to examine his territory more closely to see if there are opportunities that have escaped him. They force him to reevaluate customers and product uses. He can no longer be content to persuade old customers to buy more, but must show them additional profitable opportunities. Through probing, evaluating, and studying, he can find new potential customers.

Contests can be the means of accomplishing particular company objectives—to improve territories, secure new customers, remove seasonal sales fluctuation, or develop new product uses. Hopefully, a contest will improve the customer's welfare.

If a contest is used as a judicious spur to deliver improved performance, it has merit and will improve sales. If it is used in place of good supervision or to attain impossible objectives of some executive's imagination, its failure is a foregone conclusion. The damage created by ill-conceived contests may be disastrous and leave lasting scars.

WHEN TO AVOID CONTESTS

It is questionable how effective a contest can be among mature, highly trained, and respected salespeople who consistently perform satisfactorily. Effective sales supervision requires tactics suited to the individual salesperson, and to inflict a series of juvenile contests on him would be objectionable. However, that does not rule out all contests since a well-chosen one can make some salespeople enthusiastic and arouse a glow of response from even the most sophisticated salesperson.

Contests are of doubtful value in industrial selling, where the product is a component item in a larger item. Thus, a car manufacturer will not purchase more steel if he is not going to build more cars.

CONTEST OBJECTIVES

Contests are used to increase sales in the entire line, to increase sales of particular items, and to introduce new products. A well-conceived contest can be concentrated so that salespeople consciously direct their activities.

A contest can be directed to individual salespeople to test responses and to determine what management efforts are most productive. It can be a stimulating force to revive the sales staff whose efforts have become sluggish and unresponsive to other appeals. When a new sales manager is employed, a contest may be used to get the salespeople to respond with a tangible demonstration of their regard for the new boss. A sales increase at this time would encourage him and please management.

Sales contests may be a convenient way to develop new territories, revitalize slow territories, and build up territorial potential for new business. A contest could be used to open new geographic areas, solicit new customers, introduce new products, find new uses for old products, and create new customers.

It is not unusual to tie in a contest with an important event. The opening of a new territory could be an occasion to have a contest in all territories. To take full advantage of a new advertising campaign, a contest would be used to tie sales efforts directly with advertising. For example, salespeople could concentrate on a product currently advertised. If a firm desires to expand production, it is essential to get greater sales; and the impetus can be started by a contest.

Firms with a seasonal consumption pattern must struggle to get orders in the off-season. Salespeople must be educated to work hard for orders to level out production, and they must educate customers to place orders well in advance even though delivery is made much later. A contest can be a realistic prod to get orders now instead of three months later. The advantages are threefold—the customer is assured of prompt delivery; the salesperson gets more compensation; and the firm operates with sales, rather than producing for possible future sales.

TYPES OF CONTESTS

Contests may be directed at various sales levels for a variety of purposes, even though the objective is to provide more profitable sales. Each contest should be tailored to fit its particular objectives and clientele. Often, it must be flexible to answer a number of requirements and cover a varied group.

Contests for Company Salespeople

Most of our later discussion will be centered around these contests, but it is well to recognize that this is but one of many types of contest a firm may use to reach particular goals.

Dealer Contests

Dealer contests are conducted by manufacturers and wholesalers to move merchandise into consumers' hands. There can be a number of additional reasons for this type of contest, such as better window and counter displays, better demonstrations, and greater attention to quantity selling.

The requirements of this contest are that the dealer and retail clerks see personal benefits. To them, manufacturers' or wholesalers' benefits are incidental. The contest should be easy to use, applicable to a variety of situations, and rewarding to all participants. Prizes should stimulate retail personnel to greater effort, but not be beyond the reach of those in small and large stores. The dealer should also get a prize, perhaps different from the other prizes, when his employees receive prizes. Everyone involved should receive prizes in proportion to his contribution.

Distributor Contests

The distributor, or wholesaler, contest deals with fewer people than at the retail level, but in many ways it is more important because distributors can assure a firm that its product reaches the retailer or the industrial buyer. Consequently, it is imperative that a successful contest must provoke salespeople enthusiasm and motivate them to spend sufficient time and effort to achieve results.

Contests for wholesaler salespeople should be relatively simple and appealing. These people may be bombarded with contests from other manufacturers and may view any contest with doubt or indifference. If a product is complex, the firm must endeavor to arouse distributors' interest so that they willingly devote more time and effort. Dealer salespeople soon become disgusted with a poor contest or one that has marginal value to them. Unless a contest is beneficial to all participants, its success is doubtful.

The end result of a manufacturer's contest for distributor salespeople should be lasting and carry over to succeeding sales. A contest that is well staged should leave a feeling of solid satisfaction which continues to give future benefits.

Contests for Nonselling Personnel

Nonselling personnel refers to those people whose primary jobs are not selling. Such individuals may have great influence on sales. Salespeople's families can stimulate and encourage. Secretaries in the office frequently can make suggestions that pave the way to more sales. Repairmen who go into homes, offices, and plants often see opportunities to sell equipment, which they pass along to salespeople.

This approach can be supplementary to a sales contest for salespeople, or it can be handled independently. It rewards interested individuals for contributing specifically to sales. Such contributions become more numerous and meaningful when these people receive tangible rewards. For example, a district manager deserves no reward for passing on a customer lead to one of his salespeople for that is part of his job; but a repairman who is observing and passes on a customer lead to a salesperson is performing beyond his normal duties and should be rewarded.

A salesperson's family can become interested through the use of contingent awards. While a salesperson accumulates contest points directly, the family can be stimulated by tickets which can be used in drawings for special awards which are contingent on, but not directly associated with, salesperson awards. Such awards can be called "piggyback" prizes.

Consumer Contests

Manufacturers may use consumer contests to stimulate sales. If salespeople cooperate enthusiastically, see that proper display material is used, that adequate supplies are available in stores, and that displays are clean and prominent, they will benefit by the pulling power of such contests. In this way, salespeople smooth the way for a successful contest; the final customer gets some reward in a special price or sampling approach; and the retailer makes more profit. As a special inducement, there may be some extra reward for the retailer. For example, a display of bags of charcoal was heaped around and over a grill. After all the charcoal was sold, the retailer received the grill as a gift.

KINDS OF CONTESTS

A contest is a competitive thrust towards predetermined objectives and should be established by a careful analysis of existing conditions. A salesperson may compete with himself based on quota; his reward is determined by his individual effort. Some contests stress competition of all salespeople for specific awards, with a series of prizes ranging in descending order. In this situation, there are several winners (first, second, third, fourth, fifth prizes) and probably many losers. In some contests, salespeople are organized in teams which compete with one another for team and individual prizes. The contest must be governed by the way effort is directed; that is, each salesperson plays his own game, or there is joint effort. Successful contests are often based on current activities, such as space exploits, seasonal sports, or television shows. For example, the latest popular television show might be an excellent idea for a sales contest.

Space Contests

Space events are appealing and challenging to people who are adventuresome. Space activities can be almost endless in variety, length, and variation. There can be plenty of excitement and unlimited goals, such as "aiming for a star."

Mystery Contests

Most people are intrigued by mystery, and many like to take the detective's place in solving a problem. Intricate situations will stimulate the salespeople to solve sales problems and produce (sales) successful answers.

Treasure Hunt Contests

This familiar theme played by children and adults in social life is readily adapted to selling. This type of contest can hold interest for both younger and older salespeople.

Athletic Contests

Athletics has a great impact on salespeople. They can follow favorite teams or individuals. This type of contest can be joined in by customers, who understand it readily and can pull for their favorite salesperson by increasing their orders. Because of the wide variety of sports, it is easy to choose one to fit a contest, whether it is based on individual or team effort. For example, salespeople could be teamed together in a baseball contest, but each salesperson could operate independently in a golf contest.

Travel Contests

Each year travel experience is becoming more rewarding to greater numbers of people. Travel is a mark of higher living standards and fits in nicely with a salesperson's success concept as well as pleases his family. It is easy to stimulate interest by showing progress on a map, and distance covered may be equally appealing to salespeople of all ages and income brackets.

Big Contests

These contests consist of a number of approaches designed to stimulate salespeople by a massive attack. For example, there can be "Giant Stampede," "Power Sales Quarter," "Rich Man's Harvest," "Annual Success Carnival," and many more titles which describe major efforts, large scale increases, and substantial rewards.

Political Contests

Political contests are effective when political campaigns are in newspaper headlines. Tying in a contest with political content is stimulating when both salespeople and customers are highly motivated by a real political battle. Beware of getting involved politically, however.

Secret Contest

A secret contest blends the unknown factors of a game into sales performance. There is an element of suspense when each period brings a reward based on a different set of factors which are not published in advance. The purpose is to have salespeople perform on all products, all customers, and all activities. The surprise element would be in those areas often neglected. It would be desirable to reward all salespeople according to overall performance, but in addition provide additional rewards for some type of effort each designated period. For example, extra rewards would be given for largest percent sales increase for any one customer, for selling the most new accounts, for the account that showed the greatest profit increase on sales, for use of promotional material, for calls on prospective customers, and for specific duties. If this is a monetary reward, it could be piggybacked on increased performance; that is, the size of this additional award would be determined by the salesperson's extra effort. Thus, if the salesperson earned an additional fifty dollars through increased effort during the contest period, the secret award would be fifty dollars.

Miscellaneous Contests

Many other kinds of contests can be used on specific occasions, such as gambling contests, fishing contests, and bridge contests. Sometimes it may be desirable to have a contest with greatest appeal to a segment of the sales force who previously have gone along with other contests that lacked appeal. Management cannot expect to have any contest that will give equal motivation to all the salespeople.

CONTEST PLANNING

Contests, like most other activities, require advance planning; but unlike other activities which may be repeated, each contest is a new experience and demands exacting attention. There is no reason for having a poor contest when careful advance planning can insure brilliant execution even though results might be less than expected. Management should not confuse the mechanics of handling a contest with decisions preceding it or results following. Hopefully, management has carefully weighed the merits of having a contest; if their thinking is correct and the contest is guided properly, the results should be gratifying.

Contest Theme and Occasion

The purpose for a contest must be determined first. Management could center a contest around the introduction of a new product, profitable item sale, gaining new customers, bringing back former customers, off-season sale, season windup, inventory cleanup, or bigger earnings splurge. It is essential to have purpose, occasion, and theme specified. For example, the purpose of a contest could be to pioneer a new product; the occasion, the twenty-fifth year celebration of the firm; and the theme, "Pioneer with Product X."

Contest Timing

The timing of a contest is critical. It may be dependent on what competition is doing; it may be controlled by product availability; it may depend on salespeople time; it may be affected by season, weather, condition of the market, or financing availability.

How long to run a contest is primary. If it is too short, it may never really become effective; if it is too long, it may taper off and lose force. It is not possible to keep salespeople enthused for a long period even though excitement remains high and results appear favorable. While it would be feasible to have a one-week contest for a small local producer with a restricted sales area, it would be difficult to implement such a contest nationally. Contests of one, two, or three months are acceptable in many cases. Longer or shorter ones may be practical under special conditions.

ADMINISTERING CONTESTS

There are numerous details that must be handled to insure a successful contest. To insure that each part of the contest is handled properly, it is wise to draw up a detailed outline giving a step-by-step approach.

Printed Material

In advance of the contest, all the necessary forms, signs, slogans, and other printed material should be prepared and delivered in sufficient quantity to the home office and to each additional location as required. Written instructions must be provided for the people conducting the contest; they must read and understand instructions. Since a certain amount of material must be prepared and printed or duplicated during the contest, facilities must be available for this work when time is at a premium. It is imperative to have all materials ready in proper locations and insure adequate supplies of the product for delivery to customers. A contest can fall flat after initial impact if product delivery is erratic.

Launching the Contest

To stimulate salespeople, a contest might require a spectacular introduction. Each salesperson should become involved immediately and feel that he is an important cog in a surge of sales. He should be motivated toward outstanding performance which will be rewarded financially. When introducing a contest, a salesperson may sign a pledge, wear a special badge or button, carry some unusual sign or briefcase, or have something conspicuous to wear, show, or say that will draw attention. A salesperson wants to show others, particularly customers, that he is proud to participate in a contest.

Developing Enthusiasm for the Contest

A successful contest is the product of enthusiastic salespeople who are stimulated to perform through superior motivation. Enthusiasm can be generated by effective, imaginative presentations. Hollow-sounding clichés are redundant and bounce off the salesperson because he recognizes there is no real depth or basic value involved. Therefore, the contest should have underlying factors that are worthwhile to the salesperson as well as advantageous to the company. No matter how flowery the selling approach is, the salesperson is able to analyze a contest that has weaknesses resulting from a lack of genuine, worthwhile objectives.

Maintaining Contact

A carefully developed program will maintain contact between headquarters and each salesperson. This program could consist of weekly letters, bulletins, telegrams, and flyers listing pertinent information on the contest's progress. Statistics of sales, individual salesperson standings, prizes awarded for top weekly production, and other fascinating data will keep interest on a high level. Besides regular communications, extra bulletins can give special news which is different from regular mailings. Surprises can be stimulating or amusing and may revive sagging interest.

Dynamic Follow-up

Contacts must be continuous, dynamic, and adjusted to fit current developments. Once a contest is started, it needs regular reinforcing and careful attention to avoid spotty results. Weak application must be reinforced with bursts of hard-hitting effort to revive interest. Attention to unusual problems in certain areas will prevent breakdowns and overcome poor performance. Ineffective response could be the result of inferior salesperson effort, but there might be particular handicaps that need special attention. For example, a contest for volume would have difficulty in an area where competitive price cutting is rampant.

In a large organization, district managers and supervisors can use meetings and individual contact to give fresh purpose to the contest by passing along the latest information from the top. If salespeople become discouraged, personal meetings will catch them early and rebuild morale by picturing goals, objectives, rewards, and personal distinction. Before a group meeting would conclude, salespeople would be revitalized by learning what some of their group had accomplished already and by hearing about outstanding successes in other areas.

Family Participation

The spouse and children are friendly contest allies. The salesperson knows his family expects greater performance than usual; when he comes home, he is questioned eagerly by them. They show an eager interest and may inspire him to greater performance in order to justify family faith.

The reward element is present to tempt the family. They can readily see how they can benefit from prizes earned by the salesperson. Thus, there are a variety of family pressures that make it highly desirable for the salesperson to do his best.

Contest Scoring

Contest scores can be based on a number of performance objectives. Points can be given for greatest increase in sales, increased sales of specific products, largest single order, biggest sale for a specific day, and biggest first order. Points are awarded for greatest number of sales in a day or week, for opening new accounts, for reactivating old accounts, and for other achievements. In some contests, only one or two scoring variations would be necessary; other contests might use more.

Scoring should proceed in steps measuring attainment of set goals. Such steps should not be too large or too difficult to achieve. It would be wasteful to set a first step that some salespeople could not attain. The first step should be easy so that the line or scale used to measure progress for each person leaves the zero point rapidly. In that way, everyone shows some progress and will avoid premature discouragement. Preferably, the measuring stick should be large or divided into many units. If each unit is small, results are shown in hundreds of units. It is far more comforting to the salesperson to see his performance halfway up a yardstick than halfway up a six-inch ruler. For example, if each salesperson was to receive an extra prize of a shade tree, all would be started with a seedling. Then each week would show a different sized tree based on points. At the beginning, each salesperson would be listed alphabetically, and each would have the same sized seedling. Each weekly listing thereafter would be on performance. Another way would be to prepare a number of blank charts, giving each salesperson listed alphabetically a horizontal space. After the first period, different sized trees would be filled in, giving the realistic appearance of a forest.

A variation in making scoring more realistic is to give each salesperson a token representing his points each week or period. These tokens, like money, could be used to purchase prizes. Many salespeople and their families would find tangible items, such as tokens, stamps, stars, or token money, realistic and motivating.

Point systems must be conceived so that each participant has a good chance to score well. It is probably impossible to set up a completely objective plan, but effort equalization is important. Thus, some people might have handicaps to hold them in line with others. Some scoring could be based on preset quotas, taking care to adjust points to comparable performance. A straight percentage increase might help the person with a $900 a week quota, but could be almost impossible for the person with a $2000 a week quota.

To heighten interest and maintain enthusiasm, there can be one set of points that cumulate over the entire contest; but each week can have a separate point series that can be used for intermediate awards. A long contest may lose much of its effectiveness unless significant outstanding examples maintain interest and give tangible recognition to short periods of performance which are cumulated at the end.

Contest Prizes

Money is always an acceptable prize, even though it may not be as colorful as other prizes. The value of prizes can be the prices that would be paid at retail. Since the company would pay less, this method would give bigger prizes than awarding money.

If a contest is scored properly, every salesperson is rewarded commensurate with his performance. It is unfair to have contests involving many people with just a handful of major prizes. This approach is discouraging to the many who succeed in a smaller way and get little or no recognition.

Many firms use prize catalogs showing articles that can be secured with different point values. Thus, a salesperson with few points has a number of articles from which he and his family can choose. The salesperson with many points can choose major items or a number of lesser articles. A large number of prize options is desirable for older salespeople, who already may have most of the articles listed.

Luxury prizes are often used to appeal to those who see opportunities they normally never have. Travel is a desirable prize option; cars, furs, and boats are tempting prizes. Prizes should not be given that may cause difficulty later. For example, a country club membership for a year would be inappropriate if the salesperson could not maintain it later.

Consolation prizes should be handled with great care to avoid ridicule. No one may admit it, but so-called booby prizes hurt the individual. Instead of prizes of this nature, it might be preferable to have a minimum prize which could be awarded on points issued on entering a contest. There is no such thing as no motivation, but salespeople have degrees of motivation from low to high. A salesperson is often judged hastily and branded lazy, useless, or indifferent before management really understands him. From his viewpoint, he behaves rationally and intelligently. He feels he is worthy of prizes reflecting performance on certain criteria he considers worthy, but perhaps not tangible.

Other Contest Considerations

Using contests successfully requires careful attention to conditions surrounding each situation. Are the sales ripe for a change that would lend itself to a contest? Will a contest be beneficial to the company? The salesperson? The customer? Is the contest of temporary value? Are there potential long-term accruing benefits? Is the contest a carefully planned sales aid, or is it a desperation move to revive sagging sales?

Is a contest the best way to achieve particular objectives, or does it seem expedient because no one comes up with a better approach? Can management run a contest with present personnel or must they hire many extra people? If the present home office staff is to handle contest details, will it interfere with regular assignments? What are sales plans after the contest, and how will management handle the transition period? Is the contest a one-shot approach, or will there be more contests if this one is successful? What are measuring sticks for success?

Some sales managers who use contests regularly should experiment with other sales devices; they may be so attached to contests that they have ignored other avenues. Firms that feel contests have no place in their sales operation might be surprised to find a contest is a refreshing change of approach that will appeal to salespeople. Special sales situations may call for a contest when normal conditions would not call for such action.

A poorly executed contest can be harmful and should be avoided if it cannot be carried out effectively. A firm anxious for a contest, but doubtful of its ability to handle it, can hire a firm that stages contests. There are such firms that handle many contests each year. They have wide experience in staging contests, know how to work out details completely, and may be surprisingly modest in their charges since most of their revenue comes from sales of prizes. Sales managers expecting to use contests should become familiar with literature [1] in the area as well as with the possibility of buying services of professional contest consultants.

AFTER THE CONTEST

A contest successfully executed requires extra salesperson effort and attention; in the aftermath, a letdown is inevitable. Some degree of decrease must be accepted, but the danger to avoid is letting sales go below levels preceding the contest. Firms try to overcome this letdown by immediately staging a shorter, perhaps smaller, contest or by introducing something else that will maintain a high interest level. Whatever the approach, the sales department should prepare for this letdown with strong, imaginative sales leadership to prevent a relapse to previous performance. A contest should have a successful immediate effect, and its lasting qualities should remain and become incorporated in future sales.

QUESTIONS AND PROBLEMS

1. How can a sales contest build salesperson morale? Is this the primary purpose of a contest? Explain.
2. Discuss several situations where the value of contests is doubtful.
3. Point out several circumstances where sales objectives can be aided by contests.
4. Contests can be used for a number of different groups besides the company sales forces. Discuss several situations where other groups may benefit from contests.

---

1. "Love Those Sales Contests," *Sales Management,* (February 5, 1973): 10. Many other articles on contests are available in various issues of *Sales Management* and other sales and promotion magazines. *Handbook for Conducting Successful Sales Contests,* published by Dartnell Corporation, Chicago, gives proven ideas and techniques for sales contests.

5. Why should there be several kinds of contests? Explain and illustrate several kinds, and indicate why particular contests vary in impact.

6. What is the importance of careful planning in the success of a contest? Point out several reasons for this important step.

7. Trace the important steps in planning and executing a contest.

8. Why are interim prizes helpful in promoting a contest? What is the motivation impact?

9. It is important that every participant receive some reward. Explain.

10. How can prizes be distributed equitably? Why is a handicap sometimes used? Who is challenged by one major prize?

11. Discuss the advantages of a variety of prizes. Which one prize is universally acceptable?

12. "Consolation prizes should be handled with great care." Explain.

13. Do some sales managers place too much reliance on contests? Explain and indicate alternatives to contests.

14. What is meant by "lasting effects" from a contest? Must one insist that only such effects justify a contest? Discuss.

---

case 9–1   **LEWIS FOOD WHOLESALER**

Monday afternoon, April 2, Mr. Lewis called his sales manager, Pamela Dahl, to his office. "Pam," he said, "our inventory of canned tuna and canned peaches is above normal. We've got to unload 2,000 cases of each fast."

After discussing several alternatives, Mr. Lewis and Pamela agreed to run a sales contest in May to reduce this inventory. They agreed to give $0.02 per can discount below regular price on all sales in full case lots, when each buyer bought equal numbers of cases of both tuna and peaches ($0.02 in wholesale grocery area is considerable).

Lewis Food Wholesaler, located in Funston, employed ten salespeople. They covered Funston, 200,000 population, plus surrounding suburbs and country towns in a fifty-mile radius. Yearly sales averaged around $5,000,000. About $4,000,000 was sold by the salespeople; the other $1,000,000 came from two chain store accounts handled by Pamela Dahl plus some direct buying by customers who came to the wholesale house. Salespeople called on numerous independent stores and supermarkets each week. Some larger accounts received two calls a week. The salespeople received a salary plus traveling expenses. In addition, each salesperson received a 1 percent commission on sales over monthly quota. Normally, this amounted to $50 to $300 a month per salesperson.

During the contest period, the salespeople will not receive additional compensation except that their regular commission will grow with increased sales. However, they are expected to respond to the company's challenge to move excess inventory. The firm operates as a closely knit group, and there is a good relationship between salespeople and sales manager.

You are asked by Pamela Dahl (you are her office administrative assistant) to develop this contest for the month of May. You have about four weeks to plan, get any printing done, and secure necessary supplies and equipment for this contest. She will work with you as much as possible.

There is to be one main prize of a hundred dollar bill at the end of the contest to be awarded at a dinner for the salespeople. Each week for four weeks there will be two $50 prizes—one awarded to the salesperson with the greatest volume and the other to the salesperson with the greatest increase in sales in percent over the same week last year. Only sales of canned tuna and peaches will be counted. No salesperson can win both prizes in any one week. In addition, there will be a surprise prize each week. At the dinner, each of the nine salespeople will be given a small transistor radio.

ASSIGNMENT

You are to develop this contest and list all details. Show each step and activity. You may use your discretion in buying the four weekly surprise prizes. They should not cost more than $10 each.

CAMPBELL MANUFACTURING COMPANY

case 9–2

The Campbell Manufacturing Company produces a line of thirty-six industrial products. It sells these products nationally through a sales force of 690 people. The sales organization consists of three districts which cover industrial customers in the eastern states, the western states, and the midwest states.

The eastern district sales manager, Phil Brevy, had worked for Campbell Manufacturing Company for five years and was fifty-five years old. He had previously been employed by a travel agency.

The western district sales manager, Joe Davis, is forty-three years old and had worked for Campbell Manufacturing Company his entire career. The midwest district sales manager, Fred Middleton, is thirty-nine years old and a brother-in-law of Dick Evans, the national sales manager for power tools.

The Campbell Manufacturing Company was planning the release of a new portable power tool to the commercial market. According to Dick, "We have developed a new finishing sander that is vastly superior to any other sander on the market, both from the standpoint of performance and of price." The salespeople would call on prime potential customers for the new product, such as woodworking shops, plastic laminate fabricators, and furniture makers.

Dick said, "Our success with this new product depends on our ability to capture a significant share of the market quickly. Our competitors are planning to release a similar product in only a few months. Our salespeople must act quickly and aggressively to contact the major potential customers and make sales before the competition can release and market their product. This means a quick, intensive sales effort that should be stimulated by a sales contest."

Campbell Manufacturing Company had not been too successful with sales contests, but Dick felt this was because they had been held only on the district level. In most of the previous contests, the rewards had been minor; and in several contests, considerable sales force resentment had resulted.

On January 15, Dick called a meeting of the district sales managers to discuss the release and promotion of the new sander. The major item of discussion during this meeting was his proposal for a sales contest.

The promotion plan which Dick had developed for the release of the new sander included national advertising in trade journals, a sales contest featuring significantly large prizes, and a formal presentation and recommendation to the salespeople.

The proposed sales contest would make every salesperson a winner. The major prizes would be mink stoles or large color television sets awarded to salespeople who met or surpassed their sales quotas for the new product. Salespeople who did not meet their quotas would receive smaller color television sets valued at $400.

The formal presentation planned is to be informal. After the salespeople are assembled, a model wearing one of the mink stoles walks into the room, interrupts the speaker, and says to the salespeople, "Wouldn't you like your wife to have one of these?" Then Dick outlines the details of the incentive program—everyone would be a winner, but the mink stole or large color television (sample displayed) would be awarded only to those who met or surpassed their sales quota. Next, the advantages of the sander are explained, and the salespeople are instructed how to sell with a planned approach. The salespeople are admonished not to use high pressure. After the presentation, the salespeople are to leave the sander with the prospect, who could try it himself. In seven days, the salespeople would return, hoping for an order for one or several sanders.

The sander sold for $150; 75,000 were scheduled for production during the first six months. Dick realized that this was an expensive sales contest, but felt that it was necessary to capture the major market share. The profit margin on the sander was higher than that on any of Campbell's other products. Also, the sander was to be sold at full price in contrast to many of the other product lines, which were discounted 10 to 20 percent.

The market for the new sander was expected to be 150,000 units in 1977. The market was expected to grow at 10 percent per year for the next twelve years. Dick felt that this sales contest would enable Campbell to capture 95 percent of the market. As competitors entered the market, their market share was expected to decline 7 percent each year until Campbell sold only 50 percent of the market. Campbell should be able to hold this share during the remaining years of the product's life cycle. Without a stimulating sales contest, Dick felt that Campbell could hope for only 50 percent of the 1977 market; this share was expected to decline to 25 percent within two years as competition increased.

Dick knew that the district sales managers would be careful not to adopt a sales contest which was not profitable. The expenses of this contest would come out of district budgets. Each district manager had final responsibility of the profitability of his district and the authority to veto any national sales contests in his district. However, if salespeople in one of the three districts were receiving major benefits from a national program, the district managers knew that they would have serious morale problems in their district if their salespeople did not receive similar incentives.

Knowing that the district sales managers were key people who must back the contest, Dick asked each of the district sales managers at the January 15 meeting what kind of sales contest he would like to see implemented. Each of the district managers had already seen Dick's proposal and a letter from Fred to Dick indicating support of the program.

Fred was the first to answer Dick. He indicated support for the program, but pointed out that he was concerned with the cost. Phil felt that the system of assigning quotas should be revised because it penalized the good salespeople. By revising the quota scheme, Phil felt that the number of people who would win mink stoles or large televisions could be reduced to 10 percent of the sales force. Phil also felt that the losers should not be awarded any prize. Also, Phil indicated he would like to see the salespeople's families involved in the contest. He suggested that each salesperson's family be kept advised by letter each month of how near he was to winning.

Joe took exception to Phil's suggestions and intimated that the resentment caused by previous sales contests resulted from the families being involved in the contests. "The salespeople don't like having their families know if they do not win the top prize," Joe said.

All the salespeople would benefit from increased commission on sales of the sander. Salespeople called on large accounts once a month and less often on smaller accounts. The seven-day follow up would be extra.

QUESTIONS

1. Is the cost of this contest excessive? Explain your answer by pointing out short-range and long-range goals.
2. Can a salesperson sell this additional number of units in addition to his regular load?
3. Is Phil's position on quota revision sound? Explain.
4. What is your view of Phil's suggestion that losers should not get any prize? They still would receive commission on the ones they sold.
5. What is your opinion of Joe's statement that families should not be told?
6. What suggestions do you have to improve the contest?
7. Do you think the contest should be used? Explain your position.

10

Compensating Salespeople

Compensation is a reward for performance. Presumably, it is given for a salesperson's individual effort in fulfilling requirements of the job. Properly administered compensation should be equally advantageous to both the firm and the salesperson for a long and successful relationship. It should work like a balance with reward on one side and effort on the other. In the initial stages, compensation balance swings in favor of the salesperson because his effort is an expense, rather than a contribution, to the firm. As the salesperson progresses, hopefully his contribution overbalances his reward; and the pendulum then swings to the company's advantage. After a period of this overswing, the salesperson's compensation is increased to balance his contribution. There will seldom be an even balance because sales and payments are changing. Thus, it becomes a seesaw situation, swinging from one side to the other. The situation is balanced with some degree of regularity by a variety of incentive payments; usually in money, but frequently supplemented by promotions, better territory, recognition at conventions, and other acts that signal approbation.

Compensation is a measurable amount sought and evaluated by the salesperson and his family, for this amount determines the family standard of living. It contributes to the happiness and welfare of the recipient and establishes him in society. It is a measure of progress revealed by a rising standard of living, by freedom from pressing monetary worries, and by acceptance in the community. In an economic sense, compensation measures a salesperson's worth to his employer.

MEASURING SALESPERSON CONTRIBUTION

A well-designed compensation plan should reflect how well the salesperson represents his employer's interests in a particular territory or under predetermined standards if territories are not used. In fairness, the sales assignment should include conditions that reflect production under varying degrees of difficulty. For example, two territories with the same sales potential might have quite different company expectations because of peculiar conditions or underlying causes which make equal sales improbable.

Measurement Criteria

It is useless to make sweeping recommendations for measuring devices or standards unless such standards are meaningful. While sales volume is often used to gauge compensation, it can lead to misplaced rewards because dollar volume gave little profit. On the other hand, when a firm is burdened with excess inventory, sales volume alone may be of greatest importance regardless of profit. What may be desirable for a firm under particular circumstances might prove detrimental if allowed to continue. Therefore, an element of flexibility is needed which precludes rigid measuring devices.

Management may seek to maximize a firm's income immediately, or it may wish to develop a solid base of sales before striving for greater profit. Each of these factors may dictate kinds of measurement or may modify existing measurement to reflect current thinking. A firm may wish to create an image among customers and therefore strive to build up quality, dependability, or other factors in an attempt to soft-pedal higher prices or lack of flexibility.

In the industrial field, a company may wish to create an atmosphere of customer product satisfaction even though delivery may be delayed; or a company can build a reputation for promptness even though the product occasionally lacks quality. In the first instance, salesperson concern for the customer and his problems might be a measuring stick; in the latter case, selling followed by minimum delivery time might be most important. Sometimes immediate delivery of a product giving less satisfaction is more important than delayed delivery in order to come up with a superior product.

The position of a firm within an industry may influence measuring criteria, for seldom is there just one policy, one price, or one quality that satisfies all demands. One firm's use of a particular method of sales compensation does not dictate that another firm in the same industry should use an identical system, although the second firm may use the first firm's compensation system as a base for its own plan. On the other hand, two firms may have almost identical sales objectives, but achieve those objectives by using different compensation approaches or even different sales approaches. For example, in the pharmaceutical industry one firm distributes largely through its own sales force while another relies on wholesalers.

Over a period of time, a firm's objectives may change so that emphasis must be redistributed. This new pattern may necessitate new approaches to sales compensation so that equity remains among salespeople and effort is focused as new policies dictate.

Specific Criteria Measurements

If a company is emphasizing growth, management may use new accounts as criteria. If it stresses customer welfare, the criteria may include meeting a customer's complete needs, including selling a wide spectrum of merchandise. If profit maximization is an immediate goal, management may stress large sales of high profit items. If volume is paramount, sales may be measured by how well a salesperson establishes himself with a few large accounts. If territory maintenance is stressed, the number of calls may be significant. If point-of-purchase advertising is important, the number of displays installed may be a good measure. If a missing part may tie up factory production, speed in contacting a customer and handling his problem might govern.

OBJECTIVES OF A SALES COMPENSATION PLAN

The purpose of sales compensation is to remunerate salespeople, hopefully meeting both the objectives of the salesperson and the firm, but primarily making compensation adequate, meaningful, and important. It must be adequate to meet the desires of superior salespeople lest they be tempted to leave; retention usually is less expensive than recruiting and training replacements.

A satisfactory compensation plan may be directed toward maintaining a strong, pleased customer following. Management should usually guard against a plan that puts a premium on immediate results but sacrifices customer interests. A firm that depends on new customers may use a different compensation plan from one that depends on repeat sales to old customers.

A well-conceived compensation plan aids in directing salespeople activities towards objectives most advantageous to the firm. It is unlikely that any one plan will be most beneficial to the firm and equally satisfactory to the salespeople. A plan of this nature may pay well but require extreme effort which would displease the sales force. Management should not expect a pay system to solve many sales problems, but rather to aid in solving some.

The compensation plan cannot be too expensive or so poor that it does not attract desirable sales applicants. A firm must have some idea of what percentage of sales it can assign to sales costs. It would be easy to design a compensation plan that would please the sales staff but would become catastrophic to the firm.

Competition and the economic system tend to adjust costs of production to the lower point of price versus quality. Thus, the firm tries

to settle for salespeople cost that provides satisfactory sales representatives. If a firm sets compensation too high, it attracts excellent
personnel, but excess costs soon force them out of the market. If
remuneration is too low, sales suffer through poor quality salespeople.
A weak salesperson is too expensive if he cannot perform, and a strong
salesperson may be too expensive if someone less expensive can do
the job adequately.

CHARACTERISTICS OF A SALES COMPENSATION PLAN

Salespeople are suspicious of a complex compensation plan. If they
cannot calculate their earnings or if it is difficult to figure earnings,
they tend to view a compensation plan with disfavor. Therefore, a
simple plan is more desirable as long as it is adequate. It would be
unwise to stress simplicity at the expense of soundness and workability
because the plan must fulfill its purpose even though it sacrifices other
conditions.

Salespeople appreciate fairness. Compensation should be predicated on salesperson contribution; if his duties are spelled out clearly,
he can tell whether his performance warrants a certain paycheck. If
he feels he is being defrauded or shortchanged, he becomes unhappy.
What may seem eminently fair to management in planning may seem
quite unfair to the salespeople in the field. He should believe he is
being paid enough and that his pay is proportionate to his contribution
as compared to other salespeople. While part of a salesperson's salary
may be based on subjective factors, the more objective the plan the
better the salesperson can evaluate it.

A compensation plan should be flexible enough to meet varying
conditions, territory variations, salesperson ability and maturity, and
changes resulting from minor policy revamping.

When management studies the many variables involved in selling in
unlike territories, it is evident that numerous variations will arise which
can be handled through the compensation plan. Such variations include product changes, price changes, special sales, inventory adjustments, return privileges, and others dictated by environmental
changes and on-the-spot decisions. Latitude in interpretation may introduce elements which are unfair at times, but such minor frustrations
are less harmful than introducing new features into the plan. There
must be room for some judgment decisions to modify temporary or
unusual situations.

Selective incentive features impart a challenge to enterprising salespeople and enable them to increase earnings by a more intelligent approach to the selling job.

A relatively simple compensation plan is a low cost plan that is
easy to administer and understand. Particularly difficult to administer

are those features contingent on some other factors. How are returned sales handled? Who pays for bad debts? How long should a salesperson wait for commission? How are split commissions handled? The use of modern office equipment can expedite administration of difficult problems, but it may confuse the salesperson, who never knows how to interpret the different decisions.

Salespeople, like most other employees, need uniform earnings which are paid regularly. At least the major portion of their income should be paid promptly and regularly.

Any compensation plan is better if it includes elements that promote harmony, build enthusiasm, encourage greater effort, and develop loyalty. A plan should be tied to regular, definite increases based on measurable criteria. When extra sales materialize and a territory becomes more profitable through sales efforts, the salesperson should be rewarded on the basis of his performance and not deprived by some management decision to divert extra income elsewhere. Periodic compensation review should be an integral part of a satisfactory plan, and intervals should be close enough so that unusually fine performance in the beginning of a period is not forgotten by the reviewer when he is appraising performance at a later time.

TYPES OF COMPENSATION PLANS

Compensation plans can be divided into two types—straight salary and straight commission. Many compensation plans combine elements of both, and a bonus arrangement is sometimes introduced as further modification.

Commission arrangements are called *incentive payments,* which might lead to the erroneous conclusion that a straight salary is not an incentive. The fact is that many salaries are sufficiently attractive to attract people who give their best merely to retain the salary. However, giving a smaller fixed payment plus incentive payments has proved successful in stimulating salespeople to greater productivity. Some salespeople seem to respond better to an inviting compensation plan in which extra effort can bring success. They seem to respond better to a reward predicated on special effort than to earn that reward when it is already assured through a generous salary arrangement.

Whatever plan a sales manager may use, it should prove effective, and should stimulate salespeople to greater performance at a reasonable cost. While the sales manager may not be rigidly restricted in amount, he has rather firm guidelines on how much he can spend. He must develop his plans within an allocated expenditure framework—a budget.

Straight Salary Plan

The *straight salary plan* compensates salespeople, like most other white-collar workers, by an exact amount paid at regular intervals. This plan is usually supplemented by expense payments.

The salary plan is widely used simply because it seems the easiest to administer and to compensate salespeople fairly. Differences in performance can be adjusted by regular and special salary increases. These increases may not be sensitive to many small changes, but they tend to aggregate a series of small performances which together justify an increase.

A salary plan seems to be preferable when jobs have numerous variations that are difficult to evaluate. It is suitable for beginning sales-people, who must support themselves and their families although their contribution is negligible.

When there are wide sales fluctuations, justice may dictate a level salary income. For example, the author had a student who made one sale of large machinery early in the year, but then was unable to close another sale for three months. A series of lost sales was discouraging enough; but if that salesman had been plagued by income uncertainty during that period, his performance might have been seriously impaired.

Advantages of the salary plan

The salary plan gives a uniform, regular income that enables the sales-person to plan his life and relieves him of fluctuating money worries. It gives the company greater freedom to insist that a salesperson perform certain field duties which may seem unremunerative and perhaps less rewarding in sales and prestige. The salesperson can be assigned unpleasant tasks and temporarily may be asked to do certain jobs which would be unreasonable to ask of a commission person.

Under the salary plan, the salesperson is less likely to push aggressively and overload a customer. He is able to view the customer's and firm's interests objectively without associating them with his immediate welfare. The salesperson can be content to build for the future, rather than concentrating on immediate returns.

The salary plan appears to be the only logical way to pay people starting an extended training period. During this time, their activities are expensive to the company and contribute little or nothing to sales. As they become full-fledged salespeople, a different compensation plan can be introduced.

There are some types of selling that do not lend themselves to anything but a salary plan—sales are erratic or far between; the measures of sales performance are not accurate; the job is irregular and each sale is different; sales may be seasonal but require service the year around; sales may be wholly indirect through wholesalers.

For example, a pharmaceutical representative calling on physicians does not expect to make a sale directly, but hopes that the physician will specify his products when writing prescriptions.

Weaknesses of the salary plan

The salary plan can be excessively expensive if sales are not proportional to cost of selling. Sales may fluctuate, but costs remain constant; in periods of declining sales, costs may absorb all profit. The salary plan is rigid and may reward excessively in one period but be wholly inadequate in another.

Income inequities and salespeople differences can be handled by selective salary increases, but such action may be difficult to define and even harder to justify in the eyes of those not receiving increases. Each salesperson feels that he has raised his contribution in sales, service, expense reduction, or new accounts; if his particular type of performance merits no increase in the eyes of management, he becomes bitter. Who can say if one person increases sales while another maintains his volume that the first person merely continues to skim in an expansion territory?

Salary can lead to complacency; and a well-established firm using salary for years may base increases on longevity, friendship, and other factors not really pertinent to current production. Many salespeople feel frustrated under such restrictions and become impatient. An aggressive man is unwilling to bide his time and seeks a job with a different firm. Soon the firm is saddled with a group of plodders lacking resilience and spark.

A salary plan may appear to give sales control, but there is no assurance that it will. Unless the sales manager maintains careful supervision and follows up in the field to insure compliance with orders, salespeople may handle assignments carelessly and report efforts in glowing terms which do not describe actual performance.

Small, regular salary increases become expected and do not stimulate, but missing even one such salary increase is discouraging. Salary may be appealing to management and top-level salespeople because increments are sizeable. Thus, a one hundred dollar a month raise may appear quite fitting to the sales manager, but the person on the lower rung of the ladder is no longer content with small, regular step increases. The stepladder approach is harder to justify when each step is unequally spaced in quantity and steps are arranged differently for each individual. Such a precarious approach discourages salespeople, who choose other firms where compensation is more to their liking.

Commission Plan

The *commission plan* of payment is remuneration based on specific performance, usually sales. It is tied directly to performance and closely associated to productivity. For competent salespeople, commission is the most satisfactory method of payment because it recognizes and pays openly what other plans do in disguised form. Selling costs are calculated as a percentage of sales; and in working out a compensation system, it is necessary to develop it so that a portion of the sales dollar is represented. The commission person earns his money from visible sales performance.

Advantages of commission plan

Under the commission plan, the salesperson knows how much he is earning at all times. He sees the reward for extra performance and may be challenged to intensify his effort. Salespeople appreciate immediate rewards, and only a few are willing or financially able to work for a year or more at a low income in order to build a territory. They have also seen occasions when a salesperson goes through a trying period building a territory only to be transferred or discharged after he has built up a good sales record.

The firm knows its sales cost in advance, which aids in budgeting. If sales are small, commissions are small; if sales are large, commissions merely reflect higher sales. One of the real problems of any firm is to have an element of cost of operation that stays relatively stable whether sales increase or decrease. Many firms have failed because they could not reduce costs as rapidly as sales decreased. Hence, management may become desperate when facing a rigid salary cost schedule with decreasing sales, but will not be disturbed by increased total costs against a rising sales curve.

Since a salesperson is directly responsible for his income, he is likely to work harder and do a more extensive selling job. Since he feels this responsibility, he may be easier to supervise and in many instances thrive under mimimum supervision.

The commission plan works well in house-to-house selling. In some instances, the down payment is the salesperson's commission. This method eliminates office work and simplifies records. A salesperson who works part-time and a salesperson who represents a number of firms prefer a commission plan. Commission payment is universal for compensating manufacturers' agents.

Commission compensation is useful when representation is intermittent and/or irregular. Thus, a broker selling canned fruits and vegetables may work for a firm three months. He may represent a farmer once or twice in a season, and he may be called on by chain stores on an occasional basis. A job of short duration lends itself to commission. Whether selling novelties at a football game, Christmas greeting cards, or a once-over coverage of a territory lasting a few months, it is undesirable to establish a permanent relationship entailing permanent records.

Weaknesses of the commission plan

Often, commission plans are associated with weak control which may lead to serious abuses. The firm which expects to make a single sale tends to overlook some abuses.

Salespeople may take a short view of the situation and try to maximize income immediately. In the process, salespeople may oversell a retailer, fail to give service to an industrial buyer, force inferior products on a homemaker, neglect service calls, and omit activities which develop loyal customers and contented users.

Beginning salespeople are unlikely to be top producers and require a period of adjustment and development. During this time, commissions are inadequate to meet daily necessities. Therefore, people who might, with experience, become excellent salespeople are eliminated since they cannot afford to continue.

Most salespeople are happy with commission payments as long as the payments remain adequate or are increasing, but become disillusioned when economic recession cuts their sales. When the going gets rough, commissions drop severely, and soon even the better salespeople will look for more favorable jobs.

The commission plan is sometimes used to exploit salespeople, their families, and friends through enticing naive individuals to sell a product with limited applications and a restricted market.

There is also the problem of windfall commission, which a firm is reluctant to pay. A person who is willing to exist on lean commissions should not be restricted when fat commissions are received. Yet this situation has limitations which affect the salesperson. The author knows of one occasion when a government sale during World War II would have given the salesman a commission equal to his previous five years' earnings. The employer refused to pay this amount since the salesman did literally nothing to earn the commission and in renegotiation the government would have disallowed the payment.

Combination Compensation Plans

In *combination compensation plans,* part of the compensation is fixed and paid at regular intervals. The remainder varies with salespeople productivity when giving commission and with overall company profit when paying bonus or profit sharing.

The purpose of a combination plan is to tie the salesperson closer to his performance in a way he feels is equitable and challenging. It gives him immediate incentive to perform, and he can see results quickly. Salespeople appreciate rewards quickly rather than building up credit for the future. As long as compensation is a motivating tool, management should use it to maximize the firm's interests.

Among the great variety of combination plans available are specific ones that may meet the needs of each firm. When one plan is unsatisfactory, another plan somewhat modified may excite the salespeople. The flexibility of combination plans make them readily adaptable to a variety of needs.

Guidelines for establishing combination plans

Combination compensation plans are designed to overcome weaknesses of the straight salary plan and the straight commission plan. The former plan tends to give compensation rigidity, and the latter plan gives too much variation.

How to adjust compensation to secure maximum results can be studied from various viewpoints. If the salary is large and commissions are small, the incentive value may lose force; if the salary is small and commissions large, the salesperson may overload customers or make sales that will increase his commission but harm his firm, his customer, or both.

To have the benefits of salary and commission, it is preferable to set a salary which is substantial and leave room for an exciting commission contribution. For example, if a salesperson is averaging about $150 a week income, a salary of $100 a week might be adequate. If a salesperson averages $300 a week, a salary ranging from $150 to $200 a week could be suitable. If a salesperson averages $100 a week, a $75 weekly salary would be a minimum.

If sales are regular and commission contribution is fairly uniform and dependable, a lower salary would be acceptable. If management wanted to employ a top salesperson on a job where commissions fluctuated greatly from year to year, a substantial salary might be required. Thus, to secure a good salesperson on a job where income fluctuated from $10,000 to $25,000 a year on a commission basis but averaged $20,000 a year, it might be necessary to guarantee a minimum salary of $15,000 a year.

Types of Combination Plans

There are many types of combination plans that may be used to meet a company's needs.

Salary plus straight commission

Straight commission gives a definite amount of commission for each eligible dollar of sales. The salary is fixed; and the commission may be given for every sale, for sales over a certain quota, or almost any starting point. The amount can be based on weekly, monthly, or quarterly sales. Longer than a quarter may be acceptable in particular circumstances. If the commission is level, there is no particular reason for the salespeople to hold back or push forward sales to pyramid commissions. Usually it is important to pay the salesperson his commission earnings within a reasonable time—every month or quarter.

Salary plus variable commission

A variable commission arrangement may be worked out in a number of ways:

1. A firm may divide its products into a number of categories or groupings and pay straight commission at a different percentage on each category. For example, a drug salesperson would get a higher commission rate on pharmaceuticals than on sundries.

2. A firm may have a series of steps whereby commissions increase as sales increase within each designated period. For example, commission would be 2 percent within one bracket of sales. Commission would be 3 percent when sales cross into a higher bracket. Sometimes this higher percent may be paid only on the sales in the higher bracket; sometimes it may be retroactive to the lower bracket as well, which provides a tremendous stimulus to the salesperson. This stepped-up method is often used when the total compensation is in commissions. For example, a house-to-house salesperson may receive one rate of commission if he sells one vacuum cleaner a week. If he sells a second one, his rate of commission goes up for both sales. If he sells a third one, his rate goes still higher. This method tends to eliminate the poor salesperson, since only the ones who sell several a week can afford to continue.

3. Some companies may use a decreasing commission schedule. Up to a certain point, the salesperson will be paid his regular commission. Beyond that, his commission in one particular category will decline in percentage. It would be possible for a manufacturing firm to have level commission in one category, increasing percent commission in a second category, and decreasing percent commission in a third category. This method could prevent overselling one category and underselling another. In a manufacturing or processing operation, certain products come out in fixed relationships; and each product must be sold, although some of the products are much easier to sell than others. For example, in a packing plant operation, all portions of the animal must be sold; and in a petroleum refining plant, a number of products are obtained and must be sold in some sort of ratio. If one product is more difficult to sell than another, the tendency is to concentrate on the one easier to sell.

4. Companies may base commissions on percentage of quota performance. Commission may be based on every dollar of sales, using a small percent up to quota and then increasing the percent significantly. Commission may start when the

salesperson has achieved 50 to 75 percent of quota and increase in definite intervals. For example, 50 percent of quota may give 1 percent commission on all sales from 50 to 75 percent of quota, 2 percent on all sales from 75 to 90 percent of quota, 3 percent on all sales from 90 up to and including 100 percent of quota, and 4 percent on all sales over quota. Quota as a basis for compensation can be unfair if quotas are improperly established. Often quotas are determined in a haphazard, capricious, or unscientific way.

Guaranteed draw plus commission

A firm that gives a guaranteed draw is in essence paying a salary, since the salesperson receives a fixed amount regularly. When this amount is charged against commission, it is paid even though commissions are below the amount. In case a salesperson leaves the firm, any drawings exceeding commissions are a cost to the firm. Actually, any kind of a drawing account resembles a salary because it is impractical to recover from a person who no longer works for the firm.

When a salesperson earns adequate commission but sales are uneven, the drawing account furnishes a convenient way to level out earnings to provide for current expenses. While a guaranteed draw has the earmarks of salary, it may appear different to the salesperson, who enjoys the freedom and flexibility of commission and considers the draw merely a convenient payment method. It gives stability; and when his draw exceeds his commission, he considers it a temporary situation used to balance out those periods when he is paid for commissions he has earned.

Draw plus commission on profit

When each sale of a similar item may vary in profitability, commission may be calculated on the profit. For example, a car salesman is given a percentage of the profit from each car sold. His share is then determined by his ability to bargain with a buyer.

A similar situation arises when a firm submits a quotation on merchandise or on an installation of equipment. When competition is keen, the salesperson's percent commission is adjusted to share in major price concessions.

Salary Plus Bonus

A bonus is something added to salary. When it becomes a regular payment, salespeople tend to regard it as part of their earnings and are disappointed if it is not paid.

If a bonus is incorporated in the sales plan, it is a reward for performance and becomes attached to sales compensation. As such, it is paid to each person according to his contribution. If, however, these earnings vary depending on the profitability of the firm, the bonus takes on elements of profit sharing and blends individual sales performance into the firm's overall success.

One weakness of a bonus is that it may become a substantial part of a salesperson's income over several profitable years. If a lean year comes along and no bonus is paid, the salesperson may seriously suffer. While it is common to tie executive income to company earnings, it is less prudent to apportion salespeople's income in the same way. Executives guiding the firm have decision-making responsibilities which influence earnings, but an individual salesperson merely controls his own territory. Most, if not all, of his income should be tied up with the contribution he makes from his territory.

Smaller bonuses are often given, such as Christmas gifts. Such added compensation is usually given to all employees and would hardly be considered a bonus.

When a bonus is tied with compensation, it may become almost like commission to the salesperson. One major difference is that commission is fixed to percentage; but a bonus may be paid regularly or somewhat haphazardly depending on profits, the economy, and the particular thinking of executives that year. If a bonus of major proportions is paid equally to all salespeople, the more successful ones may grumble because their greater contribution is not recognized individually. A good salesperson dislikes being teamed with what he considers weaker people to build a group bonus. When sales teamwork is essential, salespeople should be tied together in such a way that each will feel he is fairly compensated.

Profit Sharing

Profit sharing is not common in sales compensation because so many conditions beyond salespeople's control affect profits. The salesperson doing a tremendous job is disappointed when he sees the fruits of his efforts dissipated by mismanagement or when he sees some greedy executives charge dubious expenses to the firm. Profit sharing might be considered when there are only one or two salespeople who have certain decision-making functions. Although not executives, they are strong enough to influence executives.

Point System in Compensation

The point system is a device for awarding points for particular salesperson performance. Management may feel that each salesperson should do a variety of tasks, some of which he may dislike or neglect. Points are a method to force a salesperson to work for new accounts, service accounts, set up displays, collect bad debts, push particular products, and many other tasks. The idea is to direct the salesperson at any particular time to those activities management considers important.

When compensation includes fixed and variable elements, points can be used in determining the variable part. When salary is used alone, such points may be considered when giving salary increases —in a sense, a merit award.

Management should exercise care in developing a point system compensation plan. Although it has many inviting aspects, it is a difficult plan to establish and administer. In time, it may be necessary to change and adjust points to meet differing sales thrusts. Management may find great difficulty in keeping point distribution equitable, and salespeople may become confused. As a result, salespeople may never completely understand where they are in terms of performance and how much money they will get.[1]

DEVELOPING A SALES COMPENSATION PLAN

In the development stage of a compensation plan, management must attach great importance to basic considerations.

What are the precise objectives of the plan besides paying the sales force? A brilliantly executed plan may incorporate many useful features which may not be recognized as such by the sales force, but will guide their activities to maximize company progress. Objectives may include building a happy customer following, breaking down company barriers, increasing company social visibility in its community, enhancing profitable operation, perpetuating growth, building up a quality image, developing customer reliance on company service, and developing greater buyer dependence.

The sales manager can make an exact assessment of the salesperson's job, determine the caliber of individual needed, and search for such employees. If the present group does not fit this category, judicious hiring and replacement will soon convert the sales force to the desired image; or a new sales force can be hired to reflect the image.

Having determined the caliber of sales force, the sales manager can plan a compensation level that is competitive with other firms and attractive to sales personnel. He need not operate blindly because current literature is available to advise him what is acceptable for this type of sales work. He cannot have satisfactory salespeople if he pays less than the going rate; to pay more is an extravagance his company cannot afford.

If a firm is revising its compensation plan, considerable preplanning

---

1. David A. Weeks, *Compensating Salesmen and Sales Managers,* The Conference Board, Report No. 579 (New York).

including consultation with the sales force is justified. If the present plan is not suitable, care must be exercised before plunging into a new plan which still lacks important features, safeguards, and salesperson appeals.

IMPLEMENTING A SALES COMPENSATION PLAN

Salespeople often are confused by the compensation plan because there are variable elements and some features subject to judgment determination. Frequent changes and adjustments add additional interpretation problems and upset salespeople, who like to know exactly what they will receive.

A compensation plan should be worked out carefully before implementation. Before revising a plan, management should get suggestions from salespeople. Whether or not suggestions are requested before any plan is developed, certainly suggestions should be invited after the plan is drafted. To ask for suggestions before a plan is presented will result in a few suggestions; but once a plan is drafted and given to salespeople to criticize, they are in a position to make positive suggestions for revisions and additions.

By presenting a tentative plan to salespeople and executives, management benefits from their suggestions and criticisms. Many ideas submitted may have little merit, but a few suggestions may expose weaknesses in the first plan. This procedure gives a number of interested people a part in the plan preparation and furnishes guidelines to those developing the final plan.

Management should present the final plan to salespeople for discussion and questions before implementing it. At least the salespeople then know what to expect. If the plan is explained so that the salesperson feels he must work harder but get an increased income, he will accept it.

Occasionally, a company may start with a plan that pays too much in relation to salespeople's contributions. The plan must be adjusted downward to meet going rates in comparable jobs in other firms. After the price adjustment, salespeople will still be paid as well as or better than other salespeople performing similar jobs.

Once a plan is implemented, it is good to indicate that further revision may be necessary. This procedure will tell the salespeople that the door is not closed to some changes, upward or downward. If glaring inequities appear rapidly, it may be necessary to change to prevent severe suffering; if compensation is too large, it may be condoned for a while. Sometimes these variations will correct themselves through quota adjustment or particular area conditions. For example, if a major customer moves from one territory to another, the salesperson losing him will not make quota; but the salesperson gaining him makes quota with ease and goes far beyond. In this case, the salesperson losing potential in his territory may have to receive extra compensation until he can build up his territory or until new industry moves in. The salesperson who receives the extra business may be reluctant to have any adjustment until the year's end, so he might temporarily earn quite a large income.

Rapid compensation changes are upsetting; and if some people suffer severely, morale may be lowered and excellent salespeople will quit. Unless serious difficulties occur, it is desirable to make changes cautiously because initial weaknesses may tend to be self-correcting as the salespeople adjust their operations. Some inequities may arise because of changes within a territory which cannot be anticipated. A compensation plan based on incentives might be adjusted within a year or less by territory reevaluation and quota adjustment.

COMPENSATION PROBLEMS

Whenever there are compensation variables attached to performance, a number of problems may arise. Sometimes these problems have not been anticipated and disagreement arises; sometimes there are variables which are not covered by company rules. Many disagreements can be avoided by clearly setting forth conditions governing unusual situations.

Split Commission

A *split commission* occurs when more than one salesperson is involved in a sale. One salesperson makes a sale in his territory, but delivery is made in another salesperson's territory. One salesperson makes a sale, part of which is delivered in his territory and part in another territory. One salesperson does most of the work for a major purchase in his territory, but the final closing is made in the home office in another territory. The sales manager from the home office comes into a territory and helps close a major sale by making a concession the local salesperson cannot make.

How to split commissions may vary with each firm and each situation. Presumably, the person contributing the most to the sale should receive the major portion of commission. It is important to anticipate these situations and predetermine guidelines to eliminate dissension and misunderstanding.

Job Quotations

Many products do not have firm prices; but are quoted on the basis of current need for business, competition, difficulty of installation, season of the year, production runs, need to shave prices, or substitution of materials. Each job may have peculiarities that justify a different price. Frequently, the size of an order may determine how much to shave a quotation. On a $1,000,000 order where a firm normally grosses $200,000, conditions may dictate shaving $100,000 off the price in order to get the business. Otherwise, the plant might have to close for a period.

In small everyday sales, price-cutting situations develop. For example, the author's student selling siding for homes was given a list price and a minimum price. His commission depended on the amount he could get between the maximum and the minimum. Car salesmen are often compensated on a sliding scale determined by each sale's profitability.

Telephone and Mail Sales

It is common to get sales from territories by mail and by telephone; these sales are not directly connected with a salesperson's efforts. Sometimes these orders are solicited by mail, and often special telephone operators call for orders. At times, orders come in unsolicited. Frequently, commissions vary depending on how the order is secured, profitability of order, and other variables. Some of these orders yield little in profit because of competition; others may be extremely profitable when sold at list prices. Often, complex commission arrangements are devised to handle these special situations.

Overlapping Territory

Occasionally, territories overlap or are not clearly defined. This situation is not to be confused with that of salespeople who may sell in any territory or that of territories not specifically designated. If one salesperson is permitted to sell in another territory, does he have to share commission? Is territory jumping permissible? Is it encouraged? Discouraged? Problems in clearly defining territory may arise when trading areas spill over county lines. (A trading area includes the territory which feeds a particular shopping area, city, or metropolitan area. Political boundaries frequently cut through shopping boundaries.)

House Account Sales

House accounts are particular accounts in a sales territory that are reserved by the sales manager and handled directly from his office. Often these are large, lucrative accounts deliberately withheld from the salesperson because he could not handle them adequately or would not have the privilege of bargaining which the sales manager has. In some instances they furnish volume that would make the salesperson's earnings excessive. If a salesperson is expected to do some servicing of a house account, will he receive any extra compensation? May a sales manager seize large accounts and convert them to house accounts against a salesperson's will? These and many other perplexing questions often make careless use of the house account privilege a point of disagreement.

Windfall Sales

Special circumstances sometimes permit a salesperson to make extraordinary commissions. To what extent are such windfall sales allowable? In one instance, a salesperson who was expected to sell one or two office machines on a satisfactory commission base closed an order for 200.

To avoid runaway situations, a ceiling can be set on earnings. For example, a salesperson may not be paid more than double his previous year's earnings in a windfall situation; or his earnings may not be more than 100 percent higher than the earnings of the highest paid salesperson. Another method of limiting earnings is to reduce commission rates when earnings reach a certain figure. Finally, a salesperson may be allowed all the earnings even though they are excessive. These situations are rare and do not cause major problems.

Trade-in Sales

Trade-in sales can be vexing because it is often difficult to determine profitability. Sometimes time must elapse before a situation is cleared up. Often, arbitrary decisions are made to calculate profit. In a large transaction, the actual amount of money between the purchase and the trade-in may be small; in rare instances, the trade-in costs more than the purchase. Then, it may be necessary to wait until the trade-in is sold before any commission is awarded. Often a trade-in is merely a disguised discount necessary to get the order. In many cases, commission must be based on subjective judgment open to disagreement. Salespeople may bargain successfully at times to increase their commission on particular sales. The sales executive must weigh the profit situation and the necessity for retaining a salesperson. The market situation for employing salespeople may be a factor in deciding whether to be generous or stringent.

Sales Returns and Allowances

There can be a variety of reasons for sales returns, many of which may be entirely outside the salesperson's control. A sales return is costly to the firm because of additional expenses in handling, refurbishing the merchandise, or even destroying it. Most firms have policies governing these situations predicated on the seriousness and costs involved. If these returns are few and minor, the firm absorbs the loss; if they are large and frequent, it becomes part of the selling agreement that salespeople forego commission while the firm absorbs other losses incident to returns.

A buyer may be dissatisfied and want to return merchandise. Whether the buyer or seller is at fault may not be a determining factor. Even though the buyer is at fault, he is unhappy; and the salesperson must placate him with a positive gesture. Since it may be inconvenient for the buyer and undesirable from the salesperson's standpoint to return merchandise, they often compromise; the buyer keeps the merchandise, and the salesperson makes a price concession. Neither is too happy about the adjustment, but it seems to be the wisest solution. The seller in this adjustment foregoes any profit but minimizes losses. The salesperson's commission may be paid in full, but more likely he will get a reduced commission or none at all.

Bad Debts

A number of sales go sour because the customer will not pay, may be unable to pay, or goes bankrupt. Since most business is transacted on credit, it is inevitable that credit losses will occur; when no credit losses occur, it is likely the firm is losing sales through too strict a credit policy.

If a firm has a credit department that approves all sales, it is unfair to penalize a salesperson for bad debts. He may have already been penalized by the credit department which has rejected some of his sales, some of which probably would have been paid satisfactorily. Guidelines can be set which will govern most bad debt situations, and the exceptions can be negotiated. Unless violations are frequent and large, it may be advisable for the firm to cover bad debt losses.

Supervising Junior Salespeople

Some senior salespeople can bring junior salespeople into their territories and give them training and experience without hindering selling activities; others find junior salespeople a burden. Some senior salespeople find junior salespeople so helpful that they may share commissions. Others feel they are doing their duty if they let the junior salesperson into their territories and expect the firm to pay. A few senior salespeople may find a junior salesperson a hindrance and only allow him in because the firm insists. It is unlikely a firm will pay a senior salesperson additional compensation for training a junior salesperson; but selling supervisors and selected senior salespeople may have as their regular assignment the training of new salespeople, and their own commissions and income may be adjusted to cover this work.

QUESTIONS AND PROBLEMS

1. What are the purposes of a well-designed compensation plan?
2. In preparing a compensation plan, there are a number of criteria to

consider. Discuss several of these criteria, indicating why each may be important.

3. How can a properly designed compensation plan affect salespeople? customers? the employer?

4. A workable compensation plan should contain a number of features in order to represent several interests. Discuss several of these features, pointing out how each may add to the plan's effectiveness.

5. What are the merits of a straight salary compensation plan, and what are possible weaknesses which may appear?

6. What are the advantages and disadvantages of a straight commission compensation plan?

7. Sometimes sales managers state they must have some form of commission to insure salesperson incentive. Is this statement true? How can it be modified?

8. Why is a combination of salary and commission considered a compromise plan? Is it merely a device to aid the sales manager in getting a better performance response?

9. Discuss several features of variable commission plans, pointing out what purposes such variations are designed to achieve.

10. In what way does a guaranteed draw assume the characteristics of a salary plan? In what way does it resemble a commission plan?

11. Why is compensation based on profit an unwise way to determine a salesperson's earnings?

12. The term *bonus* has become common in speaking of compensation, but there are a number of meanings attached to it aside from the principle of increased earnings. Describe some of the particular ways the word *bonus* is used, and indicate how special meanings have developed.

13. How is a point system used in sales compensation? Why may it upset salespeople? What are some of the problems in using it?

14. Two executives charged with the task of developing a salesperson compensation plan for a firm were sharply critical of each other. The first executive believed he could accomplish reasonable objectives by using a straight salary plan; the second executive strongly felt the only reasonable plan was one using straight commission. The second insisted that only when a salesperson was forced to work in order to earn a living would he give his best performance, but the first replied that a strong sales manager could motivate salespeople to do their best without a commission incentive. The president heard the discussion and presentation of each. Then he asked you to weigh both arguments, develop a paper assessing each approach, and give your opinion which would be the better way to develop a compensation plan.

15. What are several significant factors to consider in developing a compensation plan?

16. Discuss some of the problems involved in implementing a compensation plan.

17. After a sales compensation plan has been activated, a number of problems, some unforeseen, will arise to create dissension and develop

frictions which must be resolved. Discuss several of these problems, indicating how and why they might arise and how each can be resolved.

SPANEL MANUFACTURING COMPANY   *case 10–1*

Spanel Manufacturing Company produces a number of industrial supplies commonly used in manufacturing. Ten years ago, they started operations by manufacturing a popular product used widely in machine shops. Since they produced only one product they used mill supply houses, industrial distributors, and some hardware wholesalers to sell the product. Each year, they added one or more new products so that now each sale is large enough to use direct distribution.

After carefully considering present distribution methods, it was decided to sell through their own sales force as well as through the present distributors who wished to continue with them. However, they expect to increase present prices to distributors by 5 percent once they have their own sales force established. Distributor sales are handled by the home office.

Since great expense is involved in establishing and compensating their own sales force, Mr. Fraser, president of the company, cautioned the sales manager, Mr. Bartlett, to be economical in developing this new distribution system and not to build up a lot of fixed sales costs.

It was decided that initially ten salespeople should be hired. Sales varying between $200,000 and $250,000 were estimated for each salesperson. At present prices, gross margins varying from 10 percent to 30 percent were anticipated. Salespeople would be cautioned to put extra effort into selling high margin items.

Two compensation plans were under consideration:

1. Pay each salesperson $150 a week plus a sliding commission of 2 percent on all sales grossing 15 but less than 20 percent; 4 percent on sales grossing 20 but less than 25 percent; and 6 percent on sales grossing 25 percent or more.
2. Give each salesperson a guaranteed draw of $75 a week against commission. Commissions would be paid at the rate of 4 percent on all sales grossing less than 15 percent, 6 percent on all sales grossing 15 percent but less than 20 percent, 9 percent on all sales grossing 20 percent but less than 25 percent, and 11 percent on all sales grossing 25 percent or more.

To facilitate calculations, all products would be grouped in four categories on the basis of profitability. Possible sales distribution might be category 1, 20 percent; category 2, 50 percent; category 3, 20 percent; category 4, 10 percent. Under either plan each salesperson would be paid $0.14 a mile car allowance.

The gross margin covered all marketing costs and part of general administration costs and profits. Production costs covered all direct and indirect production costs, including research and product development and a proportionate share of general administrative costs.

QUESTIONS

1. Which method would be immediately better for the company? Why?
2. Would the same method be preferable for the company over a longer period of time? Explain in detail.
3. Which method would be better for the salespeople in the long run? Explain your answers.

---

case 10–2   CHICAGO WHOLESALE DRUG
                                                                          COMPANY

Mr. Mel Fleming, the owner and president of the Chicago Wholesale Drug Company, had been contemplating some major changes in his sales force. Although the company's sales had been increasing every year for the last five years, Mr. Fleming did not think they were increasing rapidly enough.

Mr. Fleming believed that it was now time to reevaluate the compensation program in effect for the sales force. He wanted to be sure that it was providing sufficient incentive to increase sales volume.

Background of the Chicago Wholesale Drug Company

Mr. Fleming started as the owner of a retail drug store in Chicago in 1967. After this store quickly prospered, Mr. Fleming became the sole owner of a second retail drug store and part owner of a third retail drug store in Chicago. In 1972 Mr. Fleming had the opportunity to buy one-half ownership in the Chicago Wholesale Drug Company. This company had been organized in 1957 by Mr. Ormand French. Mr. French had extensive background in the wholesale drug business from working for ten years with the McKesson and Robbins Company. He had become very friendly with Mr. Fleming in the last three years and decided to offer him a chance to become part owner of the Chicago Wholesale Drug Company.

Mr. Fleming had been looking for an opportunity to get into the wholesale drug business for several years. It would give him virtually an unlimited market and the opportunity to develop his business ability. After carefully examining the company's records from 1957 through 1972, Mr. Fleming decided to accept the offer to purchase 50 percent of the business. In order to make this investment, Mr. Fleming sold his interest in the three retail stores. Shortly after Mr. Fleming's purchase of 50 percent of the business, Mr. French died suddenly of a heart attack. Mr. Fleming then decided to buy out the remaining 50 percent of the business.

Sales Volume

Since the company's beginning in 1957, total sales had risen steadily:

Date	Sales	Date	Sales	Date	Sales
1957	$140,000	1963	$380,000	1969	$405,000
1958	280,000	1964	390,000	1970	441,000
1959	300,000	1965	392,000	1971	442,000
1960	310,000	1966	395,000	1972	486,000
1961	320,000	1967	398,000	1973	519,000
1962	350,000	1968	402,000	1974	542,000
				1975	572,000

The sales ranged from the low of $140,000 in 1957 to the high of $572,000 in 1975. Except for the first-year variance between 1957 and 1958 when sales doubled, sales had increased by a fairly steady amount each year. Since 1971, the accounts the company serviced had increased from 125 to 150. This seemed to account for the small rise in sales for the period, from $442,000 to $572,000. Of this amount, over $20,000 was telephone and over-the-counter sales.

The firm had been very ineffective in recent years in its attempts to make any significant gains in its total sales volume. This was alarming to Mr. French and was one of the main reasons he wanted Mr. Fleming to become a partner in the business. He hoped that Mr. Fleming could take positive steps to increase sales. Mr. Fleming was convinced that the company could double current sales volume in the next three years. He based this fact upon the vast potential of the Chicago area market and on the changes that he expected to make in the sales force.

Sales Staff

Presently the company employs four salespeople—Raymond Osborn, Clarence Emsley, Susan Branch, and Reese Olcut.

Raymond Osborn is fifty-eight years old and has been with the company since its beginning in 1957. His territory is on the northwest side of Chicago. He had the highest sales volume of the four salespeople, $190,000 for 1975. He services twenty-eight accounts in the area that range from a low of $6,000 a year to a high of $25,000 a year.

Clarence Emsley is forty-two years old and has been with the company since 1966. His sales territory is the northeast side of Chicago, which previously had been handled part time by Mr. French. He had the second largest sales volume of the four salespeople, $170,000 for 1975. He services thirty-four accounts that range from a low of $4,000 a year to a high of $18,000 a year.

Susan Branch is twenty-six years old and has been with the company since 1973. Her sales territory is the southeast side of Chicago. Her sales volume for 1975 is $101,000. She services forty-five accounts that range from $1,000 a year to $12,000 a year.

Mr. Olcut started with the company in 1975. His southeast side territory consists of forty-three accounts with a sales volume of $90,000.

Customers

Presently the company is selling about 5,000 of the major items that are used by the various retail outlets in the area. In addition to the retail outlets in the area, the company also makes an effort to sell supplies to hospitals. The company has only one hospital account. This slow progress is attributed to keen competition in this market and to the lack of salespeople's qualifications to sell hospitals. Although the two younger salespeople have college degrees, none of the present sales force has any technical background in the drug business. This makes it difficult for the salespeople to sell to major hospitals.

The job of the salesperson is part selling and part servicing of accounts. He is supposed to help the retailer set up merchandise displays and keep him informed of the numerous new products that are coming on the market.

Present Compensation of the Salespeople

All four salespeople presently work entirely on a commission basis. They receive a flat 7 percent commission on all their sales. Their wages for 1975 ranged from a low of $7,000 for Mr. Olcut to a high of $15,300 for Mr. Osborn. For each new account, a salesperson is paid a bonus of ten dollars. A new account is defined as any customer who has not placed an order in the previous six months. In many cases, it appeared as though the salespeople were deliberately skipping a few of the smaller customers for the six-month period. Then they would try to get an order from the account to receive their ten dollar bonus. In addition, each salesperson was paid $0.14 a mile traveling expense.

Mr. Fleming is dissatisfied with the present method of compensation. His chief complaint is that the plan does not accomplish the major objective of a commission sales plan since it does not motivate the salespeople significantly. Since Mr. Fleming is contemplating realigning sales territories in the near future, he decided this would be the ideal time to institute a new compensation program. This issue is made even more important since the company will be hiring from two to six new salespeople to cover new territories.

Proposals for New Compensation Plan

Mr. Fleming wants a compensation plan that would give each salesperson an incentive to increase sales volume, to open new accounts, and to service all established accounts in an efficient manner.

Mr. Fleming decided to take the following steps:

1. To set up new sales territories based on sales potential of each area.
2. To establish a monthly quota by product category for each salesperson based on sales potential, competition, geographic location, and the company's past sales in that area.
3. To pay each salesperson $75 a week salary plus $0.15 a mile travel expenses.
4. To revise the commission rate structure to a sliding scale type of commission on product categories over quota. Every $1,000 or fraction thereof in monthly sales by category over quota would give the salesperson a 1 percent increase in commission. Thus, in category 1 the first thousand dollars over quota would be 1 percent commission; the second thousand, 2 percent. As soon as sales crossed the next thousand mark in that category, the commission would automatically increase 1 percent. Each category had a different commission starting point. Category 2 begins with 1½ percent; category 3 begins with 2 percent; and category 4 begins with 2½ percent.
5. To raise the bonus for each new account to $25. A new account would now be classified as any account that did not place an order with the company in the last twelve months.
6. To start a semiannual sales contest based upon salespeople exceeding their sales quotas by the greatest percent during the period. The winner would receive a cash compensation of $200.
7. To give an additional bonus of $50 to every salesperson who could open a regular account with any major hospital in the area.
8. To give a $100 bonus to every salesperson each year the company exceeded its forecasted sales volume for the year by more than 20 percent.

Mr. Fleming believed that these proposals would enable the Chicago Wholesale Drug Company to increase sales volume. The plan would allow both the sales force and the company to prosper together.

QUESTIONS

1. What are the major strengths and weaknesses of the proposed compensation plan?
2. Do you believe the plan will enable the company to achieve its sales objectives? Discuss your answer.
3. What changes would you recommend for the proposed plan? Why?

11

Compensation—Fringe Benefits and Expenses

Adequate remuneration requires a total compensation plan made up of a number of rewarding features that cover a greater part of the salesperson's expenditure pattern.

FRINGE BENEFITS

Fringe benefits are an increasingly important part of compensation. What was once considered a sweetener to encourage applicants to join the sales force is now a significant part of sales remuneration and has become a necessity to compete for better salespeople. No longer can a firm point with pride to some special benefit; rather, it must stress the benefits it gives so that an applicant can weigh and compare benefits of this firm with those offered by other firms competing for his services.

Fringe benefits, once considered a minor cost item, have increased to the point where they may become a burden unless computed in the total sales compensation cost. These benefits are increasingly expensive and proliferating in number. Each additional concession by the firm presumably makes a salesperson happier or reduces dissatisfaction, but also each requires increased expenditures and additional records.

Fringe benefits improve the salesperson's personal situation, reduce economic uncertainties, and relieve some of his worries. Provided with a number of extra benefits, he feels safer knowing that unexpected contingencies are provided for, old age needs are anticipated, and present desires for status and recognition are available. Many of his needs that previously required careful planning and budgeting are automatically taken care of, and areas of present concern are lightened.

Many applicants appear to be as interested in fringe benefits as they are in present income. They know that present salary or commission is usually sufficient to meet or exceed minimum living needs. Even major credit purchases can be worked out satisfactorily. But it is the unexpected costs and heavy drains on present income for future benefits such as pension that cut into earnings. Even payroll deductions are a fringe benefit in that they apportion charges evenly over a period.

FRINGE BENEFITS CATEGORIES

There are numerous fringe benefits of varying importance, and special benefits may loom important in particular instances. We can divide fringe benefits into special categories—(1) working period benefits, (2) retirement benefits, and (3) morale building benefits.

Working Period Benefits

Benefits in this category include financial benefits that accrue primarily during the salesperson's work life. They are designed to give him additional financial aid over and above salary and commission in order to meet particular financial obligations.

Insurance

There are a number of different insurance coverages that give protection to the salesperson and his family.

Health insurance may cover hospital care, physician costs, and materials and services required in diagnosis and treatment. These are often called Blue Cross Blue Shield coverage or some similar name, organized in a number of states and operated as a nonprofit organization. There are many other similar organizations, as well as numerous insurance company plans. Each may have slightly different provisions, and benefits may vary. Some are quite liberal and expensive; others are more restrictive.

There are many types of accident insurance that reimburse the salesperson or a beneficiary for loss of life or disabling injuries. Most have payments of varying length and quantity to meet current needs while the person is unable to work.

Many firms assist a salesperson by paying his salary for a period when he cannot work because of sickness or accident. The person on straight commission probably must arrange for his own protection. Protracted periods of illness are often handled by major medical insurance. This insurance is less expensive because it is used infrequenty, but it can be highly important to the individual salesperson, who might become one of the small minority caught in this unfortunate situation. It is preferable to have this type of insurance, rather than depending on the firm's generosity to help in catastrophic situations.

In the latter situation, a suffering salesperson may become subject to the whims of management or the profitability of the company at a particular time. Various health insurance policies cover loss of income and costs of particular expenses. They frequently provide a weekly monetary allowance.

Profit sharing

To a lesser extent, profit sharing may be a real incentive, particularly in a smaller firm where there is a close knit group of employees. In a large company where individual effort has little effect, it would be more difficult to arouse enthusiasm because profit becomes a condition in which a salesperson's effort is but one of many contributory factors.

Bonus

A bonus may be awarded for specific performance, but it may be determined by what the salesperson does and the success of the firm. It differs from profit sharing because it may be calculated for each salesperson and vary according to his contribution (often considered regular compensation).

Use of company car

Many salespeople have the use of a company car both at work during the week and at home on evenings and weekends. He must pay for gasoline, but is allowed free use of the vehicle. This takes the place of owning a car and most certainly eliminates the need for a second car. Use of a car can be worth a thousand dollars a year or more to a salesperson.

Paid vacation

Like other company employees, salespeople are now receiving vacation with pay. In some firms, this may be the typical period given other employees. Sometimes salespeople have to take their vacations at off-season when business is slow. It is not unusual to sandwich salespeople's vacations into the selling year to cause minimum dislocation of sales effort.

Promotion

In some instances, promotion from salesperson to senior salesperson or a similar name may be accompanied by a pay increase as well as be a status symbol reward. This promotion does not indicate progression in management status necessarily, but merely a performance recognition as a field person. At times, a change in title gives the salesperson more status in the eyes of the customer.

Convention trips

Convention trips are often awarded salespeople whose performance passes certain quota or goal standards. This trip stimulates them to extra effort.

Prizes

Usually, prizes are a part of remuneration coming from contests. There can be a number of prizes awarded irregularly for special or unusual services. These prizes could come from meritorious performance in civic affairs, particular contribution to the industry in which the firm is a part, or reward for outstanding achievement. For example, a salesperson who has become prominent in a civic association, church organization, or lodge may be given time off with pay or some other tangible recognition.

Retirement Benefits

Retirement benefits cover areas of protection to the retiree and his dependents. These benefits plus savings should enable the salesperson to live comfortably after he leaves the job.

Social security

Social Security is almost universal coverage to which contribution is automatic and amount of return established by government decisions. When membership is voluntary, salespeople should take steps to join and secure benefits. In essence, social security amounts to a planned tax progression on earnings to meet the cost of operating the entire program. The federal government does not accumulate huge reserves as do insurance companies, but uses current funds. As cost increases, payroll deductions are increased.

Insurance

Many firms furnish life insurance after retirement without charge. Sometimes they furnish a portion without charge and additional amounts on a contributory plan.

Insurance takes many forms—term insurance gives specified protection for a definite period of time and then expires with no further rights; straight life insurance gives returns to a beneficiary upon the death of the individual insured; and various combination policies give protection to dependents during the working life of the salesperson and can be used as income after retirement. This type of policy incorporates both life insurance and a savings plan which features annuity after retirement or at a specified age.

Pension

Pensions are growing in importance. A company with a strong pension plan has a decided advantage in recruiting over a company with no pension provision. People are becoming more security conscious, and more protection is automatic or incorporated in the job. A firm that offers security safeguards is more appealing than one that fails to give such benefits.

Pension plans are often designated as contributory and noncontributory. In the former, part of the pension is deducted from the salespeople's salary or income, and part is furnished by the employer; in the latter, the employer pays all.

Pension plans are often tied to particular conditions which make them contingent plans. Some plans pay retirement only to employees with a minimum number of years of service; some pay after a salesperson has reached a certain age plus a minimum number of years of service. In so-called noncontributory plans a salesperson may receive some return from the plan after a certain number of years, even though he leaves the firm to seek employment elsewhere. For example, he may receive some of this retirement benefit in a cash withdrawal or a future retirement benefit. Many more variations in rights and conditions are incorporated in pension plans with a variety of contingencies and hazards, not the least of which is that the company itself may disappear through going out of business, bankruptcy, or selling out to another firm.

Problems of pension plans

Some company managements are interested in the salesperson's welfare and have extended pension plans similar to the ones in force for other employees. Other firms have pension plans in order to remain competitive in the employment market. Since the problem of retaining good salespeople is a continuing one, many pension plans are dependent on the salesperson's remaining with the firm until a certain time. If at a later date he is offered a far better opportunity in another firm, he must weigh this opportunity against the loss of pension from transfer. If he becomes dissatisfied or if his income does not increase in line with other opportunities, he may grumble and suffer because he cannot afford to sacrifice the pension he has built up.

As a result of this involuntary aspect of pensions, many unhappy salespeople have little interest in their present job and are possibly building up antagonism to the employer. The firm has tied the employee, but does the firm really gain? If salespeople had freedom to take pensions with them, there would be some job changes; but for a number of firms, these transfers would be mutually beneficial because they would end up with people who wanted to sell for them.

A pension is given to fill a genuine need. The need exists whether a salesperson works for one or another firm, and regardless of where he chooses employment his pension needs remain the same. Consequently, after a trial period of perhaps a year, a salesperson should be allowed to accumulate all contributed funds towards a pension and that money should go with him, not remain with the employer.

To implement a pension of this kind, it is preferable to use an insurance company or a similar firm established to work in this area. In addition to choosing a carrier outside the firm, the pension should be funded; that is, once the yearly or regular payment is made by the firm, the salesperson, or both, the employer is relieved of all pension obligation of that past period. The relationship now exists between the salesperson and the carrier, which probably would be an insurance company.

Management may feel this method loses some control of the salesperson, and perhaps it does; but at the same time the salesperson has a better feeling toward his employer because he is not coerced into staying. Actually, a seasoned salesperson who has been with a firm for several years is not likely to quit without serious reasons, for he may find difficulty in getting a new job.

A funded pension plan going with the salesperson may be expensive to a firm, but over time it may pay rich dividends because:

1. Each period the firm makes its payment to the carrier and is relieved of any further obligation. There would be no renegotiation of pension as is done in union contracts. There would be no extra money needed when the person retires and no demands on the firm after he retires.
2. The benefits would be determined on an actuarial basis, and the salesperson would have recourse only on the carrier.
3. Provisions could be built in to prevent a person from cashing the money before retirement. This pension system would provide solely for retirement.
4. Should the firm get in financial straits, be reorganized, closed, or bought by another company, the salesperson's pension, up to that time, would not be affected. All accumulations to date would be his.
5. The firm could charge pension contributions to current expense.
6. A firm could hire salespeople of any age. If they hired a person five years from retirement, they would be responsible for his pension only for the time he worked for them. Prior responsibility for his pension would have been covered by previous employers. If each previous employer had used a different carrier, the salesperson on retirement would receive retirement checks from each carrier involved; but the total of the monthly checks would approximate the same amount he would have received had he remained with one employer throughout his working life.
7. Management could feel free to discharge a salesperson who had become unproductive or did not fit in with current operations. Often, a firm will carry a weak person for a few years until retirement because it would be unfair to discharge him if he were to lose his pension.

Often a short-sighted executive will develop a pension plan with restrictions that are onerous to the salesperson and unwittingly may become a real burden to the firm. Because they are trying to use a pension plan not for the main purpose of meeting a salesperson's retirement needs but for the firm's ends, it may end up satisfying no one, lowering salesperson morale, and frustrating management because the added cost does not bring a commensurate rate of return.

Fallacy of a noncontributory pension plan

A noncontributory pension plan is a misnomer. By definition, it means a plan in which the employer pays into the plan and the employee contributes no money. Technically this statement is true, but actually it does not describe the true situation.

No thinking employer pays for something he does not receive. No one knowingly pays for nothing; rather, he pays for value received whether it be for product, service, or some other worthwhile tangible or intangible possession.

To look at it in another way, the employer pays this pension cost in order to secure and retain productive salespeople. It is not likely he would pay this cost if he could satisfy his employee needs without it. Consequently, it becomes a part of a salesperson's compensation that will lead him to one employer rather than another. For example, an employer may give a salesperson a 10 percent increase in salary for the coming year. Then he starts a pension plan in which the employee contributes 5 percent of his salary and the employer matches it. Or the employer may give the salesperson a 5 percent salary increase and start a noncontributory pension plan in which the employer pays 10 percent of the salesperson's salary for the coming year. In either case, the employee receives an approximate 15 percent increase in income.

There is, of course, a small monetary difference between the two methods in the pension:

Example 1

Salesperson's salary	$10,000
10% increase	1,000
New salary	$11,000

In the coming year, the salesperson would contribute five percent, or $550, to the pension; and the employer would do likewise, making a total of $1,100.

Example 2

Salesperson's salary	$10,000
5% increase	500
New salary	$10,500

The employer's contribution to the pension fund is ten percent, or $1,050.

Whichever method is used, it is clear that pension is incorporated in the salesperson's remuneration. To tie a contingency of continued employment with this firm for many years is, in many situations, depriving the salesperson of part of his compensation unless he can take his pension with him when he leaves. Since most firms have difficulty in forecasting their futures for even five years with any accuracy, it is inconceivable that they should try to forecast employees' personal and individual needs twenty years in the future. Since in the whole economy savings represent about 6 or 7 percent of Gross National Product, it seems highly questionable to tie up 10 percent of a salesperson's salary or income in an "IF" pension plan.[1]

Nonmonetary Benefits

These benefits might be termed morale builders because they are successful in aiding sales. A salesperson's wants may be divided into three categories—(1) compensation and benefits that enable him to live comfortably, support his family, and protect against unexpected contingencies such as sickness and accident, (2) retirement benefits that will assure him comfortable living after he retires, and (3) recognition or the feeling that he is important. There are many ways to give nonmonetary recognition in order to give the salesperson a lift and cause him to work harder.

Clubs

Special recognition may be given to salespeople who achieve certain goals. They may be awarded membership in a club made up of similar producers and may be presented with a pin or scroll at a special meeting. At the annual convention, there can be an awards dinner where salespeople are given particular awards depending on type of activity. For example, there could be awards for making quota, for high profit sales, for volume, and many others depending on company standards. Membership in a club might be for a year and could be retained only by superior performance.

Trophies

Each year a trophy or trophies could be given out. Some of these might belong permanently to individuals; others could rotate each year depending on individual sales performance.

---

1. Recently a man described his experience as a salesman for a well-known firm with a tremendous retirement plan if he stayed with the firm. He was selling a product subject to renewal each year. He cultivated his market and built up good relationships with customers by calling on them regularly. After he secured the first order, customers would sometimes mail in renewal orders. The salesperson received commission on all orders from his customers whether given to him directly or mailed in. Sometme later, a new sales manager came into the firm and cut all sales commissions on orders mailed in. If the salesman was handed the order and he mailed it in, he got his commission; if the customer did not wait for his call but mailed the order into the company, the salesman got no commission. This salesman soon quit. He said he had received a thorough, costly training program. He had built his territory successfully, but then a sales manager with quaint ideas destroyed a valuable relationship.

Plaques

A plaque with the name of the leading salesperson might be prominently displayed in the home office. If no salesperson could have more than one year, or only one year consecutively, many people would have their names inscribed.

Special insignia

A salesperson might have a special binder or order book with his name inscribed to signify him a leading salesperson. He could show his customers, and they would share in his pride since they helped him to achieve success.

Contest trophies

If a firm attaches great significance to contests, the winners should receive suitable recognition in trophies, scrolls, framed certificates, and similar articles. These awards can be shown to the family, especially the children. Experienced sales managers know that every salesperson should receive something that he can have at home which indicates outstanding performance.

Other sales recognition

It is so customary to praise the outstanding salesperson that the many other people who do very well seldom receive special recognition. As long as special recognition is used, the sales manager should give it to three people instead of one to encourage greater performance.

SALESPEOPLE EXPENSES

Most salespeople incur expenses that would be above normal if they were on some other type of job. Most of them are reimbursed by their employers, who rate this expense as another selling expense. There are many ways to reimburse salespeople and checks to monitor such expenses because it is easy to nudge expenses upward unless they are controlled. A prudent overseeing holds spending within reasonable limits.

Purpose of Paying Sales Expenses

The salesperson is anxious to make a sale and tries to win the buyer, who wants the most for his money. It is important to the buyer to receive the best buy possible. Sometimes a company buyer must get certain products within a time limit and consequently must place an order soon. Other times a buyer may buy now, later, or even never; in that situation, even greater sales persuasion becomes essential.

It has become common to use certain inducements to encourage the buyer to act favorably. Often, it has become customary to give the buyer something personally to gain his favor. For example, it is quite common for a salesperson to buy lunch for the buyer. This type of favor may extend from a lunch to free dinners, social weekends, gifts, and outright money gifts. This practice would increase a salesperson's expenses. Most firms permit some of this giving; but excessive spending is frowned upon and usually forbidden. Any luncheon, holiday gift, or birthday gift below ten or fifteen dollars attracts little attention; beyond that, an explanation may be necessary.

In order for the salesperson to be at a particular location at a designated time, he must travel and incur living expenses. These expenses are above and beyond costs of other jobs in the firm, and a salesperson cannot afford to pay them himself. If he were to pay these expenses, it is likely that he would scrimp to the extent that the buyer would receive an unfavorable impression. There are brief periods when a salesperson's expenses may exceed his income, but he must incur such expenses.

Types of Expenses Paid

There are legitimate expenses a salesperson incurs for which the company reimburses him; others are disallowed. Living and travel expenses are the most common types of expenses covered. Exceptions occur in retail selling and certain kinds of local selling where travel costs are negligible.

Living expenses away from home are paid, including food, shelter, and other personal expenses of good grooming.

Entertainment expenses are covered to varying degrees. In many selling situations, a salesperson is permitted to spend some money on a customer. Personal excesses can destroy a company image. Included in the entertainment category are modest gifts which may be part of the entertainment.

There could be other expenses, such as mail, telephone, telegraph, supplies, and equipment needed in everyday work. A special type of expense could be hiring an individual to do some minor work on a customer's piece of equipment purchased from the salesperson.

Internal Revenue Service and Sales Expenses

Internal revenue agents scrutinize salespeople's expenses; and if they are excessive, they are disallowed. Certain expenses are permitted by law and are not questioned; other expenses are prohibited and immediately disallowed; but there are many borderline situations which are questioned.

Laws change; enforcement may vary from year to year; and different government agents may vary in their interpretation. If sharp differences of opinion exist between a firm and government agents even after appeal and review at higher levels, the firm may go to court. These occasions should be rare and when major sums of money are involved or interpretation of law is questioned. Because of government surveillance, it is necessary that a salesperson keep close records of his expenses and is able to document and justify any expense that appears questionable. These procedures are carefully spelled out in present laws, and firms must watch when changes are made in order to comply with all requirements.[2]

Elements of a Sound Expense Plan

To satisfy salespeople and be fair to both salespeople and employer, the following elements should be incorporated in an expense plan.

1. The salesperson should be compensated for all job expenses that would not arise if he were employed in the office, warehouse, or some other activity of the firm. A salesperson selling in his hometown might not receive lunch money, but he would be reimbursed for lunch if he entertained a guest.
2. The salesperson should be allowed to maintain either a standard of living equal to his home standard or a minimum standard which does not reflect unfavorably on the firm.
3. There should be no financial gain or loss to the salesperson through his expense account. Any advantages a salesperson gains should be minor. Salespeople frequently complain about losing money on expenses. Salespeople should not be encouraged to spend freely; expenditures should not deviate significantly from amounts suggested by the sales manager.[3] Occasionally, salespeople are encouraged to claim liberal expenses in lieu of a salary adjustment. Expense money is normally designed to pay a salesperson for legitimate expenditures; whenever expenses are used as a device for other purposes, they should be challenged.
4. The plan should not hinder sales performance. It should not be so restrictive that the salesperson fails to spend money when expenditures could assist in making worthwhile sales. Some of these expenditures may be long range in effect, and no immediate results are visible.

---

2. There are many articles about expense plans, allowable expenses, government regulations regarding sales expenses, and company approaches to sales expenses. The sales manager or reader who desires current information on this subject can go to the public library and find articles through the *Business Periodicals Index* and the *Public Affairs Information Service*. The *Vertical File Service Catalog* lists brochures and monographs.

3. A salesperson said his sales manager questioned his lunch expenses and felt he was not eating well enough. The salesperson hastened to reassure his boss that he ate light lunches. When the boss insisted he should eat better, it dawned on the salesperson that it was not his lunch but the amount he turned in as lunch expense that was the problem. His expense was very low and made other people who turned in a more usual lunch cost look bad.

5. The plan should avoid areas of interpretation where disagreements can arise because of hazy instructions. When an expenditure seems legitimate to the salesperson and is disallowed by the sales manager, the salesperson usually is ingenious enough to recoup costs in some other way.
6. The plan should be easily understood and simple to operate. Complex plans require much clerical help, attention of management, and salesperson attention.
7. Payment should be prompt. Management can hardly justify asking a salesperson to have an expense float unpaid for several weeks, forcing him to dig down in his own pocket. Only rarely should expense money remain unpaid in order to force a salesperson to file reports or to perform other duties. This type of persuasion can boomerang.

Expense Plans

There are numerous plans in use. The exact plan to use depends on type of compensation, size of firm, availability of office help, beliefs of management, and other reasons.

Unlimited plan

The unlimited, or honor, plan is the simplest and maintains the least control. The individual merely turns in expenses and is reimbursed without question or checking. This plan is often reserved for executives and salespeople who operate in high-level selling activities. It is not widely used except for executives, where checking might touch sensitive spots and disturb company relationships.

It is easy to administer, since few records are necessary and there is no occasion to question expenditures. Salespeople who have this plan are expected to use discretion, but at the same time are not stopped from heavy spending if they feel it necessary. While there is a possibility of supervision since the top executive could check anyone under him, it would not be practical at most operating levels. Sometimes the sales manager wants to know both how much money a salesperson spends and how he spends it.

Exact plan

Under the exact plan, the salesperson is somewhat restricted in his expenditures, though not explicitly. He might be cautious about staying in expensive hotels, eating expensive meals, excessive use of taxicabs, and heavy entertaining. The salesperson would be prudent to keep his expenses in line with the work he is doing and the sales he makes. The exact plan reimburses the salesperson for exactly what he spends.

A weakness of this plan is that a salesperson is not likely to report an excessive expenditure but hide part of it in other expenditures.

When the salesperson travels on expense accounts, he does not jot down every tiny expense when made or remember them accurately. When he does make out his expense report for the day, the figures usually reflect approximate amounts. The exceptions are those expenses for which he has receipts; the salesperson should have receipts for large expenditures to protect himself. This plan is useful when expenses and work vary among territories.

Limited plan

The limited plan sets maximum prices a salesperson may pay for room, meals, and other expenses. This plan prevents a salesperson from paying four dollars for dinner one evening and eight dollars the following evening. These rates are determined from average prices in each territory. Every salesperson does not necessarily have an individual set of limits. Limits vary based on areas and to some extent on territories. Thus, a salesperson in a rural territory would have lower expenses than one in large cities.

Flat sum plan

Many salespeople travel the same territory in a predetermined pattern with some minor variations. Under such circumstances, the salesperson has similar expense reports each week. To avoid office work in checking reports and to eliminate disagreements on expenses for each period, the salesperson gets a flat amount and can use it as he wishes.

This plan works best for salespeople whose work is somewhat routine (a good salesperson does not allow his job to be routine) and when he calls on the same customers regularly. If unexpected situations arise justifying unusual expenditures, management can allow them as extra charges. The salesperson who travels various distances and calls on new prospects would find this plan restrictive.

The flat plan requires periodic adjustment to conform to changes in costs and may need some changes to reflect salespeople's wishes. For example, if salespeople are constantly grumbling that expense accounts are too low, it may be necessary to adjust them upward.

Expense quota plan

This plan gives the salesperson an expense allowance based on sales. Since it is less flexible than other plans, it may be determined monthly. If a salesperson exceeds the amount, he must pay the balance; if he uses less, he may receive a bonus.

While this plan does tie in with sales and gives an exact percentage, it may not vary with actual conditions of irregular sales and territories which may vary in cost of living. Over a period of time, expenses will settle at a regular percentage of sales; but, in the short run and for each territory, it seems unwise to force such a system on each salesperson. To expect such a plan to operate well is unrealistic because it is rigid and does not conform to each salesperson and his territory.

Salesperson pays his own expense

From the company's viewpoint, the simplest expense account is no expense account. This method puts all the burden on the salesperson, freeing the company from all obligations, but gives the salesperson maximum flexibility in ordering his way of life. The only recording a salesperson needs is to supply information to himself and to the internal revenue for income tax purposes.

When a salesperson pays his own expenses, his compensation is expected to be adequate to cover such costs and still reward him for his efforts. Usually, this method works best when a salesperson receives commission on sales and is paid only if he sells. It appears to be the best method when a salesperson represents several firms and sells on a commission basis for each.

There may be a tendency for a salesperson paying his own expenses to be too frugal and thus be unwilling to spend money for the customer's benefit.[4]

The house-to-house salesperson usually sells on commission in his home city or area. Therefore, he is expected to handle his own expenses. A part-time salesperson seldom gets expense money because of his intermittent service.

Checking Expenses

Most expense plans need some overseeing. Mathematical errors and questionable items may be included. If a salesperson finds that his expense report is seldom checked, it might be tempting to push to the top limit as often as possible. An audit of an expense report often shows items repeated with monotonous regularity, which makes one suspect that there could be significant discrepancies between expenditures and reports.[5]

Checking expense reports requires some experience and an ability to detect automatic items and genuinely accurate expenses. Whether an item is reported in a rounded sum or in an exact way does not necessarily indicate preciseness. An expenditure listed as $5 may be as accurate or inaccurate as one listed at $4.97; the exact amount might have been $4.93 or $5.03.

It would be most desirable to have expenditures detailed exactly unless supported by receipts, but it is unlikely the salesperson will

---

4. A salesman told the author of an incident where he spent $1,500 of his own money to develop a major sale. Then he lost the sale. A salesman must be willing to take risks in selling, but a few incidents of this kind might seriously curtail his efforts.

5. In a period of several months, a salesperson reported the same tip, or gratuity, expense every day.

remember or report exact expenses. In checking expense reports, it may be more important not to concentrate on exact dollars and cents, but rather on tendencies to exceed allowable limits, and to watch for a major variation. If expenses creep up regularly, it may be a reflection of increasing costs, not excessive spending habits.

Exceeding Expense Allowance

Each company has a different policy on exceeding expense allowances. Some spell out policies strongly; others weakly enforce control depending on circumstances. Unfortunately, a sales manager may be lenient to salespeople exceeding allowances when sales are high, but become arbitrary when sales are low.

Seldom can a policy be established that permits no exceptions. Exceptions will occur even though they may not be reported, because occasions arise which force the salesperson to exceed his expense level.

Some managers knowingly allow salespeople to earn money on expense accounts; others unwittingly permit it through lax supervision. Expense accounts should be adequate to reimburse salespeople for all legitimate expenses, but it is not desirable to use them to earn money.

Travel Expenses

Travel expenses are a major cost to many salespeople, particularly when great distances are involved. Travel is costly in time as well as money.

Transportation is essential to the salesperson going from one customer to another. To save time and energy, travel should be adequate, comfortable, rapid, and relatively free from danger and needless interruption. For example, it is foolish for a salesperson to have poor tires that delay him during his workday. It is a waste of valuable selling time to hunt for a free parking place when a parking lot is convenient.

There are a number of modes of travel commonly used. For long distance, air travel is common; but for most salespeople the automobile is the usual vehicle because of its versatility and adaptability.

To a lesser extent, salespeople use buses, boats, and trains because they are the best way to travel in particular situations. One advantage of using public transportation is that the salesperson does not have to drive. After a long drive in his own car, a salesperson may not be in best form to make a sales presentation.

Plane travel

Plane travel is rapid, pleasant, and brings the salesperson to his destination fresh for work. Top-level salespeople may have their own planes. A few salespeople travel in planes on first class, but most use coach fare or a similar economy rate. Most sales managers feel that the slight additional comfort of first-class travel is not worth the extra cost.

A salesperson arriving in a city where he must make a number of calls often rents a car at the airport. He frequently uses public transportation or a taxicab for a single call or a downtown location. A combination of plane, car rental, or taxicab transportation gets a salesperson to his destination quickly, but can be quite expensive.

Automobile travel

Travel by private automobile is the most common way used by salespeople because it is practical, fairly economical, and adaptable to individual needs. The automobile can be a means of travel for work and also be used for the salesperson's family needs. It is convenient for carrying emergency supplies, tools, and merchandise. It is often used to carry advertising brochures and displays. If a salesperson wishes to take a buyer for lunch or to see an installation, his car is there for immediate use. Some salespeople drive a station wagon or truck and sell and make immediate delivery. This method distributes travel expense over one complete operation.

Automobile ownership

The salesperson's car may be company owned or be his own car. If the company owns the cars, advantages include:

1. A company fleet may be a uniform style and color with company names on the side of the car.
2. The company can regulate the car's age.
3. The company can develop a uniform maintenance policy.
4. The company can regulate the driving and specify the amount of personal use, if any.
5. The salesperson is relieved of transportation financing and worries.
6. A pattern of cost relationships can be developed for different territories and salespeople.

Some of the disadvantages of company ownership include:

1. Financing a large number of cars
2. Maintaining service
3. Purchase and trade-ins of cars
4. Administrative problems

If a company has many salespeople concentrated so that central maintenance service can be provided and they drive many miles a year (over 12,000), it may be desirable to have a company-owned fleet. If salespeople are widely scattered over large territories, company-owned cars may be questioned. If salespeople average fewer than 1,000 miles a month, a company-owned car might not be advantageous.

When the salesperson owns the car, he is free to buy what he wants and may buy, sell, and trade as he sees fit. He does not have to report everything to his employer regarding personal driving needs. The car is his, and he lends it to his employer during working hours and is compensated for its use. The salesperson must maintain a serviceable vehicle which can be depended upon to perform well and make a good appearance to maintain the company image.

Travel allowance for salesperson-owned car

There are numerous ways to reimburse a salesperson for the use of his car for business purposes. The simplest way is the flat mileage allowance. To make adjustments and prevent inequities, flat mileage allowance may be varied from territory to territory based on the terrain, the type of driving, and miles driven. Mountainous, winding roads require a higher allowance than flat country roads; city driving is more expensive than country driving; driving in severe weather costs more than driving in moderate weather.

Driving allowances may vary according to the number of miles covered each year. For example, a salesperson driving 10,000 miles a year loses money on $0.14 a mile, but one driving 40,000 miles a year may come out ahead on $0.14 a mile. To equate driving costs, management may pay a maximum mileage amount for the first 10,000 miles and reduce the amount per mile for each one above 10,000 miles. If there are individual territory variations, mileage allowances might be as shown in Table 11–1.

Table 11–1
Rate per Mile

Salespeople (miles)	Smith	Brown	Green	Rose	Black
1–10,000	16¢	15¢	14¢	14¢	14¢
10,001–20,000	—	14¢	13¢	13¢	13¢
20,001–30,000		—	12¢	12¢	12¢
over 30,000			—	11¢	11¢

Smith drives fewer than 10,000 miles a year; Rose drives around 35,000 miles a year; and Black exceeds 40,000 miles a year.

Expenses in driving a car include operating costs and depreciation. To make reimbursement equitable, it can be divided into a mileage cost and depreciation, which is paid in a lump sum when the salesperson buys a new car. This plan helps him to make a large down payment when buying his new car. If he trades in his old car, the difference between the new car and the trade-in could substantially be covered by this depreciation accumulation. Of course, if the salesperson resigned, the firm would have to pay him the accumulated depreciation since it belongs to him.[6]

Automobile insurance

Even if the salesperson has automobile insurance, it is important that the company protects itself with insurance coverage on his car, particularly liability and property damage insurance. It is unlikely that a salesperson could meet a large judgment so it would be natural for people seeking payment to proceed against the employer. A salesperson may wish to have car insurance to cover minor costs, but the firm must accept the cost and responsibility of automobile insurance for salespeople. If the salesperson's car were destroyed and he had no insurance, the company would have to provide another car if he had no money.

Leasing cars

Whether it is advantageous for the individual salesperson to lease rather than buy a car is often a matter of choice. A salesperson lacking finances might find leasing his solution to transportation. Indications are, however, that the salesperson who is a careful buyer and a careful driver might be ahead to own his car.

It is common for companies to lease cars for salespeople and executives. In this case, the buyer is a professional who negotiates with the leasing company and gets better financial terms than the individual because the company leases several or many cars. It is customary to charge leasing expenses to company operations.

A company that needs many cars saves large sums in car investment through leasing. The leasing firm may arrange for maintenance, repairs, and a variety of services. This is important for a widely scattered sales force. If a company uses large numbers of cars in concentrated areas, they might own and service their own cars, which may be more economical, and lease cars in less concentrated areas. Special-purpose vehicles and cars used for short periods may be leased.

Use of Credit Cards

The growing use of credit cards leads to more effective expense control. When a salesperson can charge most of his traveling and living expenses, he need not carry large sums of money or use his own money and be reimbursed later. The company also receives an itemized list of expenses and is able to detect any unusual deviations. Using credit cards prevents memory lapses, hinders padding of ac-

---

6. Before implementing a travel allowance schedule, it would be wise to secure current information readily available in libraries. Helpful information can also be secured from The Dartnell Corporation, Chicago, Illinois, and Runzheimer and Company, Inc., Rochester, Wisconsin.

counts, and relieves the salesperson of some detail. If a salesperson pays his own expenses, he has a record for income tax purposes.

Reporting Expenses

Salespeople report expenses on special forms. Some use expense booklets, which cover expenses for a week. These booklets are sold by firms specializing in such material. Some firms prepare their own report forms designed to meet particular needs. Some reports are much more detailed than others, depending on the wishes of sales managers. Whatever form is used is not so important as the use of the information requested. It is nonsensical to ask for information that is never used, that is so detailed as to be petty, and that requires much of the salesperson's time and has minor significance. Figure 11–1 is a form used for reporting expenses.

QUESTIONS AND PROBLEMS

1. Why should we consider fringe benefits under three separate categories? Can you think of other ways of dividing fringe benefits? Explain.

2. Are fringe working period benefits a large part of a salesperson's income? Discuss, using a number of different situations.

3. Explain why a profit sharing arrangement may be a dubious benefit. When do you think profit sharing should be included under regular compensation?

4. Most firms might consider a bonus as part of regular compensation rather than a fringe benefit. How would you distinguish this difference?

5. Are retirement benefits more important as salespeople become older? Justify your answer by present social attitudes.

6. What is the difference between social security and a pension? Aren't they both pensions? When a salesperson has social security, why worry about a pension?

7. Discuss company pensions, bringing out their strengths and weaknesses. How can the weaknesses be overcome?

8. Why is a noncontributory plan not a true reflection of how the plan operates? Explain.

9. Why are nonmonetary benefits important to salespeople?

10. Discuss sales expenses, pointing out why they arise, what expenses are included, and why salespeople should be reimbursed.

11. List two groups of expenses a salesperson makes. Separate them into ones you think his employer should pay and ones he should pay.

12. How would you determine if an expense plan is fair and equitable? Give details.

13. Discuss the merits of each type of expense plan to both company and salespeople.

Figure 11–1
Expense Report Form

PARKE-DAVIS

EXPENSE REPORT
(See instructions on reverse)

FOR WEEK ENDED SATURDAY,	DIVISION OR BRANCH	LOCATION CODE	TERRITORY NO.	SUBMITTED BY *(Print)*	EMPLOYEE NO.

DAILY ITINERARY	SUNDAY	MONDAY	TUESDAY	WEDNESDAY	THURSDAY	FRIDAY	SATURDAY
FROM							
TO OR AT							
TO OR AT							
TO OR AT							
BUSINESS REASON FOR TRAVEL							

ITEMS		SUNDAY	MONDAY	TUESDAY	WEDNESDAY	THURSDAY	FRIDAY	SATURDAY	TOTAL
TRANSPORTA-TION (ATTACH RECEIPT, SEE INSTR. 4A)	AIR, RAIL, OR BUS FARES	$	$	$	$	$	$	$	$
	LOCAL (BUS, TAXI, ETC.)								
LODGING (ATTACH RECEIPT) OR DAILY ALLOWANCE.									
MEALS	BREAKFAST								
	LUNCH								
	DINNER								
TELEPHONE OR TELEGRAMS									
REGISTRATION FEES									
ENTERTAINMENT *(Itemize on reverse side)*									
SUNDRY (ITEMIZE)									
TOTAL		$	$	$	$	$	$	$ *	$

MILEAGE ALLOWANCE (SEE INSTRUCTION 5): ______ MILES ON COMPANY BUSINESS @ ______ PER MILE

COMPANY, RENTED, OR LEASED AUTO EXPENSES: ATTACH APPROPRIATE FORMS OR RECEIPTS (SEE INSTRUCTION NO. 6)

UNUSED TRANSPORTATION TICKETS

RETURNED FOR REFUND

NO. ______ COST ______

NO. ______ COST ______

EXCHANGED FOR NEW TICKET

NO. ______ COST ______

TOTAL EXPENSE FOR WEEK(INCLUDING CAR AND/OR MILEAGE)		$
LESS: FARE ADVANCES	$	
CASH ADVANCES		
CREDIT CARD CHARGES		
CAR RENTALS		
REGISTRATION FEES		
BALANCE DUE ☐ TO ☐ FROM EMPLOYEE		$
______ DOLLARS (STATE AMOUNT IN WORDS)		*

FOR ACCOUNTING USE ONLY	
ACCOUNT NUMBER	AMOUNT
	$

APPROVALS: *

SIGNATURE (*Employee submitting Report*) *	RECEIVED PAYMENT OR REFUND MADE *	
CHECKED BY	CHECK NO.	DATE

(*) If more than one sheet is used, totals and signature should be indicated on top sheet only.

* Courtesy Parke-Davis

Figure 11-1
(Continued)

ENTERTAINMENT RECORD

DATE	ESTABLISHMENT	AMOUNT	TYPE OF ENTERTAINMENT	BUSINESS PURPOSE	RECORD OF PERSON(S) ENTERTAINED	
					NAME	BUSINESS RELATIONSHIP
		$				

INSTRUCTIONS

1. General

This form should be filled out completely for each week and submitted within 5 workdays after completion of a trip.

2. Daily Itinerary

List cities visited in sequence. Indicate city where you stayed the night.

3. Business Reason for Travel

A statement of business reason must be included as part of each Expense Report. Examples of these are:

a. Sales visitations to customers.
b. Visits to Company locations as required.
c. Visits to another company for technical reasons.
d. Attend conferences or conventions.

4. Items of Expense (A receipt must be attached for each single expenditure amounting to $25 or more.)

a. Transportation — Enter the daily cost of transportation. Local transportation includes buses, taxis, etc. Airline and railway receipts must be attached; if unavailable indicate reason. Attach travel authorization when issued (see Instruction 8). Transportation purchased locally by a foreign branch for U. S. personnel traveling thereto must not appear as either an expense or an advance on the Expense Report.

b. Lodging — List lodging expense daily including any tax thereon. Receipts must be attached.

c. Meals — List the cost of meals. Include cost of meals with guest under "Entertainment".

d. Entertainment (Including entertainment of Parke-Davis employees) — Enter the daily total of entertainment expense on the line provided. All entertainment expenses must be described in the "Entertainment Record" above.

e. Sundry — Itemize other allowable expenses.

5. Mileage Allowance

Travel by personal car should be limited to short trips or where public transportation is not available. Mileage expense allowed shall not exceed the cost of tourist air fare or rail fare when air travel is not possible; show miles driven and cost of public transportation if applicable. Use of personal cars by sales representatives will be as authorized by the U. S. Sales Division.

6. Company, Rented, or Leased Auto Expenses

Attach form furnished by Company garage for emergency expenses incurred while operating Company car, receipt received from car rental agency, or Form 1797 for monthly leased auto expenses.

7. Advances

a. Fare Advances — Enter the cost of transportation tickets obtained by the Company. Attach appropriate travel authorization and transportation receipt, or other supporting document (see Instruction 8i), to the final report. Travel arrangements should be made through the Traffic Department, Detroit, whenever possible.

b. Cash Advances — Enter the amount of Cash (or checks) advanced to you by the Company for this trip.

c. Credit Card Charges — Enter the amount charged to the Company on credit cards such as Air Travel Cards.

d. Car Rentals — Enter the amount charged to the Company on Hertz Rent A Car charge plates.

e. Registration Fees — Enter the amount advanced by the Company for registration fees.

f. For continuing trips, when expenses are reimbursed at periodic intervals, all advances should be reported on the last expense report submitted.

8. Unused Transportation Tickets

a. If no portion of a ticket has been used (e.g., cancelled trip), initiate a memo, in duplicate, and forward both copies along with the complete ticket and travel authorization to the Traffic Department - Detroit. The original copy of the memo, when receipted and returned by the Traffic Department, should be retained for your records; no expense report need be submitted.

b. If any portion of the ticket has been used, the total cost of the ticket must be reported as both an expense and an advance. List all unused tickets, those exchanged for new tickets, or airline credit memos in the space provided. Initiate a memo, in duplicate, showing description and forward both copies along with all remaining portions of the ticket or any other pertinent information relating to refunds or credits to the Traffic Department, Detroit. The original copy of the memo, receipted and returned by the Traffic Department, must be attached to the expense report.

261

14. What is the purpose of checking expense reports?
15. Discuss the relative advantages of traveling by plane and by car.
16. Who should own the car the salesperson drives? Explain, pointing out advantages to both salesperson and company.
17. What are the advantages of car leasing to the salesperson and employer?
18. Do credit cards help or hinder salespeople? Justify your answer.

case 11–1   **PARIS DISTRIBUTORS**

Paris Distributors was a large industrial distributor of small machines and equipment, repair parts, and supplies for numerous types of machines, abrasives, tools, and maintenance supplies used in industry. It was located in northeastern Ohio. Fifty-two salespeople sold its complete line in northern Ohio, southern Michigan, and western Pennsylvania. Paris Distributors was a well-established, reliable firm with numerous customers who depended on it for particular types of merchandise.

The sales organization was strong. Its salespeople were hardworking and conscientious. Its compensation plan was one of the best in the industry. Sales turnover varied from two to four each year. Usually people left for better positions or retired. Many of the salespeople had been with the firm over ten years.

The sales manager was proud of his sales force. Careful selection and adequate training maintained a strong group of newcomers ready to take over vacant territories. Adequate compensation kept most of the people satisfied, although there were some complaints that the company was interested only in its sales production and had little regard for them as individuals.

This feeling concerned the sales manager because he felt the need for top morale in order to stimulate superior performance. He was well aware that salespeople needed emotional stimulus to maintain high production. Each year, a contest had helped to motivate them, but only for a short period. What was needed was some type of nonmonetary incentives to give the salespeople prestige, respect, a place in their community, and public recognition.

ASSIGNMENT

Devise a plan of nonmonetary incentives to achieve this goal. Feel free to develop unique approaches. Try for originality, keeping in mind the type of firm and the age range of salespeople from twenty-two to sixty-four years. At least three salespeople were in every five-year age bracket. More salespeople were clustered in the thirty-seven to fifty-nine age area.

LINK CORPORATION
case 11–2

James Doane, sales manager for the Transmission Division of the Link Corporation, thought that everything was going very well; but his best salesman, Dick Tuma, had just given him a problem. Dick was unhappy with his progress and felt that his efforts were not appreciated by management. Doane did his best to reassure Tuma that he was doing good work and that he was appreciated, but Doane realized that something more than words was needed. If Tuma felt like this, then the other people may be unhappy also. Small raises could be given, but that might not be sufficient to motivate them.

Background

The Link Corporation started in the 1930s, making oil pumps for oil burners. They were still one of the major sources for these pumps. During World War II, they started making aircraft hydraulic components. After the war, they diversified by buying a machine tool company and packaging machinery company. The tool business prospered; but the packaging business lost money, and its assets were merged with the machine tool business. The Link Corporation became the prime source for aircraft hydraulic pumps and motors after the war. Management saw that these pumps and motors could be used as transmissions in vehicles of all kinds. They have also been successful in small garden tractors and agricultural equipment.

A few years ago, the company was reorganized into four divisions: Aviation, Industrial, Transmissions, and Research and Engineering. The Transmission Division was the newest and the smallest. It was located in a new factory in Cadillac, Illinois. Corporate headquarters and other divisions were located in Wingford, Illinois.

There were only five salespeople in the Transmission Division to cover the United States. The division sold small hydrostatic transmissions for garden tractors, larger units for a limited number of farm tractors, transmissions and components for farm machinery, components for industrial use, and components to their sister division. The salespeople all had an engineering background because most of their work was in application. There were application engineers in division headquarters available for more involved applications; for complex installations, the Research and Engineering Division would help.

Up to three years' experience was required before a salesperson was considered fully capable. All the present salespeople had come from the sales department of the other divisions. Tuma had the most experience, four years. He had been a salesman in the division since it was formed. Two salesmen had been with the division only one year, and the other two had two and three years' experience. In contrast to the salesmen, James Doane had only recently joined Link Corporation. His previous position had been with Western Corporation as sales engineer and sales manager for their hydrostatic transmission sales.

The Transmission Division salespeople were all on salary with a bonus tied to the profits of the division. There was much missionary work required before a sale could be made. For new installations, there could very well be three years' work before a production order was received. In addition, engineering work had to be done by the division engineers and, for some installations, by the Research and Engineering Division.

The salespeople's salaries were competitive with those in the other divisions and in the industries they called upon. The fringe benefits were set up to match those in the air space industry, but were under those of the agricultural industry and markedly less than those of the automotive industry.

Dick Tuma was the East Coast representative. He called on a major truck manufacturer, several smaller specialty truck manufacturers, off-road vehicle manufacturers, tractor manufacturers, and several agricultural equipment manufacturers.

Doane's Proposal

Doane realized that there was not much he could do for his people in terms of salary. The salary policies were established by corporate headquarters. He thought that there were some nonmonetary fringe benefits that could be provided within the corporate framework. After three weeks' work, he had prepared the following list of possibilities:

1. Private office for the salespeople. At present when they are in the home office, they use desks in the bullpen.
2. A new title, regional sales manager. They are called sales representatives now.
3. Name plates on their offices.
4. Note pads, memo pads, and stationery with their names on them.
5. A secretary to help the five salesmen. Now they give their typing to whoever is not busy.
6. Permission to take their wives on some of their trips.
7. More flexibility in taking days off and in vacation scheduling.

For instance, vacation could be taken a day or two at a time. At present, only whole weeks can be taken.

8. Making the firm's legal and accounting departments available to help the salesmen in their legal and accounting problems. The help would be available only as long as it did not interfere with company business.

Doane felt that if he could get management to accept these changes he would be better able to reward his salesmen. He planned that the new title would be given after the person had completed three years' service successfully.

QUESTIONS

1. Appraise each of the eight proposals, indicating strengths and weaknesses.
2. Would you modify any of the proposals?
3. What other proposals would you suggest?

part three

ADMINISTRATION

12

Sales Territories

A *sales territory* is usually a geographic area which has a sufficient number of customers or potential customers to keep a salesperson fully occupied. Hopefully, it is constructed to facilitate servicing and to meet the requirements of the firm. At the same time, it should be most advantageous for efficient sales operation. Many sales managers think of a territory as a physical area, but they ought not neglect thinking of a sales territory as an aggregate group of buyers. Customers are located at their own convenience, and a sales territory must conform to them. The sales manager must consider where customers or potential customers are and then divide them into suitable territory groupings to promote adequate sales coverage. However much a sales manager might like to rearrange customers, he is powerless to do so and must adjust his actions to what is, not how he would like to have it. One way a sales manager can adjust physical territories is by dropping some customers and securing new ones who are better located.[1]

Sales territories can be widely divergent. They may be too large or too small, too rich or too poor, too concentrated or too widely scattered, have too many or too few customers, have too large or too small customers, be too difficult or too easy to cover. Territories may be too challenging or not challenging enough, too restricted or too broken up for logical traveling, carefully designed or carelessly designed, drawn arbitrarily or fitted to local situations, made to stimulate salespeople or drawn for selfish company reasons, or designed for favorite salespeople, leading to unfavorable boundaries.

---

1. It is not uncommon for firms to drop customers who are prohibitively expensive to service. Many sales managers are reluctant to lose any customers because they are volume oriented instead of profit oriented.

GUIDELINES FOR ESTABLISHING TERRITORIES

There are many problems in establishing equitable territories, and a large number of abuses and weaknesses have developed. Some abuses may be deliberate, but most are unintentional. Many of the variables change in unexpected and confusing ways. For example, a customer with several locations may shift his buying from one area to another; he may shift part of his buying, but not all of it; he may rearrange his buying in kinds of merchandise and in size of orders; he may shift his buying by the season of the year and from large quantity to hand-to-mouth buying; he may change material specifications; he may expect different financing arrangements; he may shift the carrying of inventory.

The sales manager is expected to map territories that will be fair, suitable for the customer, advantageous to the firm, and stimulating for the salesperson. A definite set of guidelines can be useful, in fact essential, to set up territories and allocate them to salespeople.

Reasonable Size

A sales territory must be reasonable in size. In one firm, a reasonable size may be a square mile in a city; a second firm may use the whole city; a third firm, the state; a fourth firm, the New England region, and so on. Mere size is not a territory criterion, but size in relationship to what the salesperson must do is a criterion. For example, some firms have several salespeople assigned to each automobile manufacturer, but expect another salesperson to cover five states.

A reasonable size means that the salesperson can handle the business in his territory in a profitable manner. That does not mean he may sacrifice long-range objectivity in order to realize immediate profit. A territory that is so large or so poorly constructed that it is almost impossible to cover will strain salesperson activities and encourage slighting of customers and neglect of essential tasks. He will cut corners and perform improperly in trying to fulfill requirements.

Sufficient Potential

A salesperson will not receive all the business in his territory. Sometimes, even a small percentage of the business is enough, if sales are highly competitive but enormous. A sales manager should estimate realistically how much business is in a territory and then determine how much his salespeople should receive. To estimate too low is wasting potential sales; to estimate too high is to set an almost impossible task. Frequently, a greater effort is required than the sales justify. It is unwise to go after business at a high cost in one territory if equally good orders may be sold in other territories at less cost.

Lack of potential may seriously hinder some salespeople, but more often territories have greater potential than the salespeople can cultivate. This situation results in territory skimming, which is often wasteful.

Adequate Coverage

If a territory is to receive adequate coverage, the salesperson must handle certain demands, learn customer habits and wishes, and schedule calls to satisfy these requirements. Often, he must make more calls than he would like just to keep sales flowing smoothly. A salesperson may have many discussions with the sales manager to work out how often customer calls are necessary. The salesperson has one idea; the sales manager has another idea; and the customer may think differently from both. Careful planning is required for good coverage of important customers in order to maximize sales.

A sales manager cannot set arbitrary relationships between sales and number of calls. Some customers may have highly fluctuating business, requiring weekly calls at one season and monthly calls the rest of the year. Hopefully, there is a sufficient variety of customers so that a salesperson can dovetail his calls; that is, if customer A requires weekly calls in December, he will require monthly calls in May, and the reverse is true for customer B.

Geographically Sensible Territories

A geographically sensible territory is one that recognizes travel problems. Sometimes the shortest distance is the long way around in mountainous country or where other impediments make the short way not feasible. It is indefensible to lump all customers together, and it is equally absurd to divide territories arbitrarily without recognizing their differences. Physical terrain and climate changes can be significant. Sometimes it is helpful to arrange a territory so that extensive travel between two customers can be done after regular working hours. It is wasteful to have a salesperson use prime selling time for travel.

Take Advantage of Favorable Conditions

Often, a territory may be favorably situated so that the salesperson can cover it with ease. There may be customer groupings, superior highways, freedom from heavy traffic, favorable climate, and other conditions which will enable speedy coverage without sacrificing attention. Another territory may have a set of unfavorable conditions which require much greater effort. The sales manager cannot arbitrarily set up two unlike territories even though they are the same geographical size and are adjacent to one another when such territories have significant internal differences.

Avoid Overextending Salespeople

The salesperson should not be given an oversized territory just because there is plenty of territory not being cultivated. It is far better to handle a smaller territory properly than to give perfunctory attention to many customers in too large a territory.

Thin coverage is not necessarily harmful. When introducing new products or in making calls where salespeople rarely take orders, there may be decided advantages in covering wide territories. The frequency of coverage required is the determining factor in establishing territory size.

Assigning a Difficult Territory

A territory may be difficult for a number of reasons,[2] and it is important to weigh such problems in assigning particular salespeople. Assigning a beginning salesperson to one of the best territories might not be judicious because he might antagonize customers and seriously lower sales. It would not be wise to assign a beginner to a territory where customers are hard to handle. When an excellent territory becomes available, it is common to transfer one of the better salespeople to it so that maximum company benefits continue.

Individual peculiarities may also determine assignments. Moving a competent salesperson to a more difficult territory against his will may be self-defeating because the promise of higher earnings or other reward is insufficient to make him respond adequately to the demands of the new territory.

Salesperson Pride in a Territory

If a salesperson is proud of his territory and satisfied with sales, he is on the way to success. Once he sees further possibilities, he may expand his energies to improve an already successful situation.

Many salespeople have justifiable pride in building harmonious customer relations. This situation may be the work of years of effort and consideration that has developed into a mutual confidence and, in some cases, close friendships. Such relationships can be valuable to a firm; in any reassignment, it may be unwise to move a salesperson unless he is willing. It may be unwise from a customer standpoint to move a particular salesperson. However, changes entered into reluctantly may soon show decided benefits for both the salesperson and his former customers.

---

2. A difficult territory has a number of factors that salespeople cannot handle readily. It requires extra attention and particular skills which salespeople do not have universally. Difficulties include physical size, unprofitable orders, uncooperative customers, competition, delivery problems, poor credit, and many others. Some, but not all, may be present in many territories.

ADVANTAGES OF TERRITORIES

Many sales managers find territories indispensable in allocating market potential distribution among salespeople. Territories become a starting point from which a sales manager can assess individual salesperson success.

Develop Effective Control

A territory is a definite sales assignment set up by the sales manager. It began to exist when the sales manager carved out a piece of potential sales by geographical arrangement or some other pattern. A particular territory becomes meaningful to a salesperson because it is his assigned work area.

Sales control becomes possible because the sales manager measures, evaluates, and prods the salesperson to perform within his area. (Remember that a territory frequently is a geographical area, but it need not be such a breakdown.) Since the salesperson is confining his activities to his territory, his success is determined by his ability to develop it properly and profitably. Proper control may dictate developing a territory quickly or slowly, depending on company objectives; profitable control may stress immediate profits or long-range profits. However, most firms cannot afford a control that primarily stresses long-range results. Unless returns are forthcoming soon, there may be no long-term approach because today's expenses have an insistence that may not afford putting off profit until tomorrow.

Improve Market Coverage

A salesperson with a definite assignment knows the job facing him. He soon learns the extent of his task and is reminded that he must fulfill certain requirements. Each salesperson is assigned a definite job, and his work does not overlap that of any other salesperson. Hopefully, territories are assigned so that no market gaps exist and no meaningful potential is skipped. All communications regarding customers within a territory are addressed to the salesperson responsible, and customer requests for assistance and information are usually channeled to him.

If the salesperson falls down on the job in any way, the sales manager can point it out to him quickly and suggest remedial procedures to increase effective coverage.

Lower Sales Cost

Sales force control using definite territories and careful assignments can lower sales costs because it is one step towards maximizing sales effectiveness. By reducing lost time, by careful routing, and by detailed attention to each person within his territory, the sales manager quickly detects when the salesperson deviates from carefully established objectives and can follow up immediately. Cost as a percentage decreases as sales increase; cost decreases when salespeople spend less time and money in traveling; cost decreases as a salesperson's entertaining is prudent; cost decreases when the salesperson works in the most economical way. Cost decreases help keep sales expense under control.

Improve Customer Service

When customers or potential customers are assigned to a salesperson, he realizes that problems in his territory are his responsibility. He cannot give the task to someone else. The salesperson realizes his success is interwoven with the success of his customers and becomes increasingly aware of the value of each customer. Likewise, the sales manager realizes the importance of rapid customer contact; and as soon as a problem arises with a particular buyer, he can signal the assigned salesperson. The salesperson then reports on how he handled the problem. If it was not solved, he reports his recommendations to handle the problem.

Arouse Salesperson Interest and Responsibility

The opportunity of improving sales, enhancing profits, and increasing customer satisfactions are some of the possibilities facing the salesperson. Once a salesperson feels secure in his territory, his interest grows; his satisfaction increases; his efforts multiply; and his attention becomes spontaneous.

When a salesperson is fully awakened to the possibilities and demands of his territory, he soon realizes and is willing to accept the responsibility that goes hand-in-hand with this assignment. He knows that if something is to happen, it is his job to make it happen. He has the dual responsibility of representing his company to his customers and bringing his customers' needs and complaints to his firm. He irons out difficulties and assures smooth relationships. Many times when he makes a sale, his work is just starting. If it is a sale to a retailer, he must assist the retailer to move the merchandise to the consumer; if the sale is to a manufacturer, he should assist to insure his product's successful use. Until both buyer and seller have gained an advantage in a transaction, the sale is not successful. Only when this goal is being achieved regularly can it be said that the salesperson is discharging his responsibility satisfactorily.

Evaluate Salespeople

A territory assignment provides one of the basic tools for evaluating a salesperson. If a territory is properly constructed, it helps show what a salesperson is doing in relationship to what he ought to be doing. Too often, a salesperson is complimented or criticized on his absolute performance without reference to potential, leading to unfair comparisons because the criteria for measuring are unjust.

A territory can be one of the sharpest tools for separating factors that make up successful sales performance; hence, it should be an almost universal criterion in measuring. It provides the base from which many other factors can be evaluated. A well-drawn sales territory is an equalizing factor that permits a salesperson to compete with other salespeople without irresponsible handicaps and management whims. A territory indicates strengths and weaknesses of a salesperson because it reflects so many conditions—salesperson activity, customer handling, attention to detail, and cooperation with the firm. In many instances, it is impossible to compare fairly a salesperson's performance unless it is based on a definite territory. Even if a salesperson is selling profitably, he might be open to criticism because he is doing little compared to what he ought to be doing. The salesperson who is breaking even or shows no profit may be contributing by bringing in volume from a most difficult territory.

WHEN NOT TO USE TERRITORIES

A territory arrangement is a structured operation with continuity, control, assessment of potential, customer relationships, and other factors which lead to orderly handling of sales. Since these elements are not present under some selling situations, the use of territories might not lead to success. A number of such operations would make territories costly, clumsy, and in some cases detrimental to successful selling.

Temporary Sales Situation

A firm may operate a short period, or it may operate a short time in one area. Because of the cost and difficulty of creating territories with any reliability, it may be preferable to forget territories and let each salesperson ferret out as many sales as possible. Coverage may be poor, but enough business is secured to warrant this approach and may be the only practical solution.

Territory Not Significant

Some firms stress individual sales, and continuity has little meaning. Thus, life insurance salespeople have wide territorial discretion and, in some cases, few if any limitations. Real estate salespeople work with customers and are not restricted to territories except when practical limitations restrict activity. For example, it may be unwise for a real estate salesperson to travel 100 miles in an effort to make a small home sale.

When a salesperson has a wide area, it may be to his advantage to be highly selective in his contacts and not worry about careful territory coverage. There is nothing sacred about covering a territory unless it has some useful justification that will be advantageous to the firm and hopefully to the salesperson.

Territory Not Useful

When salespeople work primarily with customers of their own selection, it would be impractical to set up territories. For example, people who sell newspaper, radio, or television advertising in a city may find it convenient to work on individual accounts that they establish. Sometimes one salesperson may be successful with one buyer when another salesperson has failed repeatedly. Security and mutual fund salespeople may feel that territories are restrictive and hinder productive sales. When there is a large potential of a particular kind of business and salesperson possibilities are almost unlimited, it may be better for the salesperson to determine his own sales coverage.

When territories set up artificial barriers or capricious alignments, they become hindrances to the salesperson and the firm. Many arrangements have failed because they were poorly determined or the nature of selling clearly indicated that a territory arrangement was not strategically sound or workable. The critical factors which determine and justify the need for territories in one situation may be missing in a different arrangement.

Territory Unnecessary

A small firm just starting operation may have so many problems and so much potential that a territory allocation has no significance. In its struggle to survive and become established, it will seek business where it may be found quickly and at the least cost. Territories may be something to think about later. If undesirable sales situations develop, they can be corrected later.

ESTABLISHED TERRITORIES

A sales territory is a unit of a firm's overall territory coverage. It is a convenient segment of the whole market that can be assigned to a salesperson and be controlled and operated as a profit unit.

A sales territory should be large enough to keep a person busy; it should facilitate travel; it should be convenient to work in; it should be determined by keeping both firm and customer in mind. While a territory may be a physical area, a particular group of customers, or some other arrangement peculiar to a firm, we primarily consider it here as a geographical area.

METHODS OF DIVIDING TERRITORIES

There are a number of ways to divide physical areas so that territories may be established. The particular approach used varies from company to company depending on size of market, intensity of coverage, customer profitability, and other factors.

State Unit

A state unit is a convenient political division to use if the potential market is the right size. The same state laws prevail in the entire territory; the highways may be similar; often much of the territory has similar industry. When a salesperson must cover large areas, a territory of several states might be appropriate.

One decided weakness of a state territory is size. There may be too much potential for one salesperson, but not enough for two; too much for two salespeople, but not enough for three. Another weakness is the normal business flow across state lines, ignoring state boundaries. If a state is long and narrow, its business may flow to several states with natural traffic patterns prevailing. Thus, a national wholesaler operating in Michigan covers southeastern Michigan from Detroit and western Michigan from Chicago. The western part of the upper peninsula is tied in with Wisconsin.

County Unit

A county unit is a convenient political subdivision which covers a smaller area and may reflect similar business conditions. Since the county is used as a unit for various statistical measures, it is helpful in assessing the quantity of potential sales. Data are published regularly and are readily available through government publications and through private firms whose business is to prepare and sell such information.

A county may be too large or too small a territory. It is not difficult to add additional counties to make a sales territory or to travel such a territory. Frequently, a county is too large a territory and must be split. A county may not coincide with existing industry and business development; that is, people may have a city affiliation, but be scattered in several counties. Business may naturally flow from one county to another, but may spread from a county in one state to an adjacent county in another state.

City Unit

A city territory or a part of a city is often used because there are definite boundaries. When a city is divided for several salespeople, it is relatively easy to lay out an exact territory for each person. Some minor problems may have to be adjusted to handle a city within a city. Frequently, a city may be divided so that each salesperson works with a special type of customer. In some instances, a salesperson may have only one major customer in a city.

Metropolitan Area Unit

A metropolitan area consists of a major city surrounded by numerous suburban cities or can be two or more sizable cities adjoining each other or connected by suburbs. Standard metropolitan areas have been created by the U.S. government based on counties and cities within these counties totaling over 100,000 people. While these areas, made up of several hundred counties, may cover only about 10 percent of the U.S. land area, they account for two-thirds of the population and more than three-fourths of all retail sales. "The Survey of Buying Power" published by *Sales Management* magazine presents detailed statistics on metropolitan areas as well as smaller territory groupings.

Metropolitan areas cut across state lines and represent patterns of living, buying, and traveling regardless of state boundaries. A metropolitan area tends to develop by natural geographical lines and types of industry rather than by artificial political boundaries.

Trading Area Unit

A trading area usually covers a metropolitan area plus surrounding territory. It is determined by the flow of business from surrounding territory toward a central location. Such a trading area may vary by type of business. Many people think of it as a total retail trading area —the direction most people go to do their major buying. However, what is a retail trading area for a retailer would not necessarily be the same for a wholesaler. For example, a large department store might have a much larger trading area than a food wholesaler; a hardware wholesaler would have a larger trading area than a food wholesaler or a department store. In establishing a sales territory in a trading area, the actual size would be determined by the nature of the product, the channel of distribution, the intensity of coverage, the size and policies of the firm, and other considerations.

PHYSICAL SIZE OF TERRITORY

There are a number of determining factors to be considered in establishing the size of a territory.

Travel Time

A salesperson must travel from one customer to another. Sometimes the distances covered in a sparsely settled area require considerable time. Even though a territory is small, customers may be scattered so that the salesperson must travel ten miles through a congested city to get from one customer to another.

Frequency of Customer Calls

In many cases, it is wise to schedule calls according to customer importance. Some customers are called infrequently because their order size cannot justify greater attention; some important customers are given frequent calls in order to maximize orders. Some customers prefer being called upon at regular intervals and are upset if the routine is varied. Salesperson routing should be considered in call frequency. Minor schedule rearrangement may permit significant time saving without sacrificing customer attention.

Competitive Factors

One territory may be relatively calm while another may be hotly contested. One territory may be serviced with relative ease in an orderly fashion, but a competitive one may require extra attention and customers may make demands on the salesperson's time. Call frequency and order delivery may be multiplied; customer service may be frequent and insistent; and territory problems may multiply.

Salesperson Ability

It appears unwise to determine a territory by basic potential without regard to skill and proficiency of the salesperson. It would be difficult to alter a territory to fit each salesperson as he is assigned; nevertheless, some adjustments might be necessary as people are transferred. The sales manager should not be constantly changing territory boundaries, but he should not regard boundaries as sacred and unchangeable.

Type of Sales Work

The nature of the salesperson's job determines to some extent the size of territory. If the job is strictly selling, the time spent with each customer can be determined. If, however, a salesperson performs a variety of activities—selling, display work, collecting, servicing, delivering merchandise—his time might vary widely among customers.

The job of the salesperson selling to wholesalers would be quite different from that of the salesperson selling to retailers; the salesperson selling to manufacturers would have quite a different pattern from the route person selling to homemakers.

Complexity of Product

Sometimes, a complex product may require frequent customer calls for a period of time and fewer calls later. Some products require much explanation; others require skilled repairmen. These conditions which relate to complexity modify a salesperson's ability to perform because of extra demands on his selling time.

Other Factors Modifying Physical Size

Some buyers are in the market infrequently; they require much attention for a period, but then are not called upon for years. Thus, sales of laboratory equipment to a university may occur once in five or ten years; sales of technical equipment and supplies may require one call a year; sales of science textbooks may need two calls a year. The laboratory salesperson may easily cover a state, but the book salesperson may be assigned to two universities.

The food salesperson finds customers in most physical areas, but the steel salesperson may find all his customers in one city. The office supply salesperson finds numerous customers in cities and towns, but the computer salesperson may find only one or two major customers. Because of this wide diversity in demand, each firm must assign territories in a way to best meet its needs.

CONSTRUCTING A SALES TERRITORY

A sales territory should be set up with the utmost care because it is a unit that is used to determine sales performance. A territory may be determined by assessing basic potential of customers and then adding them to the point where a salesperson has all he can handle. A sales manager may estimate potential for a large territory and then divide it among salespeople. Most sales managers will use part of each approach.

A sales manager may hope to set up each territory accurately, but it is unlikely he can do it. Even if a territory is correct today, it might be incorrect tomorrow because of business and environmental changes. The best any sales manager can do is to approximate equality based on standards previously determined.

Original Territory Construction

A firm usually does not start with scientifically established territories. It starts operating with a certain number of salespeople who are to work in roughly determined areas.

The company starts with a nucleus of salespeople who, most of the time, are unable to do the whole job. Consequently, these people are assigned territories which the sales manager feels are adequate. In developing territories, he assigns each person on the basis of his potential in relation to territory potential.

The sales manager weighs individual ability and wishes, amount of business he thinks each person should get, the physical size of each territory, the difficulty of covering the territory, the number and kinds of customers, and other pertinent factors. On this estimate, he tentatively establishes each territory. After the first rough approximation, he makes adjustments based on suggestions of salespeople familiar with the areas or of other experienced people.

Territory Refinement

A territory should not be a static unit since conditions change from year to year. Population movement may increase one territory and diminish another; industry moves from one location to another; industry purchasing is centralized or decentralized, moving potential from one territory to another; industries rise and decline; product use changes as new competing products enter the market; changing salespeople may require changing territory; company emphasis may shift from one product to another; travel conditions may improve or worsen; a new sales manager may be hired; organization structure may be modified.

As a company grows, there may be internal changes which make selling easier. Management may decide to advertise extensively, improving the selling situation. A new service policy may change buyers' attitudes and increase sales so that a salesperson is unable to handle such a large territory.

After a territory has been accepted and used for a period of time, discrepancies show up that were not foreseen. As such situations become apparent, it becomes necessary to iron out discrepancies and correct weaknesses. Such changes cannot be made constantly since it would be upsetting to both salespeople and customers, but periodically salespeople should expect minor adjustments. Salespeople should be told that territories are subject to major adjustments when management finds it necessary for the firm's or the salesperson's benefit. A drastic change would be to split one territory into two territories and have two salespeople cover the same area one covered previously. One way to prevent the present salesperson from being too upset by this territory change is to assure him of no reduction in compensation for the coming year, even though he has only half as much territory. It is not unusual to double sales by this method because the first arrangement resulted in skimming, rather than intensive selling.

As a company grows, regional or district sales offices become essential for effective supervision. A rearrangement changing direction and control from the main office to smaller offices, each controlling several territories, requires reorganization. Each district receiving closer supervision should become increasingly productive.

When changes are instituted, it is wise to sell each salesperson on the value of the change to him. Arbitrarily changing territories may upset salespeople and cause some of the best people to resign because they resent this approach. Those who stay may be disenchanted by what they feel is unwarranted exercise of pressure tactics. Even though they stay, their morale is lowered, and their efforts become less responsive.

ASSIGNING TERRITORIES

A variety of ways are used in assigning sales territories. The sales manager may wish to assign them in a particular way, but he may have to temper his approach because of individual salesperson desires or instructions from his boss. The top executive may have specific ideas on territories but realize he cannot enforce his approach too far without upsetting his sales manager or salespeople's morale. The salesperson has his own ideas, but he realizes he cannot get all he wants.

It is not likely that each salesperson can get what he wants; a certain amount of compromise is inevitable. The competent sales manager must sell each salesperson on particular advantages in his territory, giving the impression that there is no really bad territory. A salesperson failing in a territory may be as much of a reflection on the sales manager as on the salesperson.

Salespeople Differences

Each salesperson should be considered in relation to territories to be assigned. One salesperson prefers an open territory with scattered customers, another prefers a compact one; one prefers to deal with smaller firms, another likes large firms; one prefers to work regular hours, another does not worry about hours; one likes to get home at night, another does not mind being away; one does not like to tackle difficult customers, another likes this challenge; one wilts under tough competition, another thrives on it.

There may be physical reasons why one salesperson cannot handle one territory as well as another salesperson. There are circumstances in which strength and endurance are prime assets and give the young, vigorous person his opportunity; there may be situations where patience, skill, and sagacity are the prime requisites for a territory. One person may have family problems which keep him close to home; another may be single and have no family demands.

Territory Differences

The variation in territories can be staggering. Some territories are large and have scattered potential; others vary from medium to small in physical size and vary in potential. Two territories may have similar potential, but one is favorable to a firm and another gives most of the business to a competitor. Two territories may have similar potential, but one is located within ten miles of the manufacturing plant and the other a thousand miles away. One territory has a few large buyers; another has many small buyers.

Individual Assignment

It is not likely to find an assignment schedule that is perfect in matching person and territory. The astute salesperson knows that his territory is not necessarily the best. All he can be expected to do is to make it outstanding with respect to what business is available.

When a salesperson is assigned a territory, he can anticipate hard work to make it productive. While the potential is there, he must contest with competition to obtain his share. He must create a good image for himself and his firm and convert prospects into customers.

PROBLEMS IN ESTABLISHING SALES TERRITORIES

It may appear easy to draw up territories based on geographical maps and sales potential, but in practice a number of problems arise that upset easy solutions.

Existing Territories Not Suitable

When existing territories are no longer functional, they must be changed. Territories become out-of-date because of new traffic arteries, population and industry changes, and other factors. No matter how carefully changes are made in territories, some salespeople will feel they have been mistreated. One way of softening the blow to an upset salesperson is to guarantee that his compensation for the coming year will not be below the year just completed.

Too Large a Territory

When a salesperson has too large a territory, it is necessary to adjust it. If it can be made into two territories, the adjustment may be relatively easy, but painful to the present salesperson. If parts must be shifted to other territories, real hassles can develop.

When a territory is divided, the salesperson may want to retain certain accounts. If this practice is allowed, the result may be a broken territory or strange configurations that may temporarily placate the salesperson but lead to illogical customer distribution.

Too Small a Territory

A territory may be inadequate because of poor design, a large number of small accounts, peculiar customer purchasing patterns, pronounced seasonal fluctuations, and other reasons. Theoretically a territory may be sufficiently large to give plenty of business, but practical considerations make it difficult to implement.

Territory Jumping

Many firms do not require regular contact with a customer because of the operation involved. For example, a customer buys only once or once every five years. When this type of operation prevails, coverage is thin and salespeople change; territorial boundaries become less rigid, and it is not uncommon to have one salesperson go into another territory to solicit business. For example, if territory A has an aggressive salesperson and territory B has no salesperson or a beginner, management might tell the salesperson from territory A to go into territory B to try for a particularly large sale.

Some companies may designate particular areas for salespeople without having each territory exclusive, meaning salespeople may sell in other territories. In large territories, one person could invade another territory, and the second person would never know it.

Crisscrossing Territories

Crisscrossing results from salespeople being permitted to retain certain favored accounts in other territories. For example, a salesperson is transferred from territory A to territory B, but retains one customer in his old territory because of some particular relationship.

Sometimes these situations are overemphasized, particularly when one of the senior salespeople is transferred but wishes to keep a favorite customer in the old territory. If it appears the new person cannot hold his customer and he is an important buyer, some crisscrossing may be necessary. This situation may be temporary and should be corrected. It is not a desirable continuing policy.

Irregular Buying

Some customers buy in varying quantities at varying times, but must be worked regularly and persistently to increase their orders. They may be desirable customers because their orders are profitable, although much effort is expended.

The erratic buyer is one who comes and goes without any way of predicting his business in size and frequency. He may buy only once, frequently for a period, infrequently, or sporadically. Such business is often welcome because it becomes a market for excess inventory or can give factory production a boost at a slack period. If such purchases are scattered, they tend to level out sales; but if they bunch up, they can be a handicap.

Favored Customers

A territory may be small geographically or in number of customers, but the buyers can be so important that they are worth constant attention. Some suppliers of major equipment have their own technicians at the buyer's plant so that any breakdown can get immediate attention. A firm may put its best salesperson in a small territory where the actual duties are light, but he must possess consummate skill in handling problems when the occasion arises.

Demanding Customers

A territory may have an undue number of demanding customers, forcing the salesperson to concentrate in a smaller area. As long as profitable business is secured, a company may restrict a salesperson to a limited area and may even divide a normal territory into two assignments because one salesperson can cover only half of the territory.

A customer may want special delivery service or special inventory privileges. Some customers are slow payers, and the salesperson may double as a collector.

Some customers frequently return items. The quality seems to be less than they expected; the selection or variety may bother some buyers. Some retailers overstock and return shop-worn merchandise, exceeding the allowance established by the manufacturer; some send back equipment which broke down in service even though the breakdown was the fault of the user.

A firm may be generous in providing services for which most buyers are grateful and use sparingly. There are some customers, however, who abuse such privileges and take advantage of the salesperson. Services which most customers use rarely may be used frequently by inconsiderate customers. Costly arrangements made by the manufacturer for special occasions may become commonplace demands from certain customers. Such abuses come to be accepted to some extent, and a firm may put up with much if customers are profitable. If such services become excessively burdensome, the salesperson cannot function properly.

One problem which can become serious is constant demands for concessions. One buyer wants an extra discount; a second wants different credit terms; a third wants free merchandise; a fourth wants special packaging. If the firm has been granting some concessions, demands are multiplied; the salesperson must call his boss; extra time is used; and the result is one or two fewer calls a day.

QUESTIONS AND PROBLEMS

1. Discuss five guidelines for establishing territories. Indicate why they should be used.

2. What are some of the problems that arise in assigning a difficult territory?

3. There are a number of sales advantages in having territories. Discuss these advantages from the company's and salesperson's viewpoint.

4. Territories have litle merit in some selling situations. Point out such conditions, indicating why a territory is unnecessary and when it may cause harm.

5. Territories often are based on political units. When may such areas really result in poor territories?

6. Why is a trading area important in territory creation? Explain.

7. Discuss the methodology of determining territory size. Point out factors that must be considered.

8. Explain the need to fit the size of a territory to the complexity of the product.

9. Explain why a territory may need revision from year to year.

10. Draw five territories in an area you choose. Assign five salespeople to these areas and indicate why you chose each salesperson for a territory. Call the territories 1, 2, 3, 4, 5. Name the salespeople A, B, C, D, E. For example, you may assign salesperson D to territory 1. Explain why, giving details. Continue this procedure for all five territories. You may wish to show the territory design.

11. Discuss five or more problems that may upset present territory allocation.

---

case 12–1   **GENERAL HOSPITAL SUPPLY**

Leonard Austin was made district sales manager for the General Hospital Supply Company. He replaced Mr. Franz, who had retired. Mr. Austin had been a salesperson for five years and the assistant sales manager for one year under Mr. Franz.

General Hospital Supply Company is one of the leading suppliers of hospital equipment. The Tennessee district, of which Austin is sales manager, employs ten salespeople. The product line consists of anything from band-aids to furniture. The salespeople are paid on a commission basis plus an expense account. The sales territories are not divided by geographical boundaries, but by assigned accounts, resulting in different salespeople calling on accounts only minutes apart. In fact, four salespeople have accounts in the Memphis area. The Tennessee district is one of the few in the company to have sales territories districted by accounts.

When Austin was a salesperson, his territory had been divided on a geographical basis. His move to Tennessee as assistant sales manager was his first encounter with the territory-by-account concept. As assistant sales manager, for more than a year he had been able to observe the actions of many of the salespeople. He became especially familiar with those agents who worked in the Memphis area.

Louise Wilson is a salesperson in the Memphis area. Her territory extends thirty miles. Louise is constantly mentioning the distance she has to travel every day. In the past year, she had put over 25,000 miles on her car. Louise is twenty-eight years old. In the past, her sales had been good, but not spectacular. This year, her sales seemed to be slipping. She is under last year's sales for this same time period.

Fred Peale is another salesperson in the Memphis area. Austin had made several calls with Fred and concluded that Fred did not use his time profitably. Also, it was evident that his sales were slipping and he was losing accounts to the competition, who had not been much of a threat in the Tennessee district.

Thomas Bone is the third (in volume) Memphis area salesperson. His territory covers as much area as Wilson's, but his accounts are fewer and far less profitable. Austin noticed that Thomas was not trying to sell the line but was an order taker. Thomas has been employed by the company for two years and has not had a formal sales training program.

John Seaver was the first (in volume) Memphis area salesperson. Austin found John to be a fairly steady worker except that he liked to gamble. Austin couldn't prove anything, but he suspected that at certain times John was spending much of his time at the track instead of doing his job.

When Austin took over as district sales manager, he was fortunate because of the year that he spent as assistant to Mr. Franz. During his first year as assistant and the time that had passed since his appointment, he had formed various opinions about his problems. He knew that the district's sales volume was in need of a big boost. His first thought was to adjust the present sales territories into more equitable (probably geographical) areas without the duplication or crossing over boundaries that existed in the district. He felt that if he changed the method of territory alignment the salespeople would probably do a better job because of operating in district territories. A new alignment would also show the need for more salespeople, but Austin did not have any trainees.

ASSIGNMENT

Using the Memphis area or a similar metropolitan area, divide it into sales territories. Customers include hospitals, industrial clinics, and physicians' clinics. Assume each salesperson can average ten calls a day or fifty a week. Major customers require weekly calls; smaller ones are contacted every two weeks. Small customers get one call a month. Each salesperson is to call on at least three new prospects each week. Explain what you have done in establishing your territories. You should give your assumptions and any supporting information that helps clarify your decision. You will keep the same sales personnel, although you may set up additional territories if you think that is necessary. If you do make more than four territories, how would you staff them temporarily?

---

case 12–2   **FLOW-RITE PAINT COMPANY**

The Flow-Rite Paint Company has existed for over one hundred years. It has been a subsidiary of a larger national firm for about twenty years. It is a local firm that has always been based in Indianapolis. Prior to its affiliation with its present large corporation, it operated independently with primarily regional markets and some export operations. At present, it operates and produces products under both its own label and those of the parent institution. The products of Flow-Rite are grouped in three general classifications, maintenance, trade sales, and general industrial items.

Markets

Maintenance paint is marketed throughout the Midwest and nationally, primarily by means of franchised retail outlets. Trade sales products are marketed through specialty stores, institutional retail outlets, and discount houses. A large variation exists in prices relative to the distribution outlets. Using discount houses was a tremendous boon to the merchandising of trade sales products and continues to be an excellent means of distribution. The trade sales products include both latex and solvent-based wall paint, exterior quality primers and top-coats, both latex and solvent-based, wood stains and furniture refinishing kits, and floor coverings.

The industrial line is the one that is under consideration in this case. Marketed as general items are literally thousands of unique products. The industrial division of the company considers itself to be truly marketing oriented. Literally nothing is produced and practically nothing is developed that is not geared toward the individual demands of separate customers. Research and development work is done at the wish of the industrial sales manager from customer contacts by the industrial salespeople. The various products handled by the industrial sales department are too numerous to mention, but any company that uses paint in its operation is a potential prospect for the industrial salespeople.

Competition

The competition in this type of business is quite keen, and the biggest competitive threats are such nationally known names as Du Pont, Sherwin-Williams, Glidden, and several others. A direct threat to the industrial accounts come from small local firms in and around the Detroit and Chicago areas. These smaller firms do not have the overhead in their pricing structure and, in certain limited areas, can obtain business from industrial firms by price cutting due to lower costs. The small firms are not a threat in the case of specialty items, such as exterior quality automotive topcoats or heat-resistant finishes approved by the National Aeronautical and Space Administration for use on reentry vehicles in the space program.

Sales Organization

Because it is a subsidiary, Flow-Rite must accede to the demands of the parent organization. Flow-Rite was well known throughout the Midwest industrial area as a quality producer of industrial paints prior to its acquisition. Flow-Rite remained relatively autonomous in its marketing activities in the industrial area until quite recently.

The sales staff for industrial products is composed of eight salespeople, only two of whom are college graduates. Most of the salespeople have been with the company for over ten years. There are no trainee salespeople, and one full-time serviceman is retained. The sales manager has been with the company for five years, assuming his position after retiring from military service. The selling experience of the sales manager is limited, but top management feels that his administrative capabilities qualify him for the position. Prior to six months ago, territories were essentially nonexistent. Any salesperson could go anywhere that his allotted expenses for a one-year period would allow. Accounts as far as Iowa, Pennsylvania, and even North Carolina were not uncommon. This practice was a holdover from the former national image of the company. The parent corporation has now decided to limit the territories of the salespeople to Indiana primarily.

Territorial Problems

Because of the switch to realign the territories on a geographical basis, many conflicts have developed. One salesperson who is rated as the top person for both ability and earning stands to lose $3000 to $5000 worth of commissions because of the necessity of turning some of his accounts over to the parent organization. He complains that he built one strong account and serviced it for several years and now feels justified in keeping it. The account is in Pittsburgh and could be handled by an eastern branch. In addition, some accounts that were handled by the parent organization in past years had become inactive. In some cases, Flow-Rite salespeople called on those accounts and obtained some business. Because of redistricting, the parent corporation wants those accounts returned. This situation is creating a furor.

Job of an Industrial Salesperson

An industrial paint salesperson is a part-time salesperson, part-time fact gatherer, and full-time troubleshooter. One old-timer has described the industrial paint business as one crisis after another. Because of the many problems unique to each customer, the salesperson has to have an intimate knowledge of both product and customer operation. Although the assistance of several technical experts is available, the salesperson must be knowledgeable enough to get his customer out of trouble when his production line shuts down because of painting problems. Most salespeople become successful in this business only after many years of experience. Selling industrial paint is essentially a technical job along with a selling job, and engineers are interested in facts and good production time.

Compensation Plan

Salespeople are compensated both by salary and commission. Salaries vary from $7,000 to $10,000 depending on years of service and past earnings. In some cases, commissions are equal to or greater than salaries. All commissions are paid on December 31. Many of the higher paid salespeople are unhappy with that arrangement. Yearly incomes of $15,000 to $20,000 are not uncommon. Commissions are based on the profitability of the items sold. There is a 1 percent commission on 15 to 17 percent profit items, a 2 percent commission on 18 to 25 percent profit items, and a 3 percent commission on 26 percent or above profit items.

Commissions are paid on everything sold on a dollar basis after 80 percent of quota has been reached, providing the items sold have at least a 15 percent profit. Quotas and expenses are determined by consultation between each salesperson and sales manager. A typical example would be a quota of $300,000 and expenses of $6,000 per year. If the allotted expenses are exceeded, the difference is subtracted from the commission at the end of the year.

Present Situation

Take-over of accounts by the parent organization and the inability of some salespeople to earn any commission while others do well with essentially the same territories have created problems. Territories for all the salespeople at present are "anywhere" in Indiana. Some of the salespeople are losing lucrative accounts through top management redistricting. The pricing problem and threat of small companies to cut prices in competition together with the high quality of competitive products have made the salespeople's job quite difficult.

The loss of certain accounts to the parent organization may cause the loss of some excellent salespeople and probably the accounts because of the intimate product knowledge of the salespeople. Most of the products sold are not covered by patents, and any one of several other companies could easily duplicate the product and take the business if a disgruntled salesperson gave them the information.

ASSIGNMENT

Outline the steps you would take to handle the present situation. Explain each step you suggest, indicating probable results. What are the immediate problems that may arise, and are there long-range effects?

13

Sales Forecasting

The *sales forecast* is an estimate of sales in a coming period—month, quarter, half-year, or a longer time interval. It is based on a number of factors, some of which are company controlled and others which are beyond company control. It is a prediction of the future as assessed by company management.

A realistic sales forecast should be based on reasonably obtainable goals. It should reflect current operations modified by any changes in company policies in the coming period. For example, a change in advertising could bring a change in sales.

USE OF SALES FORECAST

The sales forecast should be a guide to aid in maximizing performance. Some firms tend to use it as a whip to spur performance, but such an approach becomes self-defeating because the forecast may not be a sensible appraisal, but a tool to drive salespeople. Often, a forecast is recklessly developed to satisfy management's desire and is not a measure of realistic performance. A carefully developed, relatively accurate sales forecast is useful for a number of the firm's activities.

Production Guide

A sales forecast helps to guide production in scheduling. Manufacturing is alerted to the quantities needed and can make commitments in purchasing equipment, materials, and supplies. The number of production workers can be determined and arrangements made to increase or reduce the force if necessary. The company can determine the number of shifts it should operate. Must factory space be increased through buying or leasing? How much should the firm produce, and how much should it subcontract? Will it be cheaper to install new equipment, or should reliance on other suppliers be continued? Many of these problems are easier to resolve if sales forecasts have been reliable.

Purchasing Guide

Most companies must make forward commitments. It is difficult for the purchasing agent to buy unless he knows how much is needed. He is forced to forecast demand through forward buying and must be guided by management. Forecasting is inevitable in forward buying; and even though the purchasing agent hedges purchases through qualifying commitments, he still must make some firm decisions. Unless he is guided by sales forecasting, he probably will rely on past experience.

Financing Guide

One of the critical areas in any company is to provide sufficient financing to keep going smoothly. Most companies do not have large sums of money ready to use. They prefer to finance normal operations by using mostly their own money, but borrow from banks or other sources for fluctuations above normal. Seasonal borrowing is common, as is borrowing for special occasions and unexpected contingencies.

Sales Guide

The sales forecast becomes the sales guide for the marketing department. It may be a guide to determine advertising, number of salespeople, selling expenses, sales training, recruiting, supervising, and even marketing research.

The sales manager bases his planning on the amount of business he will do in the coming period. The year's forecast becomes a basic tool for developing sales strategy; the quarterly forecast gives greater direction and an opportunity to make changes as conditions vary and sales deviate from forecast; the monthly forecast enables the sales manager to adjust rapidly, to level out or increase effort, to shore up weak territories, to change plans, and to meet unexpected contingencies. For example, a strike in a firm or in a competitor's firm can change short-range plans drastically.

VALIDITY OF SALES FORECAST

Some firms place high reliance on their sales forecasts; others use them as general guides. Such variations on forecast dependence may depend on the skill of forecasters, the nature of the industry, the stability of the economy, and other factors.

"Things do not just happen" is a saying to keep in in mind when forecasting. How well the forecaster reads the factors that influence his company sales determines how well he can estimate. The skill of the forecaster may depend on his individual ability, but that skill can be aided by how many forecasting tools he can use and how well he recognizes forecasting limitations. If a sales manager's attention is perfunctory, forecasting reliability may be questionable.

Validity Determined by Type of Industry

In an industry where the product is consumed daily, the forecast may be highly valid in guiding the sales department; if the product is seasonal and used intermittently or is a once-in-a-lifetime purchase, a forecast may be an approximation. A valid forecast is one that is sound and dependable because it is based on factors that strongly determine or influence sales. For example, bread sales are highly predictable because experience tells what to expect from people. Sales of snowmobiles, on the other hand, can vary tremendously because pertinent factors cannot be pinned down accurately. Forecasting the sales of a fad article is even more difficult because of inability to predict its life cycle.

Validity Determined by Individual Forecaster

A person with little ability in forecasting or one who takes his work lightly is not likely to have valid forecasts. By chance or by intuition, he may be successful occasionally; but most of the time his work is not dependable.

Forecasting is both a science and an art. It is a science when the individual relies on tools that measure specific factors, and it is an art when he displays keen judgment and seems to have an ability to determine what will happen. The forecaster who can use both of these approaches and has background experience in the area is likely to come up with a dependable forecast, but the individual depending on the use of only one technique will often fail to arrive at reliable estimates. Skill, practice, use of proper tools, and good judgment help the astute forecaster.

Validity Determined by Economic Factors

The immediate future often can be predicted with a high assurance of accuracy because economic conditions seldom change abruptly; the intermediate period forecast becomes less certain because the forces of change may operate as in the past, or there may be particular circumstances which will cause sales to deviate from the original forecast. Unexpected factors may alter a sales prediction; a strike in one area may curtail sales; a crop failure in a farm area can be a severe setback; a natural catastrophe can practically wipe out sales for a period.

A growth in the economy may produce strains on the factors of production so that a firm is unable to obtain material and parts for manufacturing, resulting in weakened production and interrupted deliveries of finished goods. A firm may forecast sales but be out of step with the economy, failing to recognize impending changes which will alter demand.

SALES FORECAST ACCURACY

Most sales forecasters hope to make an estimate that will measure actual sales accurately; few succeed. Yet most forecasts, if they are reasonably accurate, are useful for planning. Even though the firm's activity varies somewhat, the forecast becomes a guide because actual sales will not be too far from the forecast.

Many forecasters are happy if they can estimate sales within a plus or minus 5 percent. For example, if the estimate is $100,000 and sales fall between $95,000 and $105,000, the forecaster feels his work is satisfactory. Some firms with a stable sales pattern may confidently estimate between a plus or minus 1 percent.

Most sales forecasts are not intended to pinpoint sales, but to give a range of sales guidance. For example, a drug wholesaler would not predicate his inventory on a precise sales volume, but rather be guided by a relative approach allowing some leeway for unexpected contingencies.

A spurious accuracy can be achieved by certain manipulation. If a sales manager wanted sales to reach his forecast, he could take extraordinary measures and force uneconomic sales merely to achieve this artificial goal. If sales are coming in easily, salespeople may slack up, knowing they will reach the sales forecast with ease.

A firm may not be concerned with extreme sales forecast accuracy, however desirable that it is, but should be concerned with the range of accuracy. Thus a possible range of percentages (1, 2, 5, 10) must be considered in planning.

AIDS TO FORECASTING

There are a number of useful tools that will aid the forecaster to gain perspective, improve available information areas, sharpen his ability to evaluate, and develop his sensitivity to factors influencing sales. Some of these tools are common and easily adaptable; some are technical and require careful use; and some will be helpful if they are used with caution and understanding.

One approach that can be to great advantage is the use of company data. Applying statistical techniques to this data often yields a number of significant relationships.

Another area of great importance is the economy in which the firm functions. The state of the economy is measured by a number of statistical devices. If the forecaster is able to compare his firm's sales with data of the economy, he has a handle to guide him.

Many forecasting data are secured by talking with informed people in the industry. These individuals are close to what is happening and are able to interpret events. Other information is compiled by general publications and publications specializing in particular areas. For example, magazines in the steel industry compile a wealth of data pertaining to steel production, sales, and use. Trade associations regularly assemble data of interest to particular groups. Some of this information is available to everybody; and some, only to association members.

The United States government is a prolific source of information. Since this information is gathered in many ways and covers enormous industry segments, it may be bewildering. The competent forecaster must study this information and make adjustments and rearrangements to fit his needs. Professional firms take government data and rearrange them to fit the needs of particular users who buy this service.

The computer has opened many areas to the forecaster since it can perform an enormous volume of computations rapidly and permit him to make comparisons and study phenomena in ways which would have been prohibitively expensive or impossible previously. The computer is valuable in revising and updating forecasts on a monthly or other periodic base.

METHODS OF SALES FORECASTING

A number of sales forecasting methods are used depending on background of user, availability of pertinent data, importance of forecast, accuracy desired, length of time involved, practical considerations, and other reasons. Some are simple and easy to apply; others are sophisticated and require competent technicians to obtain satisfactory results. No single method is best, but there probably is one best method for a particular firm at a particular time because this method fits in best with the resources available. A hit-and-miss complex forecast or a naive one may be worse than none at all.

Sales Force Composite

The *sales force composite* is an accumulation of individual estimates from the sales territories, districts, and regions. Each salesperson estimates what he will sell in the coming period. These estimates are combined by each district manager for his district, possibly adjusted by what he thinks can be done, and then sent to the regional manager. The district manager can forward his total district forecast. If the regional manager desires, he may ask the district manager to forward each salesperson's estimate along with his comments. The regional manager combines the district managers' reports, makes revisions, and sends the information to the sales manager at the home office.

The sales manager combines these reports, studies the final result, makes adjustments to anticipate particular policy changes, consults with other executives, and finally arrives at a sales forecast. If salespeople report directly to the home office, each salesperson's estimate would be sent directly to the home office for consolidation.

This method might be termed a grass-roots approach because the estimates are made by the people responsible for sales. These people are close to the buyer. Each salesperson is aware of trends in his district; he discusses future needs with customers and estimates what he can do in getting new business. When the salesperson prepares his estimate, he knows he is responsible for selling that amount. Since it is his forecast, he accepts responsibility for it and works diligently to make or surpass it.

There are weaknesses to this method which must be considered. Salespeople are not known for being accurate in projecting sales. An optimistic salesperson may overestimate and give excuses why he could not meet his estimate. The next year, he will be more cautious and give a low estimate which he is certain he can sell. If compensation is based on quota tied to his estimate, he becomes extremely conservative because his sales over quota may increase his income. Salespeople may not be followers of broad economic changes, close to political upheavals, and alert to conditions which affect them indirectly. Nor are they always informed of basic policy changes in the firm in time to be able to incorporate those features in their estimate. Consequently, their estimates may be far off just because of lack of company information that will affect sales.

Correlation Techniques

A firm's sales are affected by numerous economic and social forces. Many of these forces are quantitative, and the information is compiled and published regularly. Each series of data measures factors that change as people exercise their purchasing function or other behavior. There are many series of data that report changes in economic and social life in a continuous fashion. Some are of recent origin; many date back as much as fifty years; some have been in existence for much longer. These time series data, many of them known as business indicators, report what has happened. By careful study, a firm may find that one or more of these indicators parallel the activities of the company. If he can determine or discover what an indicator will do, he has a good indication of what his firm's sales will be.

The National Bureau of Economic Research has conducted exhaustive studies on indicators and how they behave. In dealing with so-called business indicators, it has been found that each moves at a different time period in relation to business. Some change ahead of business fluctuations and are known as *leading indicators;* some change about the same time as sales increase or decrease and are known as *concurrent indicators;* some show changes after the main business activity changes and are called *lagging indicators.* "Business Economic Developments" and "Survey of Current Business" are two U.S. government publications that cover these areas extensively; numerous other sources are available. *The Statistical Abstract of the United States,* issued yearly, and the "Federal Reserve Bulletin," issued monthly, should be readily available to anyone doing serious forecasting. *Agricultural Statistics* and other publications of the U.S. Department of Agriculture are useful to those whose forecasts are dependent on agriculture. Figure 13–1 illustrates changes of sales in relation to an income index.

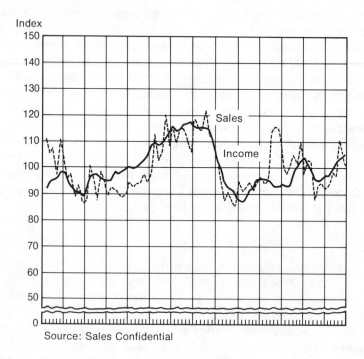

Source: Sales Confidential

Figure 13–1
A seven-year comparison of district sales of a firm with an income of that district. (Adjusted for seasonal variation and trend. Sales figures converted to index figures.)

Simple correlation

In *simple correlation,* the forecaster compares past sales of the firm or industry he is forecasting with an indicator he thinks acts similarly to his sales figures. Hopefully, he will find an indicator that moves like his sales, either leading, concurrent, or lagging. If he finds a leading indicator, he is in a fortunate position. For example, if a forecaster knows how much and the stage of construction activity at a particular time, he will know approximately the demand for builders' hardware in six months. Such prediction is indicative, not precise.

A forecaster is more likely to find a concurrent indicator because income indexes, industrial production index, and other well-known series frequently describe what is affecting the sales curve. While such an indicator is not as useful as a leading indicator, in the short run it may be helpful because of "sticky" numbers. (An indicator with "sticky" figures is one that changes slowly over time, for example, Gross National Product.)

A lagging indicator is useful in retrospect to assess actual performance against what should have been done. As a forecasting tool, the lagging indicator gives little help except perhaps to aid in constructing a hypothetical sales curve. It could possibly be used in looking forward and setting goals, particularly when sales have fallen short of reasonable expectations.

In using simple correlation, it is necessary to understand the significance of the data obtained. Positive correlation varies from 0 to 1; negative correlation varies from 0 to -1; most forecasters find positive correlation more interesting to use, although negative correlation could be equally useful.

While correlation shows a relationship between indicator and sales, the relationship varies widely. For forecasting, a correlation of 0.8 or 0.9 can be quite helpful, but lower correlations have problematical value. The forecaster must square the coefficient of correlation and multiply by 100 to obtain the coefficient of determination. Using this approach, 0.9 correlation becomes 81 percent, which is the coefficient of determination or explained variation. Simply stated, 81 percent of variation in sales can be explained by the indicator used; the other 19 percent variation must be explained by other factors. Even with a 0.7 correlation, the result is only 49 percent explained variation, which would be difficult to use in forecasting unless much other pertinent information was available.

Multiple correlation

Instead of using one independent variable or indicator, a forecaster can use two or more in correlating with sales in an attempt to reduce unexplained variation. Thus, if one indicator can give 81 percent explained variation, the addition of two more might increase that to 91 percent or more. Multiple correlation is a laborious mathematical approach that was little used before the computer era. Presently, these extensive computations are readily handled by the computer. Multiple correlation can be quite useful if no one indicator gives much help, but when several indicators together give a high correlation.

High correlation does not relieve the forecaster from caution and constant testing to check validity of continuing relationships. Conditions which caused sales and indicators to behave similarly may change. Former relationships may no longer apply. Occasionally, a forecaster may find an indicator which correlates well, but it is impossible to determine why. This apparently spurious relationship should not cause him to discard the indicator, but to use it with great caution.[1]

Projection of Past Sales

Some sales managers prefer to forecast sales from past experience. Most people, businesses, and conditions have a tendency to continue as before; change comes about slowly. From this idea comes the method of projecting future sales on a basis of past sales. The simplest method is to chart sales on graph paper and then project them forward based on past trend. Merely laying a straight edge on the sales line on the chart will indicate approximate future sales. A more accurate approach is to fit past data to a line mathematically and project it on the mathematical formula. As long as the relationship is linear (straight-line), this method is easy to use; but when the relationship becomes curvilinear, the mathematical treatment becomes more complex, and the straight-edge approach cannot be used.

This type of short-run forecasting is frequently very useful since it gives the sales manager a raw forecast, which he modifies subjectively based on plans projected for the coming period. Forecasting for long future periods in this fashion is questionable because this method assumes the future will be like the past.

Customer Intentions

What customers expect to do in the coming year can be used as an indicator of future sales. In forecasting future business, some business publications will ask representative firms about their intentions. The

1. The preceding discussion on use of correlation techniques introduces forecasting to the use of linear association analysis. Specifically, *regression analysis* expresses the relationship between an independent and a dependent variable. It is used to predict values of the dependent variable from values of the independent variable. *Correlation analysis* shows the degree of relationship of two variables. The forecaster may find a number of independent variables, each with a different correlation coefficient to his sales, and choose one that gives the best results. *Simple association analysis* relates a dependent variable to an independent variable. *Multiple association analysis* relates a dependent variable to two or more independent variables.

publication will derive data for new construction, expansion, growth, and retrenchment.

It is not unusual for salespeople to gather data from customers about what they expect to do in the coming period. From these estimates, salespeople build forecasts. These cumulated forecasts then are used in forecasting company sales. The actual interviews may be held with a number of executives of a firm. When major decisions are involved, it is important to obtain information from the executives making such decisions.

This approach gives the salesperson insight into the thinking of his customers. It is a method that helps when other methods fail, perhaps when a product is new or there is no statistical information available. While much of the data may be vague and problematical, they will give a salesperson a general understanding of a firm's forecast of the coming period.

A danger in this approach is that the salesperson or the one gathering information is not skilled enough to interpret it properly. He may take general statements at face value, interpret optimistic predictions as real expectations, and fail to make proper adjustments for the individual giving the information. The salesperson may be unable to assess optimism and pessimism accurately and to make allowances for individual variations. Also, executives may change their minds, making their previous statements inaccurate.

This type of forecasting can be useful in major equipment sales and when sales are large and irregular. Such customers may come in the market only once in five years and make a large purchase, or they may indicate an expansion program over a period of years.

Management Estimates

The executive estimate approach is widely used; it varies greatly in reliability; it may reflect composite executive opinions or merely the opinion of the top executive perhaps reinforced by "yes" men in lower capacities.

It is common in many firms to assemble the individual executive estimates and then churn them together in a final forecast. The fallacy is that by combining a number of inaccurate estimates one good estimate can be achieved. All individual estimates may be unduly optimistic, far too pessimistic, or scattered in no particular way. Thus, a consolidation of estimates may improve the final figure, but it may also be far worse than some individual estimates.

Executives who are quite knowledgeable in their particular area and have demonstrated skill in estimating may come up with very accurate forecasts. These people understand their market, keep in close touch with economic conditions, watch competition closely, and are aware of market and product changes.

Some executives, however, merely look at past sales, say they ought to do better, and then arbitrarily set a forecast of 10 percent increase for the coming period. Such forecasts are inevitably in nice, round figures, such as 10, 15, or 20 percent.

Are such estimates and forecasts useful? To the extent that they reflect good judgment, careful appraisal, and an attempt to weigh pertinent factors, they can achieve reasonable accuracy and be helpful as guides. When carelessly made or merely used as a crude attempt to bludgeon the sales force, they become meaningless or even harmful.

Combined Methods

It is not uncommon to combine two separate estimates in the hope that the final result will be an improvement. Thus, one group can base its estimate on statistical data and measurable objectives. The other estimate may be the judgment of executives, based on objective and subjective factors plus intuition. If a third estimate comes from the sales force, all three may be used.

In combining these estimates, the forecaster does not simply average them. Rather, he studies each individually and makes separate value judgments on separate sections of each forecast in an attempt to reach a consensus. In some sections, one estimate may be kept intact and another completely eliminated. Certain weighting factors may be employed in particular instances to make more relevant certain sections of an estimate. While both a segmented and a lump sum estimate may come from each source, the adjustment factors are made on various segment estimates to bring about a combined estimate.

The advantage of a combined forecast is that various estimates are developed independently by several knowledgeable individuals. Independent thinking goes into each series of estimates. It is likely that one individual would include factors another would neglect, forget, or be completely unaware of. Each estimate would be colored by each individual except for the ones based on mathematical formulae. As a result, when several executives gather and review each estimate, they become more aware of the whole situation and are likely to arrive at a composite of factors, data, opinions, and attitudes that should lead to a more accurate final figure.

Factor Models

Some firms are using models to aid in forecasting. By fitting a number of variables into a matrix which is then developed through algebraic formulae, a greater forecasting accuracy can be obtained providing the variables are pertinent and can be determined with reliability. Some of the methods already described are simple models; but in this section we are concerned with more complex approaches.

"The modeling of marketing phenomena may be viewed as having two main thrusts. The first is a scientific thrust and leads to greater understanding of marketing phenomena. Here the goal is to build either normative or descriptive models which advance knowledge. . . . The second is a managerial thrust and is concerned with the capability of management science to aid marketing decision makers." [2] Marketing models have been applied to a number of salespeople's activities with varying degrees of success. How skillful management is often determines how useful models are. Unless the sales manager voluntarily experiments with models, their use should be questioned. He may be willing to use a judgment-based model rather than a mathematical one because he is more familiar with the input of the former. Through the use of a computer, the sales manager can take masses of data and change them to useful information more relevant to his problems. There are a number of sources for securing information on models for marketing.[3]

PROBLEMS IN SALES FORECASTING

Sales forecasting at best is only relatively accurate, but it is important because it helps to determine decisions. Much time and effort is used in forecasting because it may be the first step in outlining future action. Forecasts diminish in accuracy with increasing time spans because of unforeseen economic changes and unpredictable conditions. The forecaster should be aware of a number of contingencies that can affect results.

Individual Differences

People engaged in forecasting are individuals with their own ideas, values, and degrees of optimism or pessimism. Individuals in sales who work on a forecast may be willing to take increases if top management looks on the forecast as a general guide, but they will be much more conservative if their income is strongly influenced by relation of sales to forecast. Thus, if compensation is nominal up to the forecast and generous beyond that point, they are reluctant to accept a forecast that forces them to work above average just to reach the forecast.

---

2. David B. Montgomery and Charles B. Weinberg, "Modeling Marketing Phenomena: A Managerial Perspective," *Journal of Contemporary Business,* 2 (Autumn, 1973): 20.

3. Philip Kotler, *Marketing Decision Making: A Model Building Approach* (New York: Holt, Rinehart and Winston, Inc., 1971).

Kurth H. Schaffir and H. George Trentin, *Marketing Information Systems* (New York: Amacom, American Management Association, Inc., 1973).

Leonard S. Simon and Marshall Freimer, *Analytical Marketing* (New York: Harcourt Brace and World, Inc., 1970).

Finance executives who must provide money for operation are reluctant to make commitments for funds which may be unused. They become impatient with estimates that are too low and do not foresee much greater sales, forcing them to scrounge for extra funds.

Production executives prefer sales that tend to fit in with their ability to produce economically. If the production unit has a desirable product mix in manufacturing, they would prefer sales to fit in, at least to some degree. As a result, there may be subtle pressure on forecasters to adjust forecasts to optimum manufacturing. For example, it is not likely that the forecaster would come up with a big increase in sales of an item the company could not produce fast enough. On the other hand, he might forecast an increase, if at all possible, in an item that is in abundance or can be produced rapidly and economically. The forecaster would hardly come up with a large projected increase in sales of an item on which the firm was losing money.

Top management, responsible for company success, is anxious to increase their showing in sales volume and profit. In their anxiety to please the board of directors and stockholders, they make a commitment which makes sales personnel shudder because it is unrealistic and based on desire rather than basic facts and conditions. In order to achieve some of these improbable forecasts, the sales department has to extend itself so far that costs go up fantastically because of increased advertising, greater sales effort, and unforeseen expenditures necessary to generate suggested increases.

In most firms, there are people who are perpetually optimistic and want forecasts which seldom can be justified; others who are more conservative prefer forecasts which can be achieved and hopefully exceeded. The preferred approach is one in which the forecast is accurate within small variations.

Finding Pertinent Data

The difficulty of finding information that can aid in forecasting is a constant problem. Representative data of yesterday may become unrepresentative tomorrow; sources of particular data may dry up or be altered in a pattern unsuitable for a company's use. For example, a geographic unit may be changed and become inapplicable to a firm's territories. Thus, it may be relatively easy to outline data that can be used to forecast a company's sales, but it may be an entirely different problem to secure the data.

Assembling statistical data may be even more of a problem when the firm has a changing product mix. A change in competition may force a firm to decelerate attention on one line and force attention in another direction; change in consumer demand may require a radical change in production; price variation may introduce a significant change in consumer buying. There may be occasions when no particular data in present form are suitable. The forecaster must then take existing information, adjust, weight, and reassemble it into a new artificial pattern that becomes applicable. He must literally construct his own indexes and indications of relationships.

Obtaining Information Promptly

Today's statistics become available some time later. Some data of one month's activities become available early the next month, but some are not available until the end of the following month or later. Data from one year may not be compiled and printed until six months later. Significant information may not become available in time to help forecasting, or it may be in fragmented form or of a preliminary nature that is merely a good guess.

Some major firms have developed data-gathering techniques that enable them to assemble a week's pertinent data and have them ready by the following Monday. This practice is used to maintain strategic sales positions and keep abreast of market shares. But such data are expensive to secure, available to only a few major firms, and may not be significant except in forecasting daily operations.

The federal government issues a number of publications that present statistical data in many forms. Some of this is published rather quickly; some comes in monthly publications; some is issued yearly. Magazines are a major source of information; specialized magazines often have current data in particular areas as well as periodic compilations of relevant information. Newspapers attempt to keep businessmen aware of current daily changes in statistical data and other currently useful information. Specialized organizations gather information from a variety of sources, compile it in a special form, and mail it to subscribers at regular intervals.

Policy Changes

Policy changes which alter operations can affect forecasts dramatically. Even if the forecaster is aware of impending changes, he has little experience in predicting the results of the changes. He, like other executives in the firm, can only guess what will happen. Sometimes these guesses are quite accurate since similar situations have occurred before, but other times only the vaguest ideas are possible. A policy change may introduce new factors that are unpredictable at the time. The executives may have an inkling of what to expect, but they cannot predict accurately.

Length of Forecasts

The more time involved in a forecast, the weaker it becomes. Time modifies factors that influence sales; as these modifications increase, they change sales possibilities.

Typically, sales managers want a yearly forecast for either a calendar year or a fiscal year. These forecasts are then broken into shorter periods, which may be quarterly or monthly. For many useful forecasts, monthly periods are preferred. A monthly period will vary in sales depending on seasonal factors, length of month, holidays involved, and other pertinent reasons.

Usually the shorter the forecast, the more accurate it can be. An accurate, short forecast is useful because if sales vary, immediate, remedial steps can be initiated to apply corrective action if sales are too small. If they exceed forecast, the sales manager can rethink his position and revise the forecast upward.

In addition to a yearly forecast, some firms maintain a continuous year's forecast by dropping the past month and adding the same month of the coming year. If the economy changes during the moving year, the monthly sales forecasts can be adjusted to reflect current conditions.

The practical length of a sales forecast varies not only with economic conditions but also with type of product. Some products are highly susceptible to many factors, and sales can decrease or spurt in a way almost impossible to anticipate. If the product is stable in use, a necessity to most people, reasonably appealing, priced and promoted competitively, it is likely sales will not change rapidly in a few months or a year. Thus, the demand for laundry detergents is relatively stable, but demand for expensive stereo equipment may fluctuate greatly.

LONG-RANGE FORECASTS

Long-range forecasts are made for planning long-range operations. Both hinge on a number of variables which in themselves must be estimated. Consequently, there is a series of estimates, one dependent on another and none very dependable unless the basic ones are estimated accurately. The purpose of long-range forecasting is to predict the future up to five years and hopefully beyond when it is used to make major capital investment.

Economic and Social Forecasting

Any company management looking several years in the future must anticipate changes in the economic structure. For example, a war can change demand for a product. Social forces may change demand or create new environments which channel demand to other products.[4]

---

4. The past several years have seen social pressure to decrease the emphasis on firearms and war equipment, yet parents still buy toy guns and related equipment. The pressure on smoking has increased the "kick the smoking habit" advertisements of particular products that are supposed to help overcome the smoking habit, and the reaction of tobacco companies is diversification in other products. Prohibiting the use of DDT has forced changes in some firms.

Growth in education often changes patterns of buying of particular items. The affluence of the buying public may alter living patterns. Increased prosperity may cause sales of recreational products and services to mushroom. Many products have spectacular growth periods and then plateau or even decline.

Government forces may have tremendous effects on a firm's sales curve. Prohibition of products may wipe out one industry, and government encouragement may cause another industry to flourish. Government aid to farmers is an example of possible production that is continued through artificial support. Government controls of money can cause marked reaction in the economy. Government support of road building, social projects, and other activities may alter demand for services and products. Government supporting increased medical aid for senior citizens can cause a major increase of sales for pharmaceutical firms.

Economic forces abroad can seriously alter demand for a product as presently constructed and may force a change in design to meet revised demands of a country growing more sophisticated. Weather conditions at home or abroad may affect agricultural production and set up different patterns of exports and imports. Tariffs are often used to regulate the flow of commerce among countries and prevent product dumping, which can unduly influence price. Major companies have economics departments that assess and predict a variety of economic factors outside the corporation, which may have a strong effect on company success.

Industry Forecasting

Long-range industry forecasting tries to assess competitive effects on a firm's operation. Significant changes occur within a firm over several years, and even greater changes will occur in some competitors. Competition is influenced by firms entering into the area and firms leaving the area, either voluntarily or involuntarily. Firms are normally growing or contracting so that production is seldom static whether it is in the original product or that product modified by the introduction of new sizes and different qualities.

Long-range forecasting includes preparation for future growth sales. If sales grow, at what point is it wise to alter channels of distribution? What should be the advertising level at various growth stages, and should the type of advertising change?

As a firm grows, should it decentralize production, enabling it to expedite delivery and save transportation cost? If a firm contracts and has several manufacturing plants, should it continue to produce at all plants at a decreasing rate, specialize in production at each plant, or cut down the number of production facilities? If price wars develop, should a firm be content with a smaller, higher-priced market or go into price discounting and emphasize volume? If lower qualities of a product come on the market, should a firm produce a wider range, stay in the high quality end, or concentrate in the low quality end? There is nothing intrinsically good or bad about producing high quality or low quality items. Presumably, a firm should operate in the area where it can be most successful and where it can maximize profit.

Long-range forecasting must try to anticipate these factors and to foresee trends, major developments, and basic demand shifts. As far as possible, it should test prevailing human wants and direct production to the area most likely to satisfy these desires. Within this framework, a firm must adjust to competition. Management that can foresee shifts most clearly and is willing to act responsively and rapidly with proper inventory at the best time and with the best distribution will be able to profit and grow.

PROFESSIONAL FORECASTING

This chapter has given a general introduction to sales forecasting. Several ways of forecasting widely used in many firms have been described. They are used successfully as a guide by sales managers who depend on them for charting future sales. Forecasting reaches greater accuracy in some industries than in others because of the products manufactured. Accuracy also varies because management executives in one firm are more capable than those in another firm.

Sophisticated forecasting goes far beyond the material covered here. Preparation for a forecaster's job may include specialized forecasting courses in college, a strong command of statistics, considerable facility in mathematics, and familiarity with computer use. To this should be added a good economics background, several years of forecasting experience, and regular reading of current literature in business and world affairs. The professional marketing forecaster holds a challenging position. The position is not easy; results are often uncertain; and it rarely becomes routine.

QUESTIONS AND PROBLEMS

1. Dicuss the uses of a sales forecast, indicating its importance to other departments in the firm.
2. Why can some firms forecast more accurately than others? Give several reasons.
3. Discuss relative accuracy of forecasts, and show how each forecast can be improved.
4. Discuss the importance and use of data provided by the U.S. govern-

ment. Why can this data be of greater help to small firms than to large ones?

5. How is a sales force composite forecast developed? Detail the steps. What are its weaknesses?

6. Describe the use of simple correlation in sales forecasting.

7. What is spurious correlation? Is it useful?

8. Explain the use of the three types of indicators used in correlation.

9. How does multiple correlation differ from simple correlation? Why is multiple correlation used less than simple correlation?

10. Describe the projection of past sales technique in sales forecasting.

11. How can one use "customer intentions" in sales forecasting? In which types of industry is this approach more common?

12. Discuss the use of management estimates in sales forecasting.

13. What are some of the advantages and disadvantages of using a combination of methods in sales forecasting?

14. Explain the use of factor models in forecasting.

15. Discuss several problems that make sales forecasting difficult. How can these be overcome?

16. Discuss long-range forecasts. Point out their weaknesses.

17. What is the importance of long-range industry forecasting? Can it have an effect on current operations? Explain.

BASCOM AND MENZIES, INC.   *case 13–1*

Bascom and Menzies, Inc. manufactures two lines of tools—hammers, saws, wrenches, chisels, drilling bits, and numerous other common tools—used for industry, farms, and homes. The first line is of high quality, relatively expensive, and used primarily in industry and by tradespeople, such as carpenters, plumbers, and electricians. The second line, moderately priced, moves through hardware wholesalers to retailers, discount houses, and chain outlets. The first line moves through industrial distributors, specialized distributors, and hardware wholesalers.

Sales forecasting has been done primarily by the sales manager in conjunction with the president, vice-president of finance, and the production manager. The sales forecast has been determined by the judgment and estimates of these people. Sales have been growing, but not uniformly each year. In the last ten years, sales have increased from $8,000,000 to $12,000,000. Some of this increase represents inflation.

Some years, the sales forecasts were relatively accurate; other years, they were quite inaccurate. This situation was a cause of considerable concern, particularly in planning. Some better way of forecasting seemed imperative.

QUESTIONS

1. What kind of data should be used in forecasting? Be precise in your answer.
2. Who should procure data for forecasting?
3. Should both objective and subjective information be used in forecasting? Defend your position.
4. Should independent forecasts be developed for each line? Explain.
5. What method of forecasting would you suggest using? Discuss.

---

case 13–2 **DIANE DEANE COSMETICS COMPANY**

Diane Deane Cosmetics Company manufactures a wide line of cosmetics and toiletries. The company started twenty-five years ago and, through aggressive management and a strong research and development department, has prospered. It is now one of the strong competitors in this field, although not as large as a few of the major cosmetic firms. Seventy percent of its sales are east of the Mississippi River. Sales are also heavy on the west coast. Its weakest areas are some of the midwestern states, the mountain states, and the southwest portion of the United States. Sales outside the United States make up 2 percent of the total.

Heavy advertising is carried on similar to that of other firms in the industry. Besides national advertising in women's magazines and a few other magazines, the company uses heavy concentrations in television and radio in areas of heavy sales. Newspapers are used in particular areas when that seems appropriate.

Sales forecasting has been done by the sales department. District managers estimated sales in their territories with the help of salespeople. These forecasts were forwarded to the home office, where the district forecasts would be consolidated, appraised, revised, and finalized by the sales manager and her two assistant sales managers. The sales manager sent copies of the forecast to the executive committee, of which she was a member, for study. Later, this committee met and developed a final forecast based on the sales manager's forecast plus information on policies, procedures, advertising, and introduction of new products in the coming year. Some years the forecast worked well, but for the past three years it had been inaccurate. Severe economic factors would upset sales, as would changing competitor strategy. Such factors had not been recognized too well in preceding forecasts.

The sales manager felt that the forecasters had included factors within the company quite well, but had not been sufficiently aware of general economic factors as well as other outside conditions that had affected sales. She realized that successful forecasting depended on sales generated by buyer reaction to salespeople plus buyer ability to purchase. If there were conditions that hindered users' buying, the store buyer would not order merchandise. Such environmental factors, particularly economic ones, had not been given sufficient attention in determining sales forecasts. The yearly sales forecasts had not incorporated flexibility to short-run changes.

QUESTIONS

1. How should the sales manager secure relevant information outside the company?
2. Should she make one person responsible for assembling data and assist in developing the forecast? Explain your recommendation.
3. Should management develop a more flexible forecast?
4. Would it be wise to experiment with alternate methods of forecasting? Discuss, indicating possible ways to proceed.
5. What do you think is the major problem in this case? Why?

14

Sales Quotas

A *sales quota* is a projected sales figure in monetary or physical units assigned to a salesperson's territory. Quota specifies the expected sales performance in a territory over a designated time period. A complete quota outlines total activities including dollar or unit sales, customer-related activities, nonselling activities, and other assigned duties. It becomes a partially spelled-out operating plan to which the salesperson adds greater detail. While a quota may be assigned to a district, in its final application it is usually broken down into a physical area for each salesperson. Exceptions occur when salespeople are given quotas, but are usually not assigned to particular areas, as in the case of life insurance salespeople.

Sales quotas are used as performance measures for salespeople in particular territories, districts, or regions. A quota is a useful device which aids in measuring, guiding, directing, and disciplining salespeople. Disciplining in this context is not meting out punishment, but rather a method to establish orderly and adequate work habits. New customers are essential if a salesperson is to succeed because normal attrition reduces the number of regular customers for a variety of reasons often beyond the salesperson's control.

The sales potential is the open field of opportunity ready to be harvested through successful application of salesperson effort, promotional mastery, and product excellence. If company strategy is correctly developed and adequately administered, sales should equal sales potential, for the figure is one that the firm has established as reasonable.

MARKET POTENTIAL AND SALES POTENTIAL

The sales potential of an area is based on its market potential. *Market potential* is the total amount of business in a territory available in a firm's line. Thus, for dairy producers a territory consists of all purchasers of dairy products. A fertilizer producer would count as potential all sales of fertilizer in the territory. Market potential is all demand for a particular product that is satisfied by purchasing in a particular territory within specified time limits.

Determining Market Potential

Market potential obviously is not as simple and easily defined as indicated in the preceding paragraph. An accurate determination of this potential must take into account numerous variables. These variables may include purchases outside a territory used within a territory, purchases within a territory used outside the territory, postponement of buying, unforeseen contingencies affecting demand, use of substitute products, climate variations, health of community, and individual decisions when they cumulate in one direction instead of balancing.

In determining market potential, the estimator sets up a hypothesis that the coming period will have some definite relationship to past behavior; that he can anticipate any major change both in time and in intensity; and that there will be no major upset in present demand conditions. For example, he can rationalize that people in one area will act in the coming year much like they did last year and in previous years, that any major changes are evident and can be predicted quantitatively, and that no radical change will occur. Successful determination of market potential normally presupposes a predictable buying pattern.

Since it is assumed people will act in a routine pattern, the primary job is to find out what that pattern has been, establishing new marketing potential based on that pattern but modified by current variations or changes that appear reasonable for the coming period. To aid in making these decisions, the sales manager has a number of tools that have been tested and found useful. United States Census provides much useful data which can be studied and rearranged to fit a particular firm's needs. *Survey of Buying Power,* published by *Sales Management* magazine once a year, has been used successfully by firms selling consumer products. Magazines issue supplements pertaining to special industries that many use successfully. Surveys of buying intentions by professional groups are often used as modifiers of objective market potential. Trade associations gather and compile data useful to their memberships. States compile information, and much data is available indirectly through tax collections. County, city, and metropolitan area information often seems adequate for a firm operating within that area. Thus, an ice cream manufacturer, soft drink bottler, or potato chip producer may find local information satisfactory for determining market potential.

To illustrate a specific solution for hardware wholesalers selling to independent hardware stores, management can find how many outlets operate in the territory. It may not be too difficult to estimate retail sales for each store. In many instances, the stores will give their sales figures to salespeople, and there are other ways of obtaining sales estimates. Once sales for each outlet have been established, this figure can be reduced by average markup, and the remainder ends in purchases modified somewhat by inventory. For example, if a retail hardware store sells $150,000 a year, one might assume a gross income of one-third, or $50,000, which leaves a purchase figure of $100,000.

A tire manufacturer or dealer can predict the number of replacement tires that will be sold in a territory by the number of cars registered in that territory; the same can be done for batteries and other automotive products. The number of gallons of soft drinks consumed in an area can be determined by population and per capita consumption within that area. These examples are merely indicative of methodology and do not include subjective modification gained through experience. Some products are used in a variety of ways; consequently, a number of uses must be measured. For instance, corn is used as animal food, as human food, in manufacturing, and as seed. Diesel engines are used in trucks, buses, boats, stationary installations, and in other ways. Precious metals are used in jewelry, dental work, manufacturing automotive products, manufacturing electronic components, minting money, and many other uses. A firm does not have to establish the market potential for a product in all its uses, but usually only in the area where the firm competes. Sometimes other uses must be considered, because they may indirectly affect the use of a firm's product and because other uses may siphon off major sources of raw materials.

Determining Sales Potential

The marketing potential within a territory is all the existing sales of that kind, but the *sales potential* is the amount of sales a particular firm expects to capture. Most business is competitive and in some cases highly competitive. Automobile manufacturers compete fiercely with one another; manufacturers of cleaners, soaps, and detergents are in a constant market struggle; gas companies compete with electric companies. Television and radio advertising compete with newspaper and magazine advertising. Within their competition area, television stations compete with one another as do radio stations, magazines, and newspapers.

Realistically, a firm must be satisfied with a portion of market potential which can vary from 1 percent to perhaps 70 percent of the market. Thus, one computer firm may have over 70 percent of the market while a manufacturer of deodorants must be content with 2 percent of his market. Keep in mind, however, that in one industry 50 percent of a market may be $50,000, but in another industry 1 percent of the market may amount to over $1,000,000.

A firm must compete within its own industry and with other industries. For example, a buyer may choose a particular brand of car, or he may buy a boat instead; a buyer of canned peaches may buy canned pears, or fresh pears, or no fruit at all. Price is often a controlling factor in shifting demand and in sales and market potential.

A firm must be realistic, but at the same time optimistic, about its share of the market. While it must settle for a part of the market, its relative strength often determines its share. Sometimes a firm is determined to increase its sales potential within a particular area and may succeed, but it is doubtful if the extra effort to achieve this increase was justified. Occasionally, a firm may willingly relinquish sales potential in one area because it is too costly to maintain its position. Often, a firm concentrates more heavily and increases sales potential in other areas or may even alter its marketing mix and achieve better results by changing the product line.

A firm may wish to increase its sales potential in an area, but will fail because it could not foresee how untenable its decision was. Within a framework of practical considerations governing its market, the firm must operate, penetrate, or even subsist on what it can generate in sales.

The preceding discussion points out the vital importance of market potential and sales potential in forecasting and assigning quotas. Unless a particular demand exists or can be created in a territory, it would be a waste to send in a salesperson. There must be willing and able buyers who want a product before one can sell. Lack of potential customers with sufficient income and desire would stifle any sales effort. There have been examples where salespeople were sent into a territory only to fail miserably because the people did not want their product. Many products have failed because people were not receptive. Yet territories completely unreceptive one year have become fertile selling areas the next year through demand creation. Potential was created in people's minds.

PURPOSES OF SALES QUOTAS

Quotas have many uses, varying from firm to firm. At the worst, a quota may be only a vague unrealistic figure to please the boss's wishful thinking. It can also be a way of setting impossible goals in order to get rid of a salesperson or a sales manager.

On the favorable side, quotas are used as accurate performance measurements, as guides to budgeting, and as a means of rewarding salespeople for satisfactory performance.

Determine Salespeople Objectives

Most firms want successful salespeople, and almost every sales manager would say that success is measured by profitability—net contribution of each person. Each person should be measured by a series of performance standards that make up the profitability objective. Contributing to the main objective are minor objectives that are useful in directing the salesperson's activities. These objectives break down into operating details, number and frequency of calls, which products to emphasize, customer service, and others. Essentially, a careful job of quota setting must also include other important segments of the job. Merely setting a quota figure and leaving everything else to the salesperson may be self-defeating, because under pressure a salesperson may achieve quota in a way that is damaging to his customers, his firm, and himself.

Provide Salesperson Incentives

A quota may be constructed to achieve the dual purpose of maximizing the interests of both salesperson and the firm. Many times a salesperson's activities can be channeled into specific tasks which maximize the firm's objectives. Instead of insisting that the salesperson perform certain tasks, the quota can be tied to financial or other incentives so that the salesperson willingly follows these directions because they fit into his adjusted plans.

Control Salesperson's Activities

The sales manager outlines to what extent each salesperson must modify individual effort to fit in the overall operation. The sales manager can detail the salesperson's activities in order to accomplish overall sales objectives from which quotas were originally determined. This control varies with each salesperson, but perhaps even more by type of selling. For example, the salesperson of industrial equipment may have a minimum of routine procedure, but the salesperson going from one supermarket to another may have so much routine that the district manager knows where he is every hour of the day.

Evaluate Salesperson Performance

A variety of ways may be used to evaluate performance, but it is easier to make an accurate evaluation if there are a number of performance standards as criteria. If quotas are determined in the best interests of the firm, then fulfillment of quota by each salesperson should return optimum performance for the firm.

Objectives and specific goals give each salesperson performance direction and permit the sales manager to determine exactly how well each salesperson fulfills his work. Both the salesperson and his boss know how well he performs when both are using the same measuring stick. It is unlikely the measuring stick will be exactly alike for both because they may not interpret activities eye-to-eye. But, in general, there should not be any significant difference in measurement or interpretation.

Affect Salesperson Remuneration

Tying a salesperson's income into quota is an effective way to control field performance and to guide effort in the way the company prefers. Seldom will a person respond quickly to suggestions unless there is a strong incentive to do so. One of the strongest incentives is income. When it becomes desirable to redirect field work, a quota adjustment can direct performance in the desired direction. The salesperson could not afford to do otherwise because of income loss.

Increase Impact of Sales Contests

A salesperson welcomes contests which can aid him in achieving quota sooner. He will not only meet quota requirements more easily but also receive extra reward in contest prizes. If a sales manager finds salespeople are slow or unlikely to meet their quotas, he can inject a contest to stimulate them to greater performance.

Aid in Developing Territories

A carefully constructed quota for each territory measures sales potential. The sales manager will be able to assign salespeople according to their capacity because stronger salespeople will be willing to take the greater challenges of more difficult territories. Salespeople assigned to lesser territories may not be too happy, but become reconciled when they see how large the quotas are for stronger territories.

Promote Economy

A number of ways can be used to promote economy through a quota. Sales can be compensated to insure selling profitable items in profitable quantities and discourage promoting unprofitable items and unprofitable order units. Salespeople may need direction in scheduling their travel and their use of time; they may require better expense control; they may need direction in handling customers.

Quotas are used to improve performance by creating goals that require the salesperson to reassess his working habits and solve more problems. By stressing economy with performance, the sales manager forces the salesperson to do more rigid thinking and planning in order to achieve predetermined goals. As a result, he is compelled to check himself to avoid wasting time and effort.

Aid in Budgeting

Quotas are primarily an extension of sales forecasting or are the components of a sales estimate. A firm must finance its production and administrative expenses and provide for sales financing. The size of the estimated sales divided into segments, or quotas, for each salesperson enables the finance department to project costs for the sales operation. Quotas may be arranged to call for an increase or reduction in sales force. Quotas may be set up for more than one channel of distribution, which may drastically change the need for financing at particular times during the year. For example, if sales are seasonal, using direct salespeople may require uniform expenditures throughout the year. If sales representatives operate on commission, the sales costs would peak at one period and be negligible during the off-season. Providing money becomes much easier when a firm budgets sales, production, and other expenses of operation.

CHARACTERISTICS OF A GOOD QUOTA

A quota should be complete in its coverage of a salesperson's job and yet not be so detailed to hinder the user in his daily activities. A quota should not be considered by management as an irrevocable decision, because business conditions frequently call for adjustment.

Complete Quota

A quota ought to cover a number of the activities of the salesperson in the territory. Too often, a sales manager will assign a quota, but leave its implementing to the salespeople, who will probably attempt to meet it in the easiest possible way without regard to firm or customer.

A meaningful quota should fulfill a number of wants that can be detailed specifically. It can relate to profit, to securing new customers, to giving extra service, to pushing particular items, to stressing seasonal applications, to achieving balanced performance, and to a number of other essentials. Management can get an appropriate pattern of operation from a salesperson by insisting that he do certain things, but an easier way is to reward him financially for such work. It is not possible to attempt to control all of a salesperson's activities, but quota can cover the main thrust in his work.

Accurate Quota

A quota should be reasonably accurate within a few plus or minus percentage points. A well-conceived quota should be a carefully constructed measure of what ought to be achieved within a particular territory. The salesperson should be confident that he can achieve his quota if he follows directions and works diligently. Quota should be reached with slightly above average work. The weak salesperson will have difficulty in reaching quota; the average salesperson can make it consistently with some added effort, and the superior salesperson will surpass it.

An accurate quota instills confidence because the salesperson knows that management has used its best judgment in developing it. The salesperson realizes that it is his job to achieve quota because it is reasonable. To fail means that the territory is underproductive and potential is being wasted.

Challenging Quota

A quota should challenge the salesperson. It should bring forth his best effort and force him to extend himself to reach the goal.

A challenging quota must take the salesperson's capacity into consideration. For example, a beginner would not get the same results as an experienced person in the same territory. A territory that has been worked successfully for years will give better results than an equally good, but new territory. A present, strong territory being invaded by a new price-cutting competitor will suffer reductions which should not occur in a similar territory not subjected to this competition.

A challenging quota should be inviting to the salespeson because it ought not to be regarded as a bludgeon over his head, but rather as an exhilarating opportunity for growth. A good quota should not only get superior salesperson response but also should motivate the home office and the firm to do their part to make quota possible.

Fair Quota

A quota should be fair to the salesperson and the employer. A fair quota to the salesperson is one he can handle within his limits and within the limits of his territory. A fair quota to the employer is one which he expects to achieve and on which he can base his estimates and budgets. The sum of the quotas of salespeople plus other anticipated sales becomes the guidelines of operation for the coming period.

Flexible Quota

A quota is determined for a period (often a year) in advance and consequently is only an educated guess. When conditions in the coming months do not bear out this guess, it is necessary to adjust quota to fit these new conditions. It becomes meaningless to insist on a quota which is no longer tenable. A salesperson may expect a certain volume of sales from a major buyer in his territory, but if that buyer's factory is closed by a strike for a three-month period, quota becomes meaningless.

Since a quota should reflect realism, it should be adjusted in order to reflect real changes. An adjustment may not be required for each variation because frequently there are simultaneous changes that tend to cancel one another, and the original situation remains remarkably stable. It is helpful to have a continuous quota rather than a sharp break at the end of a calendar, or fiscal, year or a definite period. Each time a month passes and is dropped, the quota can be extended for another month. For example, when October of one year has passed, a tentative quota could be set up for the next October.

Flexibility is primarily an indication of a willingness to change. Constant changing of quota can be overdone in trying to reflect minor variations, or it can be used infrequently until it becomes obvious that a quota needs adjustment. Happily, the successful application of flexibility insulates quota change from minor, rapid changes but does not overlook severe dislocation caused by major readjustments and in some cases significant, rapid changes.

Readily Understood Quota

The quota should be readily understandable to the salesperson. If it is loaded with a variety of duties that tend to overlap, the salesperson may give up in disgust because he is not clear about the exact duties. Also, salespeople usually become impatient with restrictions and tend to shun some jobs or perform them in a perfunctory way.

The sales manager should not simplify a quota if, by doing so, it loses some of its effectiveness. The salesperson who says he does not understand his quota can be required to study it. If it remains confusing, someone at the home office or a district manager can explain it.

Quota Tied to Management Wishes

Some quotas are dictated by management without understanding field conditions. At worst, such attempts are merely hopeful stabs toward the impossible or highly improbable; at best, they may be management gropings for success. A good quota comes from wise management decisions to implement carefully determined goals.

When a manufacturer plans for a coming year, he sets up a production schedule which he hopes to maintain; he makes buying commitments in line with this schedule. Such commitments may be conservative, but usually can be increased. The sales manager may be urged by the president to set total quotas in excess of manufacturing commitments, but such quotas should not exceed projected production by much. When quotas exceed projected production by more than about

10 percent, one questions the original forecasts on which production was based.

ESTABLISHING QUOTAS

Quotas may be set up by the home office, by regional or district offices in large firms, or even by an independent retailer, such as car salesperson quotas in an automobile dealership. A quota may be assigned to a salesperson by the sales manager, or it may be developed by consulting with the salesperson. When a salesperson helps to determine his quota, it may be received more gracefully than when he is forced to accept it. The procedure may be mere formality when the sales manager goes through the motions of asking the salesperson's opinion, but in reality it is meaningless because the salesperson has no veto power.

There are other occasions when the salesperson's suggestion has real impact on the final quota. In this situation, the salesperson shoulders some of the responsibility for the final quota and feels greater urgency in achieving or bettering this goal.

Certain questionable procedures may be used to the disadvantage of the salesperson. He may be pressured in a meeting to give sales figures which look good in front of his colleagues but are unrealistic in the light of tomorrow's assessment. He may treat quota lightly and accept an excessive one because he knows there is no penalty if he fails, or he has always been able to explain away failure. Many salespeople have learned that management does not take quota seriously, and they react accordingly and do not worry about making quota. If management is serious about quotas, takes salespeople into its confidence and establishes realistic quotas, the whole firm benefits. Salespeople try to meet present goals; sales management works with salespeople to fulfill quotas; production can balance and optimize operations; and finance can maintain adequate money supplies at minimum cost.

Volume Quota

A sales volume quota is customarily expressed in dollars, some monetary unit, or in unit sales of the product. For example, the quota for salesman Brown would be $250,000 for a calendar year; then this total is divided into monthly or quarterly components according to the typical sales pattern for the firm. Sometimes it may be more convenient to express quota as 100 trucks for the year, which is divided into monthly components; an insurance salesperson may have to sell a certain number of policies; a manager of a chain restaurant may have a monthly quota of number of customers served.

Sales volume quotas in monetary units are simple and have a common denominator translated into dollars, which can be readily used in determining percentage of cost, profit, expenses, and net contribution to the home office. It is easy to calculate for the salesperson and the boss and is a quick and ready measure of current performance. There may be weaknesses however which can be revealed only through sales analysis. Too often, dollar volume has been stressed without regard to profitability, customer satisfaction, or balanced product mix.

To make a dollar quota useful, it is frequently subdivided into product categories. It may be established on groupings of products, such as pharmaceuticals and sundries in drug wholesale sales; on profitability of items whereby high-profit items are segregated and grouped for special emphasis and low-profit items are carried but not pushed; on balanced sales of primary products, joint products, and by-products, as encountered in packing house operations, milling firms, and petroleum refining. It may also be established on groupings requiring different approaches, such as depending mostly on telephone sales, frequent personal calls, infrequent personal calls, committee presentations, and mail solicitation. Seldom is a single figure as useful as a major quota figure made up of components.

Weaknesses of the dollar quota are revealed during persistent inflation. Sales may increase but relatively decrease. Many firms have been lulled into false security by larger sales and larger quotas, while in reality competition has grown faster. A dollar quota, unless carefully worked out, may not be profitable if the salesperson is left to his own devices in selling. In his efforts to reach the magic number, he may offend customers, concentrate on easily sold but relatively unprofitable lines, and push immediate sales which hinder future response. A dollar quota may be unrealistic in a declining economy. Purchases of luxury items may be replaced by standard items at lesser cost; purchases may be postponed; purchases may be switched to a competitor who is willing to forego profit in order to keep his plant operating.

A sales volume quota lumps sales into an overall figure, but the use of unit quota tends to individualize each sale and bring it into true perspective. When quota is given in physical units, it is easy to compare with past sales. For example, a salesperson sells ten cars; he sells one thousand dozen of product K; he sells sixteen cartons of product M; he sells fifty canoes. It is true that this may not be more profitable because each unit may be price discounted or cheaper units are pushed rather than deluxe units. It is tangible performance and one the factory can use in production planning, particularly if quota is established in particular units.

Unit quota fits well into sales of major items, where each unit sale requires considerable effort. Unit quota is useful during rapid price fluctuations or sales under stress, where dollars would describe sales activity inadequately.

Both dollar and unit quotas lend themselves to a point system. This system attaches point values to types of selling, categories of products, special promotional drives, and many other measurements of the sales task. By judicious point reward, it becomes possible to guide the salesperson's activities into those areas most desirable from the company standpoint. Points can be given in increasing, decreasing, or a constant number for various activity levels. The total point number determines quota and may become easier or more difficult to reach depending on changes in point award. Even during a quota period, the point structure can be changed; for instance, by the addition of a special promotion which gives the salesperson additional opportunities to acquire more points.

Profit Quota

A *profit quota* is determined by specifying products or groupings of products which carry particular profit levels. Frequently, there is wide variation in product margin; and often negotiated or competitive bid prices narrow profit margins. In some situations, sales volume becomes less meaningful; but profit or lack thereof becomes predominant.

Many commissioned salespeople are compensated by a percentage of gross margin or gross profit or simply by the profit on each sale. While this method entails considerable office work to calculate, major single sales can warrant this added expense. The clerical work on many small items can be reduced by grouping them into product categories.

A profit quota reduces the frantic quest for volume and directs attention to advantageous sales. It may be preferable to forego some sales which sap the salesperson's effort and draw his attention from important accounts, but which in the final analysis contribute little or nothing to profit. One definite advantage of a profit quota is that it pinpoints attention on unprofitable items and those that involve significant losses. This method can bring an improved price structure or the discontinuance of some items in a product line.

Activity Quota

In some sales situations, much of a salesperson's job is involved in customer services. The salesperson may spend as few as one or two hours a day in actual selling and the rest in a variety of other activities. Often, these supplementary activities are as important or more important than the so-called actual selling. This situation is frequently true of highly advertised products, which are largely presold if the salesperson follows up properly with peripheral work.

Activities vary with the firm, the product, the sales strategy, and customers. They include special service and delivery calls, setting up displays and demonstrations, reactivating old accounts, prospecting for new customers, and other activities. Weaknesses of this quota include careless work, inattention to detail, neglecting work, poor follow-up, and not meeting the needs of customers and territory.

Expense Quota

An *expense quota* is related to sales or is set up in absolute terms to prevent excessive spending. In general, the sales manager is expected to operate the sales department within certain financial guidelines. While not expressly tied down to a dollar figure (although the sales budget does tend to this end), the sales manager knows that cost is tied to a percentage of sales. In the same fashion, he instructs salespeople about expense limitations which are rather precise in some aspects, but also have an overall percentage guideline. Even commission salespeople who get no expense allowance tend to keep a ratio of expenses to sales and become concerned when expenses are too high.

An expense quota has merit when salespeople become cost conscious, but it becomes a hindrance when it is so restrictive that salespeople cannot carry out regular duties.

Combination Quotas

Combination quota plans are difficult to set up and administer, but in some cases are more truly representative of actual sales situations. There is no reason why one part of a quota cannot be volume oriented and another part activity oriented. The purpose of any quota is to determine what is important and set up requirements that maximize efforts in that direction. These requirements may often include unpleasant tasks, such as handling disagreeable customers, making adjustments, collecting overdue accounts, stressing difficult items to sell, keeping sales in a predetermined balance, reactivating lost accounts, getting a greater share of customers' orders, and opening new accounts. Activity quotas may be individualized by salespeople and/or territory.

PREPARING QUOTAS

A quota is prepared for a particular territory. If there are a number of salespeople and territories, each quota must be prepared for each salesperson fitted in his territory. Another way is to set up territory quota based primarily on sales potential and then assign salespeople according to ability, experience, training, and personal characteristics. There are other territory factors besides sales potential which govern salesperson territory relationships.

Assigning an appropriate percentage of the sales forecast is one way to apportion anticipated sales. One would first build a preliminary quota by assessing and weighing quantitative data in a territory. This preliminary quota could be determined by previous sales data, careful territory analysis, and other objective data. A company usually has much factual information on each territory available in writing or in computers.

Preparing a quota objectively without considering the salesperson involved probably has drawbacks, but a company ought to appraise each territory carefully as a separate entity and determine how much sales it should generate. Later, it may have to make modifications to meet practical considerations of the present sales force. If realistic quotas must be compromised because the salespeople are not of the caliber to meet the challenge, the sales force should be upgraded.

To make the quotas challenging, an additional amount slightly above forecast can be incorporated. In the final step, a quota must be realistic for a territory and a salesperson. A territory quota developed objectively independent of the salesperson may have to be decreased to accommodate a weaker salesperson, but may be increased for the top salesperson who consistently performs above standards. Table 14–1 illustrates a volume quota.

SELLING AND ADMINISTERING QUOTAS

A quota will not function by itself. If management pays little attention to it after it is once determined, the salesperson will not be overly concerned about it either. If the quota was carefully set up and both parties agreed to it, it can be the guiding impact of sales effort throughout the quota period. It immediately predetermines an operating level and a bench mark of performance. It can be used to schedule activities and direct effort toward a prescribed goal. To make a quota work, management must be prepared to give direction, encouragement, and consistency and to remove unanticipated barriers which may appear.

Accepted Quota

The salesperson must be convinced that his quota is fair and attainable. If the salesperson is consulted and some of his recommendations adopted, he is more likely to go along with some of management's desires. He realizes he must accept many of management's sugges-

Table 14–1
Sales Quotas for High Profit Specialty Categories for a Drug Whole-saler in the Detroit District (Period covers April 1 to October 1, 1975)

Territory	Salesman	Category I	Category II	Category III	Category IV
#12/13/33	Crump	$3900	$2400	$5120	$2500
#6	Timor	1950	2025	2536	1000
#10/40/35	Kurzava	3900	2400	5120	2500
#69/39/68	Long	3900	2400	5120	2500
#50/60/36	Talarico	3900	2400	5120	2500
#4/30/34	Bruton	4000	4000	2000	6000
#1/21	Davy	3000	3000	1800	4500
#2/20	Rutkowski	2500	2600	1800	3700
#9/89	Akers	4000	3000		6000
#11/31/71	Lopez	3000	3000	1800	4500
#22/82/32	Dempsey	3000	3000	1800	4500
#18/38/19	Lieberman	3000	3000	1800	4500
#43/44 (Hospital)	Mains	2500	4000		500
#42/48 (Hospital)	Stern	3900	2400	1000	
#41/49 (Hospital)	Devon	3900	2400	1000	
#3 (Chain Stores)	King	31,970	2400	16,900	
	House Sales	153	1000		
	Total Quota	$82,473	$45,425	$52,916	$45,200

tions, but if he can blunt some of them he feels he has eliminated certain unreasonable requirements.

Table 14–1 was prepared by two sales managers in the district using the following approach:

1. Total district quota from home office divided equally among salesmen.
2. Divided by percent of volume of each salesman in these categories.
3. Past history of each category considered individually for each salesman.
4. Management judgment.
5. Adjust and smooth out figures. The sales managers appraised each salesman individually as to ability and arrived at these figures. Some salesmen had blank categories, indicating those customers did not buy in these categories.

This table represents but a small part of each salesman's quota. The other major parts of each quota were standard items much larger in sales than specialty items and were based on a straight percentage increase over previous sales. It is interesting to note how management judgment and "feel" for the market is involved. Each salesman is closely supervised in a positive way. These salesmen have a yearly income varying from $15,000 to $30,000 plus a free car and other travel expenses.

When a salesperson is asked to accept an increased or a different type of quota, he should be told why and how he can produce the results that management feels are attainable. Neither the salesperson nor management is always right or wrong; so judicious compromise and adjustment will frequently end with a better quota. Quota is both factual and emotional, and proper emotional reception by the salesperson can make the factual part more easily attainable.

Quota Based on Up-to-date Information

When a quota is prepared, it should be based on the most recent information available. This information may be far ranging and require much research.

One of the first factors to consider in administering quota is the general economy for the coming period, because few firms are immune to these effects. Most sales move in a positive or negative relationship to the economy, and the effects may not be gradual, but may affect sales in spurts. For example, a firm's sales may not be affected by several percentage point changes in the economy, but may move in a step, rather than a gradual slope fashion. In a downward economy, management's thinking is oriented optimistically, and they are reluctant to admit that conditions are really as bad as indicated.

What is happening in an industry can be a controlling quota factor because new products, new competition, changing price structures, and changing demands may be governing. Demands for a product may decrease because of substitute products or merely because people tire of certain things. Therefore, use of quota demands proper implementation of various sales tools to meet contingencies and assist salespeople's efforts.

Revising Quota

Administering quota should include revision of quota when conditions warrant. Revisions may be up or down. Quotas are often set too low or too high. Operating experience dictates revisions as conditions change. Quota revisions may encompass the entire quota, or they may involve piecemeal changes in some areas. A change of quota for one salesperson does not necessarily call for a change in another salesperson's quota. Territory conditions may change in different directions among territories, while some sections of the country are remarkably stable.

Operating in a dynamic economy with prices changing constantly, with delivery times fluctuating, with routine sales effort being interrupted by contests and special advertising, it is seldom possible to work out any quota exactly as planned. If it did work out that way once, it would be a coincidence. If it continued that way for several periods, it would indicate someone was controlling or manipulating sales.

Quotas are subject to periodic revision reflecting current operating conditions, which may have changed substantially from the time the original quota was determined. To expect a salesperson to live up to his quota when conditions change could hurt him. A flexible approach tends to fit the best interests of salespeople and the firm.

CONDITIONS UNFAVORABLE TO SALES QUOTAS

Quotas should not be used if they impede sales activities. Too often, a sales manager may feel that a sales tool must be used and fail to realize that a tool is only useful when it makes a helpful contribution. Quotas may be useful frequently, but there may be some sales situations where they are of questionable value and a few situations where they are harmful.

Quotas are unimportant if a firm has no problems in selling its output or if there is no chance to increase sales. A firm that supplies parts or components to another firm can sell only as much as the buyer can use. Industrial purchasers buy for specific purposes, and increased selling pressure will not cause them to buy more. If, as a result, a customer is oversold and loses money, he will refuse to buy later. Putting too much merchandise on a storekeeper's shelves causes loss and resentment.

In sales of very large units, quota is ineffective. If a salesperson makes one sale a year or one in two years, a quota would have little meaning. In construction contracts and in heavy machinery sales, quota appears inappropriate. Quota is meant to be a challenge to performance, but there may be sufficient challenge already present to motivate the salesperson.

When management uses quota as a device to try to get increased sales without relation to potential or conditions in the economy, its value is questionable. The salesperson rapidly learns that the quota has no realistic basis, that chance is the determining factor, and that management does not expect him to make quota. When quotas are established and management does not follow up, their values are minimal.

If sales are largely beyond the salesperson's control, a quota makes little sense to him. To set a quota accurately can be costly in time and money. The sales manager should weigh its importance against the cost and see if the effort is worthwhile. A firm with a short life may find quotas too costly because of the short time involved and because of inaccuracies existing in a short-time situation. If a sales force has a rapid turnover, many of the people barely get acquainted with the firm. To spend time and money on carefully constructed quotas is unwarranted. While quota is a useful device and is highly recommended for many firms, it does have decided limitations and should not be used if its success can be severely limited or highly problematical.

[handwritten margin note: CONSTRAINT]

QUESTIONS AND PROBLEMS

1. What are the purposes of a sales quota?
2. Why do we separate market potential and sales potential? When are they identical?
3. What are some of the tools used in determining market potential?
4. There are numerous problems hindering sales potential determination. Discuss several of these problems.
5. Name several specific uses of sales quota.
6. A sales quota is a flexible tool directing sales effort. Discuss the implications of this statement.
7. How can a sales manager determine if a quota is fair, reasonable, and provides salesperson incentive? Explain.
8. Flexibility is emphasized through the whole chapter. Why is flexibility so important in quotas?
9. Develop one salesperson's quota in a hypothetical firm. Use information from your reading and experience. Make assumptions and state them clearly.
10. Does an expense quota have merit? Explain.
11. Why should each salesperson be involved in his quota determination? Give several reasons.
12. When may quotas be a hindrance? Under what conditions may quotas be unwise?

SPEARS WHOLESALE DRUG COMPANY   *case 14–1*

Mr. Napier, president of Spears Wholesale Drug Company, had just completed the company sales forecast for the coming year. Since this was the middle of December, Archie Van, the sales manager, would have to work rapidly to set up quotas for his nine salespeople to match the sales forecast.

Mr. Napier and Mr. Van had spent much time in reviewing economic conditions in their area and had concluded that a seven percent sales increase was attainable. While Mr. Van was satisfied with this increase in some territories, he knew that other territories could not possibly show such increases. Five territories would absorb a seven percent increase without too much trouble, but considerable readjustment would be necessary in the other four. After carefully appraising as many factors as he was able to obtain, Mr. Van tentatively established the following quotas for these four territories:

> Territory F. Salesman Anson, 1 percent decrease
> Territory G. Salesman Bard, 9 percent increase
> Territory H. Salesman Cannon, 6 percent increase
> Territory I. Salesman Dub, 13 percent increase

Understandably, it would be difficult to sell the quotas to the salespeople, especially the latter four. Mr. Dub would be quite upset over his big increase, particularly since Ms. Anson was given a decrease. Indications were that Ms. Anson might find her quota very difficult to meet.

QUESTIONS

1. Why was there such a variation in quotas? Give several reasons.
2. How can you account for the big increase in Mr. Dub's quota?
3. What must the sales manager do to sell each person on his quota? Can he effectively satisfy each salesperson?

---

case 14–2   **VARIABLE MACHINE COMPANY**

Variable Machine Company produced a standard line of five machines ranging in price from $2,000 to $10,000. These machines were used in different industries and were versatile in use. These machines varied greatly in maintenance, parts, and supplies necessary for successful operation. Thus, the machines selling at $2,000 and $10,000 required a minimum of service and repairs and consequently had generous profit margins.

Machines selling at $4,000 and $5,500 required more service and usually required about $200 a year in repair parts and accessory equipment to operate successfully. These two machines carried about the same gross margin as the first two mentioned.

The fifth machine, listing at $7,200, used about $100 a month in parts, supplies, and material to operate. This machine would list at

$7,700 if it carried the same profit margin as the first two mentioned, but the price was lowered deliberately to capture a share of a large and fiercely competitive market. Once a particular brand of machine was purchased, it was customary to buy parts, supplies, and materials afterward from the manufacturer who supplied the machine or from his designated distributors. These after-market products, supplies, and materials had a generous gross margin. Even with minor discounts allowed, the profit was large.

All the machines had an expected ten-year life. Management wanted to increase sales of all machines and related equipment and supplies, but was particularly anxious to sell the machines responsible for related purchases. The firm covered the major industrial areas of the United States, but had been unable to capture a uniform segment of the market. For example, while their sales totaled 10 percent of the market, in the $2,000 and $10,000 machines, they had captured 14 percent of the market; in the $4,000 and $5,500 machines, they had 9 percent of the market; and in the $7,200 machines, they had 8 percent of the market. It was very difficult to maintain relative position in the market with the $7,200 machine because of competition, price cutting, and deals which may have been unethical but nevertheless occurred.

Up to this time, quota had been established on a machine unit volume basis. For example, if salesman Bottom sold ten units of the $2,000 machine this year and conditions for next year looked attractive, he would be given a quota of eleven units. The same procedure was used for each machine. But this system did not encourage the sale of the $7,200 machine beyond what it was now, since the salespeople already worked harder on this machine because of their commission on parts, supplies, and materials.

The successful use of quota should encourage salespeople to exert themselves harder in directions management wished. It was therefore decided to use a combination profit-volume quota to direct salespeople towards more profitable goals. It was hoped that such a quota would increase profits the coming year without increasing total sales earnings more than 10 percent.

Salesperson commission was 10 percent on the $2,000 and $10,000 machines and 10 percent on the $4,000 and $5,500 machines. When several machines were sold on one order, a 2 percent discount was given, and salespeople took a 1 percent cut on commission. Salespeople received 5 percent commission on the $7,200 machine, 20 percent commission on parts and supplies sold direct, and 10 percent when sold through distributors. About 20 percent of salespeople's commissions came from parts, supplies, and materials. Salespeople received $0.14 a mile car allowance. Last year machine sales, not including parts, supplies, and materials, averaged $150,000 per salesperson.

ASSIGNMENT

Draw up a profit-volume quota plan to meet the objective. Keep in mind that salespeople get commission on all sales in their territory, although only half as much commission on sales made by distributors. Distributors occasionally sold a machine but did considerable volume in parts, supplies, and materials. Price discounting did occur, but it was discouraged.

Marketing Research as an Aid in Sales Management

The purpose of this chapter is not to present a detailed marketing research operation, for that is a complex field in itself, but rather to indicate the approaches and tools that can be brought to bear on sales management problems. Far too many sales managers ignore the possibilities of marketing research or are content to use it piecemeal or as a supplement. They do not use it as a tool, a fact-finder of paramount importance which could help guide and give precision to the thrust of the sales department, thereby discouraging waste of resources in relatively unproductive areas.

Most major firms have well-developed marketing research staffs that feed information to sales executives, but thousands of smaller firms do not have this assistance. Since most of them feel they are getting along satisfactorily, they have little inclination to develop marketing research. Also, many sales staffs feel that marketing research is vague, costly, and suitable only to the big company. Perhaps they fail to understand that even the addition of one research person to the marketing staff can be of great help to decision makers.

The variety of market research studies are not equally useful for all firms; rather, each must choose the ones that will furnish information it needs. Besides the pressing studies, such as market share, market penetration, consumer profiles, consumer awareness, there are many others. Two governing factors in choosing are the cost and feasibility; some studies would be desirable but impractical to secure, and others are too expensive. The firm interested in marketing research should start with that type of research which yields the most useful and valuable information.

PRODUCT RESEARCH

Few products can remain the same from year to year if the market is to be satisfied. Buyers want something a little different, something that shows improvement over the present models.

Product Suitability

Is the present product suitable for its market? The firm may produce and sell a product successfully, but never know that it is tangential to demand and that a change in product might increase sales enormously. By discovering new uses for a product through market research, management may extend the product into meeting diverse demands. For example, many food products carry recipes on the package suggesting uses that are somewhat different from the primary use.

Many products have segmented markets which can be uncovered by careful delineation. The product in a slightly altered form may appeal to new users. Just the simple change of adding quick and instant varieties to cooked breakfast cereals has opened up more space for them on the grocers' and consumers' shelves. Some buyers prefer a detergent alone in a box; others like to have a prize in the box. Some prefer an item that is inexpensive and can be discarded quickly; others like to keep it longer and want a better one. Some clothes buyers stress style above quality; others like both. While the sales manager states that present customers are well satisfied, the research person may find that additions or changes may greatly increase the number of customers because the change has widened appeal.

Sizes and Packaging

Many firms regularly study their packaging for adequacy and as a promotion vehicle. The proliferation of packages of different sizes is an attempt to obtain greater market share by increasing the purchase size or by reaching new customers. Company researchers have learned that a purchaser of a larger size will often use the product more generously than if he bought a smaller size. Single-serving packages have captured new market segments. At one time, the cartridge fountain pen captured much of the market because of its convenience —it was more expensive, but much handier, than an ink bottle. Salt is sold in small, convenient boxes, but it is available in large bags at less than half the price of boxes. Glue and other difficult-to-handle products might be packaged successfully in small quantities suitable for single applications.

Packaging has a number of purposes which should be explored further. Packaging is usually a means of handling and shipping a product. It is also a means of holding and storing the product over a period of time so that it remains fresh, clean, and uncontaminated. Packaging furnishes convenience and ease of handling. For example, frozen vegetables are packaged in bags which can be used to cook the contents. In some instances, packaging is edible and can be consumed with the product. Many products, such as bolts, screws, and washers, are packaged by the manufacturer or by the store for ease of handling, for protection, and for display.

One of the major uses of packaging is to advertise and promote on store shelves. Products in attractively designed packages have been found to outsell products handicapped by poorly designed containers. Repeated tests have shown that often the attractively packaged product will outsell another product displayed less attractively, even though the latter is a better product. When competitive products are grouped together on the retailer's shelf, one will often look better than another and may outsell it because of packaging alone. Novel packaging attracts attention and frequently results in a sale. On the other hand, if a package is too different, it may vex the retailer because of the space it takes; its very novelty may relegate it to a less choice position or eliminate it after a brief trial period.

Some products are sold more readily because the package is convenient to use. Opening the package is easier; measuring out contents is facilitated by a spout; opening or measuring aids are a part of packaging. For example, there are sardine cans with attached openers, bags which have their tops sewed so that they unravel easily, and cans with marks or indicators which measure the amount of contents removed.

Branded Products

A research department can develop studies on company brands. If a firm has a number of brands, it is possible to study interrelationships to determine effects of one on another. Problems to be explored include how introduction of a new brand affects an existing one; what happens if a new brand is substituted for an old one; and what is likely to happen if a new brand is tied to an existing brand. Should new brands be added for a different quality of product, and what will be the effect on sales of existing brands? Should a company depend on one universal brand, or should each product be branded independently (in which case, each brand would be promoted separately)?

Some brands are made for retailers and other middlemen, but some firms and dealers frown on this common practice. Some firms sell the generic product unbranded, competing with the branded item because of lower price. For example, a customer buying dry, white beans is less concerned with brand; if two bags are side by side and both products look alike, it is likely the customer will purchase the cheaper one.

The firm needs to know how much more most buyers will pay for a branded than an unbranded item.

The research department can determine recognition value of a brand and its exposure strength on a retailer's shelf. Many firms feel their brands are significant to buyers, forgetting that the product may not be important enough for most buyers to remember brands or associate them with particular manufacturers. For example, it is unlikely that many buyers remember the brand names of toothpicks, clothes pins, clothes lines, shovels, drill bits, or cheese cloth.

Product Varieties and Uses

Marketing research can be used to investigate introduction of new varieties and also to make market tests to determine how much enthusiasm a new entry would generate.

If a study of new varieties is undertaken, creativity suggests trying new sizes, a number of colors, different materials, specific kinds to fit seasons, geographic locations, ethnic groups, and the foreign market. In producing for the foreign market, it is unrealistic to expect a product to meet the desires of several countries. Therefore, it may be necessary to vary a product to fit each nation where it is sold.

Studies in the use of reclaimable material may lead to a strong profit item. For example, one manufacturer of laboratory equipment found it could salvage certain pieces of wood and use them to construct a different table which appealed to buyers.

Alternative uses and completely new applications for a product may be discovered, but it is wise to check such uses carefully before plunging into a sales campaign. A new use which looks promising may be ignored because its market is small; a new application may require repackaging which is too expensive; a new use may require a different channel of distribution; a new use may require excessive promotion costs; a new use may fit an application which is becoming less popular.

In investigating a new application for a company product, it is important to learn if the need is met by some other product. It may be difficult to upset present arrangements. One of the challenging market transitions is the struggle for the container market by steel, aluminum, paper, plastics, and other materials. Possibly, the material that will become popular is the one that will make easy disposal of the discarded container to reduce pollution.

New Product Development

Marketing research is used to ascertain probable demand for new products or modified old products. It may assess size and characteristics of an area or population to forecast potential.

Before a new product is produced or even before extensive development is started, a thorough study of many factors may be used to determine the feasibility of such an undertaking. Research can explore potential buyer income, competition from similar products, competition from unlike products serving the same general area, and appeals needed to generate demand. For example, Detroit was introduced to soccer, a new, major spectator sport, in the late 1960s. In spite of vigorous promotion and excellent publicity, it failed to generate sufficient enthusiasm to continue. Perhaps it may come back some years later and be accepted. Particular car models were never accepted and soon disappeared; models in favor one year lose their appeal the following year; clothing popular one season is completely changed when the same season comes the following year.

Marketing research may be responsible for predicting change because it will bring pertinent data to the attention of decision makers. Marketing research can explore widely or in depth, can analyze broadly or minutely, and can be a means of assembling pertinent information, both specific and general. The importance of both kinds of information is that the specific product or service may have general appeal, but it must be timed correctly to be introduced successfully.

Many products and services can be extended in use and appeal, but someone must pioneer such extensions. Research fits in at this point, because specialized employees can be assigned to specific jobs of studying old and possible new markets for increasing or enlarging demand.

TRANSPORTATION ALTERNATIVES

Careful investigation of alternative uses of transportation facilities may indicate substantial savings in money, time, protection, or packaging. For any product, there may not be one best way of shipping. For example, a manufacturer discovered that he could ship furniture uncrated in trucks if the distance was less than 1,000 miles; beyond this distance, he found it advantageous to crate furniture and ship by rail. The same firm found it cheaper to ship by rail for 600 miles and then by water for 2,500 miles rather than by rail for 2,500 miles. One manufacturer found that the higher cost of shipping by air was more than covered by reduced inventory costs. The introduction of air transportation has opened up new production areas for some products—orchids from Hawaii, fresh fish from distant or difficult-to-reach locations.

Another area of transportation investigation is packaging, crating, or containerization to use space economically. Other considerations involve joint shipping by firms to secure economical rates.

Marketing research studies of shipping costs to central locations and for fresh reshipment to customers can aid in economical locations of warehouses. Comparative studies can show advantages of a single assembly location or multiple assembly locations justified by savings in transporting parts. Advantages of using a single-assembly plant can be compared with shipping parts and assembling them abroad for foreign sales.

MARKET CHARACTERISTICS

Seldom will a manufacturer know most of the characteristics of his market; never will he know them all. A broad look at any market reveals many interesting areas ripe for exploration.

Size of Market

Many firms are unaware of the potential market and the amount of the potential they can expect. In a competitive market, a firm must expect to share the market, but there is a constant struggle to increase the share. Even to maintain its share requires vigilance and effort.

There are many ways market research can assess, appraise, and evaluate a market. One of the first steps is to determine potential, which may be done in a variety of ways and from different approaches. For example, analysis of population, income, area, and habits may show a variety of market factors that may be useful. Textile manufacturers must adjust to demand changes in cloth. The demand for easy or no-ironing fabrics has changed demand for cotton cloth; the change in men's clothing reduced demand for suits; changes in clothing affect the entire market for some textile plants.

Quality of Market

Markets may be quality segmented and require products to be lower or higher priced to meet wider demand. There may be significant demand for used or rebuilt equipment to meet primary needs of some users or as standby equipment in some operations. For example, a firm may have an old delivery truck used once or twice a month for special products; it may have a sump pump to drain low areas during an occasional flood; it may need an electric generator to meet power failure emergencies. Frequently, a product is sold as a protective device, yet the buyer fervently hopes he will never need it.

Management may know that different qualities can be sold, but choose to concentrate on one only. They wish to know which quality would be most advantageous to produce. Management may wish to know if a product should be produced to appeal to a broader market or if it would be preferable to narrow it and introduce another brand to appeal to a different market segment. Are particular markets extensive enough to cultivate, or is it preferable to concentrate on smaller, more lucrative areas? Investigation of physical areas may suggest future distribution into new areas.

Inventory Needs

Correct handling of inventory saves in investment, shipping, and order filling and keeps customers satisfied. By studying inventories, a firm can balance advantages and disadvantages and have the most satisfactory arrangement for the customer and for profit maximization.

Impressive savings can be generated by proper inventory control. Customer needs must be satisfied, but some buyers can be switched to a slightly different product, order size, or container which will affect inventory. Sometimes a customer buys a certain size or in a specific way because he has never been approached about alternatives.

Different packaging may lead to inventory readjustment, to new quantity concentrations at different warehouses, and to experimenting with unified national controls to expedite delivery from a number of sources. For example, if a firm has a number of plants, it may be possible to ship all the production of one or more plants to most customers because purchases are large. In addition, it may be possible at each plant to have a small warehouse of items produced at other plants for shipping with major items frequently purchased concurrently.

Product Distribution

Seldom does a firm have optimum product distribution to satisfy customer wants and needs. Even if distribution is adequate one year, changes may warrant revisions to meet new demands the following year. These changes may take place as a result of altering the product form, the container, or the means of transportation. For example, coal is hauled in railroad cars or ground into fine particles, mixed with water, and shipped by pipeline; fertilizer packed in bags can also be shipped in bulk; some fertilizer is shipped in liquid form; gas is compressed and sent by pipeline and in liquid form shipped in special containers.

Merchandise may be shipped in quantity to a warehouse near large users and stored to be available quickly; it may be shipped to a user on consignment and stored in his warehouse. This method insures that the user need never skimp since he always has an adequate reserve supply immediately available at no extra expense.

Products may be sold more readily if financing is fitted to the buyer. Strategic plant location may facilitate distribution. For example, when the basic oxygen process in steel making was introduced, suppliers shipped in oxygen, established an oxygen plant for one user, or established a central facility and piped oxygen to several users. It is common to establish satellite plants in chemical complexes to use by-products or joint products from the original producer.

The few examples cited are suggestive of the opportunities for varying and improving distribution patterns. It is not enough for a firm to maintain a present distribution system because it may become outdated; the marketing department must search for ways to improve the existing system or perhaps scrap it for another type. This process may require efforts of several marketing research people to work in the distribution area and to combine their efforts with engineering and finance people to discover ways to serve customers.

Market Price Comparison

The marketing research department can make intensive price studies and make comparisons among a series of price variations. It can assess the impact of special deals, particular price concessions, varying payment terms, and many other variations. Unlike retail sales where prices frequently are stable and not subject to customer negotiation, wholesale and manufacturer sales often vary because of competition, expediency, clearing out inventory, and even the so-called practice of dumping. While laws state that all buyers are to be treated alike under the same conditions, it becomes quite difficult to police thousands of minor variations; and it may be even harder to find identical situations.

In thousands of smaller businesses, conditions may vary from those of major corporations, and pricing ingenuity will be even greater because the small firm has flexibility denied its major counterpart. Therefore, a research person may have greater latitude in working with the sales manager in exploring price as a selling tool. While price has a direct appeal to the buyer if he can make savings, he may be willing to forego price appeal in favor of other conditions worth more to him. For example, a buyer may be willing to pay a higher price for a case of one-half dozen cans of a product than for a case containing two dozen because the smaller supply is adequate for his needs. A month's supply of a half-dozen cans might in the long run be cheaper than a four months' supply of two dozen cans, even though the price of the latter is lower.

Another type of price comparison may arise through the use of an alternate approach which promises advantages which have never appeared before. Often, necessity has required approaches which seem unorthodox but which have succeeded at considerable cost savings. Thus, there could be price variations by combining prices of several items in a package, deferred pricing, consignment pricing, and other variables.

Appraisal of Innovation

Innovation has a number of characteristics which are difficult to assess. At the same time, they carry challenging appeals that make today's product subject to modification and change. Innovation is the lifeblood of many firms, but it can be disastrous for some who use it without sufficient understanding and caution.

Many firms are aware of the need for innovation and are anxious to try it, but they hesitate to proceed because of fear of many unknowns. The research staff can reduce unknowns by studying areas that lack ready information; by analyzing demand, supply, and competition in particular situations; by opening up a number of facets worthy of careful attention; and by presenting a number of alternatives depicting what may happen under each. They may set up simulation exercises which would attempt to reflect what might happen under a variety of conditions and assumptions. Research probably will not tell which innovations will succeed, but it can give odds on which ones are more likely to succeed or fail and why—and the *why* is terribly important. Research can help to calm the enthusiasm and the excitement of innovators and subject suggested changes to realistic assessment. It must not eliminate new ideas and discourage creativity, but it can put a restraining hand on crackpot solutions to difficult problems. Many an impractical suggestion which at first had tremendous appeal is never used after careful study reveals unforeseen obstacles.

As a result of using marketing research and in-depth probing of projected product users, it may be possible to catalog innovations into three categories—those that have immediate application and should be incorporated into production as soon as feasible, those that appear to have promise and should be investigated more thoroughly before being tried, and those that are impractical and should be abandoned. These three groupings are not entirely mutually exclusive but tend to overlap; they at least signal caution on go-ahead action.

Competitive Effects

Most markets are fiercely competitive and subjected to a number of marketing strategies devised by each firm to maintain or gain strength. Often this struggle becomes an effort by some to desperately try to maintain themselves in a market, even though their products have last position because of lack of innovation. This situation develops because of failure to create newer, cheaper methods of production or an unwillingness to compete with a firm that insists on dominating a territory no matter what the cost.

If a manufacturer insists on being market commander in a certain area, the research department of another firm can find out the approximate cost of this approach and indicate that to challenge the competitor in this territory would be prohibitively expensive, while concentration on other areas would be more rewarding financially.

Research is needed to monitor competitive efforts to be sure that a company is maintaining its position. When salespeople report changes and new developments, the immediate effects in their new territory may seem so great that they give an alarming report to the sales manager, which research reveals to be exaggerated. Some competitive actions may appear relatively harmless, but research shows that the cumulative effects over time can be disastrous to a firm unless immediate steps are taken to counteract such a thrust. For example, a firm may find a lucrative market dwindling because a strong competitor has merged with another firm that produces complementary items, which then are sold together as a sales package. When one automobile manufacturer purchased a spark plug manufacturing firm, within a year there was considerable realignment in spark plug purchasing by this manufacturer as well as by one of its major competitors.

Introduction of new brands often does not increase overall sales, but merely means a readjustment of market share. Introduction of lower-priced competing products may cause greater consumption, but the total expenditure may decrease. Thus, the increasing demand for margarine as a spread for bread indicates a growing market in pounds but does not help butter sales; buyer shift to lower-priced economy cars may not decrease the number of cars sold, but the automobile manufacturers' revenue may decrease significantly; large increases on car insurance costs for smaller cars with large engines may dampen the sales of these cars.

Strenuous competition may sour the buying public on an industry, and the abuses of a few may bring government regulation which damages the entire group. Because of these many changing conditions, the marketing research group needs to follow them closely, to try to assess their impact, and to raise warning signals to management.

SELLING TECHNIQUES AND AIDS

Research can be a valuable tool for discovering and modifying selling aids and in evaluating their uses under a variety of conditions. Some firms tend to concentrate on a limited number of techniques and are reluctant to experiment with others, even though such techniques are used successfully in selling other products. Thus, a firm selling to industrial buyers would distrust house-to-house selling approaches because the two situations have so little in common. What some of these industrial salespeople forget is that they are not selling products, but selling people, and that they should never overlook potential sources.

Products Channels

A firm with an existing channel of distribution ought to be aware of possible alternatives or substitutes. If using salespeople is successful in one geographical area but not in another, it may be wise to abandon salespeople in the unprofitable area and change to commission agents or wholesalers, depend on catalogs, use mail selling, or drop some customers and contact others by phone. There may be no important reason for using an identical channel in all areas.

If a firm is unsuccessful in distributing its products, it may allow someone else to sell the line. This method is often done by the manufacturer who sells all of his product in private brands. If a firm does not have sufficient volume to maintain a sales force or cannot cover sparse territories selling its own products, it may pick up related items by representing other manufacturers. It then becomes a manufacturer selling its own products and a wholesaler of other items. Some manufacturers become frightened when they lose money and drop out of some areas or try to increase prices without exploring other alternatives.

Want Books as Aids

A customer buying the same merchandise repeatedly often uses a want book to record items he needs. This device is common in many retail outlets. When the regular salesperson calls, if he has the confidence of the buyer, he merely copies the items the buyer has listed on his order blank. This practice relieves the buyer of the need for going over the items again unless it is to specify quantities or to hear about special deals.

An industrial buyer might have a similar listing of items he calls in to his industrial distributor or gives to this firm's salesperson. A salesperson who has the strongest relationship with a buyer frequently gets the routine purchases at favorable prices.

Preprinted Order Blanks

Preprinted order blanks are given to buyers to make purchasing easier. These blanks may be issued weekly and arranged to make them most useful to the buyer. Some firms issue these blanks in booklet form once a year to facilitate ordering. For example, school science laboratories give one yearly major order for dozens or hundreds of items that are used by instructors and students.

A firm's research staff can develop these order blanks in a number of ways and change the makeup, pricing, order size, and continuity to arrive at one which best meets their purposes. A firm may have a number of these blanks because different buyers require different merchandise. Thus, an order blank sent to a chemistry instructor would vary from the one sent to a biology instructor; a list sent to a specialty store would differ from one sent to a general store. A well-developed order blank mailed or given to a buyer in advance of his needs is a powerful aid in getting orders. It is easier to check items on a preprinted order blank than to write one out. Most order blanks include a blank sheet attached for listing infrequently ordered items.

Product Specifications

Product specification can be complex and appears most important in particular categories. Made-to-order purchases are usually based on specification. Commercial and industrial buildings are constructed to architects' specifications; often, equipment in the buildings is made to specifications. An enterprising firm can use research to find how important it is to get its specifications into the final architect drawings.

Preparing catalogs and specifications is a costly procedure done by leading firms in an industry. Smaller firms sometimes forego all these costs and take orders based on competitors' specifications. Although somewhat handicapped in production, a small firm may easily overcome this extra cost by avoiding the specification preparation cost.

In some areas, a firm may have standard items and items prepared to specifications. The problem becomes one of comparing profitability of standard items to the profitability of special items. Sometimes, these special items command a much higher price and easily cover increased production costs.

Personal Call

The personal sales call is the most effective selling technique. This approach needs constant study to maximize its usefulness. Studies have revealed careless and ineffective selling techniques that waste the time of salespeople and buyers and often irritate buyers because of salesperson ineptness.[1]

A firm, through research and experimentation, can develop a pattern of salesperson behavior that should maximize his effectiveness. In some selling situations inventory examination is useful; a careful demonstration may prove advantageous; motion pictures of processes and construction techniques at the plant can be instructive; a detailed discussion of precise applications may be useful; comparisons with competing products may be revealing; possibilities of change and adaptation can be explored.

Mail as a Selling Tool

Research into the use of selling by mail can have several objectives. Mail alone may do a fairly good selling job. Increased sales may come from personal selling, but it is expensive. Often, infrequent sales calls are supplemented by excellent mailings. Some firms find that envelope stuffers along with invoices have increased sales.

---

1. Robert W. Littlewood, "Aiming at Profit Targets," *Marketing Times,* 22 (July/August 1975), 27–29.

Telephone

Many salespeople fail to use the telephone as an effective selling aid. The research department can study telephone uses by salespeople within a firm and possibly similar use by salespeople in other firms and obtain a composite approach that will aid salespeople who have not taken full advantage of telephone technique.

Many unnecessary personal calls are made by salespeople who do not appreciate the use of alternate methods, such as telephoning, for contacting buyers, answering inquiries, handling complaints, or securing information. Adequate research into the use of supporting techniques multiplies sales effectiveness and reduces overall distribution cost.

Return Privilege Aid

The return privilege, though often abused, is a strong selling aid. A buyer is more willing to accept a product if he has a return privilege, whether it is at the retail, wholesale, or manufacturing level. Many firms have differing policies on merchandise returns because unlimited return privileges have proved excessively expensive.

The return privilege is widely used and consequently needs regular review to establish its cost and importance. Marketing research can monitor this service and suggest changes to tighten or loosen this privilege. A return privilege may be enforced selectively if study reveals favorable results in general, but abuses in particular areas.

Credit

Most commercial business transactions are on credit, as are many retail transactions. When credit sales are the typical method of selling, salespeople and customers are irritated when the credit department rejects sales. While most firms have credit guidelines, it is doubtful if the salespeople know these guidelines too well. As a result, salespeople take credit chances with doubtful buyers.

Because of its importance and universal acceptance, credit needs to be monitored constantly to show changes that call for greater or lesser restraints. Research may reveal other approaches to credit restraints, which would make them less restrictive. Imaginative suggestions might be accepted by the credit department. Thoroughly documented studies of sales gains versus credit losses could benefit both departments in developing a better understanding of each other's functions.

SALES PROMOTION ANALYSIS

Analyzing sales promotion efforts (including advertising) is essential for the best use of scarce resources. These efforts include forms of advertising as well as programs to stimulate salespeople and/or dealers.

Advertising Research

Present research is growing more sophisticated, and attempts to measure advertising are being refined. Most firms admit to wasting advertising money, but are incapable of developing sharp appraisal to determine where the trouble lies. Many ineffective advertisements appear; these efforts are not deliberate, but arise from lack of knowledge.

Advertising research merits continuing examination by research staffs to improve quality and have greater returns on this expenditure.

Direct Mail Promotion

Management may discover how to use direct mail effectively by analyzing markets and buyers and by checking availability of pertinent mailing lists to cover specific areas. Direct mail may give as effective coverage as general advertising at a fraction of the cost. Since all sales costs (whether direct salespeople or direct mail) are charged as marketing cost, any revision in promotion devices that does the same job at a lower cost is inviting.

Demonstrations

Salespeople often have devices to demonstrate products, such as slides, motion pictures, or models of the product. Careful research on these approaches will aid in singling out the one most useful for particular situations. This area also includes the evaluation of trade shows and exhibitions, which some firms regard highly while other firms question their contribution.

Point-of-purchase Advertising

There are advantages to using literature in stores and descriptive material attached to the product. Enormous quantities are wasted by people who pick up literature as a matter of habit, but have little or no possible use for the products. Often, store managers do not bother to display literature. Much more research is needed in this area and in developing changes to make this kind of promotion more worthwhile.

Trial Use

When products are put out for trial use, they should be closely checked for the cost and effort involved compared to results obtained. A trial use approach may be successful, but other methods might be satisfactory at a lesser cost. Research people can analyze alternate methods and compare costs with results.

Product Introduction

The success of the introduction of new products or modified existing products may be determined by the timing. Many products fail because they are introduced at the wrong time. A firm must study its market to see how it will react to another product. If the product is a completely new innovation, it becomes doubly hard to anticipate market reception because there is no experience on which to predict results.

Product Guarantees

Product guarantee is an example of the use of sales promotion which has often been a tremendous aid in selling but later has become a costly expedient. Many firms offer guarantees unaware of their ultimate costs. While it is not possible to predict exactly the cost and problems involved in administering guarantees, it is often possible to anticipate some of the major repercussions and prepare for them. A quick, but unsatisfactory, way to eliminate guarantee effects is for a company to go out of business; some guarantees have literally driven firms into bankruptcy. Careful attention in the beginning would have foreseen the need for adequate safeguards and financial reserves to cope with the problems.

ECONOMIC STUDIES FOR MARKETING RESEARCH

Someone in a firm needs to keep in close touch with the country's economy. This job is often given to a research person on the marketing staff, since only larger firms have an economic analysis department.

Sales do not just happen. There are causes that make sales fluctuate; one of the greatest causes is the economic welfare of buyers. While many individuals in a firm read daily newspapers, daily business publications, and other periodicals, someone is responsible for keeping up with the enormous flow of economic literature. He may attend meetings where the economic climate is discussed and talk with economists from other sections of the country and other countries. He probably develops statistical data reflecting current conditions and suggests possible interpretations for the future. His study may reveal economic conditions which can have serious repercussions in his firm's industry; when these conditions occur, the firm can be alerted to expected market changes. Many firms are able to isolate specific economic conditions that affect them, even though the general economy shows little change. They are prepared to meet these new conditions early enough to prevent serious operating dislocation.

There are a number of nonrecurring and extraordinary economic incidents which need to be watched. Changes in competition may result from mergers of firms. Decisions of some firms to drop out of an area can mean significant sales increases; marked declines in sales may be expected if a large firm decides to come into an area of marketing.

MARKETING AUDIT

The marketing audit embraces all of the operations of the marketing department or marketing division of the firm. It is a study that covers the objectives and policies of the firm's marketing department, the physical organization, the marketing mix, the operations and procedures of the department, the personnel policy, the sales promotion activity, and customer relations.[2]

A thorough marketing audit is a comprehensive study of the entire marketing operation. It brings all marketing activities into focus, scrutinizes each job, and presents an analysis of the effectiveness of each unit in the entire structure. It is designed to uncover weaknesses or problems and to suggest steps for eliminating or overcoming weak spots.

Because the marketing audit is expensive and time-consuming, it is more common to make a perfunctory study of some phases of the marketing task and then focus on specific areas that seem to need most attention. This situation comes about because some areas are relatively sound, some have minor weaknesses, some have weaknesses that cannot be corrected, and some have glaring weaknesses that need immediate attention. Without going into the technical detail of handling the marketing audit, it is worthwhile to review some of its broad aspects in relation to specific segments of marketing.

Marketing Objectives and Policies

Many firms do not have clearly defined objectives. Because a firm does not know exactly where it is going or what it wants, the marketing department operates blindly, hoping that as long as it makes money for the firm all is well.

Policies may be overlapping or leave gaps uncovered; their timing may be a confusion of long-term and short-term arrangements that upset continuity and decision making. In trying to untangle management statements and directives, the auditor might ask, "Where are you going? What do you want? How do you expect to get there? What are your short-term and long-term objectives?" This kind of approach forces management to rethink its purposes and directs thinking on specific operations.

---

2. For a detailed explanation of conducting an audit, see H. Webster Johnson and William G. Savage, *Administration Office Management* (Reading, Mass.: Addison-Wesley Publishing Co., 1968), Chapter 27.

Marketing Organization

In some firms, the marketing organization has been planned; in others, it has just grown. After years of operation, it may be difficult to decide which of the two types is performing better. The planned department may be operating on its old outdated plan, or it may be operating on revised, up-to-date planning. The department which seemed to grow without formal planning may be hopelessly behind, or it may be guided by a skillful marketing executive who has adapted as occasion demanded and now heads a remarkably efficient sales organization.

Marketing Mix

Products are changing constantly, and one that dominated one period becomes less important later. Studies have shown firms actively pushing items in a broad line that contribute little to volume or profit, or contribute to volume but not to profit. Some companies have determined that 75 percent of their products provide 10 percent of dollar volume and little, if any, profit.

The marketing mix considers breadth of product line, importance of each item, customer appeal, importance of various customers, and related problems that are cause for revision of production commitments. The variation in marketing mix can also have important effects on production. A change in marketing mix might improve profitability by reducing both marketing and production costs.

Operating Methods and Procedures

A review of operating methods and procedures entails study of channels of distribution, size of orders, credit policies, delivery schedules, pricing, return privileges, and the job of administering the sales force. The use of criteria for evaluating purposes assists in giving a balanced judgment and affords an easily understood method of presenting data. This area is extensive and may require traveling with salespeople, analyzing profit returns, evaluating recruiting and training of salespeople, and other specific duties.

Personnel Policies

A review of personnel policies, compensation of the marketing staff, hiring and terminating procedures, periodic review procedures, and interest in employee welfare is an important segment of the marketing audit.

Keeping employees healthy, progressive, and enthusiastic will determine a firm's success. Almost any study of personnel administration in the sales area reveals inequities of territory, training, compensation, and consideration of specific requirements resulting from acts of omission and commission. Salespeople are hurt and feel slighted when they receive inadequate support from management.

Sales Promotion Activities

The area of sales promotion and various types of advertising needs attention to assess each method. This area is difficult to analyze; at best, inexact answers are obtained. This situation arises from the difficulty of measuring results, particularly delayed promotion effects. To justify large expenditures for promotion, it is wise to provide measurements that will give management better ideas where to concentrate attention.

Customer Relations

Any marketing audit must include an appraisal of customer relations, including responsiveness to complaints, adjustment of disputes, return privileges, credit extensions, deliveries, and other associated activities. It is important to keep a healthy lifeline between customer and supplying company; often, this must be maintained by salesperson contact as well as by careful attention to detail from the district and/or home office. If the marketing audit is periodic, each audit ought to delve into company-customer relationships to see if there is evidence of improvement or deterioration. There is a danger of slighting customers or of making a corporate change which will be to the customer's disadvantage.[3]

PERFORMING MARKETING RESEARCH

Marketing research has a number of techniques, tools, methods, and procedures which make it possible to secure meaningful results,[4] some of which may be valuable in guiding future marketing activities and some which give warnings of what to avoid or discontinue. A few are discussed for the benefit of the sales manager who has not been

---

3. The reader will find useful information in *Analyzing and Improving Marketing Performance; "Marketing Audits" in Theory and Practice* (New York: American Management Association, Management Report No. 32, 1959); for performing an audit see Dan Crone and John H. Burns, "Management Audit," *Ideas for Management,* Systems and Procedures Association, 1962, p. 68, and William P. Leonard, "The Management Audit," *Systems and Procedures,* edited by Victor Lazarro (Englewood Cliffs, New Jersey: Prentice-Hall, Inc., 1959).

4. The information in this section is a brief glimpse into the field of marketing research. It does not attempt to give detailed methodology or operations. Marketing research is a difficult area and deserves special training. There are several excellent textbooks on the subject, and new ones appear every year or two. Frequently, excellent publications come from other countries. The American Marketing Association in Chicago can give current information, and their publications should be a part of libraries of professional marketing research practitioners.

exposed to this discipline, which is growing rapidly and is now a department in most major firms.

Market Testing

Although some people question the use of market testing, it is still one of the more useful approaches for many firms. The firms that question this approach do it because it reveals their strategy to competition and may spoil a time advantage of a new product which, if successful, may be duplicated by others in a matter of weeks.

Many firms in less competitive situations find market tests to be a helpful approach in analyzing future demand, particularly the volume of demand. Exposure of any new product is likely to evoke interest and generate some demand, but products which are introduced without sufficient market testing may sell slowly, but not in sufficient quantity to be profitable.

Market testing may be used for new products and for entering new territories with established products. Many firms wonder what would happen if their successful products in one area were expanded to a nationwide basis. Market testing may include experimenting with different channels of distribution, different promotion techniques, different packaging, and a variety of ideas which need market examination before adoption.

Personal Interviews

Marketing research finds personal interviewing one of the more successful approaches in securing information. A personal interview may be structured (follow an exact prescribed pattern), unstructured (a guided but perhaps rambling interview which covers the information wanted, but data must be extracted from the conversation), and semi-structured (interviewer follows a pattern to some extent, but encourages digression which may lead to uncovering unsuspected facts).

Some types of interviewing merely consist of asking and recording answers to specific questions; others use depth interviewing, which consists of probing questions and follow-up discussions intended to reveal hidden reasons for acting in certain ways. Prepared questionnaires are normally used in carrying out the usual interview, which is not in depth.

Mail Questionnaire

The mail questionnaire is often a less costly way of doing a marketing research survey. If a large enough proportion of the mailed questionnaires are completed and returned, large physical territories may be covered rapidly at a minimum cost. To insure greater returns, some questionnaires include a reward or a promise of reward for filling them in and mailing them back. It is possible that such inducements may affect the sample reliability.

If questionnaires are returned by a small percentage of users, the results may still be sufficiently accurate to predict the product's universe (total users of the product). A number of devices are used regularly in order to encourage greater questionnaire response, many of which do not give the respondent any tangible reward.

Observation Techniques

Observation is one of the common approaches to securing marketing information. An observer may be stationed in a store to see how people buy, how salespeople handle customers, to check strength of different shelf locations, to check on amount of stealing, and to compare various ways of shelf stocking or merchandise arrangement. An observer may check the number of units sold, the number of people who pick up the product but then replace it without buying, and many other factors of customer behavior. An observer may accompany salespeople on their calls and check what they do and how they do it. An observer may watch a sales trainer to see why one is more successful than another.

An observer may be stationed in the home office to trace order handling procedure; he can inspect the physical order filling; he can watch the packing of merchandise and follow up on shipping procedure.

This observation may be done constantly over a period of time at one location, or it may be an intermittent approach (work sampling) that attempts to uncover weaknesses or changes that are going on either consciously or unconsciously.

Research Firms

Some companies have a complete research department; others have a small department and hire outside firms to do most of the research. There are nationally recognized research firms that perform a variety of services. Information on many of these firms can be obtained from the American Marketing Association in Chicago. Research firm listings are found in the yellow pages of the telephone books in major cities. Many of these firms have field forces or access to field forces that can handle interviewing and other types of work in many locations simultaneously. Some have offices in major world cities. Unless a company has a steady amount of research and can justify setting up permanent staffs for specific duties, it probably is better to hire outside services as needed for much of the work.

Panels

A *panel* is a reporting service covering a specific number of users of a product in particular areas or nationwide. For example, a panel member reports all his purchases over a period of time on forms provided by the research firm. These purchases are reported by brand, size of container, price, where purchased, and other information and mailed to the research firm at regular intervals. The information is consolidated and presented to the client to give him data on the movement of his product as compared to competitors' products and for other purposes.

Panels may be created in a number of ways, ranging from the one just described to the kind where a group of individuals meet only once to discuss a particular subject. This latter type of panel gives opinions and suggestions; the first type of panel is a compilation of members' purchasing behavior.

Publications

Newspapers and magazines compile large amounts of information and arrange for special studies of general interest to the readers. Some may even perform specific kinds of research in a limited way for their major advertisers. Some newspapers operate continuous panels. Some magazines perform major marketing studies which are made freely available. Trade publications compile continuous statistics, and some have special annual issues of vast amounts of pertinent, detailed information. For example, each year *Sales Management* magazine issues a "Survey of Buying Power" which gives data that is widely used by firms in establishing sales forecasts and setting sales quotas.

Government Sources

Federal and state governments are sources of vast quantities of data. Every research person should be familiar with census data published by the Census Bureau of the United States Department of Commerce. This vast source of material grows every year. The United States Department of Agriculture is another excellent source of statistical data. Libraries have a number of indexes that assist the reader in locating sources of prepared data.

INTERNAL AND EXTERNAL DATA ANALYSIS

The researcher has a wealth of external source materials which may be helpful in developing useful information. These sources include the ones mentioned as well as many other source materials that apply to specific subjects. For example, trade associations gather data useful to members. Some of this material is restricted to members only, but much is readily available to the general public. An example is data published by the Motor Vehicle Manufacturers Association of the United States, Inc.

Internal company data are often one of the most useful data sources because it is the only available source of pertinent data on the firm. A judicious blending of internal and external data will give information that can yield rich dividends.

There are large quantities of statistical data and much other information available in printed form in literally thousands of publications and sources. In addition to securing original data, the job of a research person may frequently be more concerned with finding and rearranging existing data into forms useful to him. He must constantly seek current and less recent information.

QUESTIONS AND PROBLEMS

1. Why can there be a question of product suitability? Is there more than one answer to product use? Explain.
2. What is meant by purpose of packaging? Illustrate with several examples.
3. Is constant monitoring of brands important? Why worry about brands? Explain.
4. Discuss the importance of transportation in product research. What are some of the factors in transportation that may hinder sales of specific products?
5. Many firms consider new products one of their strongest selling features. Why is this new product worship so prevalent? Give examples from your own experience.
6. Why must a firm study its market constantly? Are markets stable or fluid? Discuss.
7. Is it essential to study the relation of inventory and distribution to particular markets? Will product quality have an effect on inventory? Why?
8. What can the marketing research department do to measure price factors as they affect customers and markets?
9. How can marketing research contribute to innovation positively and negatively?
10. Point out several ways marketing research gives information on competitors. Why is such information vital to the firm?
11. Why is it necessary to assess effectiveness of selling techniques? Is one technique sacred, or are they all vulnerable? Explain.
12. Discuss the advantages of assessing the uses of several selling aids, indicating where and how each may be effective.
13. Give reasons for using marketing research in the credit area.
14. Why is sales promotion so important in marketing, and why does management need to research the area thoroughly?
15. There are a number of sales promotion techniques used to market a product. Why can't a firm experiment with each to find which ones are the most effective?

16. Need a firm be current on economic factors to succeed in its sales operation? Explain.
17. The marketing audit is a complex operation. Trace some of the steps and procedures you feel important to make it useful.
18. Discuss several of the tools used in marketing research. Why is it necessary to conduct marketing research in a number of ways?
19. Sources of data are extremely important in marketing research. Explain this statement, and fortify your explanation with examples.
20. What is a panel? Can panels vary in makeup? Purpose? Duration?
21. Distinguish between internal and external data.
22. Write your impressions of the value and use of marketing research as an aid to the sales manager. Give specific conclusions of your own about its importance.

DIALOGUE BETWEEN MARKET RESEARCHER AND A POTENTIAL CLIENT

case 15–1

Purpose

Demonstrate in dialogue form the general selling technique of the market researcher to the potential client. The service involved is collecting information on home buying to reduce risk for the builder.

Background

1. The market researcher, Ms. Jerome, represents a market research company.
2. The prospect, Mr. Backstrom, is the president of a firm that builds and sells homes in metropolitan Boston.
3. Backstrom's firm is a medium-sized builder with no funds set aside for market research.
4. Backstrom has limited knowledge in the field of market research.

First Meeting

Backstrom: Mr. Andrews of the Ames Company in Dallas gave me your name, Ms. Jerome. He said that you helped diagnose his problems and that you probably could help me.

Jerome: Is there some immediate problem, Mr. Backstrom?

Backstrom: No, I want to head them off before they come. Let's say that I want to increase my sales and profits in the future.

Jerome: Have you used market research before, or did Mr. Andrews tell you how he used it?

Backstrom: I have never used market research before, but I heard you surveyed Dallas for Mr. Andrews to determine the number of potential customers in his area.

Jerome: Yes, that was the most recent study that I made for him. Since I gave Mr. Andrews the report, he has increased the number of salespeople, and sales have increased steadily. Let's get back to your company. Do you receive any industry journals or special statistical reports with information about your industry?

Backstrom: Well, I used to subscribe to national journals, but the information was too general to be of any use to me.

Jerome: Here are some pamphlets that I picked up at the library that are published by the state about this area, as well as one published by the leading mortgage company in the area. The statistics indicate where families are moving and the location from which they are moving in the Boston area. You seem to be building and selling your homes in areas where many people are moving. What do you know about the people who are buying your homes, Mr. Backstrom?

Backstrom: Well, I would say they are just average people who can afford homes in the $30,000 to $60,000 range, since that is all we have to offer.

Jerome: If you had more information about the types of people living in your homes, such as age, income, number and age of children, and location of former home, as well as information about their expectations from the builder and salesperson, and their postpurchase satisfaction, then you might be able to make better decisions based on this information.

Backstrom: All that information would be helpful, but how can you get it?

Jerome: There are several ways, Mr. Backstrom. Some methods give more and better information than others, but they usually cost more. Why don't you let me design a growth proposal for you which will summarize some of the better techniques that can be applied to your company. Before I leave, will you give me one of each of your advertising brochures and any other form materials used by your salespeople or your company in communicating with potential customers?

Backstrom: Certainly.

Second Meeting

Jerome: Here is the main copy of the growth research proposal, Mr. Backstrom. Let me explain it to you. Since you want to increase your sales and profits in the future and avoid as many problems as possible, this proposal is designed to cover your broad marketing area. After examining the forms and other types of materials your salespeople use, it appears that you already have much information that you are not using.

Your secretary told me that you get a number of complaints about your houses, both before and after the buyers move in. This number of complaints is probably about normal for a builder of your size. I know you are trying to solve these problems with letters to your customers, but I am recommending a new kind of action.

I suggest tabulating your complaints by supplier or subcontractor. By doing this, you can keep records on these people and threaten them with evidence of bad products or workmanship when complaints are made. You can also determine which companies are responding promptly to the complaints you report. This recommendation is probably the most important one since it pertains to the real quality of your product in the eyes of the buyer. You must keep in mind that present owners of your homes are the most important advertising you have. If they are satisfied with quality and workmanship, they will tell their friends. If they do not think you are trying to solve their problems, they will also tell their friends.

The second kind of information that you have is your salespeople's prospect cards. Each salesperson fills in a file card on those people who look at your homes who he thinks might be probable customers. If you analyze the cards, you can tell where your prospects come from, which aids in determining into what neighborhoods your advertising should be directed. If your cards are modified slightly as I have suggested, you can pick up more information about what the prospect saw in your home that he liked and what your homes did not have that the prospect would have liked to see. The recommended actions cost little and will give much additional information. If you wish, the information on the newly designed cards can be sent to my office every three months so that we can tabulate it for you. In this way, you can measure any trends in prospects.

My last recommendation of the growth research proposal is to conduct a telephone survey of those people whose names are on your prospect cards. At the end of the proposal is a questionnaire and recommended set-up for the tabulation. I suggest two hundred interviews. One hundred will be with people who have looked at your homes and then bought; fifty will be with people who have looked at your homes and then bought competitors' homes; and fifty will be with people who have looked at your homes, but have not made any purchase. Notice that most of the questions can be compared among the three groups.

You can compare the demographics and find what motivated your customers to buy, what motivated your competitors' customers to buy (and why they didn't buy your homes), and what kind of people did not buy at all. Further, I suggest that we make an evaluation of your use of my recommendations from the survey, six months after they are first used.

What are your reactions, Mr. Backstrom?

Backstrom: Useful suggestion, Ms. Jerome. How much?

Jerome: The first few recommendations will not cost you anything except some of your secretary's time. She should be able to do the tabulating of the customer complaints that I can help her set up. She can also tabulate the information you are now getting on your salespeople's prospect cards. If you change to the newly recommended prospect card, the cost of printing, coding, key punching, tabulation, and a written report will be $500 every six months. The most valuable piece of information that I will be able to provide now will cost $1500. This price will cover interviewing two hundred prospects, coding, punching, tabulating, cross runs, and a report with my recommendations.

Backstrom: That's not as bad as I thought it would be.

Jerome: Good! Look the questionnaire over; indicate in the margin if you would like to make any additions; put your initials on it; and send it with the list of prospects to me. I will have the written report of our findings to you within four weeks after I receive the names.

QUESTIONS

1. What is your opinion of the services offered? Explain.
2. Did Ms. Jerome do a good selling job? Discuss.
3. What is important for a continuous relationship between Mr. Backstrom and Ms. Jerome for several years?
4. How can marketing research have a continuing value to Mr. Backstrom? Give several reasons.

THE K AND L MACHINE COMPANY   *case 15–2*

The K and L Machine Company has produced a complete line of office equipment for over twenty years. It started as a one-machine business in the late 1800s; through a process of growth and merger, it has become a leader in the industry. Although management has not pushed to expand the market on every fringe, they have permitted expansion where needed to maintain market share.

Competition among machine companies has increased to a point where extensive product innovation, systems assistance, and customer consideration are often the deciding factors in maintaining a market position. A much expanded research department located at the home office in Omaha produces many product innovations. A few years ago, the research department developed paper that would make copies without carbon paper. How to market this new paper posed a problem.

Management realized this paper was a major market attraction which, if merchandised properly, would attract a greater market share for the entire K and L line. The benefits of selling this new carbonless paper in office forms in conjunction with the machines were many; but the salesperson's highly technical job as a systems engineer permitted little time for designing and selling custom forms. Management, being a conservative group, was undecided as to a course of action.

Would this type of service substantially aid the product line sales, and would it pay for itself? What type of sales staff should do the actual selling, and how could a machine-oriented sales organization break into a job shop type of printing operation? Perhaps it would be wiser to wholesale the new paper and capitalize on the new features it offers through name branding.

Although the market for machine sales would be the same in many cases as the forms sales, the selling techniques would be different. A forms salesperson would sell a six-month or a year's supply and would expect repeat sales. He would have to broaden his market to include retail business. The forms person would have many small orders compared to large orders of the machine salesperson. This situation dictated a new compensation plan, where the commission rate would have to compensate for the smaller orders and an incentive plan for new orders.

The present sales organization consisted of highly trained systems engineers who oriented themselves to machine operations. Their territories also reflected the highly specialized type of selling machine sales demanded. Their market consisted of medium to large operations in a general geographic territory or in a special account territory. The present system was not set up to handle the new marketing necessary for successful forms sales. The forms company which K and L was considering acquiring has an experienced, but limited, sales staff located on the west coast. K and L was considering using these people to head a forms department in the larger branches. Another consideration was to transfer a machine salesperson to head a forms department. This move would require a salary increase to offset the machine salesperson's previous income. Problems of this nature are bound to occur with the adoption of a new marketing policy. K and L was also considering using wholesalers to market this product. This method would eliminate many problems, but might mean fewer profits for the company. The real selling feature of the carbonless paper might be lost.

Management had to make a major decision about the advisability of this new venture. A test market situation had been discussed as well as the acquisition of a large forms company. The deciding factors involved the actual cost of implementing a system of this kind and the benefit it would have on the competitive position of the company.

QUESTIONS

1. How could the marketing research department help management to reach a decision?
2. What specific things could the marketing research department do?

16

Marketing Costs and Budgeting

Management should be concerned with all marketing costs and use an overall marketing budget as a guide to spending. A *marketing budget* is the total estimate of all sales and other marketing costs over a future period. It represents a figure which not only covers all sales costs broadly interpreted but also acts as a brake on unrestrained spending or unplanned expenditures.

Sales costs analysis and budgeting are not to be regarded as straitjackets to hamper reasonable sales expenditures, but rather as guides to future action resulting from the best thinking of management at the time. If later events suggest budget revision, there should be no hindrances that forbid change to reflect conditions which had not been anticipated.

MARKETING COSTS

The scope of this presentation covers those costs which are closely connected with the sales organization. Too often, however, the sales department will be so intent on its own direct activities that it will fail to appraise correctly efforts made by other departments in the marketing organization.

Before a sales manager undertakes to develop a sales budget or to set up a marketing budget (in some firms the terms are synonymous, in others they differ), he needs to visualize the efforts of all people in the firm who are working towards improved selling operations. For example, it is helpful if the sales manager understands how research and development strives for new products or modifies present ones in quality, appearance, packaging, convenience, and other appeals. Changes in production methods, assignment of products to factories in new locations, warehouse locations, and similar factors may materially affect sales costs, even though salespeople would accept such changes as normal operating procedures and fail to recognize them as effective sales cost reducers.

The sales executive cannot overlook changes generated from adjustments in channels of distribution. Adding or dropping salespeople, changing from exclusive to selective distribution, or introducing alternate channels in some territories must be considered in viewing sales costs. It is likely some changes will lower costs and others will increase them; but, taken by itself, increased or decreased sales costs may be good or bad. There is little reason to cut sales costs if the result is fewer sales and less profit; increased sales do not automatically justify higher sales costs. When a sales executive begins looking at sales costs as ends in themselves, he is weakening his position. He loses sight of the ultimate end of the sales function, which is to move merchandise or services profitably. In a broader sense, he must increase customer satisfaction while increasing his firm's profit.

The marketing mix that determines which items are to be pushed and how to assort various products into groups has a bearing on costs. One cannot overlook market responsiveness to a firm's products and to modify approaches to meet market demand. For example, product A and product B may have equal market sales, but product B may be much more profitable. Management would rather sell product B, but competition is fierce. Product A is much less profitable but less competitive. It may be better to sell a large volume of product A at a lower profit margin and to maximize profit through volume than to contest for product B, which is highly profitable, but where no firm can have a marked advantage.

Another area would be to assess the relative use of alternatives in the sales effort. Each marketing activity presumably directly or indirectly enhances sales. How to use various types of sales promotion, advertising, direct salespeople, dealers, mail order, and other ways present a constant problem which cannot be dismissed by merely continuing present practices. Methods adequate at one time may become prohibitively expensive; approaches previously successful may be declining in impact; and today's techniques may lack relevance tomorrow.

It is dangerous to assume that continuing present procedures will be equally successful even if yearly or periodic modifications are introduced. Sometimes this approach may succeed for years; at other times it can lead to failure because of pronounced changes in the particular industry. For example, many city restaurants have been forced to close because their evening trade has practically disappeared. People patronizing such establishments have transferred their business to other areas. In some cases, there have been radical changes in customer choice of evening entertainment. Existing forms of distribution may give way to other methods, which may be more costly or less costly but may be more appreciated by the customer. Sometimes the higher cost approach can be successfully maintained by customer willingness to accept higher price.

Cost in distribution is something the sales executive must accept, but it is a means to achieve a result and not an end in itself. Consequently, in studying sales cost or the total marketing share of gross revenue, management cannot concentrate on cost without looking at its reciprocal of value offered to the customer. In consummating sales the executive cannot look at marketing costs as absolutely high or low, if it takes 2 percent, 20 percent, 50 percent, or 75 percent of sales. From the firm's standpoint, it justifies the cost that gives optimum return.

Sales costs among firms in the same industry may vary considerably. Lacking other criteria, what competitors are doing may often be a guide. Presumably, these data represent the best results of others in the business. It is not likely that a firm can remain in business if it differs substantially from competitors unless its marketing is quite different; its total expense pattern is divided differently; or its expense allocations are quite different.

Types of Marketing Costs

Viewed narrowly, marketing costs might be construed to encompass those costs directly related to selling. However, there are numerous peripheral costs which arise from performing related marketing duties that have been found necessary or helpful. Sales executives feel that expenditures of this nature are worthwhile and contribute materially to successful distribution. For accounting records and for statistical analysis, it is necessary to assemble these costs into categories.

Direct selling costs

Direct selling costs are those that arise from using salespeople in territories and include such expenses as travel, telephone, entertainment, sales office expense connected with sales supervision, and sales compensation. These are the sales costs generated by the field sales organization that can be directly allocated by salespeople, territory, district, or other distinctive unit of operation. Such costs occur only because there is a field sales organization actively soliciting orders. This situation can be contrasted with a firm that uses a selling agent who takes charge of all selling functions. In this situation, all direct selling costs would be his; the firm's only cost would be sales commissions to the selling agent.

Sales promotion costs

Sales promotion costs, broadly interpreted, include a variety of activities that supplement the salespeople's selling activities. Often, sales promotion is differentiated from advertising by saying that advertising is promotion directed to the final buyer or user, while sales promotion consists of aids that are used by dealers or other members in the channel of distribution to influence the buyer. For example, advertising could be an advertisement in the local newspaper, but an attractive retail counter display would be a sales promotion device. It is impractical to become too precise in terminology, since some items might fit either category depending on use or circumstances.

Sales promotion costs may include conventions, exhibits, mailing costs, samples, and other aids used to further sales indirectly. Both advertising and sales promotion are intended to assist in the active sale of the product with or without the assistance of the salesperson.

Warehousing and handling costs

At what point to draw the line between manufacturing and distribution costs is not always clear; nor is there universal agreement in such cost allocation. If a firm commences distribution costs when the goods are in the warehouse, the costs included would be for storage which covers all building expenses—temperature control, rent or taxes, light, maintenance, handling of merchandise, filling and packing orders, and other closely connected activities. If a manufacturer has a number of warehouses, the cost of shipping from the plant plus the unloading and placing in the warehouse would be included. If a firm has two corporations in which the manufacturing corporation turns over its products to the sales corporation, the latter's handling and warehousing expenses would all be marketing costs. In a wholesale firm, all costs in securing, storing, and handling can be considered marketing expenses, since the entire organization exists for a marketing purpose.

Transportation costs

Transportation costs include all freight, express, and parcel post charges as well as the expenses of the firm's own shipping department related to outbound shipments. Freight on incoming shipments in manufacturing is properly regarded as expense which is included in the price of the manufactured products; wholesalers and retailers may properly add freight on incoming shipments to the price of the item to get a total cost or landed cost (invoice cost minus purchase discount plus freight-in).

Financial costs

Financial costs include the cost of borrowing money to finance inventories and other regular and irregular expenditures.[1] The account-

---

1. This might involve an analysis of both implicit and explicit costs. Rigid analysis at this point might dictate alternative ways of financing at different periods.

ing cost would be included, as would credit and collection expenses, bad debt losses, and sales returns expenses.

General sales costs

These expenses cover home office sales supervision, sales administration, sales office expenses, marketing research, and all other marketing expenses that cannot readily be allocated to any other categories. Each firm has a number of sales expenses, and some firms may have special expense categories which are literally impossible to pin down to a particular area and consequently are put in this group simply because there seems to be no other place for them.

Analysis of Marketing Costs

There are many ways of analyzing marketing costs to secure information. The analysis may show direct costs, indirect costs, travel costs, customer costs, product costs, size of order costs, return goods costs, credit costs, order filling costs, and other kinds of costs. Much of this cost study approach was covered in chapter 7, but there are additional elements that need attention.

Functional cost analysis

One of the common approaches in marketing cost studies is to break down and study costs by functions performed. Each firm has a number of functions it performs, some of which may be unlike functions of another firm. Most firms have functional cost groupings, such as selling, credit, and transportation. But many other functions may be added, depending on whether it is a manufacturing or wholesaling company, whether sales are made to large or small buyers, whether there is a variety of product operations within the distribution job. Some firms show functions under large groupings; others separate them. One firm may delineate fifteen, while another has twenty functions. They both operate in the same kind of business, and both are much alike. For example, two similar firms may sell merchandise to a retailer. One delivers to the store; the other delivers and stocks the merchandise on the retailer's shelves. The same two firms deliver to another retailer who insists on stocking his own shelves; thus, neither of the two firms has a stocking function.

Analysis by type of expense

Some firms find it easier to concentrate on particular costs which are cataloged in their accounting records as salespeople travel expense, salespeople salaries, advertising expense, and others. A firm may set up neat categories in which a certain type of expense is allocated and then study each category. For example, study may reveal that salespeople are spending too much on travel, meals, or hotel rooms; advertising cost may be creeping up on folders and bulletins; returned goods costs may be signaling product or customer problems. This type of analysis is basic and is performed regularly to determine that sales functions are going on normally. This type of analysis would likely cut across functional lines, so that one natural expense, such as travel expense, might well be divided among several functions.

Analysis by type of expense might start in the sales department, but actually spread throughout the whole firm. For example, in analyzing salespeople's airplane travel, it may be shown that first class is not warranted and coach is quite satisfactory. Further study may lead management to conclude that salespeople and supervisory personnel and higher management can travel at coach rates. Savings of this nature may not seem large at first; but when such savings are translated into their effect on profit and it can be shown that the cost difference is equal to profits from sales of one hundred thousand dollars, the impact is significant. Then, management becomes painfully aware of how some of their pet expenditures cut into the overall profit.

Analysis by direction of effort

Analysis of direct cost application to territories, products, and customers has been examined in chapter 7. At this point, it is mentioned to emphasize that it is a way of directing sales effort in the best possible ways. The other two approaches—by functional and by direct or natural type of expense—are primarily ways of studying to keep costs in line, reduce costs, or slow down the rapid rise in costs. Most cost studies are concerned with absolute cost increases and relative increases. Often, it is not the increase in cost that causes concern; but the fact that costs are increasing faster than sales is a cause for alarm.

Allocating Marketing Costs

Allocating marketing costs may result in much confusion unless a plan is set up which is designed for a specific purpose. There should be a definite allocation pattern which includes how and where to allocate.

Specific approaches to allocating costs

Direct costs can be assigned directly to the accounts which have been set up in the analysis pattern,[2] which may consist of functions or some other designation.

Indirect costs are allocated to functions which describe activities or related groups of activities—advertising, transportation, selling. These

---

2. Analysis of sales expenditures, sales costs, and sales categories should be regarded as a statistical analysis for studying the sales operation and hopefully to improve certain aspects and is not to be thought of as an accounting operation to improve accounting data.

in turn may later be allocated to such bases as product, customer, territory, and other groupings.

The duties of a specific salesperson might be confined to selling product A half the time and the other half devoted to securing new customers for the entire line. In allocating his expenses, it would be necessary to assign some of his costs directly to product A. This same salesperson might be paid a fixed salary which could be allocated easily (direct cost), but his traveling costs might vary greatly (variable cost) from week to week and be difficult to assign. Many other costs have their own patterns of fixed and variable elements.

Another problem of allocation might be solved by the responsibility and benefit criteria. An example is an expensive project undertaken for a particular user, but others are assessed part of the cost because they also use it. For example, a special delivery service may be started for one important customer, but its cost may be lowered to this user because other users along the route may benefit from the service. The important customer is responsible for the service and may have to take the greater cost, but others benefit from the service and are charged accordingly.

Another cost category may include those costs beyond the control of the sales department. In many cases, they may relate to administrative overhead. These may be fixed costs which are arbitrarily allocated. It is questionable if such costs should be charged directly to the sales department because their contribution cannot be measured except in a very general fashion. Such costs might better be charged to income from operations or to overall income.

Application units in allocating costs

Expense allocations must be made to specific accounts, groups, or categories by clearly defined methods. If management has a number of dollars expense to be distributed, it must be done in some particular fashion, that is, by application units.

Delivery expense may be distributed to a product by weight, by cubic space, and/or by distance shipped.

Warehousing expenses would be calculated by space used for periods of time. This expense might be further divided into handling costs plus space and time costs. Such a breakdown can be justified because merchandise must be put in and taken out of the warehouse whether it stays a week, a month, a quarter, or a year. If merchandise is frequently brought in and taken out, the handling cost would be a major cost in relation to space and time cost. Specific allocation could be made by box, package, or the container which represents the handling unit.

Filling orders may be assigned cost by order line extension. For example, one drug wholesaler estimates that it costs fifty cents to fill each line on an order. This charge may be arbitrary, but it tends to focus handling costs on small line extensions and points out the desirability of getting unit package orders equal to the manufacturer's packaging.

Direct selling costs can be charged directly to the territory of each salesperson. These costs consist of all charges that would not have occurred if this territory had not been covered. Each territory should generate enough revenue to pay for all direct costs, including merchandise and transportation, and leave a remaining amount for selling administration, overhead costs, and profit. The application units could be number of orders, number of customer calls, costs of servicing customers for credit, returned merchandise, and other services.

Costs of branch offices would be distributed to the territories supervised by the branch in a ratio of time devoted to each territory. If a branch had three territories—one requiring 40 percent, the second 30 percent, and the third 20 percent of its time and effort—branch office cost would be distributed to each territory in that ratio. If these time ratios changed among territories, appropriate adjustments would be necessary.

Indirect selling costs, including supervision, training, and general sales administration that cannot be directly assigned to any specific territory or unit, would be assigned in some time-unit relationship to each district, territory, product, customer, or other established category. Assigning indirect costs is not based on factors that can be directly determined, but rather reflects the best judgment and estimates of concerned management.

Specific advertising and sales promotion may be assigned to territories and then to products, customers, or other breakdowns. For example, newspaper advertising of a product may be assigned to the product sales in that immediate territory; store demonstration costs of a product are assigned to that product in that area or may be assigned to a particular customer, depending on whether analysis is to determine costs of moving a particular product to each customer or to determine costs of moving the product through different stores. Coupon costs may be assigned directly to the territory or distributing unit generating such returns. For example, if store A sells one thousand dollars of a product in one period and has a return of ten coupons, and store B sells the same amount in the same period but has a return of fifty coupons, the cost for each store is quite different. Subsequent analytical study of this difference could reveal pertinent facts that might lead to further studies to improve sales performance.

Standard Costs in Distribution

Standard costs are accepted in manufacturing and can be adapted to sales costs. Admittedly, there are areas in which standard costs of distribution are difficult to determine; but there are many situations to which they can be applied, particularly when sales activities are routine. These situations hold true for many wholesalers and manufacturers when regular calls are made daily, weekly, or some similar period. Many salespeople follow a pattern that varies only slightly from week to week.

Distribution standards can be measurements of satisfactory performance under conditions prevailing at the time they are established. They should be regarded as measures of attainable achievement. They are realistic performance measures of salespeople who are willing to perform aggressively. This performance must be standard in activity and in achievement; that is, a specified number of sales calls made each day should generate a specific sales volume.

Distribution standards are developed carefully through study and assessment of each sale or other activity. A distribution standard is determined by conditions existing at the time. Such a standard may be high or low later, but as a measuring stick it becomes useful in comparing it with performance in successive periods. Regardless of its original accuracy, it is unlikely that it will measure actual costs in periods of inflation. If different means of distribution are introduced, old standards may no longer apply. Standard costs may also deviate materially from actual cost in business cycles which reflect many different conditions.

Application of standard costs

Applying standard distribution cost will require breakdown into a variety of application units for measuring purposes. For comparison, examine the following data:

	Actual	Standard
Cost per call	$ 27.40	$ 25.50
Cost per order	44.50	42.00
Cost per display installation	22.00	20.00
Weekly expenses	102.50	100.00
Weekly travel expenses	40.00	39.00

In the preceding data, actual cost exceeded standard cost in each instance, indicating weakness in a salesperson or an increased (inflation) cost structure. Perhaps the salesperson could justify the higher cost through increased activity or a profit return above normal. A standard cost is a measuring stick which can be used on all the salespeople to maintain some kind of orderly check on each person's activities. The mere fact they are being checked will tend to keep salespeople more careful in spending.

Some sales executives may not think in terms of distribution cost standards, but yet have established guidelines which are similar. They set a series of maximums for expenses, many of them in considerable detail (price of hotel room, each meal). They are often tied in with sales quotas, profit margins, and sales incentives.[3]

MARKETING BUDGET

The *marketing budget* is essentially a blueprint of expected expenditures for marketing activities for a coming period. In many companies, these expenditures cover a multiplicity of marketing activities; in others, they consist primarily of projected costs of the sales department. These costs range from home office expense of the sales department to sales expenses within territories and all expenses in between, such as sales supervision and district office expense. Included may be all or particular portions of advertising expense and often all sales promotion expenses. While the more proper term may be marketing budget, many firms will consider this term synonymous with sales budget.

Marketing Budget Uses

Proper preparation of a budget recognizes the need for planning, which in turn requires clear delineation of objectives, alternate methods of achieving such objectives, and possible readjustments in present operations. To develop well-laid plans, it is helpful to consult various levels of sales executives, including supervisors and salespeople, and members of the staff of facilitating functions, such as credit and warehousing. Each activity is outlined in advance, and each responsible individual is forced to think through what he expects to do in the budget period, how many employees he will need, what supplies and equipment must be purchased, and what additional new costs will appear. A review of this process shows that at each level responsible planning must be used to assure orderly development of future operations as outlined.

A budget becomes a guideline for operation and, hence, a control mechanism. It tends to prevent unplanned activities and forces management to follow a preset pattern without major modification or snap judgment decisions. When changes are made, they usually must be justified and are carefully considered before introduction. As soon as actual operations deviate from planned operations, a cost signal is raised which comes to the attention of the concerned manager. He

---

3. The student or sales executive who wishes more detail in sales cost analysis can refer to Charles H. Sevin, *Marketing Productivity Analysis* (New York: McGraw-Hill Book Company, 1965); Harold H. Maynard and James H. Davis, *Sales Management*, 3rd ed. (New York: The Ronald Press Company, 1957), Chapters 27 and 28; Theodore N. Beckman, Nathanael H. Engle, and Robert D. Buzzel, *Wholesaling*, 3rd ed. (New York: The Ronald Press Company, 1959), Chapter 29. A number of trade associations publish information of this nature that would aid firms in particular industries.

then recognizes that something unplanned has occurred and investigates what has happened and why. He wonders if this change is an improvement or a sign of weakness or breakdown in control. The computer may be useful in locating deviations quickly and alerting management to unexpected changes.

A company budget leads to greater coordination because it ties in so many activities. Each manager sees that his is not an isolated activity, but a part of a whole operation. The budget is almost like a jigsaw puzzle in which each part must be in its proper place if it is to convey meaning.

A departmental budget can be not only a control mechanism, but also in retrospect a means of evaluation. A manager may be evaluated on his performance, cooperation, foresight, judgment, discipline, and other factors. This evaluation may be a means of appraising an individual's contribution to the firm's success and his own success in fitting into present management. If a manager does not fit in an organization, it may not indicate incompetence (the organization may be ineffective); but if he is competent but presently unsuccessful, he will likely sell his services elsewhere where he is able to maximize his own ability. If a company is poorly organized and managed, it still may be moderately successful because of peculiar advantages; but if a number of capable people resign over a period of a year or two, it should signal top management to evaluate themselves.

Budget Preparation

The marketing budget is only one part of a firm's overall budget. Each unit of a firm needs a budget for guidance, and each subbudget must fit into the overall budget.

The sales forecast may be the starting point for a firm's total budget. Marketing, production, finance, office, and other units prepare individual budgets based on operation expectation. Marketing prepares its budget by assembling all necessary cost data. This information is gathered from district offices, regional offices, marketing costs in the home office, and other units generating expenditures.

Planned expenditures

The budget is a plan of expenditures (use of money plan) for a coming period and should be complete enough to provide accurate information. It should cover all personnel costs, including salespeople, supervisors, managers, office help, and any other marketing employees. If there is to be a change in employment status, it must be included. It should cover all departmental costs involving physical requirements —heat, light, rent, and others. It should cover all costs of purchased services and equipment—signs, posters, displays, training equipment, and other items. It must cover all travel expenses, entertainment, and fringe benefits not included in compensation. Finally, it should cover those expenses which are not included in a major category, but cover a number of unclassified areas.

Steps in budget preparation

1. Determine how many subunits or groups are to make up a budget—district, region, territory, department, area.
2. Have each budget center detail its probable needs for the budget period, frequently one year.
3. In assembling and combining smaller units into a larger unit, the person in charge of the larger unit should go over individual sub-budgets with the people who prepared them to reconcile views and to insure that each understands company objectives.
4. Each management level combines the budgets below it and sends it to the next higher level with appropriate information detailing changes and why they are anticipated.
5. The marketing or sales budget is combined with other top budgets to make one overall budget for the firm. This process involves the sales or marketing manager and gives him and other top management a picture of the expected marketing operation for the coming period.[4]

Flexible budget

A budget is a guide, not a straitjacket, and should be used as an aid to operation and as a warning signal when real costs vary significantly from budgeted costs.

Seldom is a firm able to forecast sales with great accuracy; within and among territories great variations will occur. When such deviations appear, it is impossible to use existing budgeted figures, and they must be revised to meet actual situations. For example, if a major competitor mounts an extraordinary promotion campaign in an area, it may be necessary to counteract with increased promotion which will make the original budget promotion item obsolete. If sales increase rapidly in an area, it will push up costs to handle this increase. If sales decrease in an area, it may be necessary to lower expenditures in that area, but probably not in proportion to the sales decrease. Unfortunately, a change in one activity or cost sector will not be reflected proportionately in other cost sectors because many costs are semivariable and may change infrequently in sizable amounts.

A budget should be revised when the current situation dictates a change. It should not be revised to accommodate changes resulting from poor management. If real cost deviates significantly from bud-

---

4. For greater detail in budgeting, refer to Ovid Riso, ed. *Sales Manager's Handbook,* 11th ed. (Chicago: The Dartnell Corporation, 1968), Chapter 25 and *The Controller,* Volume XVIII, No. 12 (Controllers Institute of America).

geted costs, it is the duty of top management to assess this change, try to determine the causes, and judge whether they are controllable or noncontrollable.

Budgeting Problems

Often budgeting is considered a financial exercise required by management occurring once a year and prepared by looking at past operations, forward to anticipated operations, and guided by the current profit situation. If everything appears encouraging and management is contented, looseness in budgeting may be encouraged; if conditions are bad and money tight, management may demand budget cutting that is wholly unrealistic. Usually, it is impossible to budget for severe declines because most people are naturally optimistic.

Coming budget period much like last period

Too great a reliance on the past may blind management to problems appearing on the horizon.[5] Management cannot ignore a multitude of factors that may change in either direction—war, population, money, strikes, demand, new product developments, changes in competition, availability of labor, wealth, fashion, taxes. To budget well, management needs to study the future budget period carefully.

Sales decrease

Seldom does management budget for decreased sales unless in a recession. While one or two industries may suffer severely, most other industries go ahead with no noticeable impediment. All firms are not affected alike, and firms within one industry may be affected unequally. If a firm is well organized, it should be able to expand and contract as conditions require. Expansion may be accompanied by many difficulties, but increasing profits will help cover up inefficiencies. When contraction occurs, few firms are able to pull back fast enough; the cost structure decreases slowly. The result may be significant losses, even though sales retreated moderately.

Costs must increase

The economy since World War II has been faced with an increasing cost situation, slow some years and rapid other years. Following a period of spectacular increases, budget makers become acclimated to 6 to 9 percent yearly increases and fail to adjust to plateaus where costs are stationary. Many departments may enthusiastically budget and get a sizable increase that is curtailed a few months later when

---

5. Examples can be given of automobile forecasts which were grossly overestimated, of analysts on Wall Street whose earning estimates were found a short time later to be wildly exaggerated, and of factories partially completed left standing unfinished because of a shortage of capital and slackening demand for the product.

business conditions no longer warrant these increases. Sometimes changed procedures and a different emphasis in activities will permit a department to operate for long periods without cost increases.

Data are accurate

The person fashioning a budget may accept all data he receives as accurate rather than estimated. If, for example, experience shows that sales forecasts usually are 15 percent higher than sales, a department affected by that estimate should make an appropriate allowance because top management probably will cut that department's budget estimate anyway. It is embarrassing to receive a deep cut in the budget estimate and then be able to operate successfully under it. This situation soon gives the department the reputation of asking for too much; consequently, the department may be cut severely when sales decrease.

Conditions will improve

In a period of decline, management is hopefully looking forward to turning the corner and may make unwarranted assumptions that jeopardize a firm's solvency. While it is desirable to prepare for an expanding economy, a few premature moves in that direction can prove costly. Management must face the fact that some industries will never improve, some firms will never grow stronger, and all product sales will never increase some time in the future. Although overall total sales in the economy may improve, there is no assurance that every segment will improve at all, or equally.[6]

Major equipment and expansion expenditures

The problem of budgeting for major equipment and expansion becomes one of making correct decisions and accurate timing. Introduction of sophisticated equipment to aid sales may be desirable, but costly. Thus, the extensive use of electronic data processing may help the sales department but increase the cost burden far more than the contribution. Some firms buy equipment and then learn how to use it, in the meantime sacrificing large sums of money because of inadequate preparation.

Sometimes a firm will expand into a new channel of distribution because of particular advantages, but fail to properly assess the increased costs that will result. "It may be desirable, but can we afford it?" is a statement that is used over and over again. Being too impetuous in innovating and expanding can be disastrous, but waiting

---

6. The phonograph, once very popular, lost its popularity to radio and television; but years later made a comeback and now struggles with a new competitor, the tape recorder. Horses were largely replaced by tractors on farms, but horses have made a startling comeback. Statistics in Michigan show that horse population in the 1970s will exceed that of any previous decade. Of course, the primary use of horses has changed.

too long can be equally dangerous. It may not be the prerogative of some budget makers to make major policy decisions regarding introducing products or changing channels of distribution, but such decisions are often controlled by budgets, that is, fund availability.

QUESTIONS AND PROBLEMS

1. When a sales executive begins looking at sales costs as ends in themselves, he is weakening his position. Explain this statement, showing the fallacy of the sales executive's thinking.
2. How do alternative approaches to sales effort result in different costs?
3. What are some of the dangers of comparing sales costs of one firm with another firm?
4. Define implicit and explicit costs (covered in your course in economics).
5. Describe and illustrate (1) functional cost analysis, (2) analysis by type of expense, and (3) analysis by direction of effort.
6. Illustrate cost allocation by the responsibility and benefit criterion.
7. Describe and illustrate the use of application units in cost allocation.
8. How would you apply standard costs to distribution costs?
9. Define marketing budget. Why is this budget important?
10. Show the importance of the sales forecast in budgeting.
11. Why should a budget be flexible? Discuss, giving several examples.
12. What are some of the problems in budgeting, and how can they be handled? Relate problem and solution specifically in each example.

WINSLOW DISTRIBUTING COMPANY   *case 16–1*

Winslow Distributing Company is a large wholesaler of parts and supplies to the oil industry. It is located in Louisiana. Fifty salespeople cover a territory extending five hundred miles. Profits vary among sales territories because of potential, salesperson ability, and sales expenditures.

Salespeople's expenses vary greatly. Some of this variation can be attributed to territory size and competition, but too much comes from salespeople who are big spenders. They justify their expenses by big sales which they say require heavy entertainment expenses as well as the necessity for them to maintain a high standard of personal living to impress buyers. Yet the most profitable territory is handled by Mr. Antrim, a salesperson whose expenses are among the lowest.

Mr. Samson, the sales manager, recognizes that closer expense control is necessary. He asks you to draw up a plan incorporating cost standards that can be used to measure various costs incurred and to give tentative standards for each salesperson cost and expenditure. You may use trade association data, published information supplied by firms specializing in gathering such information, library sources, and U.S. Census data.

ASSIGNMENT

Prepare this plan, giving detailed expense breakdowns. You may talk to wholesalers in some instances to secure information. Consult your business library, trade association publications, and special source services.

---

case 16–2   # ASKAM AND NAMBO, INC.

Askam and Nambo, Inc., manufacturers of automotive accessories, sold to wholesalers, chain outlets, discount houses, and retailers and has operated for fifteen years without using formal budget procedures. Informal budgeting had been used, but in a casual way without too much attention to details.

Last year's sales were over $6,000,000. Sales were satisfactory, but fluctuating expenses resulted in unsatisfactory profits. For several years, expense control had been poor; but whichever department was to blame always gave an excuse. The president felt that many of these excessive cost situations should have been anticipated and adequate provision made in advance in the price structure. Therefore, he called all major department heads together and said that henceforth every department would have to operate under a budget. He directed each person to learn more about budget procedures and to give instructions to subordinates, who would also be preparing budgets. Within a week, each department head would be given a list of sources on budgeting. Some of these sources would be provided; others would have to be secured at the library or through individual purchase.

ASSIGNMENT

You are to provide this list of sources. It should include books or chapters in books on budgeting, monographs, magazine articles, trade association sources, and management association sources. Published handbooks would help department heads in their particular areas. Your list must be specific as to titles and exact publications, including dates.

17

Customer Services

The area of customer services covers many activities and promises. A product may become more useful if it is supported by the manufacturer who stands ready to keep it usable and important to the user.

Many products are abandoned before they have been given a fair chance, and many pieces of equipment are abused because the buyer has never become sufficiently trained to use them properly. A little care and forethought or carefully supervised operation in the beginning could avoid troublesome hours later. Firms are aware of this situation and have built into their price provision for special services which can be costly.[1]

A discussion of customer services is expedited by considering two major areas, industrial goods and consumer goods. Breaking the consumer goods area into dealer aids and consumer benefits gives greater clarity and definition.

INDUSTRIAL GOODS

Industrial goods may be categorized as all goods used in production of consumer goods and industrial goods. Thus, the vacuum cleaner which is widely used in homes may also be used in industry; a kitchen mixer may have a first-cousin heavy mixer used in bakeries.

Industrial equipment may be difficult to use or operate. Major expenditures demand intelligent operation because of costly equipment and because the end use can be very expensive if the final product is not suitable.

---

1. Computer manufacturers have learned that it is better to charge a somewhat higher rental and meet requests for extra service graciously than it is to price too low and irritate users by numerous extra charges.

Presale Services

Before a sale is made, much exploratory work may be necessary. Technical problems must be studied and tentative solutions explored. Comparisons between present method and suggested new method or modifications are invited because the buyer moves carefully before approving expensive changes.[2]

A manufacturer often must design and develop a whole system or procedure to meet a buyer's requirement.[3] Some of these changes require great skill and may have to be tried out to prove their effectiveness.[4]

The successful manufacturer must innovate and solve buyers' problems. Too many manufacturers, architects, and designers let someone else dream up ideas and then adopt them if they think the ideas are feasible.

Installation

Installation of equipment can be highly technical and precise. Often, manufacturers suggest or even insist on installing their equipment.[5] Proper installation often includes a period of time when the equipment is used and adjusted, and operators are taught how to use it properly. Optimum functioning is guaranteed only if the user follows instructions meticulously. One reason a supplier is reluctant to have the buyer install his machine is that too often the buyer's mechanics do not read directions or do not follow them.

Some types of machines and equipment are very fragile and require extreme care in handling; some are precision tools and are easily jolted from accuracy; some are complex and require skillful operators.

Warranties

Warranties are promises made by manufacturers, producers, and other agencies that the product or service will meet specific conditions, tests, and uses. Should the buyer find a warranty untrue, he can go to the warranty issuer for satisfaction.

---

2. It is not uncommon for a manufacturer to spend large sums of money developing equipment or approaches to sell a particular buyer. Normally there are several manufacturers competing for the same business. The losers (the buyer may decide to do nothing so they all lose) must absorb this expense as a cost of operating the business.

3. One salesperson spent three years studying a firm's operation before suggesting a procedure which used his equipment. In the fourth year, he made his first sale to the company.

4. Several firms have developed methods for automobile emission pollution control. New automobile power plants are being examined regularly.

5. One manufacturer found that some of his equipment was frequently installed improperly, which led to malfunctioning.

Warranties vary greatly in kind and quality. Some are merely statements devoid of real meaning; others are reliable. Some warranties may sound reliable, but are really meaningless in context. A warranty on a minor inexpensive product of little importance has little significance because the buyer would not bother to exercise his privilege.

A warranty may be so restrictive that the chance of using it would be nil. Fine print in a warranty document may restrict its practical application. A warranty may relate to situations that rarely develop, but not cover common applications that arise frequently.

Warranty wording

Special care in warranty wording eliminates later misunderstandings. The present trend is to word warranties in clear, understandable language, avoiding hidden meanings and reducing fine print modifications. If there are important restrictions in use, installation, servicing, and maintenance, they should be stated clearly. A buyer may question warranties and guarantees of such firms as automobile manufacturers and outboard motor manufacturers that attempt to tie guarantees to particular maintenance establishments and the use of so-called genuine parts and supplies when there are equally good competitive products at lesser prices. Some manufacturers are inconsistent in insisting on genuine parts and avoiding what they term gyp parts. While insisting on genuine parts for their products, they are securing or manufacturing gyp products for competitors' lines. A proper warranty interpretation should not differentiate in an unreasonable way. To question an alternative solution which is reasonable is objectionable.

Warranty abuses

Warranty abuse is common not only in the consumer area but also in industrial areas. While many warranties clearly state provisions of protection and responsibility, it often becomes impractical to enforce such provisions. For example, if a major industrial buyer wants an adjustment clearly beyond warranty or if the selling firm can prove equipment abuse, the seller is still unlikely to refuse extra services because he wants to maintain a healthy relationship with the customer.

If a warranty could involve major replacement cost, it is wise to spell out conditions carefully and emphasize these conditions to the buyer. There are some machines that will malfunction even with minor deviations from instructions.

Sometimes it is necessary to insist on the buyer using particular supplies to keep a machine operating properly. Substitute competitive products may not be equally effective. If frequent manufacturer service is common and free, it may be necessary for the manufacturer to insist on providing all operating and maintenance supplies, which are sold with a satisfactory profit margin. Only in this way can the manufacturer afford this free service.

Repair Services

Adequate repair services are often the key to making sales. Strategic locations of parts and supplies prevent delays in transportation which might tie up machinery. Some types of equipment are so difficult to repair that factory servicemen must be used. These people are on call night and day for immediate service. A highly visible repair facility is truck service. Downtime (period in which equipment cannot be used) must be kept to a minimum, which may mean 24-hour service, particularly for smaller firms with limited equipment.

A firm that furnishes excellent repair service and is able to supply parts for its equipment is at a decided advantage over competitors with poor service. For example, some machinery manufacturers are able to supply parts for their machines, ten, twenty, thirty years old or even older; but other manufacturers are ill-prepared to meet requests for parts for machines older than ten years. Some manufacturers have large inventories of parts and supply them quickly; others have to manufacture to order, delaying shipment an extra month or more. One way to avoid delay in parts shipment is for a manufacturer to have local inventory supplies either in his own warehouse points or on consignment with local distributors.

Performance Standards

Industrial sales are often predicated on performance standards. It may not be the original purchase price, but the cost in use which determines which machine to buy or whether an old machine should be replaced.

A performance standard guarantees particular output per unit of time (100 pieces a minute), particular hours of operating time between maintenance periods, length of time a tool can be used, or how long a liquid solution can be used before it must be replaced. Performance standards may be physical, chemical, or other kinds.

Cost in use may be more important in making sales than original cost, particularly in industry. Even if the original price is far greater for one brand than another, it can be justified if its eventual use cost is lower. If initial higher cost is difficult to finance, special financing or leasing may overcome this barrier.

Trade-ins

A trade-in often is a significant bargaining issue in making a sale. Most owners are likely to overvalue present equipment when trading for new equipment. Even if the old machine is literally scrap, the owner still attaches great value to it. Sometimes prices of new equipment have enough leeway so that a significant amount may be allowed for the trade-in even if it is discarded. Often, reconditioning old equipment makes it salable to another user with less demanding requirements or one who cannot afford new equipment.

A sale may be negotiated by a trade-in of unlike equipment or by helping a customer dispose of some obsolete or unwanted equipment. This situation often happens in commercial establishments, when the firm making the sale of bakery or laundry equipment agrees to dispose of an old piece without charge.

Delivery

A sale may come after long negotiation, but a customer wants prompt delivery. In negotiations, the ability to deliver within a certain period may decide who gets the order. When a machine is fabricated to order, a lead time of a year or more may be necessary.

Delivery may be arranged piecemeal over a year or more. Initially a large order is placed, but delivery is arranged by product use. For the buyer, this means minimum storage and spread out financing; for the seller, it may require large storage space or result in spaced out production.

Storage

Storing merchandise is expensive in money and attention. Frequently, it is advisable to hire a storage firm to perform this function.

Forward buying is common in some areas. For example, contracts are arranged in advance for agricultural products for canning and preserving. Seasonal agricultural production makes it mandatory to store products if at all possible; some, of course, cannot be stored but are used in a short period.

Seasonal demand requires storage to even out production. Some firms close down for part of a year; but when they open for processing, their suppliers must have arranged in advance for delivery of supplies. Economies of production dictate a production pattern that may involve storage. Difficulty of storing supplies by producers or fortunate purchases may force a buyer into heavy storage. Advance orders force manufacturers to secure accessories and parts perhaps months in advance in order to assure a supply when needed.

Packaging

Packaging is important to customers for use and resale. Convenient packaging includes size, quantity, shape, protection, ease of removing contents, color, and other qualities. Awkward packaging leads to overuse, spilling, waste, and sometimes physical danger.

Packages should be put in cartons to fit the needs of the buyer. If a dozen cans are sufficient, it is a disservice to pack in two-dozen cartons. If a fifty-pound drum is most convenient, it should be used.

Some manufacturers will package to fit a customer's needs, which may include storage on the user's premises. Some types of packaging fit in with the user's handling equipment; some may be shipped in bulk for convenient storage and to eliminate unpacking. Several types of bulk or packaging combinations are often used to meet various user requirements.

Abuse of Service

Buyer service abuse can be a major problem. Some of these situations are the result of willful abuse; some arise through misunderstandings; and a few arise when the buyer honestly feels the seller is dodging his obligation.

Willful abuse may be tolerated because the seller doesn't want to lose a customer. Abuse may arise because the truth is difficult to determine. For example, improper operation of a machine may be subject to interpretation, particularly when the transgression is slight. When subjective evaluation is involved, accuracy becomes approximate. To solve major disagreements may require some leniency on both sides. If one participant is adamant, the other participant may give in, but reluctantly. The amount of money or time involved in the disagreement often determines how easy it is to achieve final settlement. A salesperson who sees a major problem arising over a minor issue may quietly settle it with the buyer without recourse to a higher management level.

A few buyers may pay little attention to service abuses and violate them with impunity. Such firms are difficult to handle and bear constant watching. When they ignore specific agreements and try to take advantage of the seller regularly, management must weigh consequences of severing the relationship. A loss of one or two major buyers of this nature may put a great strain on a seller's market. Surprisingly, some buyers will behave more reasonably when they are forced to adjust or else lose this source of supply.

Alternative Applications

A true customer service is aiding in developing new users for your product. Innovative salespeople frequently find they can broaden use for their product or service by broader product utilization. Conversely, if the salesperson finds it is to the buyer's advantage to use less, the salesperson should tell him. A short-term loss may result, but later the buyer may be able to buy more of some other product the salesperson sells or recommend his product to buyers in other firms.

The short-run situation may loom so large that the salesperson refuses to look at the long-run situation realistically. If a sales manager faces this problem, he should take steps to correct it by stressing to the salespeople the importance of favorable buyer relations. His efforts can be strengthened if the salesperson compensation plan is slanted toward this objective.

CONSUMER GOODS AND SERVICES

There are a number of services manufacturers give to wholesalers and retailers that make distribution more effective. Some are of a service nature, and others are monetary.

Guarantee Against Price Decline

If a manufacturer reduces prices, he agrees to compensate dealers for the difference between what they paid for their inventories and what they presently would pay. This practice encourages dealers to carry adequate inventories without fear of loss through price cutting by the manufacturer. Such privileges are not blanket, since they would not cover over-age inventories and special situations.

When a dealer has this cost protection, he will feel freer to meet a greater variety of demands. The manufacturer benefits because a bigger inventory share is carried by the dealers, relieving the manufacturer of a burden and avoiding immediate shock (cushions) of a sudden spurt in sales.

Dealer Agreements

A manufacturer may enter into a number of dealer agreements which protect the dealer. One kind gives a dealer special privileges, such as restricting new competing outlets in a period of time and/or number. A manufacturer may arrange special displays which attract customers. Manufacturers' demonstrations in dealer establishments are common.

Sometimes a manufacturer will replace old merchandise free. This practice may be more for his protection than the dealer's, for the manufacturer cannot afford having dealer shelves stocked with old, dirty packages of his product. Manufacturers may agree to certain promotion activities to stimulate sales.

A manufacturer may have special financing provisions for qualifying dealers. Automobile manufacturers have arrangements for kickbacks, which are special allowances for a particular volume of sales. There are agreements as to use of parts in making repairs of equipment and agreements concerning nature of inventories.

A manufacturer with a loyal dealer group will have closer and better arrangements than one with constantly changing dealers. A franchise arrangement frequently calls for a close relationship between the principal and the franchised dealers or outlets.

A manufacturer dependent on wholesaler, retailer, or distributor distribution enhances the relationship and binds it together by particular arrangements that make continuing the relationship advantageous. A producer with goods that are eagerly sought may encourage agreements with dealers because they are eager to handle his merchandise.[6]

A firm that franchises dealers or outlets may put rigid requirements on their franchises, because they have learned that the only ones that succeed are those willing to follow these requirements. A few failing franchise operations can injure the whole chain.

Return Privileges

College bookstores return new books that are no longer used in a class; retailers return unsold dresses to manufacturers; defective merchandise may be returned, or it may be destroyed and the dealer be reimbursed. These are examples of return privilege arrangements among manufacturer, wholesaler, and retailer.

A manufacturer gives the return privilege when he has made an error in filling an order; sometimes the dealer keeps the merchandise, but receives a special discount which becomes the cheapest way to handle such an occurrence. Merchandise damaged in transit may be returned or retained by the dealer when he gets a monetary adjustment. Substandard merchandise is often retained by the dealer for a reduced price.

Return privileges are expensive to the manufacturer and are discouraged for minor problems. Some dealers do not bother returning merchandise if a small amount of money is involved.

Delivery Service

Manufacturers offer dealers a variety of delivery services to fit individual needs. Some firms prepay delivery charges, often with limitations on order size and type of delivery. For example, a seller may offer to pay delivery charges on a fifty dollar order shipped by truck, but not by air freight. Freight prepayment may be governed by distance —prepayment or free delivery in a metropolitan area, but not outside this area.

Some retailers accept delivery only at certain times in the day. Attempts by manufacturers to make store deliveries at night have been rebuffed. Retailers get lower delivery costs because suppliers use a variety of ways to lower or eliminate costs; sometimes high transportation expense is reduced by more expensive packaging.

---

6. Eli Lilly & Co., a pharmaceutical manufacturer, distributes through wholesalers. Because of its reputation, wholesale druggists are eager to handle its products.

Storage on Dealer Premises

When a manufacturer is willing to finance inventories with wholesalers and retailers, he takes on major burdens but does insure an adequate supply in the distribution channel. Dealers are willing to carry large inventories if they are on consignment, that is, financed by the manufacturer. To the dealer, this means an adequate supply and assortment; to the manufacturer, it provides adequate stocks and control to the final buyer.

Packaging for the Dealer

At one time, manufacturers would package their merchandise in one way, and wholesalers and retailers would have to accept them. Different types of outlets and varying consumer use have forced manufacturers to package in a number of ways—not particularly what they want, but what the buyer wants.[7] Many a competitor has gained on other firms by imaginative packaging. The progressive manufacturer packages economically whenever possible, but he cannot overlook means of assisting each unit in the channel of distribution in doing an effective job. This situation may call for expensive, but attractive packaging. Expense is relative, not absolute; and if a particular type of packaging becomes an effective promotion device, it may replace other promotion activities.

Advertising and Public Relations

Manufacturers cooperate with dealers in advertising and promotion to stimulate sales. Manufacturers supply advertising literature and mats which are used for newspaper advertisements. These mats are supplied free, enabling the retailer to use carefully prepared material. A manufacturer frequently pays half the cost of a retailer advertisement that features his product.

Manufacturers contribute to wholesaler and retailer activities. At conventions, they set up displays so that dealers can learn about the latest items. Manufacturers advertise in dealer publications not only in magazines but also in convention programs. Much of this advertising has questionable value, but it does build rapport and establish good relationships.

Manufacturers often aid dealers in passing legislation. They contribute money and legal aid. If a local dealer organization holds a social gathering, manufacturers are solicited for gifts. They are asked

---

7. At one time men's socks were packed in plain boxes, a standard number of pair to the box. Today they are packed in such boxes but also in transparent envelopes of one, two, or three pairs, envelopes attached to cards, and other ways to facilitate retailing.

to supply tickets for sporting events and often furnish customers free entertainment.

SERVICES TO FINAL BUYER OR USER

Manufacturers furnish the final buyer and/or user with a number of services which enhance the product's appeal. In today's society, the producer is subject to greater responsibilities for his product. With service he can move closer, enhance his reputation, and build stronger ties with the ultimate user.

Trade-in

Manufacturers sometimes have special offers in which a consumer can trade in his old unit for a new one with a substantial allowance. The manufacturer will reimburse the retailer for this service, but the offer is extended by the manufacturer directly to the user. Some manufacturers have a policy of accepting special customer orders with trade-ins, which are primarily concessions to buyers since they may hinder orderly production.

Packaging

A certain amount of differentiated packaging is done in an attempt to gain competitive advantages without much regard for consumer needs; but much packaging is an attempt to anticipate consumer wishes, even though costly to suppliers.

Attractive packaging may not enhance a product's utility, but it may add color to a room or space. A convenient package (size, ease of opening, special protection) does not make a better product, although it may prove to be a better product in use. If a package is easy to open and close, it may give better protection to contents; if it is easy to pour, less may be used each time; if it is compounded in a certain way, it may eliminate requirements such as shaking, using only at specific temperatures, and other controls.

Packaging is used to distinguish products quickly for the user. For example, one user wants light chocolate, and another wants dark chocolate; one user prefers one blend of coffee to a different blend. A package may contain just enough product for a single application —individual bandages are more convenient than rolls of cotton cloth and adhesive tape. Many medical products are packaged with the primary objectives of sanitary protection and convenience.

Manufacturer Instructions

Products to be assembled usually are accompanied by instructions to aid assembly. Some products have instructions for use on attached labels or printed on the article. For example, outboard motors will carry printed instructions on the motor for mixing oil and gasoline. Many products include manuals covering operation and maintenance. Clothing has labels with washing instructions. Medicines are clearly labeled with use instructions, ingredients, and cautionary suggestions. Some products include detailed instructions and are protected by mechanical devices to prevent malfunctioning.

A manufacturer may send company representatives to train buyers if product use is complex. Repair kits with complete use instructions may be offered to provide economical maintenance. Special instructions are frequently supplied for installation and use of accessory equipment. Dangerous products are equipped with cautionary information to prevent misuse.

Consumer Warranties

A number of manufacturer warranties are so restricted by specific conditions that they have little meaning to the consumer; others are simple, straightforward, and broad. The restricted warranty reflects the manufacturer's responsibilities, but the broad one more nearly measures the consumer's viewpoint. Even if some malfunctioning results from a degree of customer misuse, not the fault of the manufacturer, it is better for the manufacturer to accept the loss. For example, a tire manufacturer may disclaim loss caused by a road hazard (technically correct); but neither is the user to blame, although he suffers the loss unless the manufacturer accepts it. The goodwill created by the manufacturer in making adjustments compensates for such losses.

Consumers receive performance, time, and quality warranties which aid the manufacturer to sell. In essence, consumers literally buy product use rather than just the product itself. A consumer cannot acquaint himself with all the conditions which produce malfunctioning of the dozens of products he buys. Some manufacturers put reasonable restrictions on use of other brands of parts and supplies in making repairs and in operation; others go to ridiculous lengths to shut out competition.[8]

A loosely worded warranty is that of consumer satisfaction. This warranty is indefinite to the issuer because he not only warrants his product but also consumer satisfaction, which covers many variables not necessarily inherent in the product. Such warranties may be successful if the amount involved is not great or if prices are high enough to cover this service.

---

8. A well-known outboard motor manufacturer in his operating manual recommends his own particular brand of oil only, implying that other branded oils are not acceptable. Yet professional operators of these outboard motors, or those who rent motors or have guides using these motors, use other brands satisfactorily.

Warranties should not be written with fine print. Customers have learned that the large, plain warranty words are so restricted by fine print at the bottom of the page that the warranty becomes practically meaningless. Legislation is now trying to curb such abuses. A manufacturer is more ethical if he details what the warranty covers and the restriction involved in the same-sized letters.[9]

Service Abuses

Manufacturers deal with a broad spectrum of buyers whose ethics vary widely. Some consumers are fair and do not make unjust claims; some try every possible way to take advantage of the seller. Between these extremes are most of the buyers, who are considered reasonable.

A common problem arises from product misuse and/or abuse. It is not uncommon to buy an item in a size that is too small for the job and then complain when it malfunctions. Frequently, consumers will not give proper maintenance to a product and then ask for an adjustment when it breaks down. Examples include improperly inflated tires, improper maintenance on cleaning and oiling moving parts, failure to clean textile products according to directions, protection against weather changes, and many other conditions.

Some customers abuse their privileges by excessive service use. Each trifling problem calls for service attention. This problem can be tempered by a modest charge beyond a certain number of occurrences or a minimum charge for first calls followed by graduated fees for succeeding service calls. Whether to add restrictions or to absorb the costs of some unjustified requests depends on the extra cost involved. Sometimes it is preferable to charge a slightly higher initial cost and then absorb most service costs with minimum customer irritation.

A firm must be prepared to accept a number of difficult decisions in service and guarantee areas. Service decisions involve judgment, but the company representative should probably resolve any controversial decision in the customer's favor.

USER RESPONSE TO SERVICES

The product a firm sells is essentially a bundle of satisfactions which provides the user with services, pleasures, and necessities. A customer enjoys his purchase; he may not enjoy it; or he accepts and uses it with reservations. The key to satisfaction is in use, whether it is a car to drive, a painting to look at, or food to eat.

When food is purchased for consumption, any accompanying service that will give it supplementary attributes makes it more inviting. For example, recipes tell how to use it in appetizing ways; frozen

---

9. "The Guesswork on Warranties," *Business Week* (July 14, 1975), 51–52.

foods give immediate selection prepared for cooking; cake mixes make it easy to bake. When a person buys medicine, he receives instructions on how to use it and dangers involved. New wearing apparel has information on washing and cleaning.

In the industrial area, operating instructions accompany equipment and machines. Frequently, the seller will send someone to instruct the buyer. Extensive experimentation may be required to achieve maximum performance. Use of some machines may require changes in raw material. Special accessory equipment may be needed to complement operations.

Retailers and wholesalers receive many services from manufacturers that often ensure successful operation. Franchisees are dependent on the franchise seller for assistance that will aid them. Examples of these services are securing business locations, assisting in designing and building structures, designing and installing equipment and shelving, developing promotions, and setting up credit systems.

This section has indicated some of the many ways a product's usefulness may be increased. As a buyer finds more and better ways to use his purchase, the expenditure takes on greater value. It becomes what every sale intends to achieve—mutual advantages to both buyer and seller. How will this benefit the seller, the one who extends the services?

Create Goodwill

Repeated evidence of bankruptcies of firms with impressive buildings and marvelous equipment indicate some other ingredient is essential.

A customer is disinterested in the type of management or equipment of the manufacturer but is tremendously interested in the product he purchased. He is not too concerned about where his new car was assembled or what type of sales staff the manufacturer uses, but he is greatly concerned about repair services and how well his car performs.

The goodwill which develops from satisfactory use places the manufacturer in an enviable position. Satisfied users tell others about the performance of their cars, the washability of fabrics, the comfort of shoes, the tastiness of food. People using competing products which are not satisfactory listen intently to what satisfied users say about the products they use. Those contacts grow and permeate groups, and others are inclined to try products their friends like.

All services will not create corresponding satisfactions with all uses. A segmented society will find a product useful, but not always exactly in the same way. One buyer likes the delivery service; a second buyer likes the color; a third buyer appreciates the carefree maintenance; a fourth buyer enjoys the durability; but all give increasing satisfactions.

Ask a buyer why he patronizes a particular store, and he may be unable to give a good answer. Ask a buyer why he uses a certain brand, and his reply may not sound too convincing. The true answer in each instance may be one or a combination of factors not readily apparent. Yet the ultimate effect may be goodwill that is evident in a number of ways.

Promote Sales

Increasing sales is usually the primary purpose of services, since they are in a sense fringe benefits. The buyer may be vaguely familiar with these extras, or may assume they exist; but once he has used some of them, he really appreciates them. They loom large in a repeat purchase, particularly when a competing brand does not include these extras.

The reliability of a firm is one of its important assets. If a firm has a close relationship with buyers, it usually has furnished considerations buyers want. A close tie between buyer and seller does not rest on imagined causes, but on solid performance in ways that please the buyer. He learns to depend on one firm and/or salesperson because he is confident that the product and all that goes with it are best for his needs.

With an ever-expanding core of satisfied users, it is inevitable that sales grow. In most instances, the issues involving services are resolved to the buyer's satisfaction and are a continuous boost to a pleasant buyer-seller relationship. If management creates the right atmosphere in the buyer's environment, it will build up an asset the firm calls goodwill, which literally means an individual's preference for the firm's product.

Increase Loyalty

Loyalty increases through a continuing happy relationship between buyer and seller. Value measured on a balance is tilted in the buyer's favor by a series of services that increase product usefulness. Loyalty may not be measured in dollars immediately, or it may not be demonstrated in increased purchases by one particular buyer. He may be getting all his needs from a firm now.

Buyer loyalty may be valuable to a seller in many ways. The buyer is willing to accept mistakes of the seller—late delivery, back orders, and other problems. He mentions the firm to others as a source of supply. When the firm is being criticized by someone in a group, he defends it. He blunts criticism, encourages the salesperson, and speaks well of the firm.

When critical issues arise, he gives the firm the opportunity to explain. When failures occur, he listens with patience. A genuinely friendly relationship grows, which tends to perpetuate sales and produces a strong base for future expansion.

QUESTIONS AND PROBLEMS

1. Discuss the importance of customer services as a selling aid.

2. Why does a manufacturer insist on installing the equipment he sells? Why not let the customer install it?

3. Explain the use of warranties on an industrial product. Does a warranty protect a buyer? Give examples.

4. Some manufacturers establish repair outlets in strategic locations in their selling area. To what extent do you think this is necessary?

5. What is the purpose of a performance standard? Discuss how it aids in selling.

6. List several customer services that might appeal to industrial buyers. Are these expensive for the seller?

7. Explain ways of handling customers who abuse the service privilege.

8. What are the advantages of guarantee against price decline to (a) the manufacturer, (b) the wholesaler or retailer?

9. How can return privileges help the retailer? Is a merchandise return the fault of the seller or the buyer? Explain.

10. Name four customer services often extended in consumer goods sales to make selling easier for a manufacturer's salespeople and for a retailer. Discuss each seller separately.

11. Discuss some of the effects on buyers who receive a number of services free. Do you think the costs more than overbalance the advantages to the seller?

12. What are some of the long-run effects that may be anticipated from extra customer services? How would you assess their value?

AVERY & SELLS, INC.   *case 17–1*

Avery & Sells, Inc. had developed a substantial firm manufacturing and marketing a number of electrical household appliances.

Twenty salespeople sold their products to department stores, discount houses, large retailers, and to distributors in a few sparsely settled states. Their major sales were in heavily populated areas. They covered the United States, but not equally well in all areas.

The appliances had an excellent quality image. In ten major cities, service centers were established to service their appliances and to furnish parts for private repair shops. The company had built a reputation of fast delivery of parts, because each service center had large and complete parts inventories. Their own centers gave superior and rapid service to all appliances brought in by customers.

Next year the company expects to introduce a line of home dishwashers, a highly competitive item. To compete successfully, it will be necessary to advertise and promote extensively. It will be essential to develop some type of home service to handle repairs. Presently service centers' personnel make no home calls. All repairs are made in each service center.

Several plans for servicing are being considered:

1. Extend present service centers' work to handle home service calls on dishwashers.
2. Establish separate centers to handle dishwasher repairs.
3. Establish arrangements with independent repair shops to service their dishwashers.
4. Offer no repair service, but explain to customers that most independent repair shops could handle service satisfactorily.

ASSIGNMENT

Select a way of servicing dishwashers that will be satisfactory to customers but will not put too heavy a financial drain on the manufacturer. Defend your choice.

---

case 17–2   **DANGLER EQUIPMENT COMPANY**

Dangler Equipment Company manufactures industrial machines with multiple uses. Most of its machines can handle various operations by using parts and equipment that can be added to present machines. Each type of machine may handle up to five somewhat dissimilar operations. The company manufactures a number of different machines, but each does not overlap work done by other machines it produces.

It has been the policy to give service generously to customers who demand it. Some customers are careful not to make many demands; others use the privilege excessively, sometimes making requests that are unreasonable. A small number of buyers have increased their demands steadily so that they now abuse their privilege and often become offensive. If most of the buyers exercised a similar abuse of privilege, Dangler would soon go into bankruptcy.

Top management is acutely aware of the problem. Net income decreased 15 percent last year because of excessive service costs. Indications are that net income may be off over 30 percent this year unless this service cost pattern is corrected.

The seriousness of the situation becomes apparent when the purchasing agent of Slocum Company requested an expensive repair job on a machine sold by Dangler. The repair job would cost about $5,000. The breakdown occurred because a new employee at Slocum assigned to operating the machine disregarded several basic fundamental instructions. As a result the machine malfunctioned, twisting and breaking many gears and other parts. Since this is a precison machine, it must be completely reconditioned before use.

In reviewing the situation with Mr. David, the sales manager, Mr. Ashton, the president, wound up with, "They're just pushing to see how much they can get away with." Slocum's purchases amount to about 2 percent of Dangler's sales.

ASSIGNMENT

Dangler has become overly generous in giving free service and parts to keep their machines operating satisfactorily. Now they have reached a breaking point. They must curb this spiraling cost. Competition in the field is intense.

Devise a plan to handle the problem. Defend your decisions and choices. Forecast possible repercussions in Dangler sales.

18

Planning for Operation and Control

The sales manager comes into an operational situation which may be successful or marginal. He inherits a functioning sales department and, for a time, may leave it unchanged. If it is operating well, it may be unwise to tinker with it, but merely keep it going at the same pace. In time, weaknesses will develop that will require some alteration that can lead to improvement.

The other extreme is the sales manager who inherits an organization which may be functioning poorly and needs a complete overhaul. This situation will require immediate attention and drastic action, particularly if the firm is in a precarious situation.

A more usual situation is to step into an organization that is effective, but can stand considerable improvement. The type of present sales organization may determine the direction of action, but any organization will not operate long by itself. Within a short time, the sales manager must act to leave his individual imprint on the sales department.

PLANNING

Planning is developing a tentative blueprint of the future. It attempts to foresee coming periods and develop a method of action to meet tomorrow's demands.

Planning can be divided into three future time spans—(1) short term, which is about one year or less; (2) intermediate term, which is about two to five years; and (3) long term, which may be more than five years. These time intervals are not rigid because the nature of the firm's operation may dictate different time planning periods.

The shorter the time period involved, usually the more accurate the plans. The longer the time period, the more nebulous plans become. A sales manager cannot see far into the future with certainty; so the farther he looks, the more planning becomes an exercise in guessing.

The sales manager's planning should not be dreaming, but should deal with positive future steps to be translated into action. Planning leads to orderly action and carefully worked out approaches. It prevents hit-and-run operations, overcomes groping procedures, and gives direction to positive, progressive leadership.

However, a sales manager should not overlook the dreams of the future. Translated into reality, dreams may become the seeds of creativity, the stimuli to imagination, the focus of vision, and the promises of tomorrow. Planning marks the difference between the dreamer and the person who creates and performs. It separates the plodder who goes along well enough today from the adapter who recognizes the necessity for change and prepares for it.

PLANNING STRATEGY

Planning strategy for the future demands basic, concentrated thought on a number of requirements. It must resolve generalities of planning into long-range objectives.

Planning Future Objectives

Unless a firm has planned for future objectives, it is likely to operate in a hesitating manner. This situation may not be evident when everything is functioning properly and the business is successful. As changes take place, management does not respond promptly; and gradually there is a divergence from successful operation. Even this divergence may not be perceived for a long time, since the leaders are unable to separate normal divergence indicators from trend changes.

There are many primary objectives management ought to consider. Must we change our organization? Should we decentralize? Will our product demand change? What types of competition will we face? What about taxes? Will government relations change? What will be our labor situation? These are a few of many areas that deserve attention to provide for orderly transition.

Some managers contend that specific long-range planning is impossible because unforeseen contingencies upset the best plans. Experience shows, however, that carefully thought-out plans have a better chance of succeeding than no plans because they can be modified and adjusted to fit new situations. Devising new plans on the spur of the moment does not work well in practice. Improvising is often necessary, but it seldom succeeds as well as carefully planned action.

Planning Marketing Strategy

Marketing strategy is particularly important in the present, but it should not be neglected for longer periods. This year's operating strategy must be implemented, however well planned, but any one of the current difficulties ought to be eliminated as soon as possible. Every effort should be made to provide alternatives to handle difficult situations before they occur. Preventive measures will often eliminate major problems.

New approaches to marketing a firm's product may develop future sales. Today's channels may impede sales in the future, necessitating use of alternative or additional channels. Fresh promotional devices can create greater demand at lesser cost. Price flexibility may bring increased sales opportunities.

Planning marketing strategy requires careful appraisal of existing market operations plus consideration of other approaches. Management must appraise the success of the present method and consider what may happen if it changes or modifies existing procedures. Primary demand change, beyond management's control, may increase or decrease sales and introduce new selling dimensions.

Competitive strategy requires managerial alertness and a willingness to innovate. Management must refine existing procedures, remain alert to incorporate new features that seem promising, and drop those procedures that have outlived their usefulness.

Planning Inventories

Inventories require a major financial outlay. Inventories are subject to obsolescence, shortages, surpluses, and deterioration. Excessive inventory increases costs; inadequate inventory means lost sales.

Transportation affects inventory cost. Often judicious transportation arrangements affect total company profit. Frequent small inventory replenishing may become prohibitively costly because of transportation. Significant savings result from carload or truckload shipments. Combination shipments with other firms may save substantially in shipping costs. Shipments in original packages save labor costs. Direct shipment from a manufacturing plant to the buyer bypasses the inventory warehouse and gives savings in handling and storage.

A large savings arises from properly balancing inventory size, warehousing, shipping, and delivery. Larger firms use computer control to balance inventories among regional warehouses and to maintain adequate stocks.

Planning proper inventories demands careful use of manufacturing equipment to insure maximum production efficiencies. It is necessary to balance manufacturing costs, size of inventories, shipping costs, costs of backordering customer orders, and many other problems. Careful planning can generate savings, expedite merchandise flow, optimize costs, and still satisfy the customer.

One particularly knotty problem is planning a seasonal demand inventory. Past experience is a guide; but weather factors, changes in customer demand, competition, and other contingencies often reduce plans to guessing. Nevertheless, these decisions must be made so that production can be geared over the year in an orderly fashion. Underestimating demand results in crash programs and shortages which are costly; overestimating demand results in costly inventory carryovers which destroy profits. Planning tries to gauge future seasonal demand at a profitable level. People who plan recognize that the best they can do is to estimate within an acceptable range and be willing to accept a certain amount of inventory excess or shortage.

Planning Promotion

Promotion, interpreted broadly, includes advertising, point-of-purchase displays, aids to dealers, and possibly the sales force. The sales force is not included in this discussion.

Planning promotion frequently rests heavily on advertising, particularly in consumer products. Often, advertising is the chief sales-creating technique. The salespeople merely contact dealers, arrange displays, stock shelves, and check inventories.

Advertising, correctly focused, can be effective at a reasonable cost; poorly focused, it becomes an expensive luxury. Advertising planning requires careful appraisal of alternate media and then choosing particular ones. Each of the media will have a representative touting his medium; so the buyer must exercise independent judgment in selection. Much effort and money are wasted unless advertising is synchronized with distribution. Advertising must be channeled to take care of lucrative markets. It must be used at the most appropriate times of the year and must appeal to the correct buying segment of people. Planning advertising involves a constant search for better ways to reach the buying public. Management should not overlook the use of computers and simulations, whereby a number of alternatives can be tried experimentally as indicators of future possibilities.

The use of literature requires careful planning in creativity and in use. Large quantities of brochures, leaflets, and flyers are sent to salespeople and dealers without definite plans for their use. Many sales managers assume that once they have delivered attractive literature to their dealers, their job is done because dealers will use this material effectively. Experience indicates this is not true. Vast quantities of such material are dumped into wastebaskets or left unused. Some of this waste of dealer material can be corrected by making the dealer pay part of the cost of the literature. Company salespeople can arrange display material in retail stores.

Most retail stores welcome some point-of-purchase material. Merchandise attached to cards with descriptive information aids customers. Some manufacturers overwhelm retailers with advertising literature and create resistance and antagonism. Too many man-ufacturers distribute advertising literature with little thought of retailer needs or capacity. Manufacturers forget that they must share retailer space and attention with many other firms.

Planning Training

The salesperson training program may be formal or informal. The size of the firm and the number of salespeople employed will dictate to some extent the completeness of a training program.

If a significant number of new salespeople are hired each year, it is practical to have a complete program handled by a training group; but if only a few are hired each year, the training must be delegated to one or more people on a part-time basis. In each method, it is de-sirable to exercise the planning function so that training is efficient, current, and effective.

Every year, new training aids make instruction easier and more in-teresting. Programmed learning approaches permit individual trainees to learn independently. Compact visual aids enable a beginning sales-person to carry information and to study in the evening.

Irregular salesperson replacement and occasional hiring of a new person may seem to give a sales manager an excuse for minimum training. But this rationalization is not permissible. Sales training is essential whether there are two or twenty-two trainees. Ways can be devised to handle a variety of situations if proper planning is used. Often, basic preliminary sales training can be secured through school courses or by reading salesmanship texts. All sales jobs have some things in common—personal appearance, getting along with people, report writing, planning daily activities, demonstration techniques, sales closing techniques, and customer attention.

Planning for the Staff

There is a tendency to create a staff, assign tasks, and let these as-signments become rigid. Managers tend to think in terms of their particular authority within their areas and lose sight of the functions. Each staff member (whether in the home, regional, or district office) may be operating effectively within the present framework; but does little to foresee changes, to suggest possible improvements, and par-ticularly to suggest new methods which might jeopardize his job.

When time indicates a change is desirable, such a change is in order. Early preparation will alert concerned individuals to changes and modifications in their jobs and in their authority. Stability may dictate an unchanged operation for longer periods; but flexibility wthin an organization reduces rigid thinking and application, elim-inates complacency, and upsets a job-for-life attitude. It may be some-what unpleasant to work in such an atmosphere, but it does keep the staff alert to the necessity of watching for and adjusting to new developments. It keeps them in a position to urge changes at the proper time, rather than waiting until they are long overdue.

Planning organization includes possible changes in selling direct versus use of distributors. These two methods need not be mutually exclusive. A combination can be justified when markets alternate in size and compactness.

Planning Activities

Activities should be planned and justified. Too many activities are used because they make favorable impressions or lend authority to the sales department. Many activities are considered proper, but bear little justification in use.

Meetings that take the sales force from its selling job may be useful, but often cost more than they produce. Neglecting such meetings when they have important purposes can be even more costly than having them.

Planning different kinds of meetings calls for different skills. Small, short meetings are readily handled by subordinates; but special attention must be given to conventions and other major gatherings. Regional conventions versus a national convention should be weighed carefully. Small group meetings should be compared to large group meetings to determine which are more effective and how to implement them successfully.

One of the most difficult areas is dealer meetings, distributor salespeople meetings, and similar meetings where management does not control the participants. These meetings must be made attractive and inviting so that people will attend and become responsive to the message. These people have responsibilities to many sources and usually will give attention to their important sources. If a firm's merchandise is less important, it may be neglected; if a firm does not have a strong profit stimulus to motivate them, it must emphasize ease of selling, rounding out a line, service to customers, and many other suggestions to awaken interest. Planning for these meetings has overtones that are quite dissimilar to planning for a firm's own salespeople meetings.

Planning Product

Product planning is an important function of top management. Many firms have strong research departments developing new products, but their activities can be directed by suggestions from sales executives. Many so-called new products are merely modifications of existing ones. Competition may force changes, even though a firm is reluctant to change or is not ready for a change.

The sales executive responsible for selling a product line should be management's eye as to when a change is necessary or desirable.

When he sees the need for product additions or modifications, he must be ready to convince other top management of the need.

Another use of planning is considering allied lines not presently manufactured. Excellent manufacturing or distribution capabilities may mandate extension into other products. Such a decision will require more careful study and planning than adding a similar product to the present line. Many firms have ventured into new areas with disastrous results. Usually, this situation indicates lack of careful analysis and planning. Beckoning successes often blind management to dangers which are unknown, ignored, or not considered serious.

Planning a product must be continuous, for the market is never static. Long-range plans must be modified as the periods involved come closer. There is usually some long-range plan which changes into an intermediate time period and then rapidly approaches current planning.

Planning for Contingencies

Regular planning covers ongoing procedure and performance as well as future projects. A sales manager can plan to establish a pattern of action to fit situations as he foresees them. But what about unexpected situations?

The sales executive cannot speculate about what to do for bizarre happenings, but he should be ready to handle unexpected contingencies. The sales executive must have plans for countering unusual competitor efforts. He should be reasonably ready to handle problems of inventory and moving merchandise when storms or other natural phenomena interfere. He should prepare for transportation worker strikes. He should make provision for sudden shortages of inventory if his firm runs into production difficulties. He should plan for installation hindrances that may hold up completion of a job.[1] Because sales situations change, planners cannot work out a master set of answers but must be ready to handle new situations that may necessitate some departure from existing approaches.

PLANNING FOR COORDINATION

An essential prerequisite for successful operation is coordination. Coordination requires careful planning to insure that one operation synchronizes with another properly and that each activity contributes its

---

1. Some firms have encountered installation problems because they were not familiar with union regulations in an area. Some installations are held up by other contractors who did not complete their job on time. Some installations are held up because the building owner runs short of funds or wants to delay finishing the building. Sometimes a building construction is speeded up, and the firm cannot speed up its production. This situation brings overtime and other costs. Changes in design are troublemakers. Unanticipated transportation problems arise. Installation blueprints are inaccurate.

share. Improper coordination brings about clashes, interruptions, delays, wastes of manpower and equipment, and cost escalation. Management can approach coordination from several avenues of operation.

Coordinating Timing

Timing marketing activities is crucial to successful operation. Creating a successful selling program depends on a number of factors which are important at different time periods.

Advertising must be arranged so that its impact is greatest when product sales need the most support. Advertising too early or too late loses much of its impact; placed in the wrong media, it does not reach the buying audience; executed poorly, it has little appeal. Promotion literature should be in the dealers' hands in ample time to be used in the introduction of a new product or a new season. Advertising and promotion literature should feature appeals that are timed to the season, the mood of the buyer, the style cycle, or whatever factors prevail.

Sales conventions should be held to create minimum selling interference. Sales meetings should not encroach on a salesperson's prime selling time. Sales reports should not force salespeople to use their selling time in writing. Salespeople should be required to have their reports in at times when they are most useful.

Sales recruiting and training should be timed to have new salespeople ready for replacements and to staff new territories. It is futile to set up new territories or implement new strategies if the firm is not prepared to staff such operations.

Synchronizing activities necessitates careful planning since each activity usually needs starting at a different time. Since each activity must be completed at a specified time and each one takes a different time span, it is important that this time is worked out carefully, allowing extra time to take care of unforeseen contingencies. Such timing has added importance if one activity cannot be started until a preceding one is completed. When there are a series of such activities, the cumulated time can cover long periods; and any excessive delays can result in serious sales problems.[2]

Coordinating Product Movement

In an extensive distribution system with many products, product varieties, and package sizes, the scheduling of movement becomes involved. Some airlines depend on moving freight for manufacturers who would otherwise be unable to have the right items in adequate quantities at the proper place at a specified time. Most people inexperienced

---

2. Additional information on timing control is given in such flowcharting techniques as CPM (critical path method), PERT (program evaluation and review technique), and other methods developed to expedite flow.

in this work have little appreciation of the difficulties involved in timing product movement. Even the most experienced people in the area reconcile themselves to problems and lost sales, because the items cannot be delivered on time. Because of the cost involved, it is imperative to control inventory closely. As a result, a certain amount of backordering must be accepted.

New inventories must be tied to product on hand in warehouses. Sometimes it is better to shift inventory from one location to another, even though new products could be moved in more cheaply. Product movement must be coordinated with economic lot manufacture, which may dictate major inventories in a few locations or small inventories in many locations.

Products may be packaged, boxed, strapped, or shipped in bulk. They may be shipped in returnable or nonreturnable containers, on pallets, or in other packaging devices. Shipping costs may be decreased by combining shipments with other manufacturers in carloads or truckloads.

Coordinating Delivery

A number of issues develop when delivery is coordinated. Delivery may be at the convenience of the seller, but usually the buyer dictates when and how the merchandise is to be transported. Deliveries may be scheduled for a buyer at irregular intervals and in varying quantities. Sometimes a delivery is determined by a customer's ability to pay. Economic conditions, weather conditions, and many irregular conditions and contingencies may upset previously developed plans.

Some manufacturers have coordinated production and shipping to a point where manufacturer warehousing is minimized, resulting in considerable saving. Consignment selling permits economical shipments to distributors and industrial product users who are willing to carry large stocks. In addition to transportation savings, the supplier gains an advantage because he can maintain adequate inventories in the distribution channel.

Various types of delivery equipment give control of quantity, time, and cost. For example, transportation between foreign countries may be dominated by ships, barges, and other water means. Land transportation may use the railroad, trucks, and airplanes. Lowest cost results from large shipments; if dangerously low inventories occur, interim small shipments by airplane correct the poblem. It is not uncommon for salespeople to make small emergency deliveries to satisfy customers, but this approach should be held to a minimum.

Coordinating Supervision

Supervision is not an ongoing function that, once set in action, continues to operate effectively. Supervisors change, and people with varying abilities are transferred from one district to another. Salespeople working harmoniously with one supervisor may experience difficulty in adjusting to another supervisor with different tactics.

The skilled sales manager plans his personal supervision to the individual salesperson. When the sales manager shifts authority to a supervisor, he should inform him of individual salesperson differences and caution him about problems that might arise in a new territory. It is cheaper in time and money and easier on the supervisor or district manager if the boss outlines preferred approaches and sets guidelines. Many a salesperson's morale has been lowered by a new supervisor, who is insensitive to his needs and desires. The result is frustration for both supervisor and salesperson, which usually results in lowered sales and unhappy customers.

Too often, supervisor training is assigned without careful thought about the task to be done and the individual assigned to the job. Blanket training of supervisors may cover many facets of the assignment, but the sales manager, or someone he has assigned to the task, must individualize part of the training for each supervisor.

Coordinating Contingencies

The phrase "putting out brush fires" is often used to cover unexpected situations that seem to rise out of nowhere but must be solved. Inevitably, unexpected problems will arise for which no policy has been established. Sometimes they seem to dominate the sales manager's work and leave him too little time for constructive planning. While these situations cannot be eliminated, their frequency can be reduced by planning so that many will be anticipated and possibly avoided. The careful planner has time to work constructively toward future objectives; the careless planner is constantly embroiled in current problems that require all his time and energy.

PLANNING FOR GROWTH

Planning is a tentative format of the future. Planning for growth therefore is an outline of expectations for some definite future period.

Management should plan for growth in time intervals—one year, two years, five years, ten years. Different time length planning can go on concurrently. Sometimes a more distant period is merely a continuation of planning for a shorter period; planning for a second year is an extension of first-year planning. However, planning for five years may be quite different from planning for two years.

Company growth is not automatic. It must be planned, worked on, and carefully nurtured to succeed. Many pitfalls are present to hinder growth—product change, competition, change in demand, population movement, and financing. Planning must be continuous since changing conditions upset carefully conceived plans.

Growth planning may be centered in product areas. To what extent must present products be altered? How long is the life cycle of some products? Will it be advantageous to invade other fields? Shall other product lines be introduced? If so, what will they be? Is it wise to introduce new shapes or kinds—soap in bars, flakes, liquids; clothing in new sizes, colors, materials; products for both industrial and consumer use?

Products may be modified to meet new environmental requirements —automobiles, cleaners, fire-resistant textiles, safer toys. Innovations may make obsolete present products, which then must be modified or replaced.

Growth may entail expansion into new territories. The local firm becomes regional; the regional firm becomes national; the national firm becomes international. Expanding into new territories introduces numerous problems. There are not only problems pertaining to a firm and its products, but also political and environmental problems which develop when a firm expands into additional physical areas.

Expansion and growth call for increased financing. Much planned growth must be tailored to resource availability. Some firms are limited by capital constraints. A firm may find expansion difficult because of raw material requirements. Plant location may hinder expansion because of transportation costs.

Planning for growth requires extension along different lines, avenues, and approaches. Management does not just plan for growth; it plans specifically in a number of areas and in various ways. For example, a firm cannot plan a more extensive product line without considering how it will be distributed, how it will be financed, who will buy it, what prices should be, and many other factors. Planning is not a single thrust forward; the big conception of a forward thrust must be broken into many smaller thrusts in order to determine if the planned overall suggested strategy is feasible.

PLANNING FOR CONTROL

Control is essential if a firm is to succeed because it brings direction and stability to operations, promotes harmony among employees, and adjusts functions within operations. Control is a force to assure smooth performance in all activities and to prevent excesses and deviations which might disrupt or impede progressive realization of objectives.

Information Sources for Planning Control

With a large sales force, a sales manager must rely on supervisors for information about salespeople and territories. Even though this information may reflect supervisor bias, it is a useful substitute for direct observation, which is impossible. Supervisors are close to selling territories and can keep informed of current relations between buyers and salespeople.

Salespeople's reports can be one of the most important information sources. Salespeople ought to know the conditions of their territories and be aware of any impending changes. Without field information, planning is difficult since the sales manager's knowledge of any one area is incomplete. He cannot plan with any certainty without a continuing knowledge of present markets. Planning for the future requires up-to-date information, including customer expectations.

Excellent records give a strong background for planning. While individual customer purchases may change drastically, it is unlikely that most of them will. Most changes are gradual and can be anticipated. Company records give a spectrum of what has happened and may be used to forecast an operating pattern.

The sales manager may analyze past behavior and compare performances in preceding periods when he plans. Many firms have one or more staff members assigned to analyze data and prepare charts, mathematical studies, and reports for management. This material shows the direction of sales in territories, profitability of lines and customers, trends in kinds of merchandise sold, and a variety of specific information which helps to sharpen planning.

Changing transportation patterns can necessitate revisions in planning sales and operations. Management cannot ignore developments which make present transportation expensive; study may reveal new approaches. Transportation may change because of changed market location, resulting from population movement. The increased attention being given to product movement (logistics) may become a significant factor in intermediate and long-range planning.

Forecasts are basic raw material for planning. Forecasts are the present best thinking of top management to give the sales manager a responsible guide for projecting sales operations. Forecasts should project a number of company activities to guide the sales manager, since all of a company's operations result in a product that must be funneled through sales. Forecasts, being of different lengths, help the sales manager to plan operations for extended periods.

Quotas assist the sales manager to plan the immediate future. They add a degree of certainty which permits careful budgeting of territorial costs. They become the basis of planning and provide a sales platform. Quotas reach every salesperson and tell him realistically what management expects. Quotas affect individual salesperson status because they measure expectation developed from information about the company, the territory, and the person in the field.

Many sources of information may be used to support projected goals. The predetermined goals supply direction to effort. Succeeding plans and efforts are supplementary to and subservient to these goals. If they are realistic, sales planning can be implemented to the correct objectives; but if they are hazy or unrealistic, planning goes ahead, but it will be hampered by higher management's weaknesses.

Goals should aim at progressive development of resources, management, production, and sales. If this development is visualized in terms of market, price, and competition, planning can prepare to reach that segment of the market which appears reasonable. Each activity can be synchronized to achieve maximum performance and reach its objectives.

Planning simplifies operations and directs personnel to follow charted paths which outline the task. In essence, planning is the device which enables personnel to determine what they should do and how they should do it.[3]

FACTORS OF PLANNING CONTROL

Short-term planning deals with future performance within the firm's resources and existing markets. The sales manager must plan within a number of constraints—company policies, resources, funds available for the selling function, caliber of salespeople, competition, and the market.

Company policies are operation guides to be heeded by the sales manager. Policies set a general operational framework, which limits the sales manager. The sales manager is never quite free to do what he wants to, but must fit his sales activities within the game plan. Policies often dictate caution and conservatism, especially when committing major funds or personnel.

Lack of resources is often a limiting factor that will force modification of some plans and even defeat others before they can be tested. These resources can be indigenous to the firm or be outside the firm. For example, the firm may fail to secure essential distribution resources. Ambitious plans may be thwarted by lack of capable personnel. It may be possible to hire excellent sales personnel, but a long training interval is needed before they learn to handle the firm's products and customers.

Finance is a common limiting factor in marketing aggressively. Large sums of money may promote success, but such sums may not be available. The sales budget sets a maximum operating frame. Within this restraint, a successful sales campaign must be originated and effectively pursued.

The wise sales manager examines his budget and plans carefully because he must justify higher expenditures through better sales per-

---

3. Goals and planning should be considered in terms of a firm's resources, not in terms of a competitor's resources, which may be quite different.

formance. He must control expenses, set up expense distribution patterns, allocate funds for regular and emergency expenditures, and preserve a balanced cash outflow that keeps adequate field representation throughout the period. This situation dictates control of salesperson activities to avoid spending too heavily in some areas, leaving other important areas inadequately financed. Even if the sales manager spends more than budgeted, such action is frowned upon by top management. It is far more comfortable to underspend and exceed sales expectations than to overspend and still fail to meet quotas.

Profit is a result of successful selling at a favorable price. Competition interferes with plans. To prevent unprofitable operation, a sales manager may have to replan performance goals and shift emphasis from one product category to another, from one type of customer to another type, or change emphasis in certain geographical areas. A plan that appears feasible when created may have to be drastically altered when its execution results in minimum or no profits.

Management must be alert and flexible. Translating present into future conditions may be naive, futile, and disastrous. Too often, planning attempts to reduce future unknown events into familiar terms, which leaves little room for tomorrow's conditions.

PLANNING AIDS

A number of planning aids are useful in specific instances. The input-output table shows in which areas products are sold and used to produce other products. Input-output analysis is a sophisticated tool which may assist the planner once he understands what it is for, how to use it, and the limitations inherent in it.[4]

National and international business forecasts give broad spectrums of anticipated economic behavior, which may reflect in future sales.

---

4. L. Atkinson and T. C. Reimbold, "Dynamic Industry Forecasting for Business Planning." Paper presented at the Fifth International Conference on Input-Output, Geneva, 1971. New York: United Nations, Department of Economic and Social Affairs.

"Input-Output Analysis in Business Planning," New York: The Diebold Group, Inc., Document No. PP26, 1969, 5 pp.

"Input-Output 1969 and the Corporate Planner," Cambridge, Mass.: Arthur D. Little, Inc., 1969, 20 pp.

"The New OBE Input-Output Tables." Paper presented to the National Association of Business Economists, 12th Annual Meeting, Boston, Mass., September, 1970. Washington, D.C.: Office of Business Economics, U.S. Dept. of Commerce.

Harry W. Richardson, *Input-Output and Regional Economics (New York: John Wiley & Sons, 1972)*.

K. R. Polenske and J. F. Smith, "Alignment of 1960 BLS Consumer Expenditure Categories With the 80-order OBE Input-Output Industrial Classification." Washington, D.C.: Report No. 5, U.S. Department of Commerce, 1968, 44 pp.

Publications give information on specific product use in regional areas by industry and users. Tax statistics in some areas indicate what competition is doing.

Economists of financial institutions forecast business direction for both short- and long-term periods. Income forecasts and buyer intentions for coming periods are valuable planning aids, as are population movements and new construction information. Trade association data present facts and ideas for planning.

PLANNING RESULTS

The results of planning tell what is happening and what will probably occur. The sales manager plans strategy to guide operations and implement present policies as well as to orient thinking towards new achievements. Management objectives are realized through maturation of previous plans which proved feasible when translated into action.

If management has made correct decisions and the sales department has planned properly, successful operation can be continued along a carefully proposed path. If plans do not materialize as projected, rapid feedback tells management to change quickly before greater harm results. Flexibility in planning and execution permits redirection of effort into more promising channels. Sensitivity to failures permits shift in directional effort almost instantaneously before great harm occurs.

When an operation has been planned, management knows the methods used in execution and is quick to detect minor breakdowns. With an unplanned, or hit-and-miss, approach, management soon notices that operations are not going well, but is unable to pinpoint the problem because the performance pattern was not defined carefully.

If alternative planned approaches have been used concurrently in separate geographic areas, on different products, or in separate company divisions, comparisons of results quickly identify preferred approaches. In sales, such approaches might entail use of more salespeople, of specific advertising using various media, of different selling plans, or other variations. The effects of planning can be measured by successes or failures from implementing plans which not only measure performance but also give direction to future operations.

QUESTIONS AND PROBLEMS

1. What is planning?
2. Differentiate different time lengths in planning.
3. Is there a relationship between planning and dreaming?

4. Why is it essential to plan for future objectives? Isn't it enough just to plan? Explain.

5. Discuss the need for planning marketing strategy.

6. In several chapters in this text, we bring up the topic of inventory. Why is inventory planning so important?

7. Does each operation of a sales department need some planning? Discuss. Include specific illustrations.

8. The text discusses a number of activities, such as promotion, new products, training, product installation, and department organization. Why is planning a necessary part to be incorporated into each activity? In your discussion, single out two activities to show effects of planning.

9. Give several examples of correct timing to coordinate effective sales strategy.

10. Show how coordinating efforts expedites delivery of products. Give examples.

11. What is "putting out brush fires," and why must these activities be fitted into the regular operation?

12. Illustrate planned growth and explain its importance in the life of a company.

13. How can adequate information sources bolster planning?

14. What limiting factors must be recognized when planning?

15. How can management use an input-output table in planning? Reading one or more of the sources mentioned will aid you in giving a more complete answer.

OSTEN VIBRATORS, INC. *case 18-1*

Osten Vibrators manufactures a line of vibrating equipment used for rubbing and massaging. It is planned to introduce a piece of equipment especially designed for massaging the hand and arm. This equipment has been developed and tested. There is no competing product exactly like it.

Production is no problem. Once it is determined to go ahead with the manufacture, this new piece of equipment can be produced in sufficient volume at the end of six months.

The sales manager realizes that if the decision is made to produce and market this equipment, he must be given sufficient time to prepare for its introduction, which probably would be more than six months. Just the promotion material alone would require several months, and it would be essential to have a name for the equipment.

After a long discussion in a meeting attended by top management which included the sales manager and the marketing research manager, it was decided to go ahead with the new product. The target date for introducing it on the market would be one year.

ASSIGNMENT

The sales manager has designated you to handle the details of marketing this product. You will work directly with him. The president of the firm stated that a suitable name would be selected within three months. Your first job is to draw up a plan and timetable for introducing the product. Once this plan has been reworked by the sales manager, it will be your job to implement it. Prepare your plan, and have it ready for inspection in two weeks.

---

case 18–2   **PRINTMOR COMPANY**

The Printmor Company is a well established and respected producer of letterpress and offset printing equipment. The company is nation-wide, but its heaviest concentration of sales and service offices is in the Midwest.

The company has just completed a new offset press called the Mark V. This press is the most advanced of its kind. Because of its high price and lack of trained servicemen, Printmor has decided to introduce this new product on a limited scale. Therefore Printmor's sales department, working in cooperation with its advertising agency, has decided to base initial promotional operations in the metropolitan areas of Detroit, Chicago, and Cleveland. These areas were chosen because a large percentage of Printmor's regular customers and potential customers are located here.

Tom Burns, the marketing and sales manager for Printmor, feels that two distinct problems must be solved in introducing the Mark V. First of all, since the Mark V is a new and highly technical press, a new sales structure must be established. Secondly, an innovation of this type will require a new advertising and promotion campaign.

As a result, Burns and the account executive of the advertising agency have prepared the following sales program for introducing the new Mark V offset press. This program will be submitted to Printmor's top management for approval. Following is the direct sales program developed by Burns.

Sales Force Development

Although the Printmor Company has a sales force, the complex nature of the Mark V requires that a new force be selected and trained. The problems to be overcome in setting up a new sales force are as follows:

1. How many salespeople are needed and what are the qualifications?
2. What territory will each cover?
3. What will be the best way to compensate them?
4. What is a method of measuring salespeople's performance?
5. How will the sales force be selected?
6. How will these people be trained?

Only three of the six sections will be discussed.

Number and Description of Salespeople

The salespeople to sell the Mark V will come from the present sales force, since it is felt that the Mark V will eventually replace most of the firm's existing offset market. These proved salespeople have a thorough knowledge of the technical aspects of offset presses and of the offset market.

To determine the number of salespeople needed to cover these three metropolitan areas, the following procedure will be employed. To illustrate this method, the Chicago metropolitan area will be used as an example.

The total number of printing establishments in the Chicago area who would be interested in the Mark V offset press is approximately 500. These 500 potential customers are broken down into three sizes (size being determined by the number of presses in operation). The first size consists of small companies with five or fewer presses in operation; the second, medium-sized companies with six to fifteen presses; and the third, large companies with sixteen or more presses. It has been determined that in the Chicago area there are 248 small, 185 medium-sized, and 67 large printing establishments.

Since the large concerns offer the most sales potential, the salespeople will visit them once a month. In the medium-sized company, they must call every other month; and for the small shops, every three months. This comes out to twelve calls per year for large companies, six for medium, and four for small.

Experience has shown that the average sales call lasts an hour, and that three hours per day are devoted to lunch and travel time. In an eight-hour day, the salesperson can make five sales calls. As will be explained later, our salespeople will spend only three days out of a five-day week for actual selling. They can make fifteen calls per week and, on the basis of a fifty-week year, 750 calls per year.

Combining the preceding information:

Company Size	No. in Territory	Calls per Year	Total Calls per Year
1	248	4	992
2	185	6	1110
3	67	12	804
	500		2906

Since a salespeson can be expected to make 750 calls per year, the number of salespeople needed for the Chicago metropolitan area can be computed by dividing the total number of calls by the calls per year of an individual salesperson.

$$\frac{2906}{750} = 4 \text{ salespeople needed in Chicago}$$

This method would also be used for the Cleveland and Detroit areas.

Territory

From the market research conducted by the advertising agency, it was discovered that any printing establishment would be a potential customer for the Mark V. Some companies could use one or two presses, and some could use more. On a map of the Chicago area, all printing company locations were plotted and given a rating of 1, 2, or 3. These numbers represented the size of each establishment according to the number of presses in use—1, small; 2, medium; 3, large. This area is divided into four sections. This division was made on the basis of equality. That is, since each salesperson would be required to make 750 calls a year, the different sized printing firms and the amount of time needed for travel are computed as equally as possible among the four salespeople. Naturally, because of the various locations of these customers, there will be some variations.

Compensation

Although the Printmor Company will have only a limited sales force at the present, for the new Mark V it does consider the future. Realizing that the probability of the Mark V going on a nationwide level is high, management wishes to establish a compensation plan that will be applicable now and to a larger sales force in the future.

Since each salesperson will be highly trained in the mechanical operation of the Mark V, it has been decided that every salesperson will have a twofold responsibility. First, and most important, he must sell the Mark V; and secondly, he must be able to repair and service it. Naturally, at first the latter responsibility will be almost nonexistent. However, after the Mark V has been on the market for a while, this activity will present a problem. It has been decided that after this press goes on a national scale, each salesperson will spend two days a week as a service and repairman.

Three important advantages are gained by this plan. First of all, the company will not be required to hire and train a separate service department. Secondly, a professional salesperson will create better customer relations than just a repairman. Finally, a highly trained salesperson can promote parts and accessories sales.

Since each salesperson will be performing a dual role, the "salary plus commission on all sales" method of compensation has been decided upon. The straight salary will cover the service and repair responsibility, and a commission will cover the sales duties. The going rate for repairmen in the industry is $7 per hour. Therefore, each salesperson will receive $112 salary per week. For each Mark V sold, a 5 percent commission will be paid. Since the press costs $10,000, a $500 commission will be paid on each sale. A 10 percent commission will be paid on all parts and accessories sold. This plan offers three distinct advantages:

1. It is simple and can be easily understood.
2. An incentive is present and is related to the main function of the salesperson (selling the Mark V).
3. It is fair and proportionate since each salesperson has the same amount of service and selling time.

ASSIGNMENT

Shown in this portion of the plan are three of the six parts mentioned at the top of page 411. Your assignment consists of (a) discussing and analyzing planning as a management function. Are the approaches indicated proper, significant, and complete? and (b) discussing and analyzing the basic merits of each of the three sections.

part four

MARKETING

19

Managing Product Offerings

The sales executive must deal not only with a sales force and its many activities but also with a tangible product or intangible services. The product may be a standard one, or it may be tailored to customers and markets.

When a product is standard, the executive must exercise ingenuity in selling. When a product is flexible and presents opportunities for alternatives, selling is easier although more choices lead to greater complexity.

More products facilitate selling because it is easier to please the customer; but they may increase product management problems because of varieties, styles, sizes, and qualities. Greater variety leads to increased production problems as well as excessive inventories. This situation is prevalent in highly competitive marketing operations and becomes a problem in product financing.

The sales manager develops product emphasis in line with company policies. Within this framework, he has latitude permitting him to exercise ingenuity in a number of directions. Some of the major aspects of the product managing job are presented in this chapter.

PRESENT PRODUCT LINE

A company manufactures and distributes a particular product or products. It may even distribute products which it purchases from another firm. The number of products may vary from one to several thousand. Product prices may vary from thousands of dollars to pennies. It is not likely, however, that this variation will exist. Probably there will be concentrations of product-price relationships at different levels; that is, one firm will sell locomotives; a second, automobiles; a third, furniture; a fourth, kitchen utensils.

Size of Present Product Line

A number of factors may determine the extent of the present product line. Type of distribution, competition, available capital, desire to grow, and plant capacity are a few factors which have determined how products have been added in the past and may govern how they will be added in the future. Occasionally chance or providence may have been determining factors, but such occurrences dwindle as a company grows. For example, an accidental research discovery may be the beginning of a new chemical product; but it is unlikely the firm will put it in production until it has been thoroughly researched, the market appraised, and a pilot plant operation has worked out most of the production problems.

Wide Product Line

Some firms produce a large number of related products to meet a total market. A manufacturer of kitchen utensils produces many items to fit particular needs; a manufacturer of drills makes a large number of styles and a great number of cutting bits; a pharmaceutical manufacturer produces a wide variety of products to meet the needs of medical doctors and perhaps the needs of veterinarians.

Many firms find it advantageous to produce a wide line because of manufacturing capabilities and research availability. Another firm will choose to expand because of availability of capital and other resources. Some firms are forced to expand because of their method of distribution; others expand because of customer demands.

Narrow Product Line

Some producers are content to merchandise a narrow product line. Instead of trying to widen their distribution area, they are content to sell a few items and concentrate on superb performance. Sometimes a narrow line lends itself to merchandising through distributors; sometimes the area of specialization prevents expansion. For example, extractive industries, forest products firms, and farms are limited by nature; process industries, such as petroleum refineries and dairies, are limited by existing raw materials and by manufacturing plants; weight of product may dictate shipment in a restricted geographic area or to users of large amounts. Occasionally, an entrepreneur is satisfied to stay at present size and refuses to take larger challenges.

A narrow line does not automatically indicate small sales. Some producers with one or two items have enormous dollar volume. A shipbuilding yard may spend a year producing one or two tankers. A construction firm may spend years on one project, but another construction firm may have hundreds of projects each year. A flour mill produces enormous tonnage of one kind of flour each year.

Variations in Present Product Line

It is entirely possible that numerous changes should be made in the present product line. Management may find new ideas that can open up new markets or revitalize and stimulate present buyers. An attentive ear to suggestions of customers and salespeople can lead to development that will enhance offerings. These changes may develop in a number of directions.

Variety in number

A greater number of items may be produced to enlarge the market. A new line of regular products suited for left-handed people may be added. Clothing for the extra tall or extra large individual may be added. A firm may add queen size and king size beds to the regular bedroom furniture. A tool manufacturer may add wood bits and masonry bits to his regular line of metal cutting bits.

Color variety

The addition of colors to products pleases buyers and gives greater choices. For years color has been an important feature in clothing, and this same feature has been added successfully to hard goods. Automobiles, refrigerators, furniture, boots, and many other items originally appearing in only one or two colors have blossomed forth in many colors. Incidentally, this color variety compounds inventory problems. Paints are now available in far more colors than they used to be. To alleviate paint inventory problems, manufacturers produce a standard white paint and use color additives to achieve color variety. Color television has eroded the black and white television market and may almost supersede it.

Material changes

Uses of new material supplement the product line and, in some instances, wipe out the use of the old material entirely.

Wood furniture shares the market with metal furniture, plastic furniture, and furniture made from newly created materials. Wood boat production has been replaced by fiber glass material. The delicate bamboo and the sturdy steel fishing poles are being supplanted by fiber glass and graphite rods. Nylon has replaced other material in both soft and hard goods.

Size variety

Some firms concentrate on a few fast selling sizes; others try to meet the entire range of sizes for a particular product. One firm caters to sizes in production quantities; another firm gains strength through custom-built needs in addition to regular sizes. A buyer may prefer to use one particular source because he can get all his requirements and refuse to deal with another firm with better prices, but a very narrow range of product.

Models

One company will concentrate on one or a few models; another will try to have enough different models to meet the entire market. General Motors' line of cars is extensive enough to meet most market requirements; International Harvester has a wide line of trucks; Mack tries to cover one segment of truck demand; while Checker concentrates primarily on taxicabs. Companies become known for particular products. For example, one manufacturer is well known for its woolen clothing; a second, for soup; a third, for coffee; a fourth, for catsup; and a fifth, for baby food.

Packaging

Superior packaging may spell the difference between success and failure. Even everyday industrial goods can profit from attractive packaging.

Effective packaging includes a number of sizes, shapes, colors, and materials. A package has a twofold purpose: (1) to protect and (2) to attract.

Protection of contents is a primary purpose of packaging. That means protection against heat, cold, moisture, physical handling, vermin, and other hazards. In an industrial plant, it may include protection against fumes, exposure to weather, heat, and other conditions pertinent to any particular industry or environment.

Imaginative packaging can save money and minimize inventory loss. A well-known candy always packaged attractively has a second outside wrapper for holidays. If some remains unsold after the holiday, the special wrapper is removed, leaving the box in its normal wrapper. Many durable packages have a variety of uses after they have been emptied. The common glass container has a number of after uses, as does the bushel basket; but few remember the large wood candy pails of years past, which were greatly appreciated by farmers. Resale of used containers is a profitable business. In some instances, the package costs far more than its contents.

Some packaging is devised to fit particular users. For example, many buyers have found that packaged bacon is more convenient than the bacon square; other users prefer bacon in metal cans; a few individuals prefer the specially prepared bacon used by hikers.

All of these factors weigh heavily in the sales manager's work in presenting, managing, and selling his product line.

CHANGES IN PRODUCT LINE

Most product lines are subject to meet new conditions. This change may come about because the firm wants to expand, or it may result from the necessity of lowering manufacturing costs.

Simplification of Product Line

Companies are forced to reassess product lines from time to time because too often there is a tendency to proliferate styles, varieties, and sizes. Special demands may command an addition to the present line, but seldom is there a compensating reduction elsewhere. Soon there is a great number of slow-moving items cluttering inventory and creating excessive financial burden. Even though a particular item or size has lost majority favor, there are inevitably a few customers who want it. There arises the decision as to when to risk displeasure of a few customers in order to terminate an unprofitable item. The sales manager cannot eliminate an item merely because of small demand, but must also consider the impact on certain customers. He dares not refuse a user of an unprofitable item, because he is a major customer for other purchases. One way to handle a product manufactured at a loss is to discontinue production, but buy it from another source and resell it. A more successful method is to switch the customer to one of the newer products which may meet his needs at a lower price. When a customer must be switched from one item to another, the sales manager should try to make the change inviting.

Standardization of Product Line

The sales manager may find it impossible to meet all customer requirements and still keep the product line manageable. A firm may not be capable of extending its product line and, as a result, must concentrate on a specified number and give up the idea of selling all users.

The firm may set limits in its manufactured items featuring particular products. In agriculture, there are standards and grades to facilitate marketing. For example, a bushel of mixed sizes of apples or a bushel of mixed varieties would sell much cheaper than one carefully sorted. Standardization and grading enable the buyer to make purchases without ever seeing the product. The producer can separate inferior quality products, which may be marketed locally or diverted to byproducts.

How rigid standards are enforced in quality may determine what level of user to sell. Some buyers are satisfied with an average quality; others demand a very high quality and are willing to pay a much higher price. Some buyers must be content with low quality.

Management may decide to use a few standards and limit its line drastically, or it may feel it wise to commit greater finances to inventory and produce a wide line using many standards. Some may disregard standards (a standard is a measure) and have a large variety of items which may lack uniformity and dependability.

New Uses and Applications

Product changes arise because customers demand different items or management finds new opportunities. The sales manager must be able to detect and isolate new uses for his product. Sometimes such uses arise from new products or changes in promotion.

Some new uses may come about accidentally, but a more successful approach is to have a carefully formulated plan with someone or several people alert to possible changes. A prepared approach will uncover many more possibilities than one left to chance.

DROPPING PRODUCTS

Few product lines remain static for any length of time. To avoid change may be to court disaster. Some changes may be drastic, as when an automobile manufacturer brings out a new car, a new model, or an entirely different vehicle. Often, a new line of cars replaces a series that is phased out completely.

Profitability of Product

Almost invariably, the purpose of a product is to make a profit for the manufacturer. As long as it is reasonably profitable, it will be pushed. When its contribution becomes negligible, management considers phasing the product out and replacing it with one that is profitable.

A product may be necessary, even though not particularly profitable, if it is of key importance in the line. If sales go down, is it possible to reverse the trend by promotion? If competition becomes rugged, are there ways of tying in a losing product with a profitable one? These are two of several alternatives to be considered before abandoning it.

Some firms are reluctant to drop an important product even though profitability has vanished. They cannot force themselves to recognize the inevitable process of change. Instead they may try repeatedly to stimulate it through promotion and minor modifications, hoping to restore it to its former position.

Position on Growth Curve

A study of many products has shown that each has an individual growth curve. Sometimes this curve shows a slow steady period of growth, a period which has a plateau showing no great change, and then a decline in the curve, showing decreasing demand. Such a curve may cover months for one product and years for another.

A growth curve for a fad product may show a steep increase almost immediately, a short high plateau, and a rapid, sometimes precipitous, decrease in demand. In between these two curves are many other growth curve configurations illustrating demand behavior for a number of products.

The sales manager can chart each of his products on a projected sales curve. Such charts may not be accurate, but they will be indicative of the stage of each product on its curve. From this information, the sales manager can plan strategy, assign funds, and determine the degree of effort each product should receive. It would be unwise to put major effort on an item that seems likely to decline rapidly, because the payoff would be small. It would be negligent to slight a product in the ascending phase of the growth curve, where additional effort would carry great reward.

Product Leadership

If a firm's product has been a leader in the market and shows signs of weakness, the first impulse is to bolster it with harder selling or promotion to keep it at the top. It is wise to examine the product in its present environment to see whether it is structured to maintain its position or if demand changes will relegate it to lesser importance, leading to a final phasing out period.

A firm may find product leadership depends on maintaining its primary product in a dominant position, or it may mean maintaining leadership with a succession of new products. There have been several examples in the past two decades when pharmaceutical companies have suffered severely because their primary products have lost original advantage and their firms' research laboratories have been unable to develop new products to maintain company sales.

Fear may be a strong influence to prevent dropping an out-of-date product. Just because it has been successful, management hopes it will continue to be. Another danger for clinging to an old product is that management has no alternative.

Market Position

The market position of a product may determine whether it should be dropped. Just because a product is lowest among competitors does not signal abandonment. Even at that level, it may be quite successful. The smallest of the four U.S. car manufacturers has sales exceeding one billion dollars a year.

A firm may inaugurate an expensive promotion to maintain a product market position, even though the results do not give sufficient financial return. Maintaining market position with one product may stimulate sales in other items, thus making the whole operation worthwhile.

If it is difficult to maintain market position, it may be time to reassess the operation to determine if dropping a weak product will hinder or benefit the other products. Unless a product is profitable, maintaining it because of pride or some sentimental reason is hard to justify.

Interwoven with Other Products

One of a firm's products may be so interwoven with the other products in production or demands that it must be kept. If the product is part of production, then it must be sold. For example, meat packers must sell the entire animal, not only choice portions; the farmer must dispose of several grades of apples; the petroleum refiner has a number of products he must sell.

Customers may insist on buying certain products from the same supplier. It is not likely that the grocery buyer will want to buy his meat requirements from one source and then be forced to look for one minor item from another source. The industrial buyer purchasing a line of drills would not like to have to find a separate source for one size if he depends on one major source.

Small, Insistent Demand for Product

When a product declines in popularity, sellers often phase it out because it becomes unprofitable. Often, customers can be switched to another product which is equally satisfactory. To some buyers, there is no substitute; and they will brave almost any annoyance to get what they want.

Before dropping a product, a firm may have to review various alternatives. If there is no ready substitute, perhaps the product should be kept; and possibly raising the price will take it out of the loss category. The buyer may be a major customer whom management does not want to offend. Competitors may have dropped the item; and though in itself unprofitable, this product can be a ready wedge to get new customers. The product may be dropped from direct distribution, but made available through wholesalers. A buyer may be willing to order a particular product by mail rather than using the regular channel.

Management may show great reluctance to drop a relatively new product which is not selling well. Too often, there is a tendency to exert tremendous selling effort to a faltering new product rather than to assess the true situation, admit to a mistake, and drop it.

WAREHOUSING THE PRODUCT

Managing the product line requires advantageous warehousing. Each type of product and method of distribution requires its own type of warehousing.

When rapid delivery is essential, warehouses must be located strategically to prevent delay. Major warehouses may carry full lines of products; smaller ones, only part of the line. Perishability may be a deciding factor for where and how much to stock. Production may dictate large stocks at some periods and lesser ones at others.

Whether to have one, few, or many warehouses may be governed by costs as well as the need for speedy delivery. Whether warehouses should be company owned or rented depends on the nature of use.

If the same relative amount of space is needed the year around, a company may find it advantageous to own its own warehouses; if warehouse use is uneven and intermittent, it probably would be preferable to rent space.

INVENTORIES

Management might consider warehousing and inventories part of the same supply problem. In many instances this is true, but there can be numerous occasions when they are independent rather than interdependent.

When a firm has long production runs of staple, nonperishable products and owns ample warehousing facilities, financing may be the balancing factor determining inventory, especially if the product is high in unit value. For example, an automobile manufacturer stores very few new cars, but does have a major problem in parts inventories.

Seasonal production, as in agriculture, requires major warehousing plus enormous financial investment. Carrying such inventories is expensive but can even out selling price by overcoming gluts at one season, while customers are deprived entirely of the product in another season. Even dairies are forced to divert milk to other dairy products commanding lower prices at one season of the year in order to insure sufficient supply of milk for consumption at another period. The frozen food producer, as well as the canner, must build up inventory when the product is available. Holidays create special demands at particular periods, but inventories to supply such demands may be created over a period of weeks, months, or even a year.

Two products can illustrate the precarious nature of some inventories. The manufacturer of electric fans builds up huge inventories which may be moved in a period of a month or two in summer. A glut of inventory may have to be carried over to the next year; a seemingly excess inventory can be wiped out by one week of excessively hot summer weather. Salt for highways and sidewalks must be stored in advance at particular locations. Wholesalers and retailers must stock supplies for consumers. If severe weather normally appears, the inventories are used as anticipated; if the weather is mild, huge stocks are left for another year (storing salt in summer has problems); if severe storms occur early in the season, supply is depleted and customers criticize suppliers for lack of foresight in planning inventory. A firm tries to plan for the average; but in any one-year period the average may be far wrong, for average sales seldom coincide with real sales of any one period. Each sales manager must study his particular demand curve and plan inventory to meet as many demands as his firm can afford. To meet all demands becomes impractical in most instances,[1] but to meet only a few demands may irritate buyers and cause them to seek more promising sources of supply.

ADDING A NEW PRODUCT

Adding a new product may be a major decision of top management or the board of directors, or it may be of lesser importance and be decided by the sales manager, usually in conjunction with the president and perhaps one or more managers. A new product is added when there are specific good reasons for the addition. Often this action will affect other items in the product line, and it also becomes one more demand for allocation of scarce resources.

Why Add a New Product

There can be many reasons for adding a new product. These reasons can result from within the company, from outside competitive pressure, from customer wants, from new environmental conditions, and from government suggestion.

Expand the size of the firm

Active management wants the firm to grow and show greater sales and profits. The small company becomes the medium-sized company, and, hopefully, in time grows to be a large company. Some firms start small but must grow large in order to survive. For example, the small snowmobile manufacturer becomes large, is absorbed by another firm, or goes out of business. Requirements in some areas prohibit a small firm from staying small and surviving. In many instances, advertising and promotion costs are far greater than a small firm can handle. Sometimes a small firm finds a niche that larger firms cannot handle profitably and holds that particular market.

Salvage waste products

A manufacturer may have scrap and waste products which become valuable only if he can use them constructively. A waste product with little or negative value may be used in a new product that returns a handsome profit.

Pollution control

Although pollution control has become increasingly important, it has been a problem of long standing for some firms. The cost of disposing

---

1. Electric utilities must meet surging demand at particular periods for a product that cannot be stored and hence have idle capacity at other periods. Consumers Power Company and Detroit Edison Company pump water into a pond dug into a hill on Lake Michigan during low electricity demand. Then that water is allowed to flow back to generate electricity during the high-demand period.

of waste increased with industrialization. To reduce some of these costs, imaginative entrepreneurs have developed new products using wastes as raw material. While such utilization has not reduced material cost to zero, it has reduced cost of waste disposal and has put to use materials that have been eyesores and harmful to the environment.

Utilize plant capacity

A plant represents a fixed investment. The more production that can be forced out of a plant, the lower the fixed cost becomes. Alert management may find opportunities in developing products which are either new or similar to competitive ones. Available plant capacity signals management to search for means to use this resource. If it appears impossible to increase sales of present products sufficiently to sop up this excess capacity, management should seek other possible products. Caution suggests that production is only one element; if a new product is to become successful, its marketing implications must also be assessed.

Availability of capital

Successful companies often find extra capital readily available for growth. If other conditions in a firm are favorable, capital availability tempts management to expand in their own area or perhaps in other areas that appear lucrative.

Management availability

A firm rich in top grade management only partially used may seek to add products. It is not unusual to have such a firm add new products successfully because they have successfully developed know-how and have already demonstrated capacity.

Retaining customers

Customers may want changed product lines or changes within a product line. Retailers want products that appeal to customers; wholesalers prefer product lines with a competitive edge; salespeople find elements of newness and improvements attractive to buyers.

In an industry where change is typical, new products and product variations are essential. Sometimes it becomes a matter of opinion whether a change in a product deserves to be recognized as a new product. Probably the nature of the product and the industry will determine this. If the product is highly advertised and widely distributed, a firm would be more likely to designate the changed product as a new product to obtain a fresh appeal. If the product is a staple of many years, changes might be noted as improvements in the present product. For example, both the publisher and author of a revised, or second edition, of a textbook prefer that the buyer see the new book as having major changes (a new book) rather than the same book with a few changes.

Changing customer requirements may force drastic product changes. These requirements may result from environmental demands, new uses, competition of new substitute products, or many other reasons. Changes may be incorporated to make the product line more attractive in appearance, use, durability, and price.

Competition may dictate product changes. For example, the Ford Model T was finally discontinued and superseded by the Model A. Textbooks are supplemented with readings books, programmed instruction, and visual aids. Many staple foods have been processed and packaged to make them specialty items. When one firm added a new line of syrup with butter, the chief competitor responded immediately with a similar line; when one firm produced a high protein, ready-to-eat breakfast cereal, competitors responded shortly with their own versions; when a firm comes out with a new hair-care preparation, competitors rapidly develop products to serve the same purpose.

Diversification

Any firm restricted to one item or a few items finds itself in difficulties if sales sag because alternatives are limited or, perhaps, almost nil. Sales suffer drastically if a product is a derived demand component of another product.

Diversification opens new opportunities, new choices, and chances for balancing performance. It permits redirection in sales efforts, opens new sales horizons, balances financial applications, and provides a more regular profit flow. With all these advantages, diversification entails new hazards because spreading management and sales effort in more directions may sap vitality of major thrusts and end with general mediocre performance.

Diversifying into a family of products or even unrelated items enables a firm to take advantage of a widely varying economy. To prepare for a number of contingencies also opens up a number of economic advantages in product, price, and geographic areas. For example, a strike in one area may hinder sales there but have little effect in another area; a drought in one farm area may seriously lower farm purchasing power in that locality but have no effect in another area; one area may have lost enthusiasm for a particular product, but demand for it may continue strong in another. Introducing a new product may be slow and expensive, but the cost pressure may be mitigated by other lines with favorable sales volume.

Ready-made distribution

A firm may have an excellent distribution system that makes it successful. Often there is spare time which salespeople could use on another product. A judicious rearrangement of duties with possible personnel additions might open up new opportunities for merchandising an additional line of products.

A firm in this position may distribute a line for another company, or it may manufacture it. Usually it is wise to add a complementary product which fits the present channel. A distributor of cosmetics may add a line of deodorants; a distributor of small electrical appliances could add small electric tools used in the household; a salesperson for farm equipment coud add heaters for animal shelters.

Management should avoid adding lines with dissimilar outlets and buyers. A salesperson handling textiles to department stores would have problems if he were asked to handle a line of machine tools. This would be an extreme example of dissimilar items, but often those that seem compatible may not be distributed together. For example, a company selling food products through its own sales staff might try to add a grocery item that has been moving through wholesalers only to find that they cannot do it successfully.

Ethical Considerations of a New Product

Society increasingly voices concern over products entering consumption. Restrictions of today were unheard of a few years ago. Controls limit product freedom and inhibit experimentation with products that may have questionable use effects. At one time, the manufacturer's major concern was "Will customers buy?" Now another concern is "What effect will my product have in use?"

Safety Requirements

Product safety has taken on new dimensions. The automobile manufacturer is forced to introduce safer cars—safer for the rider, the pedestrian, the insurance firm, and the environment. The food producer must be more meticulous in detailing food contents and possible bad effects, if any. Tobacco products are meeting more stringent requirements in informing users of possible harmful effects. Pharmaceutical manufacturers are compelled to use more safeguards in producing and testing various drugs. Household appliances and cleaning products are struggling with new demands, which often are created by hysteria rather than documented information. In part, this concern is a result of carelessness, deliberate disdain, and lack of knowledge or ineptitude of producers. But much of this concern arises because of new knowledge that uncovered many harmful effects from product exposure or usage and also because society has been jolted by obvious physical environmental deterioration. Possibly, society overreacts; but management must cope with such situations because they must operate today and in immediate tomorrows, not in the far future. Management must be able to meet safety requirements, directly because of legal requirements and indirectly by the implied safety desires of society. All this must be consummated with minimum cost as governed by competition.

RESEARCHING A NEW PRODUCT

Some firms introduce a new product without sufficient background to determine its probable success. A product that appears attractive may have serious drawbacks in the marketplace, one of which may be insufficient demand. The result can be disastrous. Other serious difficulties may appear that hinder successful selling.

A variety of problems, somewhat different depending on type of product, arise in any product introduction. One way of approaching the product-related problems would be to identify the product as (1) an addition to a present product group, (2) a new product, but with similar characteristics to present products, or (3) an entirely new product.

Addition to Present Product Group

If a new item is to be added to a product line, the problems of production and distribution may be minor. Presumably, related demand will insure a ready, though small, market; and total cost of adding will be minimal. If there is evidence of sustained demand at a moderately profitable price, there would be little risk in going ahead because even a small increase to total profit is welcome.

New Product Similar to Existing Products

A new product similar to the present line can mean products in use, products in distribution, or some other similarity. For example, a manufacturer of ladies' toiletries can introduce a line of men's toiletries; a firm distributing through grocery stores may find another item that will move through the same channel; a firm selling industrial equipment with an excellent financing arrangement may make another line of equipment that depends on adequate finances for successful selling.

Many new risks appear in merchandising a new product of this nature. Primarily, the demand factor looms as paramount, for management never knows how much can be sold. A frustrating situation develops if low-level demand over an extended period signals eventual defeat. A serious danger exists if there is insufficient primary demand. Even if there is adequate demand, intensive competition may make acquiring a sufficient market share prohibitively expensive.

New Product Hazards

New risks appear in trying to develop and sell an entirely new product. Snowmobiles opened a new form of recreation. Some of the pioneers reaped handsome immediate rewards but were soon driven out of business by stronger, well-capitalized firms with an ability to evolve excellent distribution. A large firm may survive a bad product, but a small firm may be wiped out. A small firm may introduce a product with minimum cost as compared to a large firm and can succeed even if volume and return are not great.[2]

Overassessment

In assessing opportunities for a new product, management may be blinded by the chances for success and ignore the pitfalls of reality. If management finds families use certain quantities, it may generalize and forget other families might use much less or none. Even if adequate potential demand exists presently, what assurance is there that it will continue?

DEVELOPING A TIMETABLE FOR A NEW PRODUCT

Bringing a new product to the customer requires careful planning and timing because of the many facets that must be considered and implemented. Since some of these activities require long time periods, it is essential to start each part with plenty of lead time so that the orderly flow of work is not held up.

Making the Product

The task of making the product is assigned to the manufacturing division. It involves many actions that we will not consider here because it does not call for sales involvement. But it is important that the product be attractively designed and have convenient features appealing to buyers. These features apply to consumer goods and to producer goods.

It may be worthwhile to market test a product extensively before volume production. Even though earlier market testing indicated buyer demand could be generated, further buyer suggestions could pinpoint improved design, color, and features that would enhance the product's attractiveness. Often, a product stumbles along in sales because it was launched before sufficient time was given to add important details.

To bring an improperly developed product onto the market leaves damaging aftereffects on unhappy customers. In the desire to show early profit in a costly product investment, it is tempting to put a

---

2. An employee of a tractor manufacturer stated that opportunities to modify existing equipment on tractors is handled in low volume by small firms, but could not be handled by the manufacturer because of excessive overhead.

product on the market early, even though manufacturing has serious reservations about product performance.[3]

Preparing for Distribution

Preparing distribution methods may involve a minimum of coaching salespeople at one extreme and, at the other extreme, developing another sales division staffed by newly recruited salespeople or by salespeople transferred from other assignments.

Time and Performance Schedule

If a product is to be launched under the most favorable circumstances, pertinent details must be carefully handled. Since many necessary jobs of unequal time requirements are involved, it requires careful preparation so that each job is started early enough to insure its completion at a particular time.

If a new organization is required, it must be set up and functioning before it must handle large quantities of a new product. This organization in itself may be a major undertaking with its own problems in developing, recruiting, training, and assigning territories.

Product promotion is an essential ingredient in sales. Therefore the amount and kind of advertising must be planned, display material originated and produced, informational literature and brochures created and printed, sampling and store promotion timed accurately, synchronizing and scheduling of activities carefully worked out, and follow-up procedures be ready to insure proper use of promotional materials.

Adequate inventories to meet initial and continuing demand must be arranged. Inventory must be balanced in sizes, styles, colors, packages, and other dimensions (if these apply) to satisfy buyer wants. They must be strategically located to make them available rapidly. Transportation should be arranged to expedite product delivery.

Perhaps the only way to be sure of keeping every step and every activity under control is to list everything that must be done from beginning to final distribution. Management should detail various elements under every part of the operation spelling out what, how, and when each activity must be performed and then arrange to resource all of this with people, money, equipment, and technical aids.

---

3. For special literature on current product development, the reader should refer to current articles, monographs, and books. For broader treatment on the subject, refer to to *New Product Planning,* 2nd edition, compiled by Donald E. Megathlin and Winnifred E. Schaeffer, American Marketing Association, Chicago, 1966. This is a bibliography on new product planning. *New Product Development,* Joseph O. Eastlack, Jr., editor, American Marketing Association, Chicago, is a useful reference. Marketing management textbooks have sections on product development.

Developing feedback procedures

The sales manager must stay informed of what is going on in the initial stages of the sales operation. Since each subfunction will not develop equally well, it is important to learn of malfunctions rapidly in order to give support where problems appear. Unless the entire operation is kept under constant supervision, breakdowns will occur that can seriously impede the entire effort until corrective measures and remedial steps are instituted.

Even in those areas where feedback indicates progress is continuing as predetermined, the operation may call for readjustment upward because original forecasts were too low.

QUESTIONS AND PROBLEMS

1. Discuss the advantages and disadvantages of (a) a wide product line and (b) a narrow product line.
2. How can a firm simplify a product line without antagonizing customers?
3. Indicate how money can be saved by using standards.
4. Explain a product growth curve, and tell why it is important.
5. Why is market position of a product important to a manufacturer?
6. Does small demand for a product automatically signal its discontinuance? Explain.
7. Why is warehousing important in product management? Justify your position.
8. Describe several conditions which justify fluctuating inventories.
9. Give several reasons why a firm may wish to add a new product.
10. What are some of the advantages and disadvantages of product diversification?
11. Point out some of the current restrictions which may hinder production of a new product.
12. Why is product safety becoming an increasing burden on manufacturers?
13. Explain some of the economic hazards of producing a completely new product.
14. Trace the development of a timetable for producing and marketing a new product.

COMPUTER COMPANY   *case 19–1*

In a field dominated by a single giant, IBM, Computer Company produces and sells computers. In addition to IBM, the relatively small

Computer Company competes against Burroughs, Sperry Rand, Honeywell, and National Cash Register, each firm being much larger than Computer Company.

Over the last fifteen years, many small firms, such as Computer Company, have entered the computer field only to go bankrupt or have avoided bankruptcy by selling out to firms in other fields which felt that they could use the failing firms' technical staff and/or tax loss carryover.

Computer Company's sales manager was faced with the prospect of seeing his firm soon go broke as so many other small firms were doing, merging with a larger firm, or devising a sales strategy which no one else in the computer field had succeeded in doing—a sales strategy which would be profitable immediately.

Merging with a larger firm was not desired. The sales manager, like most of the other of Computer Company's founders, had left a job with a large corporation. He had previously been general manager of a major computer firm. These dynamic young founders felt that they could succeed in their own computer firm by capitalizing on the larger firms' inability to spot some important developmental and marketing opportunities in computers. They felt that the large firms were too slow moving and inflexible.

The alternative that the sales manager and the other founders considered was deciding which of the openings left by IBM they should assault with their limited resources. Due to the firm's small resource base, such a strategy would have to be profitable quickly.

Among the openings thought to have been left by IBM were small, desk size computers, small desk size computer terminals, hardware for check sorting and other bank processes, software for use with IBM computers, process computers for industries such as steel making, computers for stock exchanges, super fast "brute force" computers for scientific and engineering uses, hospital computers for patient monitoring as well as patient billing and payroll accounting, or producing computers for the defense department as components of various radar, missile, and other military systems. Each of these gaps in IBM's armor was carefully evaluated by the sales manager.

Small desk size computers offered a very promising long-term potential, but to exploit this opportunity effectively would require a large national sales and service network complete with parts depots. The firm's sales management felt that pursuing this course of action would take time and money that Computer Company did not possess.

Computer hardware for check sorting and other bank services offered significant sales potential. This alternative would entail the need for a sales and service network which would be smaller than that required for small, general purpose desk computers. Burroughs was enjoying success in this area, having already been well entrenched with banks due to Burroughs' widely used conventional, precomputer bank machinery. Burroughs had spent many millions of dollars to develop computers which would protect its traditional bank business. Burroughs already had a sizable sales and service network.

Small desk size computer terminals for use with IBM computers appeared to offer too small a market to suit Computer Company's present ambitions.

Software for use with competitively made computers offered a large, growing potential for business. Opting for this strategy would not necessitate a nationwide service network, and it could apparently be handled by a sales force of the size that Computer Company could afford in the present circumstances. However, Computer Company would have to buck the forcing type of sales tactics of competitors. Furthermore, this market would not offer an opportunity to utilize fully the talents of one of the firm's founders, a scientist.

Process computers for continuous process manufacturing such as steel making were an area where custom designed computers could be successfully sold with a sales and service force small enough so that Computer Company could afford such a marketing effort. Selling such custom-made installations offered a quick profit because the users would customarily make an outright purchase of their computers rather than leasing them.

Hospital computers for monitoring of patients was exhaustively researched by the Computer Company's sales department because it knew that coming government payment of medical expenses coupled with the increasing proportion of the population of geriatric age would mean an explosion in hospital patient populations. Computer monitoring of patients conceivably could help offset increasing hospital labor costs. It was the sales manager's conclusion that the breakthrough in hospital use of computers was many years away due to his belief that hospitals generally lacked the caliber of management which would recognize today's potential for computer usage in hospital care and administration.

The sales manager early in his considerations concluded that the stock exchanges offered too small a market potential for his firm's further consideration.

Producing computers as parts of defense department systems was undeniably a large business, and it was certain to get much larger. Computers produced for the defense department were paid for upon delivery, providing a prompt, small, but quite certain margin of profit. The sales manager's research indicated that producing computers for the defense department also provided a means of getting the government to pay for part of Computer Company's necessary continuing research program. To handle defense department sales would require only a handful of sales personnel for dealing with the federal government. Also favoring government contract work was the fact that the federal government was politically desirous of fostering competition in the production of computers. IBM's past performance in this defense activity did not give it any advantage in new bid negotiations. Government work was also inviting because the government would warehouse its own spare parts.

Apparently promising for Computer Company was the production of "brute force" high speed computers for the scientific community. This area was largely untouched by any of Computer Company's competitors. It was also an area which could yield a prompt profit because these computers would be purchased outright, rather than leased.

In making his formal, comprehensive report to his fellow founders of Computer Company, the sales manager strongly recommended that Computer Company embark upon a sales effort to land as many federal government computer contracts as possible. He further recommended that his firm develop methods of inexpensively converting the products developed with defense department funds to civilian use in the virgin area of super fast "brute force" computers for scientific use. The sales manager indicated that his combined marketing strategy of going simultaneously for both the defense and scientific high speed markets offered the best likelihood for sales success over the next few years.

QUESTION

What sales strategy should Computer Company have adopted?

---

case 19–2   JONES ELECTRIC COMPANY

Background

This dialogue concerns the objections of the buyer to the product which the salesperson has presented. The salesperson, in each case, must overcome these objections with adequate and convincing answers. Once all objections have been overcome, the salesperson must then close the sale. The product is an electric frypan. The salesperson is attempting to make the sale to a department store manager.

Narrator: The salesperson, Ms. Gerard, has already demonstrated the use of the product to the buyer, Mr. Fox. At this point, we will listen to the conversation.

Gerard: Now that you've seen the frypan demonstrated, Mr. Fox, I am certain that you recognize its superiority over competitive brands. How many of the frypans do you think I could send out on the next delivery date?

Fox: Wait a minute. I'm not sure whether I want any, so don't rush me. Did I hear you correctly when you said that it sells for $34.95?

Gerard: Yes, sir, that is right. I'm sure that you can readily see that with its many features the frypan could sell for much more.

Fox: Are you kidding? That's five dollars more than the similar competitive model, and I'm having trouble even giving them away. I really don't see where there is five dollars worth of difference between your model and others on the market.

Gerard: Actually, there is one very important difference between this frypan and other brands. The fact that this pan is completely immersible in water is an innovation in itself. You must agree that this is far better than having to take the heat-control mechanism off each time that the pan is washed. This convenience is very appealing to the homemaker. Ease of washing is also emphasized by the teflon lining.

Fox: I suppose so, but five dollars is still a lot of money.

Gerard: I have to agree with you that the slightly higher price seems to make competitive models appear more desirable. But, let me point out that the unique features of this brand have made it the best selling electric frypan in this area in spite of the fact that it's only been on the market for a month.

Fox: That sounds better. By the way, you've only shown me one size. If that's the only one you've got, I don't want it; it's too small.

Gerard: This frypan is the one that I use for demonstration only. It has to be small so that I can fit it into my briefcase. Actually, we have a complete line of different sized pans and different types and sizes of lids. This brochure shows the entire line.

Narrator: Fox looks through the brochure and agrees that the selection is very complete. He then picks up the frypan to look it over.

Fox: Boy, is this thing heavy. What's it made of, lead? I don't know that I want to sell something that is going to be this difficult for someone to handle.

Gerard: Actually, it is only about a pound and a half heavier than comparable competitive models. The reason for the added weight comes from the extra sealer and parts which are necessary to make it one unit. Notice that on the competitive models, if the heat-control mechanism is left on, it is just about as heavy. Also, a little of the extra weight can be attributed to the new alloy we are using. This one is about 25 percent more conductive than any other on the market.

Fox: Is that so? Does it really make that much difference?

Gerard: When a metal is more conductive, as this one is, the cook can be sure of a more even temperature over the surface of the pan. Thus, more uniform frying takes place.

Fox: I just don't know. I've had a lot of trouble with that darn teflon business on regular frying pans. It seems that it peels off after about two years of use. I don't want to have 50 percent returns for faulty materials. I really don't think that I'd better add this pan to my line.

Gerard: I think that I mentioned earlier that every electric frypan has a five-year guarantee against failure of parts and materials, including the teflon coating.

Fox: Now that you mention it, I remember that you said something like that. Sounds all right. But even still, I hate to be tied down with nothing but teflon pans. Stainless steel is a pretty big seller, and I don't remember seeing any in your line.

Gerard: The usual reason that people purchase a stainless steel frypan today is they cannot find the same size or shape available in teflon. As you can see in the brochure, practically every shape and size of pan available in stainless steel has been duplicated in teflon. In fact, many new styles have been added.

Fox: I really can't argue with you there. But, I've always found that no matter how well a thing is sealed it begins to leak after some usage. With the frypans, this could be very dangerous. They could easily short circuit and electrocute somebody if water got inside. I don't think that I want to take the chance with something this new and risk the possibility of lawsuits.

Gerard: You don't have to worry in the least, Mr. Fox. These pans have been thoroughly tested by the Underwriters Laboratory and found safe for use in the home.

Fox: Is that so? I guess they're all right then.

Narrator: It might appear at this point that the salesperson has Mr. Fox fairly well convinced that he should handle the product. However, a little further pushing is still necessary.

Fox: I really don't think that I ought to take on an additional line at this time. Maybe in a couple of months, I'll consider it.

Gerard: I really don't think that you can afford not to handle it now. With the Christmas season coming, I feel certain that this will be one of your largest selling appliances and probably one of the most profitable. Remember, it is outselling all competitive brands. Let me send you the usual initial order, which should give the product an adequate trial.

QUESTIONS

1. Did Ms. Gerard make the sale? Give reasons for your decision.
2. If you were product manager for the line, would you have your salespeople use this approach? Explain.

20

Distribution and Pricing

Selecting a channel or channels of distribution is of major importance because it may be the determining factor separating success from failure. The method of distribution determines how, where, and when marketing resources are used and directs the flow of products to the user. If this flow is smooth, regular, and adequate, the user is given the opportunity to buy; but if it is irregular and fails to reach potential users at the proper time, the firm is jeopardizing its future.

Pricing, treated later in the chapter, is another major factor determining a firm's success. Unless pricing is directed and managed to reach particular objectives, it is likely to hinder growth and possibly force a firm into bankruptcy.

Choosing the best distribution channels and pricing methods in a complex and changing marketing environment merits careful attention to many factors. Cautions and perhaps experimental approaches may be considered if the firm is permitted this luxury because mistakes can be quickly rectified. Time is usually an essential factor hastening decisions because necessity for moving the product forces a choice or choices of methods. As soon as factual pertinent data are readied, management can begin weighing and deciding. The more adequate the data, the easier will be the decision making.

MAJOR DISTRIBUTION CONSIDERATIONS

Management must consider a number of elements before establishing channels because weakness in distribution may hinder effective performance in other operations. Neglecting or overlooking one phase of distribution may have serious consequences. An inadvertent slip in the beginning may be costly to correct and possibly could bring on discouragement and withdrawal from a market.

Inventories

Inventories are crucial in most distribution systems. Location, size, financing, and timing require careful preparation, continuous monitoring once established, and a responsive sales force to eliminate overstocks or overselling. Few firms are fortunate enough to require no inventories, but even these firms are frequently beset by production irregularities more serious than the problem of handling inventories.

Whether a firm should have a single, regional, or district location for inventories is often a serious consideration. A single location may require smaller total inventory than several locations, but delivery may be slowed and transportation cost increased. Multiple warehouses increase warehousing costs but facilitate distribution. A firm with several plants in various locations may find regional warehouses practical because each plant can send unit loads (truck, carload) to each warehouse at major transportation savings. Large inventories of a seasonal product cannot be prevented, but they may be relieved by immediate shipment to some buyers who are willing to take on the extra storage function, usually for a price concession. Multiple warehousing requires greater inventories which need careful management to prevent excessive quantities in one area and an inadequate supply in another area. It may be impossible to prevent a temporary imbalance in inventory because buyer demand can be erratic. It is unlikely any inventory system can afford a "never out" policy. Such a system would be excessive in cost, physically difficult to maintain, and would ignore human error.

Warehousing

Warehousing may be a simple or relatively complex process. The simplest type would be outside storage such as gravel; a complex type would be cold storage with its variety of temperature controls. Another type would be warehousing narcotics which requires special security, as would warehousing of jewelry, precious metals, furs, and other valuable merchandise.

Warehousing of products to be used for collateral for loans would require special consideration of locations. A similar situation arises in connection with storing products for aging purposes, for tax exemption, for shipment to foreign countries, and other special situations.

A major consideration is single or multiple warehousing. Since storage is a facilitating function, it should be carried out at a minimum cost but within the framework of meeting marketing requirements. If storage fluctuates in quantity or is seasonal, public warehouses may be cheaper than owning them; but if storage is more or less uniform for most of the year, it may be practical for the firm to tie up its own resources in structures. Unavailability of public warehouses may force a firm to build its own.

A firm may shift a major part of its warehousing by selling through distributors who are required to carry a minimum inventory. Intermediate warehousing between the firm and the final buyers may be promoted by consignment selling. Most dealers are willing to carry larger inventories if they are owned by the manufacturer. Opportunities in sharing warehousing may be uncovered through diligent efforts.

Of some importance to marketing is storage of raw material and parts for manufacturing. Inadequate inventories in this sector may increase production time and result in serious finished inventory deficiencies.

Transportation

Transportation costs can vary from an insignificant fraction of the selling price (jewelry) to over half the selling price (coal). Transportation often determines location of manufacturing plants as well as storage facilities. Water transportation, or a combination of water and land transportation, may give substantial savings over land transportation alone. Air transportation may be higher than land delivery but save time and storage costs. Time savings often open new markets. Air transportation may open a higher standard of living (fresh fruits and vegetables to Nome, Alaska).

Transportation costs vary widely depending on size of shipment. Carload rates and truckload rates are far cheaper than smaller shipments. Various ways of packaging and packing may increase or decrease shipping costs. Substantial savings can result by combining shipments with those of another manufacturer. Freight forwarding services can increase speed of shipment, thus reducing time in transit and perhaps permitting smaller inventories. Furniture manufacturers ship uncrated furniture in trucks. Transportation costs increase, but crating costs are eliminated and delivery time is shortened. Careful auditing of freight bills may bring major savings.

A careful study of costs of both inward and outward transportation may be one of the most important tasks before locating a plant. After locating a plant, an important task is comparing different styles of packing (knockdown equipment, special containers, special railroad cars, and trucks) because even a 1 percent savings in transportation can make a significantly different profit for the firm.

Risk

Risk in the channel of distribution can take a number of forms with varying impact on success. The risk of not securing adequate sales outlets, retaining good ones, and adding new ones requires constant vigilance. Adequate company representation is extremely important to the customer, whether a firm sells a common consumer good, an industrial product, or a major purchase item.

One of the major physical risks is protecting goods in the channel, including physical protection as well as protection against obsolescence and contamination. Too large inventories may lead to sluggish movement of merchandise; too small supplies may develop shortages and slacken sales. Large inventories require heavy financing; small inventories may put inordinate pressures on production and force many small production runs rather than large economical ones. An unbalanced inventory may force heavy sales concentration on burdensome stocks.

The many risks of the market, which may not respond to sales efforts and the vagaries of customers, can easily upset plans of orderly distribution. A firm may have to change production, transportation, and channel plans to cope with rapid changes of demand. Predicting market demand in fashion areas is extremely hazardous, and some of the hazards can be mitigated by highly responsive distribution channels.

It is prudent to use insurance companies and other professional risk carriers to shift as much as possible, but there still remain sufficient entrepreneurial and personnel risk to challenge channel operation.[1]

Competence of Sales Force

The sales manager strives to provide a competent sales force that is economical. Restricted funds set an upper quality limit in most firms because channel costs cannot deviate significantly from similar costs of competitors. Whether to use company salespeople extensively or to depend on wholesaler salespeople is often decided on a cost basis. For example, selling through company salespeople to retailers might be more effective in volume than using wholesaler salespeople, but costs force the use of the latter.

Choosing a method of distribution is a major decision since company success is predicated on successful selling. It is common for a firm to make changes in its distribution channel. Changing conditions and the development of new retail outlets force reconsideration of present policies.[2]

Communication with User

The most effective channel of distribution may depend on the importance of communication with the final buyer, who in most instances

---

1. A young man heading a small service corporation was advised to retain the other present owners who secured the work to be performed. As long as these outside sales people had a considerable amount of money invested in the firm, they would be zealous in procuring work for it. Were he to buy their ownership, they might lose incentive to supply him with work, particularly if they could cultivate competitors.

2. One wholesale druggist chose to work with independent drug stores and hospitals primarily with much less emphasis on direct-buying chain drug stores. When discount houses added pharmacies and supermarket chains owned drug stores, this firm had to revise its policies. Another drug wholesaler adopted the policy of selling every outlet it could reach. One major pharmaceutical manufacturer channels its sales through drug wholesalers; other similar manufacturers sell direct to retailers, chains, and wholesalers.

is the user. If little buyer communication is needed after the sale, one type of channel may be suitable; but if a continuous buyer relationship is essential, another channel may be desirable.

If the product is a major purchase requiring installation and servicing, a relationship must be established with each purchaser. If a sale requires intense selling effort but minimum or no follow-up, selling effort must be centered on rapid and effective sales closes that might require highly specialized direct selling. If afterservice is important, the channel may require area service establishments or careful selection of representative wholesalers.

Since the primary job of sales departments is to keep satisfied customers, it is imperative to develop special types of communication to fit particular situations. How often and where salespeople communicate with customers and prospects and how and when customers want to reach them may often dictate the channel a sales manager must use.

SPECIFIC DISTRIBUTION PROBLEMS

After outlining the major considerations which are important in selecting a channel of distribution, management must consider a number of specific problems pertinent to particular selling jobs. Policies may be broadly outlined and deal in generalities, but each sale is specific and deals in practical realities in a particular environment. Some of these problems require individual examination.

Size of Sale

A sales manager with top-notch salespeople making large sales has a different supervision task than one leading a group of ordinary salespeople selling low-priced merchandise supported by heavy advertising.

Major unit sales require careful preparation. There may be technical problems involved, committee buying, demonstrations, bids, pricing variations, and other complicating features. Routine selling requires supervision of routes, handling details, salesperson stimulation, attention to filling orders, handling back orders, settling complaints, and a host of minor operations. Losing a large sale can hurt a firm, while losing a minor sale is merely annoying. The size of sale, either in one large or in many small units, often determines the best distribution channel.

Type of Buyer

Most regular buying is done by professional buyers and purchasing agents. Sometimes a purchasing agent will negotiate a large order for a year's supply to be delivered periodically. He will issue other purchases daily to industrial distributors. Chain store buyers may order in enormous quantity with delivery scheduled to a number of warehouses. Some buyers go to the salesperson's factory to inspect production, or the salesperson will take him to installations showing the product in use.

Committees representing schools and institutions often visit the factory or an installation in another institution. Some buyers insist on bids on certain items which have precise written specifications. Some large sales of raw materials are based on guaranteed prices for certain periods; others have fluctuating prices determined by the market at the time of shipment.

These illustrations are merely suggestive of the thousands of variations and deviations set up by individual buyers. In most instances, the salesperson must conform to the buyer's wishes. New ways of appealing to buyers (packaging, pricing, shipping) often give entry to a new salesperson, who succeeds because of some impressive innovation with evident advantages.

Number of Calls

The marketing channel is governed by the number of customers that must be contacted and the frequency of calls. Infrequent calls require a different number of salespeople than is required for numerous repeat calls or maintaining a close relationship with large customers. If many smaller customers are handled partially by telephone or mail, salespeople can cover more customers without sacrificing effective coverage.

New Company

A new firm may find it expedient to use one specific channel because of the difficulty of penetrating a market. Often, a new firm may have to use wholesalers or other distributors because here is a ready-made channel with access to buyers.

If a new firm is to go direct in selling, or if a well-entrenched firm decides to market a new product, it is possible and perhaps necessary to concentrate the entire selling effort toward one specific objective.

Financing

Strong firms with well-developed marketing departments have sufficient money and talent within the firm to develop proper channels. Any firm, small or large, often is handicapped by inadequate money sources which force it to tailor its distribution effort to what it can afford. Financing distribution is a common problem for new firms and many small firms; yet judicious programming can help them develop gradually, maintaining stability but at some sacrifice in channel effectiveness. A sales manager must guard against saddling the firm with an expensive distribution channel which might be profitable over a long period but could prove disastrous over a short period.

Product Line

A product line may have few or many items. The firm may have an extensive, wide line with each item furnishing satisfactory volume, or it may be made up of a few items with heavy sales and many items with minor sales volume. Some of the items may have large sales but slim profits; some items have large sales with excellent profits; some items sell in small volume but return worthwhile profits. Many items may have irregular sales and low profits but are needed to offer a full assortment.

Unless a firm's product line can support strong individual sales, it would be unwise to use company salespeople. It would be preferable to sell at wholesale to distributors who carry the products of many manufacturers. A company salesperson may have only ten products to offer, while the distributor's salesperson can supply a thousand.

Low Gross Margin Products

Some firms' products command low gross margins. These margins are caused by competitive factors, loss leaders, service items, convenience, or other reasons. Sometimes a competitor will have one or more items as by-products in his manufacture and will unload them at low prices. Sometimes cloth manufacturers dump excessive inventories that upset regular profit margins.

Whatever the cause for low margins, the influence of this factor must be considered in using a channel of distribution. The sales manager must choose the best channel within his budget. Even though a better one is available, its cost may be prohibitive. The sales manager must avoid choosing an inferior channel just because it costs less; inferior performance could jeopardize the life of the firm.

Competitive Factors

Most firms face vigorous competition that forces them to maximize the use of scarce resources in order to survive. Frequently, unprofitable firms become profitable through vigorous cost-cutting efforts. Careless management will acquire expenses that subtly creep in and grow almost unnoticed.

Even more dangerous is a sales operation which continues unchanged while competition discovers new ways of distribution that are more economical. The sales manager must watch that channel costs do not increase faster than competition allows and at the same time assess alternative approaches that permit the firm to hold or lower sales costs without impairing efficiency.

CHANNEL MIDDLEMEN

A channel middleman moves products from the producer to the consumer. In a broad sense, he controls or assists in all the activities, such as transferring titles to merchandise, physical movement, financing, and carrying inventories.

The manufacturer may have his own sales department to handle the entire process to the retailer or consumer; the manufacturer may be content to produce, but depend on the retailer to handle channel activities; the manufacturer and retailer may be content to handle their own functions and hire professional middlemen to perform the major channel activities.

Direct to User or Retailer

The most effective, but possibly the most expensive, channel is selling direct to the final buyer. Establishing a sales force to make these sales is costly primarily because each sale must have sufficient margin to cover direct salespeople service. This channel is usually the best one if the cost factor can be sustained.

Direct selling to retailers and to industrial buyers is profitable when sales are large and/or gross margins are generous. Small sales and low margin sales will not cover direct selling costs plus other marketing costs. Direct house-to-house selling is used by some firms, but their total marketing costs are high.

Selling directly to industrial users is common because these sales are large, require extensive personal sales attention, and carry gross margins sufficient to cover the high costs.

Missionary Salespeople

A missionary salesperson is a special case in direct selling. His purposes are to introduce a product to customers, secure initial orders, and open up a new territory. Often he turns these orders over to a wholesaler to fill and then to handle the account on repeat orders.

Even with direct selling salespeople, it is not uncommon to use special, or missionary, salespeople in established territories to introduce a new product or to secure new customers whom the regular salesperson has failed to reach. This procedure is expensive; but it can be justified because it is a single, not a recurring, expense.

Broker, Manufacturer's Agent, Sales Agent

A *broker* is an agent middleman who brings sellers and buyers together to consummate a sale. He does not take title or finance any transaction. He is paid a commission by the seller or the buyer (but not both), depending on the one who asked for his services. The broker is paid a commission for a sale; if there is no sale, the broker receives no commission.

A firm may find a broker useful when it has no sales force, when sales are irregular, when sales representation is needed only part of the year, when there is no regular continuing relationship with buyers, or when special occasions require the sale of special or large quantities of merchandise. A special case is the food broker who may have continuous representation with a supplier, in which case the broker really becomes a manufacturer's agent.

A *manufacturer's agent* is an agent middleman representing several manufacturers in a particular geographic territory. He does not take title to the merchandise he sells; he usually does not handle the merchandise; he sells at prices specified by his principals; he is paid a sales commission; he pays his own traveling expenses.

The manufacturer's agent, also called a manufacturer's representative or sometimes a sales representative, usually represents several manufacturers of noncompeting lines that are generally sold to the same buyers. Prices might vary between two hundred dollars to a thousand dollars, although there are numerous exceptions below and above these prices.

A manufacturer may find the use of a manufacturer's agent advantageous because of low selling cost, minimum costs during periods of weak sales, and no travel expenses. A well-established manufacturer's agent can gain immediate entry to many important buyers and create buyer confidence in the product.

A manufacturer has less control over a manufacturer's agent and may find it hard to get adequate representation in a territory. Just because a manufacturer's agent takes on a line does not automatically insure distribution. He may be lazy, indifferent to company wishes, or a poor salesperson. He may take on a line of products; but if he finds it difficult to sell, he may give it little attention, preferring to spend his time on other manufacturer's products which he finds easier to sell or yield him greater commissions.

A *sales agent* is a middleman who takes the entire responsibility of selling a manufacturer's output. He becomes in essence the manufacturer's marketing force, although not an employee. He may represent several manufacturers and hire salespeople to assist in selling. He does not take title and is paid by commissions.

The sales agent is more commonly used in some areas than others. If a manufacturer fits one of these areas, he might investigate the use of this middleman since it relieves him of all selling. However, a weak sales agent can be disastrous, while a strong one might be better than the manufacturer's own sales force. A strong sales agent aids not only in selling but also in determining what to produce; a dictatorial agent may force the producer into areas he dislikes but cannot resist.

Wholesaler, Jobber, Distributor

Wholesaler, jobber, and distributor are names often used interchangeably. In drugs, the title is wholesaler; in hardware, it may be wholesaler or jobber; in sales to industrial buyers, it may be distributor. All are merchant middlemen who buy, inventory, sell, and deliver merchandise. In number more than a quarter million, these entrepreneurs move enormous quantities of merchandise and farm products from hundreds of thousands of producers to millions of retail stores, commercial, and industrial users.

Firms may depend wholly on this channel approach; firms with a wide line of products, most of which are sold through their own sales force, may move parts of their lines through these middlemen. Some firms with direct selling sales forces use merchant middlemen concurrently; for often the salesperson from a manufacturer can call infrequently, but the wholesaler's salesperson makes calls weekly or even more often.

Many services performed by wholesalers are inviting to the manufacturer. These services include buffer stocks of merchandise which may represent hundreds of thousands or even millions of dollars to a large manufacturer; steady, frequent, and quality representation to millions of retailers, industrial establishments, and commercial and service users; assistance to retailers to keep them strong; expert financing; repair and replacement services; specialized services peculiar to each type of product which promote sales and facilitate end use.

The two major channels of distribution are through the manufacturer's own sales force or through wholesalers. When a manufacturer uses the wholesaler (merchant middleman) route, he still may have a sales force selling to wholesalers, but this would be a much smaller number of salespeople than if he were selling direct to retailers and industrial users. For example, a manufacturer could reach a hundred thousand retailers and other major buyers by selling to two thousand wholesalers.

CHOOSING A CHANNEL OF DISTRIBUTION

In choosing a channel, a manufacturer must decide: (1) Can he handle the channel function best himself? (2) Is it better to use channel professionals in the distribution function? (3) Should he use a combination of his own salespeople plus professional channel people? One cannot say arbitrarily that one method is better than another but rather that under a firm's particular circumstances one method appears better than other methods.

What the Firm Wants

If management intends to use its own sales force almost entirely, it must cope with the problems of hiring, training, compensating, and supervising salespeople and supporting the sales force with excellent administration. Many companies have used this approach and have been successful. For a market-oriented and financially strong company, this method may prove most effective; for a production-oriented company, this method may be less inviting. Thousands of firms superior in production have struggled with their marketing efforts, and their success has been marginal; other firms have performed marketing functions superbly but have struggled with production; the firms that handle both production and marketing successfully are almost always successful. Many firms with long-term success have superior research and development capacity.

The company that hopes to use channel middlemen must decide what type of end distribution it is seeking. If it wants its products in every possible retail outlet, it must depend on thousands of wholesalers. For example, a product such as toothpaste would go through food wholesalers, drug wholesalers, sundry wholesalers, general merchandise wholesalers, and perhaps others; cotton gloves might go through all the preceding wholesalers plus hardware wholesalers, rack jobbers, and soft-goods wholesalers.

Many of the products sold in hundreds of thousands of outlets are pulled through the channels by extensive advertising. Some of the products are convenience goods which are impulse items; others may be minor specialty items which are not too important but must be carried by retailers.

Selective distribution implies using a select few of the many middlemen available. At the retail level, prestige is often attached to the few outlets chosen. At the wholesale level, a manufacturer hopes to secure better coverage from carefully selecting representatives than by selling to everyone interested. The middlemen selected know they have been selected carefully and are more likely to do a better job.

Exclusive distribution between a manufacturer and wholesaler is probably the most favorable of arrangements to the wholesaler, providing he is prepared to accept the responsibility. Since the wholesaler has no competition from other representatives, the manufacturer expects him to do an outstanding performance. Exclusive distribution permits a close manufacturer-wholesaler relationship and leads to careful attention and sensitive response to manufacturer needs.

What Middlemen Are Available

A new firm may wish to secure adequate representation through carefully chosen wholesalers only to find that the best wholesalers already are handling top-competing lines and are reluctant to take a new-comer. Firms in major lines, such as household appliances, have discovered the best outlets are tied to strong competitors and the only distributors available are not as strong or well known as the more successful ones.

Some distributors may already handle several competing lines and will not pick up a new line unless a strong demand exists. Most middlemen are happy to handle a winner, but are reluctant to spend much effort to help a firm achieve a strong demand for its product.

To gain adequate distribution in a territory, a firm may have to set up a new outlet—help a new distributor get started to represent their firm and perhaps help the distributor obtain additional lines complementary to their product.

Many wholesalers may wish to handle a firm's products, but some are very small (a wholesaler can have one or two employees with sales of $100,000 a year or at the other extreme a wholesaler has several hundred employees with sales in millions of dollars each year) and give little help; some may not be effective operators and consequently generate very small sales; and some may be disinterested and consequently are of minimum help.

Occasionally a firm may find another manufacturer with a strong sales force who is willing to sell the firm's product as a complementary line. This sort of piggyback arrangement can be helpful to a firm commencing operation and may continue to be a favorable distribution method to both firms. The new firm gets a ready-made distribution channel; the other firm reduces its sales costs through sharing salespeople's time.

What the Firm Can Afford

A sales manager may have a choice as to channel of distribution. His choice may be the most logical, but the cost may be prohibitive. Then a compromise distribution arrangement will be the ultimate decision based on company finances and what can be secured.

Many firms have started small with limited means and depended on someone else to sell and distribute their products. Some firms have prospered and remained with the original distribution system because it is satisfactory; others, once they have become established, have changed to what they feel is a more promising system.

Changing from one group of distributors to another type of distribution may cause hard feelings because the ones who aided in a firm's growth and success are summarily dropped. However unhappy such changes are, they become inevitable and are common in the business world. This detachment between a firm's executives and its distributors may grow as time retires the original group of executives and younger people appear.

Some firms may find that using more than one channel of distribution simultaneously is advantageous. A channel that is adequate in one period may become inadequate later because of changes in the distribution pattern, changes in the economy, changes in size of producer and/or distributor, and often changes in thinking by the principals. Many of these changes are made possible because of increased financial resources, permitting greater flexibility.

PRICING STRATEGY

Correct pricing of a firm's product can give effective competition in the struggle for the buyer's dollar. Adequate pricing projects profitable operation. Pricing from a social viewpoint represents a balance of satisfactions to both producer and consumer, making it advantageous to both.

Pricing is a two-edged tool responsive to the needs of buyer and seller. While it may seem to be only in the interests of the producer to establish price, management must recognize the equal importance of pricing so that as many people as possible are able to buy. Such an approach may not maximize profit in the short run, but it may maximize consumer satisfaction and over time prove most profitable to the seller.

A firm seldom has the luxury of price freedom. Its decisions usually cannot be unilateral because of competitive pressures, both direct and indirect; government surveillance; public opinion; imports; and consumer resistance and apathy. For example, if price is too high, a number of potential customers will dismiss the thought of buying because the product is out of their price range. This feeling affects most people, whether it pertains to houses, cars, clothing, furniture, or even industrial machinery and equipment. A firm must price within its environment. Unless the product or service is distinctly unique, it will be subject to everyday business situations that will strongly affect its marketing acceptance.

PRICING OBJECTIVES

The pricing concept must reflect the importance of price in a firm's success. Price may be determined for one objective or several; it may have only one major objective; it may have an immediate objective; it may have a series of objectives; it may have an immediate survival plus a long-term objective. To understand a number of these objectives requires careful analysis.

Enter a Market

A new product enters a market for the first time. Price may be an entry factor only insofar as it may discourage or encourage purchase of this particular product rather than other products.

A new product may be so marginal to users that they will buy only when the price is attractive. A relatively high price can be used if a prestige factor can be created or if vigorous promotion will increase sales. There may be a strong desire to use high introductory pricing to recover high beginning costs. Sometimes a firm will use a low price to break into the market. It is difficult, if not impossible, to bring in a new product similar to others at a price above that of well-established competing prices.

If a market is small or has certain peculiarities, a particular pricing approach may be superior to another where a market is large. A product with a short-term life cycle would be priced differently than a staple product. The number of special conditions influencing price vary from one situation to another, but management should determine what conditions are present and then use price as one factor in market entry.

Rapid Market Penetration

If rapid market penetration is desired, pricing can be used to expedite this approach. A new product may be a fad and consequently short-lived. It may call for a relatively high price, allowing generous profit margins.

The return on a pharmaceutical may be over a long or short period, depending on how useful it is, how long it may last, how rapidly competition enters, and how long before a superior product appears. Often, research and development is a major cost and a firm expects to recover all such costs over a definite time period. Therefore, the selling price may have little relationship to its present production cost.

Gradual Market Development

A conservative pricing approach is used to introduce a product into a market gradually. It is not necessary to have a lower price than competition since other means may be used to push the product. As long as price is not out of line with competing products, it will not have a pronounced effect.

If the price is higher than competition, the product must be sold on superior qualities by using demonstrations, promotions, heavy advertising, and personal selling. If the product is distinctive and possesses advantages over similar products, these advantages must be dramatized or brought out forcefully to attract attention. Then a price differential may be less important than product features.

If a new product must develop a market, it is necessary to create primary demand, which may be a slow process. Unless it is a fad or has some particularly appealing feature, it is not likely to sell rapidly.

Fight Competition

When a product lacks distinctive features that set it apart in the buyer's eyes, it is subject to price competition. Some of this price competition may be overcome partially by various marketing strategies, but it is unlikely that a product can overcome significant price disadvantages.

Competitive price effects may vary depending on the nature of the product. If it is a repeat-purchase convenience product, small price variations may be significant; if buyers are brand conscious, price may have a lesser effect. If a product becomes a major, infrequent purchase, minor price variations can be overcome by salesmanship; but even such products must be price justified when purchased by industry.

Vigorous price competition tends to make a product unprofitable. Some manufacturers try to sidestep this problem by retaining a normal price on their regular line and then offering a "fighting" brand which is priced lower. Such a brand presumably is lower in quality and is intended to meet the demand of the very price-conscious customer and hopefully relieve the pressure on the better-known, widely advertised national brand.

Maintain Market Position

A firm's product may have reached a strong, or even a dominating, position in the market. Many such products, while satisfactory, do not possess characteristics that are outstanding and may have lukewarm customer loyalty. Then sales are maintained by aggressive promotion, product availability, and attractive pricing.

Survival

When price is the most significant factor promoting product success, it must be reckoned with at all times. Many firms forced out of business by rugged competition could have survived by a more realistic price control.

A firm with a number of products may have to decide whether certain items in the line are worth keeping. Sometimes immediate profitability would dictate dropping a particular product, but the importance of having a full line assists in merchandising related products. Survival pricing may be temporary because of price war, competitor inventory dumping, or a desperate attempt of a competitor to remain alive.

Complete a Product Line

A company may wish to introduce a new item to complete a product line but experience difficulty in gaining acceptance because of numerous strong competitors. Seldom can a company introduce a new product and expect it to be as sought after as its most successful product.

The new product may be moderately successful but boost the older products to greater success. Its introduction may allow the firm to supply present buyers completely, thus shutting out competition. Nevertheless, it would be difficult to justify a new product unless it makes a significant contribution; this can happen if the price fits the market. A company should not keep an inferior new product to fill in a product line.

Spread Overhead

A manufacturer may be able to use waste material or by-products to make another product which in itself may not be profitable but produces enough revenue above direct costs to absorb considerable overhead. Idle equipment might be utilized in manufacturing to produce marginally profitable products that would cover some overhead. Contract manufacturing for other firms might help in absorbing overhead costs.

Equipment and Supplies

It is common to price equipment, replacement parts, and supplies for machinery installations at profitable levels. Once a firm has installed equipment, it is likely to buy accessories and supplies for that installation from the seller of the equipment. In numerous instances, a firm may receive minimum return on its machinery and depend on other sales for the profit.

A piece of equipment that uses large amounts of material can be sold at a low price, and the profit will depend on supplies. For example, supplying ink, stencils, and special paper for an office duplicating machine can be very profitable; supplying rivets for a riveting machine is lucrative. If a firm is the sole or dominant supplier of replacement parts, the price is set to its advantage.

Short-run Pricing

Over a short period of time, it may be necessary to obtain as much revenue as possible because the public will demand the product briefly and then abandon it for something else. Under these circumstances, a high price is logical as long as price does not hinder sales. The purpose is to balance various prices against anticipated sales volumes, using the one that maximizes profit. It is not uncommon to use a high price which may capture a very profitable segment of the market and never bother to penetrate the market in depth. This approach would appeal to the manufacturer with limited resources. Another situation involving short-period pricing revolves around excessive inventories. Frequently, buyers receive special inducements to relieve a manufacturer of large inventories.

A firm desperately needing business will often take jobs at low prices just to keep the factory in operation. Some firms give favorable prices to buyers who are willing to wait for delivery and to buyers who give orders and pay for merchandise in advance of shipment.

Long-range Pricing

A stable price over a longer period of time typifies long-run pricing. This pricing may incorporate brief periods of rapid price fluctuation, but the tendency is toward stable prices. Even long-range pricing may embody many minor price changes (even daily changes) to meet market conditions.

A long-range price is one that allows a manufacturer a profit as long as he is competitive. Undoubtedly, there are many long-range prices that permit excessive profits because of peculiar circumstances, but usually competition tends to stabilize price at a level where success demands keen effort.

Long-range pricing tends toward stability but does vary. As more efficient production develops, prices may decrease. Vicious competition may erode prices and leave companies precariously balanced at a minimum profit position or even a loss position for long periods. Rising costs of materials and manufacturing may signal a series of price increases, which do not disturb the stable pricing structure.

PRICING METHODS AND APPROACHES

There are a number of pricing methods used to determine both regular and special prices. Pricing methods vary because products differ, competition is not uniform, market and geographic differences exist, demand differs in different markets, a certain degree of testing and experimentation may occur, company leadership differs, and government intervention occurs.[3]

Pricing methods evolve to fit buyers, to fit sellers, to fit peculiar conditions, to meet particular situations, and often to set up a different approach one step ahead of competition. Management should not regard pricing methods as fixed. Time and ingenuity will bring new methods as well as variations of old methods that are better suited for present needs.[4]

Pricing specials are used to reach new buyers, to introduce new

---

3. In one industry, the leading manufacturer determined the price. Small competitors were permitted to shade prices to get a small share of the market, but they were careful not to price so as to raise the wrath of the big company.

4. For pricing under inflation, see "Pricing Strategy in an Inflation Economy," *Business Week*. (April 6, 1974), 43–49.

products, and/or to convert users of competitive products. The "cents off" package is common in grocery stores, even though the buyer seldom knows what the real price difference is. The "extra merchandise," "two-for-one," "one-cent sale," and similar methods are effective ways of stimulating sales.

Manufacturers often use extra merchandise as an inducement for a retailer to buy. For example, if the retailer buys a dozen cases, he will get an extra case free. This does not disturb the basic price for a dozen cases. Sometimes a retailer will be offered a free premium with a large purchase. Some firms regularly make tie-in sales of two different items. The price may be attractive, but the overall sale is larger and more profitable. Sometimes, tie-in sales are used for slow-selling items; usually there is a price reduction involved.

The use of coupons as a special pricing device is a common approach. A coupon may be mailed or given away in stores, entitling the holder to buy a product at a special price. Frequently a coupon may be attached to the box or placed inside the box, enabling the user to obtain a second box at a reduced price. Occasionally, the coupon within a box may promote a new product.

Cost

Most companies expect to price a product to recover all costs and make a profit, but there are short periods when this may not be true and longer periods when some products do not carry their share of the cost burden. In these situations, more profitable items must carry the less profitable ones.

Pricing on the cost approach may be developed from several sets of cost data. One common way is to consider costs under two categories, (1) direct or variable costs and (2) indirect or fixed costs (overhead). *Direct costs* include all costs that arise as a result of manufacturing; *indirect costs* are those that go on whether or not there is physical production and sales.[5]

Commonly, labor and material are regarded as direct costs. Other manufacturing costs are overhead costs. Salespeople costs would be direct costs in marketing, while supervision and home office could be considered administrative overhead.

Beginning manufacturers often fail to realize how small direct costs are in relationship to retail selling price. They can hardly believe that the labor and material used in making a product characteristically vary between 10 to 25 percent of the retail price. For example, for an item retailing at $5, the actual material and labor costs in making the item would probably be something less than $1.25. Consequently,

---

5. A third division of semivariable costs is sometimes used. To gain an understanding of the costing process, it is necessary to study cost accounting books which detail cost divisions and explain how they are derived and developed.

management may price their product too low and end up in bankruptcy.

Many operations of a firm go on regardless of how much is manufactured and how much is sold. These costs are known as indirect, or overhead, costs and must be included in price. Most of these ongoing costs are relatively constant, unlike direct costs which fluctuate with production. The more items produced, the smaller these fixed costs are per unit. Therefore, it is advantageous to make and sell as many units as possible. In practice, management forecasts the probable production for the coming year, assigns to each item its share of direct and indirect costs, adds something for profit, and comes up with a manufacturer's selling price.

If all goes well, this number of items is produced and sold; and at the end of the year, the company has a profit. If sales and production fail to reach the forecasted quantity, a loss is incurred. Although direct costs vary directly with production, indirect costs are relatively fixed; and at the end of the year the firm is saddled by unabsorbed fixed costs which theoretically were assigned to units which were never produced. In a happier situation when production and sales exceed the forecast, the firm is in a very profitable position. Not only does it make its regular profit on the forecasted quantity, but it makes a large profit on the excess produced. This extra production absorbs its direct costs, but there are no indirect costs since they were absorbed by the forecasted production.

Management should understand the concept of the break-even point. Examine the following information for one year.

Product A

Selling price	$5
Direct cost	2
Remainder for overhead	$3

For each unit sold at $5, there is $3 to cover indirect costs (fixed costs). Fixed costs for the coming year have been estimated at $2,700,000. Before any profit for the year is received, these fixed costs must be covered. Since there is $3 per unit sale available, divide $\frac{\$2,700,000}{\$3} = 900,000$ units. For 900,000 units, all revenue from sales goes to direct and indirect costs. After this number has been sold, $3 of every unit sales is profit. The following examples indicate profits at different sales levels.

Forecasted sales for year (1,000,000 units)		$5,000,000
Direct costs (variable)	$2,000,000	
Estimated indirect costs (fixed)	2,700,000	
Total cost		4,700,000
Profit		$ 300,000

Sales for year (900,000 units)		$4,500,000
Direct costs (variable)	$1,800,000	
Indirect costs (fixed)	2,700,000	
Total cost		4,500,000
Profit		0

A 10 percent decrease in sales below forecast results in 100 percent decrease in profits.

Sales for year (1,100,000 units)		$5,500,000
Direct costs (variable)	$2,200,000	
Indirect costs (fixed)	2,700,000	
Total cost		4,900,000
Profit		$ 600,000

A 10 percent increase in sales above forecast results in a 100 percent increase in profits. Figure 20–1 illustrates a high break-even point of a similar manufacturer.

Profit for periods less than a year may be calculated by dividing the forecast into monthly or quarterly figures and assigning that period's share of overhead accordingly. If sales are uneven throughout the year, it would be logical to assign overhead proportionately to sales. For example, if the third quarter had half the year's sales, it would be fair to apportion half of overhead to this quarter. If profits are computed on a yearly basis, no real profit situation is reached for the year until fixed costs have been recovered. After that, the profit situation improves rapidly since only variable costs are incurred.

In some firms fixed costs are at a high level and variable costs are low (fixed costs 70 percent, variable costs 30 percent); but the reverse is true in other firms (fixed costs 35 percent, variable costs 65 percent). When fixed costs are high, small decreases in sales can be dangerous.

A high level of fixed costs demands a high level of operation or high prices, which may not be feasible. To maintain a strong sales position, the sales manager must operate aggressively, marshalling his sales staff to consistently superior performance and using sales promotion activities wisely and effectively. Examples of high fixed cost firms are utilities—gas, electricity, telephone—and railroads. Low fixed cost operations have less equipment and high variable costs—labor and material; service industries are an example.

Competitive Pricing

Many products made by different firms are so similar that the buyer is unwilling to pay a premium for any different brand. Usually he chooses the one with the lowest price. Minor price differentials may have little effect, but no one of these products can stray far from the present normal price. Household detergents, gasoline, bread, and many other similar products illustrate this fact. Even automobile manufacturers price similar models within a few dollars.

Figure 20–1
Break-even Chart

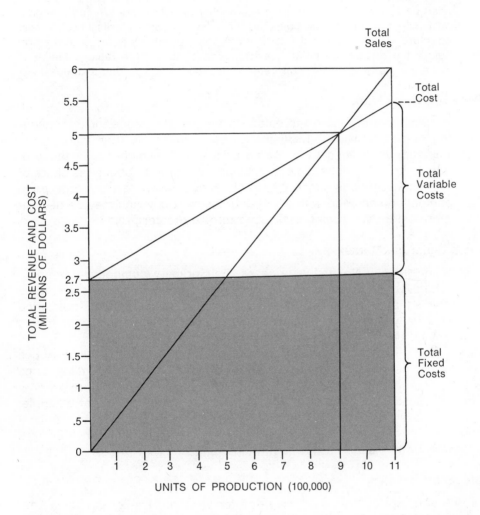

Note: Total sales equals total revenue. Total cost combines variable and fixed costs. Where the two lines intersect is the break-even point. This point is at 900,000 production units of sales, which give a total revenue of $5,000,000. The area between these two lines beyond the break-even point is profit. The time period is one year. Since the break-even point is high, this firm might attempt to raise prices or increase productivity. Profit on forecasted sales of 1,000,000 units for the year would be narrow. This illustration may approximate a real situation if one assumes that fixed costs remain constant at all levels of operation, variable costs continue the same over the period (overtime would vary the cost), price does not vary, and the product mix remains unchanged. Any variations affecting these assumptions would alter the break-even point. It is useful to determine when profit appears in a selected time period.

This illustration and the preceding arithmetical ones are break-even points used by people in business to indicate where profits start. When the economist uses the break-even point, he incorporates some profits into the cost structure. In the economist's break-even point, profit has accrued to the firm before the break-even point; but it increases much more rapidly after that. For more thorough discussion, refer to economics and pricing textbooks.

Price Above the Market

A manufacturer may try to establish his brand as superior to competing brands by wide advertising and promotion. He tries to reinforce this superiority idea by charging prices slightly higher than those of competitors. He depends on consumer following to obtain his share of the market. If he is successful in his efforts, he will avoid strong price competition and end with a larger gross margin which may be used in more extensive promotion or used to give greater profits.

Price Under the Market

Some firms prefer using price as their primary competitive weapon. Whatever the prevailing price is, they will have a slightly lower price. This situation is typified by private brand gasoline outlets. Their price is usually one or two cents below national brand prices.[6] In foods, private brand goods sell for less than national brands.

Some national brands try consistently to be below prevailing prices of competition. It is not unknown for a firm to package identical items in two or three different packages and sell each for a different price. Frequently, the channel of distribution determines price. For example, it is easy to find three different restaurants serving almost identical food at three different prices. But while all satisfy hunger, there are many other features that justify charging different prices.

Single-price Policy

A single-price policy is one price for an entire line or part of a line. Some stores sell all neckties at one price. Some stores have clearance sales—all dresses previously marked from $19.95 to $59.95 might be only $15.00. Restaurants feature buffet meals at one price regardless of what or how much a person eats.

---

6. This practice does not necessarily occur in unusual markets where there is scarcity in supply or some other disturbing factor.

One-price Policy

A one-price policy gives the identical price to each class of buyer. If one buyer pays $1 for a particular item, all buyers must pay $1. If the same item is sold for ninety cents in dozen lots, all buyers pay that price. This approach avoids discrimination as well as government laws forbidding discrimination. It eliminates price discussion in retail stores since there is no price deviation.[7] All customers know they are treated alike.

Discount Policies

Pricing is easier when a list price or a suggested retail price is used. Discounts are given from this price for quantity purchases, preseason delivery, early payment, and other variations. Also, there are various position or functional discounts for retailers, wholesalers, and distribution. For example, a discount of 40, 20, and 2 means that if the retail customers pay $1, the retailer pays 40 percent less, or 60 cents [$1.00 − (40% × $1.00)]. The wholesaler pays 48 cents [$0.60 − (20% × $0.60)] plus 2 percent cash discount on the forty-eight cents. Note that in a chain discount each discount is applied to a lesser base figure.

Single discount

Some firms use only one discount from a list price. In sales to industrial buyers, the list price may be used for one unit, a discount off list for one dozen units, and no additional discounts for greater quantity except perhaps a cash discount. Some firms have a net price without any trade discount but do allow a cash discount.

Cumulative discount

A *cumulative discount* is a quantity discount based on a series of sales. Thus, if a retailer makes a number of purchases from a supplier, the quantity discount is applied to the total sales for a period.

For example, if one buyer made a single purchase of one hundred units in one month, he would be entitled to the same discount as the buyer who made ten purchases of ten units in the same month. The purpose of cumulative discounts is to tie the buyer to one supplier rather than scattering his smaller purchases among a number of suppliers. Cumulative discount helps build relationships between retailer and supplier. It is helpful to the route person (bread, milk) who makes frequent regular calls.

Cumulative discounts can be used in industrial buying to justify larger discounts for major customers. Often one customer buys one-fourth or more of a firm's production. Cumulative discount does not

---

7. There can be price deviation on damaged or soiled merchandise or out-of-fashion goods. Other special situations may cause price variations.

refer to the firm which places one major order a year but takes partial deliveries of that order throughout the year.

Cash discount

Cash discounts are given for prompt payment. They are common in the industrial and commercial fields, but not customary in retail sales. Retail sales are commonly net sales with interest charges added for late payment.

Cash discounts vary from industry to industry. A common discount structure is 2/10, n/30. This structure means that a 2 percent discount is given if the invoice is paid in ten days; otherwise the whole invoice amount becomes due in thirty days. Firms cannot afford to ignore a 2 percent cash discount since it amounts to 36 percent simple interest in a year (30 days − 10 days = 20 days extra allowed if you fail to take the discount. 360 days ÷ by 20 days equals 18 twenty-day intervals. 18 × 2% = 36%.)

Some industries give cash discounts of 5/10 or 6/10. Such cash discounts are exorbitant and really become disguised trade discounts. Firms desperately in need of money would be able to factor their accounts receivable for less.[8]

Trade-in

The trade-in of an older piece of equipment on a new one affects price materially. Often, sales are determined by the trade-in offer. Such offers are flexible and often governed by how "hungry" the seller is.

Trade-in of used machinery and equipment is common in buying new equipment. Imaginative sellers often make a sale by taking unlike old equipment in trade (a used car on a new boat). A trade-in is often used as down payment on the new purchase. The balance is frequently financed.

Leasing

Leasing equipment is growing each year. This method permits the user to charge leasing cost to current expenses. Leasing permits use of equipment a buyer could not otherwise secure because he lacked finances. Many leases are negotiated with the provision that lease payments can be applied to the purchase of the equipment later.

Geographical Pricing

Price is influenced by distance because of additional freight. One area may be more competitive than another, and prices are shaded

---

8. Factoring is a financial transaction whereby the seller receives his money immediately by selling his accounts receivable to a finance firm. There is a financial cost involved. A somewhat different procedure is to borrow money by pledging accounts receivable as collateral.

accordingly. Some price variation may occur because of the channel of distribution used in a particular area.

Peculiar conditions within an area may invite different pricing. For example, heavy sales concentrations within a small area may justify price reductions while wide sales dispersal in another area will call for increased pricing. A few large buyers may dictate a price structure for one area quite different from another area with numerous small buyers. Variations in terrain, climate, transportation, and type of industry could be reasons for justifying price ranges and variations.

Negotiated Pricing

Many prices are negotiated according to current prices of material and labor, escalator provisions if a longer period is involved, present order backlog of firm, extent of competition, and other factors. Some companies are unable to quote a job accurately and refuse to give an exact amount because they cannot foresee contingencies.

Sometimes it is to the advantage of the buyer to arrange an indeterminate price on a major purchase, preferring to work out arrangements on a continuing basis. Otherwise, because of uncertainties involved, a bidder would give an unnecessarily high price to combat unforeseen contingencies.[9]

One type of negotiated pricing requires the buyers to pay all costs and give the supplier a fixed fee based on a percentage of cost as his profit.

An advantageous price is often negotiated when a buyer gives an order three or six months in advance of delivery, when he accepts delivery and pays for merchandise in advance of need, or when he places an order giving a wide latitude in delivery time.

Combination Pricing

Combination pricing covers a wide arrangement of prices which may be modified or changed to meet specific contingenices.

One type of pricing is to accept an order for a year's supply to be delivered monthly. At the time of the order, a firm price would be given up to three months; succeeding prices would be governed by the current costs of material and labor.

Another pricing method may contain a firm price for all costs except material. The total price each month would be determined by the current price of raw material. This type of pricing is used by companies where raw material is a major portion of the final price, for example, where the raw material involves precious metals.

---

9. Two situations may develop in bid pricing. (1) The bidder is uncertain of what is involved and bids high. (2) The bidder needs business desperately, bids low, gets the job, and finds he cannot fulfill it. This can explain widely varying bids. In construction, most quotations that are accepted require a performance bond guaranteeing completion of the project.

The farmer may sell his products at a combination of prices depending on the end use of the product. For example, milk price is determined by its use for whole milk consumption, ice cream, butter, evaporated milk, and dried milk; fruit price is determined by its use as consumption of fresh fruit, canning, freezing, or drying. Fruit may be contracted in advance with specific prices for each grade, but the quantity in each grade is indeterminate.[10]

LEGAL PRICING RESTRAINTS

Government has entered pricing in a number of areas, restraining pricing freedom and forcing firms to operate under particular guidelines. Among the important laws affecting pricing are the Sherman Antitrust Act, the Clayton Act, the Federal Trade Commission Act, the Robinson-Patman Act with its various amendments, the fair trade laws, the unfair trade practice acts, antidumping laws, and many others. Rigorous treatment of these laws is available in marketing literature; this text contains some guidelines which should alert the sales manager to pursue this subject in greater detail as need dictates.

Price Discrimination

Serious abuses crept into pricing structures, favoring some buyers but discriminating against others. Some firms received favorite treatment and were able to compete fiercely against less favored competitors. To overcome this imbalance, the federal and sometimes state and local governments passed measures to restrict this type of pricing.

Price equality exists within the law when all similar buyers, wholesales, retailers, industrials, are given similar terms. For example, each wholesaler would pay the same for one unit, for a dozen, a gross, a truckload, or a carload. Some restrictions may govern large discounts on large quantities when such discounts are unrealistic.

Functional discounts are legal. For example, the retailer pays less than the consumer; the wholesaler frequently pays less than the retailer. Such discounts are legitimate because they recognize the particular service performed by each middleman. There may be other price concessions for preseason orders, flexible delivery dates, reduced prices through early payment, and other inducements which are proper. The reason for quantity or other discounts is to realize money savings because the buyer relieves the manufacturer of certain costs. Beyond this point, price concessions are deemed unrea-

---

10. A flower grower sells his carnations each week to regular outlets at agreed prices. In order to maintain an adequate supply, he usually ends with a surplus. He sells these extra carnations at a small fraction of his regular price through another channel of distribution. This makes it possible, at times, to buy quality carnations from street vendors at less than half the price charged by regular outlets.

sonable. Advertising allowances by the manufacturer to the retailer are quite common but are subject to abuse. Often a large buyer receives a considerable monetary allowance for special-featured advertising. This same consideration is not offered to many other retailers, particularly smaller ones.[11] While governments are against discrimination in general, they are particularly zealous in protecting small firms from being abused because of their inability to hold their own against large competitors.

Full-line Forcing

Many firms manufacturing a full line of some type of equipment or supplies try to compel their dealers to stock their entire line and sometimes forbid the dealer to handle competitive lines. This is enforced by threatening to withdraw their entire line. Such demands have evoked criticism and led to legal restraints forbidding suppliers to use such tactics. One way some manufacturers have secured more effective distribution control is through consignment sales. However, a manufacturer needs strong financial resources to implement this approach. While the manufacturer is anxious to sell his entire line, retailers may be reluctant to handle some items because they are less attractive and salable than competing items.

Illegal Combinations

It is illegal for firms to agree to identical prices. When several firms bid on hundreds of tons of material (salt for city streets) to the exact fraction of a penny per ton, it is hard to maintain there is no collusion. Pricing restrictions are involved when firms agree to operate in exclusive territories and do not invade another firm's territory (utilities and other monopolistic enterprises are excepted since they have prices regulated by government).

The public objects to a firm's placing orders with subsidiaries and arbitrarily shutting out competitors who have no chance to get this business. Large conglomerate corporations are almost able to control major markets and exclude competition because a conglomerate may operate in many areas. For example, a large conglomerate may own a nationwide bus line which rides on tires produced by one subsidiary; buys gasoline, oil, and other automotive products from another subsidiary; feeds its bus passengers in restaurants controlled by another subsidiary; arranges recreational travel on its buses through its own

---

11. The same per unit allowance for advertising is meaningless to the small retailer who sells one suit a week while his competitor sells a hundred or to the grocer who sells a dozen pounds of coffee a week while a large competitor sells thousands of pounds. For example, the grocer selling ten pounds of a particular brand of coffee a week with a penny a pound advertising allowance gets ten cents to advertise the coffee. The large competitor with sales of 100,000 pounds a week gets $1000 to advertise coffee.

travel agency; and houses these guests in a hotel/motel subsidiary. The restaurant subsidiary buys most of its supplies from other subsidiaries, and this tying process goes on and on.

Predatory Pricing

Predatory pricing is differential pricing to eliminate competitors. A nationwide firm may wish to secure a greater share of the market in a particular area. If price is chosen as a weapon, the firm will arbitrarily lower prices in one area to drive out competition. Once it has reached its objective it raises prices to more than gain back losses of the price war. This situation of course eliminates the local firm which has no outlets in other areas. In general, legal pricing is cost-justified pricing. Many exceptions occur, but seldom will a firm sell at loss prices except when temporarily forced to by fierce competition or for a short time to achieve a particular objective.

Fair Trade

Fair trade laws were passed by states to maintain uniform selling prices. *Fair trade price* is a minimum price established by the manufacturer and must be used as a minimum by every retailer, with some exceptions. Strong at one time, fair trade laws have gradually decreased in importance.

Unfair Trade Practice Acts

Some states have an unfair trade practice act. This law essentially means that no one may sell merchandise below cost (cost is usually considered as the price the retailer pays plus freight in). Usually, the law states that a percent markup must be applied to cost to arrive at a selling price. Frequently this markup is very low, below markups needed for successful operation. The purpose is to prevent loss-leader pricing, that is, selling below cost. There are exceptions to provide for damaged, obsolete, and old merchandise or special pricing situations.

Labeling Restrictions

Some labeling restrictions are price oriented and controlled by law. It becomes illegal to establish a price which is deceptively higher than it is sold on the market. Stores that advertise "regular price" and "our price" have been legally forced to change their price tags since their "our price" was their regular price. Some products are sold at the price marked on the merchandise; other products have a more flexible price, and the price marked on the merchandise is subject to bargaining.

QUESTIONS AND PROBLEMS

1. Why is it important to start a firm with the best channel of distribution? Explain.
2. Discuss the use of strategic inventories and warehousing in promoting successful operation.
3. Why must a firm assume risk? Are there ways of reducing risk? Explain.
4. Compare the selling of major items with small items. Is the buyer different? Is buying different?
5. How can financing affect a distribution channel?
6. Compare the distribution of a long line with a short line of products. Can this difference determine the distribution channel? Explain.
7. Is there a great difference between distributing products with a high markup and a low markup? Discuss the implications of each.
8. Briefly point out the differences in operation of five important channel middlemen.
9. Why should a firm clearly delineate its objectives before choosing a channel of distribution?
10. Discuss the difficulties encountered in choosing people in distribution from the point of (a) availability and (b) cost.
11. Why is it important to determine pricing objectives? Explain the effects on a firm.
12. The purpose of pricing will often determine how to set a proper price. Why doesn't a firm just set a price that will yield a satisfactory profit?
13. Why may a product be introduced to complete the product line when the company knows it will be priced unprofitably?
14. Why is it customary to price parts and supplies with a generous profit margin? Explain the reasoning used.
15. Contrast short-run and long-run pricing. Why is the differentiation in pricing needed?
16. Why is it so important to stress overhead cost in pricing?
17. Draw a break-even chart. Obtain additional information from marketing and economics textbooks. Compare your chart with the one in this textbook and charts from other books.
18. Discuss several of the pricing methods described in this chapter. Illustrate conditions or products that might favor each method.
19. What are the advantages of (a) cumulative discount, (b) cash discount, and (c) trade-in in pricing? Explain each one separately.
20. Why is leasing included in pricing?
21. Indicate how negotiated pricing can be useful.
22. How can you justify different prices for an identical product?
23. Should a sales manager be well informed about legal restraints on pricing? Discuss, illustrating some special pricing effects.

case 20–1   **PINE SKI RESORT**

The Pine Ski Resort was located in Minnesota in an area of heavy tourist travel in both summer and winter. The Pine Ski Resort was a large ski area with excellent facilities, including snow-making equipment, ski lifts, a lounge, and a newly purchased helicopter. The helicopter was used to take equipment for repairs to the top of the hills and to give customers ten-minute rides in the area. The rides were $5 each.

The Pine Ski Resort's only competition came from Mountain Ski Resort, which was fifteen miles away, did not have as many facilities, and did not offer night skiing.

Pine Ski Resort sold lift tickets at the following rate:

	Day 9 A.M.–5 P.M.	Evening 6 P.M.–11 P.M.
All areas	$6.00	$4
Beginners' area	4.50	3

Children under 12 years were $1 cheaper.

Mountain Ski Resort's rates were as follows:

	Day 9 A.M.–dark
All areas	$5
Beginners' area	3

Children under 12 years were $2 cheaper.

The Pine Ski Resort had made a profit for the last five years and had considerably more business than Mountain Ski Resort. It also offered ski lessons and maintained a full-time staff of ski instructors.

When the energy crisis developed, Pine Ski Resort's expenses climbed rapidly. Because of inflation, more people had started to go to Mountain Ski Resort, which was cheaper and offered gas at cost to customers to return home. At present, the Pine Ski Resort was profitable only because of night skiing, and they were afraid what might happen if Mountain Ski Resort opened night skiing. Pine Ski Resort's customers took less advantage of the lounge and the ski lessons. These were considered too expensive to most customers.

QUESTIONS

1. What new prices, if any, should Pine Ski Resort adopt to meet competition?
2. How can Pine Ski Resort cut expenses?
3. If you were the owner of Pine Ski Resort, what policies would you adopt to maintain or increase sales?
4. This case is an example of an unexpected contingency which hampered operation. How should this situation be handled? Is pricing the answer?

NORRIS TOOL COMPANY

The Norris Tool Company was founded in 1931 as a small precision manufacturing jobbing shop. (Jobbing shops bid competitively on the construction of metalworking tools and special machinery parts. This prototype work consists of short-run lengths and very exacting machining.) Norris Tool had a competent management-owner group which consisted of people with engineering backgrounds. The work force was made up of highly skilled journeymen.

As the firm grew, more plant space was required. In 1944 a second plant was purchased. This plant was designed for long-run production manufacturing to meet wartime demand. It was during this time that the company contracted to make special hold-down clamps for major auto manufacturers. The application proved successful, and Norris Tool designed and built similar clamps for sale to the metalworking industry. (This type of product was not patentable.) Word-of-mouth advertising and a quality product aided in providing Norris Tool with a nationally known product. These clamps were manufactured in large quantities at the newer plant.

In the last fifteen years, more than a dozen firms have entered the market with complete lines of hold-down clamps. Some of the firms were large conglomerates that had thousands of distributors around the world. Soon, competition provided a solution to almost any clamping problem by expanding the sizes and styles in the lines. Norris had continued with its original basic line and had spent little effort in developing additional styles because clamps had always been strictly a sideline (but an extremely profitable one).

By 1975, most of the founders of the company had retired or passed away. There were openings for new people in engineering and management. Mr. Dan Bauer, president and major stockholder, brought in two engineers who were young and full of ideas. Mr. Brown was to be more of a sales engineer, and Mr. Clark was to be primarily a design engineer. Bauer saw an opportunity to exploit the excess capacity of the manufacturing plant by expanding the standard products line, one of the areas in which he hoped to use his two new engineers. Norris' strongest standard line product was the hold-down clamp; so the initial effort by the engineers was toward filling out the line to meet competition. Bauer believed that expansion of the clamp line provided the easiest and fastest return on investment.

Ten years ago, Norris Tool had employed one full-time sales engineer. Upon his retirement, all customers were serviced on the phone or by occasional visits by inside engineers or management. Out-of-town accounts were handled strictly by phone. The clamp customers were rarely contacted by phone or in person. With a new sales-oriented engineer, Bauer wanted to build clamp sales by establishing a national network of manufacturer's agents.

Compensation

The new sales engineer was paid a monthly salary and a semiannual bonus. All other office and plant employees were also paid a bonus. This bonus was set at Bauer's discretion and was dependent on corporate profits for the year. Bauer thought that a salary was best for Brown because of the many nonselling activities.

Bauer had counted on paying the independent manufacturer's agents a commission only on actual monthly sales. (A manufacturer's agent is an independent businessman who pays all his own expenses. He is allowed to use the prinicipal's name in a protected territory under a specific contract which normally runs at least a year. All orders are sent directly to the principal, who takes care of shipping and invoicing.) The method of paying commissions only on actual sales is standard in the industry.

In 1976, Brown and Bauer began to recruit and sign manufacturer's agents. They soon found that the margin allowed for commissions to agents in the pricing structure was below most competitive commissions. They also found that a majority of the best agents in an area were presently carrying a direct competitive line. These lines were all full lines and were therefore "bread and butter" lines. Brown suggested that they concentrate on agents with compatible, but not competing, lines.

Many top professional agents expressed an interest in the quality Norris line; but when commissions were discussed, the typical comment was, "A person with my qualifications cannot possibly work with only 15 percent, and you won't get anyone who's good to do missionary work for this commission." Norris did find a few people who would accept a 15 percent commission, but these people were not up to the standards set by Bauer.

Brown knew that Norris was on the low side, but he also knew that there was not enough margin available in their present prices. A recent study by Brown indicated that costs on the clamp line had risen so much that the only reason Norris was making a profit was that many customers did not take advantage of the 20–30 percent quantity discounts. Prices had recently been raised, in some cases as much as 30 percent. This did not leave an "honest" 15 percent margin for representatives. If times were good, Bauer thought that prices could be raised again in a year. Sixty percent of sales were from out-of-state orders. Brown learned from a study of last year's invoices that 82 percent of the $300,000 of clamp sales were from five midwestern states.

One alternative to giving a 15 percent commission to agents was the use of this margin exclusively for trade advertising. However, Brown found that the ratio of advertising dollars against sales dollars could not come close to justifying selling through advertising alone. Advertising inquiries of the past year were studied and related to new customers and revenue. Also, a follow-up mail survey of advertising inquiries was made. Indications were that advertising could increase awareness of Norris' brand name, but that personal engineering assistance was required to convert leads into sales. The study found that the results of an advertising program were spread over a long period and became cumulative over a period of time. Thus, measurement was difficult when justifying advertising dollars. Brown felt that results were needed soon to protect present customers from going to the competition. Leading indicators in the metalworking industry projected a very questionable year ahead. If sales in general declined, it would mean a halt to present development plans.

A close look at the past advertising budget showed that no more than 3 percent of sales could be trimmed off advertising expenses and used elsewhere.

QUESTIONS

1. Do you think the choice of manufacturer's agents was the best channel? Discuss, pointing out alternative choices and why.
2. How would you handle the price situation? Give details.
3. What is the role of advertising in industrial selling?

Selected Bibliography

BOOKS

Ammer, Dean S., *Materials Management,* 3rd ed. Homewood, Ill.: Richard D. Irwin, Inc., 1974. Presents the purchasing side of marketing. Salespeople need to understand the buyer's viewpoint.

Berenson, Conrad, and Henry Eilbirt, eds. *The Social Dynamics of Marketing.* New York: Random House, 1973. A book of readings on current marketing problems. Emphasis on social and ethical issues.

Bowersox, Donald J., *Logistical Management: A System Integration of Physical Distribution Management, Materials Management & Logistical Coordination.* New York: Macmillan Publishing Co., Inc., 1974.

Butler, William F., and Robert A. Karesh, eds. *How Business Economists Forecast.* Englewood Cliffs, N.J.: Prentice-Hall, Inc., 1966. Presents research methods used by leading business economists. Very informative.

Chao, Lincoln L., *Statistics: Methods and Analysis,* 2nd ed. New York: McGraw-Hill Book Company, 1974. A useful aid in forecasting techniques.

Davis, Kenneth R., *Marketing Management,* 3rd ed. New York: The Ronald Press Company, 1972.

Douglas, John, George A. Field, and Lawrence X. Tarpey, *Human Behavior in Marketing.* Columbus, Ohio: Charles E. Merrill Books, Inc., 1967.

Engel, James F., David T. Kollat, and Roger D. Blackwell, *Consumer Behavior,* 2nd ed. New York: Holt, Rinehart and Winston, Inc., 1973.

Green, Paul E., and Donald S. Tull, *Research for Marketing Decisions,* 3rd ed. Englewood Cliffs, N.J.: Prentice-Hall, Inc., 1975. This more advanced research text uses more difficult techniques.

Johnson, H. Webster, *Creative Selling,* 2nd ed. Cincinnati: South-Western Publishing Co., 1974. A complete basic text on salesmanship.

————. *How to Use the Business Library with Sources of Business Information,* 4th ed. Cincinnati: South-Western Publishing Co., 1972. Over a thousand direct sources of business information. Many of these list sources which give access to thousands of additional sources.

Katona, George, *Psychological Economics.* New York: American Elsevier Publishing Co., 1975. Reviews the major findings of the Michigan Survey Research Center. Discusses the use of surveys in contemporary social research.

Kotler, Philip, *Marketing Management: Analysis Planning and Control,* 2nd ed. Englewood Cliffs, N.J.: Prentice-Hall, Inc., 1972.

Kurtz, David L., and Charles W. Hubbard. *The Sales Function and Its Management: Selected Readings.* Morristown, N.J.: General Learning Press, 1971.

Luck, David J., Hugh J. Wales, and Donald A. Taylor, *Marketing Research,* 4th ed. Englewood Cliffs, N.J.: Prentice-Hall, Inc., 1974. Introduces marketing research approaches and techniques.

Stanton, William J., and Richard H. Buskirk, *Management of the Sales Force,* 4th ed. Homewood, Ill.: Richard D. Irwin, Inc., 1974.

Webster, Frederick E., Jr., *Marketing Communication: Modern Promotional Strategy.* New York: The Ronald Press Company, 1971.

Wotruba, Thomas, *Sales Management: Planning, Accomplishment, and Evaluation.* New York: Holt, Rinehart and Winston, Inc. 1971.

PERIODICALS

Business Week, New York (published weekly), covers current business activities. Each issue has information on marketing and often on sales management.

Harvard Business Review, Boston (published bimonthly), includes articles for the executive level. Some issues present specific articles on sales management.

Marketing Times, New York, is published every other month by Sales and Marketing Executives International, Inc., which is an organization of more than 25,000 members. It has many local chapters in the United States and other countries. The magazine focuses on sales management. Included are many sources of information on sales and sales management.

Sales Management, New York (published twice a month), covers sales and sales management areas. Its annual "Survey of Buying" issue is widely used in forecasting and territory potential.

OTHER SOURCES

American Management Association, New York, publishes a variety of studies and other literature on business and related areas. Some of its publications in marketing (including sales and sales management) are excellent.

American Marketing Association, Chicago, with a membership of over 19,000 and numerous local chapters in various cities, has a wide list of publications in marketing including sales and sales management.

Business Periodicals Index, published by the H. W. Wilson Company, New York, currently lists articles from over 160 business magazines. These listings are under numerous headings, which include several in the sales management area. Most major public libraries and university libraries have this publication in a series of volumes.

Dartnell, 4660 Ravenswood Ave., Chicago, Ill. 60640, is a publisher specializing in handbooks, surveys, studies, textbooks, brochures, and other literature for the sales manager.

The Wall Street Journal, published five days a week in New York, carries daily business and political information. The sales manager will find it a quick source of specialized and general current information.

Index

81

86